The Lord's Supper
in the Reformed Tradition

COLUMBIA SERIES IN REFORMED THEOLOGY

The Columbia Series in Reformed Theology represents a joint commitment of Columbia Theological Seminary and Westminster John Knox Press to provide theological resources for the church today.

The Reformed tradition has always sought to discern what the living God revealed in Scripture is saying and doing in every new time and situation. Volumes in this series examine significant individuals, events, and issues in the development of this tradition and explore their implications for contemporary Christian faith and life.

This series is addressed to scholars, pastors, and laypersons. The Editorial Board hopes that these volumes will contribute to the continuing reformation of the church.

COLUMBIA SERIES IN REFORMED THEOLOGY

The Lord's Supper in the Reformed Tradition

An Essay on the Mystical True Presence

JOHN W. RIGGS

WESTMINSTER
JOHN KNOX PRESS
LOUISVILLE • KENTUCKY

© 2015 John W. Riggs

First edition
Published by Westminster John Knox Press
Louisville, Kentucky

15 16 17 18 19 20 21 22 23 24—10 9 8 7 6 5 4 3 2 1

Scripture quotations from the New Revised Standard Version of the Bible are copyright © 1989 by the Division of Christian Education of the National Council of the Churches of Christ in the U.S.A. and are used by permission.

Excerpts from "A Pact," by Ezra Pound, from *Personae,* copyright © 1926 by Ezra Pound. Reprinted by permission of New Directions Publishing Corp. and Faber and Faber Ltd. Excerpts from *Book of Confessions.* Office of the General Assembly, Presbyterian Church (U.S.A.). Used by permission.

Book and cover design by Drew Stevens

Library of Congress Cataloging-in-Publication Data

Riggs, John W. (John Wheelan), 1950-
    The Lord's Supper in the Reformed tradition : an essay on the mystical true presence / John W. Riggs. — First edition.
        pages cm. — (Columbia series in Reformed theology)
    Includes index.
    ISBN 978-0-664-26019-4 (alk. paper)
    1. Lord's Supper—Reformed Church. 2. Reformed Church—Doctrines—History. I. Title.
    BX9423.C5R54   2015
    264'.042036—dc23

                                                                        2014049521

PRINTED IN THE UNITED STATES OF AMERICA

♾ The paper used in this publication meets the minimum requirements
of the American National Standard for Information Sciences—Permanence
of Paper for Printed Library Materials, ANSI Z39.48-1992.

Most Westminster John Knox Press books are available at special quantity discounts when purchased in bulk by corporations, organizations, and special-interest groups. For more information, please e-mail SpecialSales@wjkbooks.com.

CONTENTS

INTRODUCTION

Because of the complexities of both primary and secondary material; and because of the numerous disciplines covered (New Testament, church history from prior to the common era in the Mediterranean basin through the twenty-first century, historical theology, liturgical history, liturgical theology, and constructive theology); this study has taken almost ten years to complete. It serves as a bookend to its sibling book, *Baptism in the Reformed Tradition*, which appeared in the Columbia Series in Reformed Theology in 2002, so that the two books encompass Reformed sacramental theology. The final chapter of this Supper study also completes sacramental ideas that were already present in the baptism study, but that had no appropriate place there, and that took some time to develop as fully as are given here. First, a few retrospective comments on the baptism book; then some comments about this Supper book, noting advances that it tries to make along the way; and, finally, the many thanks that are owed to so many people.

The baptism book was a shot across the bow of the modern, Protestant liturgical renewal: "You are going the wrong direction and do not even know it." The argument was relatively simple. Among the remarkable achievements of the Roman Catholic liturgical renewal movement was its description of ecclesiology. The church is fundamentally built from the initiation of believers into the Paschal Mystery and sustained by the Spirit. The Roman Catholic Rite of Christian Initiation of Adults (RCIA), which has very specific liturgies that work together and that incarnate a particular theological grammar of *initiation into the Paschal Mystery*, was uncritically adapted by Protestants as *initiation into the visible church.* (No Protestant can possibly ascertain initiation into the *invisible* church because no one can see human faith; but more on that below.)

The only broad Reformation-era tradition that has ever thought of baptism as fundamentally an entrance rite into the church is the Baptist tradition. When Karl Barth in IV.4 of his *Church Dogmatics* embraced baptism as initiation into the visible church, he realized (much to his credit) that for him baptism no longer was a sacrament. Barth realized that he had placed himself rather more in the Baptist tradition of an ordinance; and done so under considerable influence from the much overlooked work of his son, Markus Barth, in *Die Taufe—Ein Sakrament?*

For the Reformed tradition baptism remains not an ordinance but a sacrament that is an outward and visible sign of an inward and spiritual grace. Baptism *primarily* communicates the divine presence that claims this or that particular person as a beloved child, always and forevermore. Baptism cannot fail to do that, because God's grace does not fail to do that. Baptism *secondarily* initiates someone into *the visible church*; but whether that person is, or has been, initiated into *the invisible church* that is comprised of believers, and is thus initiated into the body of Christ, can in principle never be known by any human being. Why? Because whether someone has faith, and thus takes to heart the prior self-communication of the Divine that claims her or him, can never be known by any human being. (Here *a foundational difference* about "faith" exists between Roman Catholicism and Protestantism, a difference that lies at the heart of being "initiated into the Paschal Mystery.")

As a Reformation example of exactly this point, Martin Luther, in his essay on rebaptism, protested that Anabaptists think that they are God and that they can see someone's heart when they rebaptize, because someone claims to have come to faith. Baptism, argued Luther, is grounded in the divine offer of grace, not in someone's putative coming to faith. You may know someone's public confession, Luther rightly observed, but you can never know whether another person has faith.

A Reformation example also exists for the distinction between the primary and secondary aspects of a sacrament. John Calvin complained that Huldrych Zwingli, by construing a sacrament to be an outward and public confession of faith, had made primary what ought to be secondary. Pledging faith is consequent upon the prior divine offer of grace, which should always remain its *primary* aspect.

By taking over a liturgical approach from Roman Catholicism, for which "initiation" means initiation *into the Paschal Mystery*, and by applying it out of its native ecclesial, theological, and historical context to Protestant baptism as initiation *into the visible church*, Protestant liturgical scholars had inadvertently made what was secondary into what was primary. They had unwittingly turned the sacrament into an ordinance. Roman Catholic scholars, both in print (see the review by Jeffrey Gros in *The Christian Century*) and in the Catholic-Reformed Dialogue group of which I was a member for eight years, saw this point easily and clearly.

The baptism book found acceptance among Protestant historians, historical theologians, and systematicians; but not all Protestant liturgical scholars were happy, as one might imagine, since the book had caught them with their diptychs exposed. One liturgical scholar even criticized the book for having a chapter on Luther, "baptizing" him into the Reformed tradition, as I recall. Such lack of familiarity with (especially Continental) Reformation secondary scholarship, and lack of familiarity with Calvin, who thought himself a true follower of Luther in sacramental theology (as compared to the epigones who frequented Lutheranism), and who subscribed to Augsburg (Variata), sadly happens too often within the liturgical field.[1]

The most helpful criticism of the baptism study was that I had not sufficiently clarified what Reformed theology understood by the validity of a sacrament. I have tried to address that issue in the first chapter of this Supper study. Whether I have succeeded in clarification is, of course, another issue.

Sacramentally speaking, this Supper study makes the same point that the baptism book insisted upon. For the Reformed tradition, with a few exceptions, the Supper is a sacrament and thus primarily and truly communicates the Divine. Whether the recipient opens her or his heart (faith) to the divine self-communication, and realizes saving well-being, cannot be told from the outside; and this remains the basic issue that distinguishes the validity of a sacrament from the efficacy of a sacrament. Historically speaking, this current study shows that the Reformed tradition, deeply humanist in its approach,[2] discovered in Augustine a eucharistic theology as ancient as any: when believers receive the bread and cup, Christ engrafts them yet deeper into his mystical body and thus *truly* nourishes them with his body and blood. Biographically speaking, I first came to see this Augustinian tradition by reading German Roman Catholic historians such as Josef Geiselmann and Johannes Betz, whose works were introduced to me by my doctoral teacher, Edward Kilmartin. Whether Kilmartin would approve of where I went with that scholarship is quite another matter.

By looking back to the earliest days of critical theological reflection upon the confession of Christ's presence in the Supper, back not only to Augustine but to writers such as Tertullian, this study argues that Reformed eucharistic theology holds a teaching that can be found among the breadth of the earliest known catholic eucharistic theologies. No eucharistic theology can claim to be more anciently catholic than the position held in the Reformed tradition. In the concluding constructive chapter, this study argues that Reformed eucharistic theology is also utterly apostolic by its appeal to the Jesus-kerygma.

The final chapter also offers a re-visioning of Christ's mystical true presence that (on my view) is thoroughly Augustinian and Reformed. In the aspects of the (Augustinian) mystical true presence, and of re-imagining that tradition for Reformed theology today, I realized late in this study that John Williamson Nevin really was my ancestor in Reformed theology. I never intended that to be the case. Nevin simply was right, and he remains *the* watershed person in the study of Reformed eucharistic theology, even with the very helpful corrections of Thomas Davis, most of which I have followed.

Along the way, and as unintended consequences of pursuing this material, the study offers a number of nuanced contributions to some different areas of liturgical history and theology. Among them are:

- A careful explanation of how the table-sharing of Jesus became a sacrament that embodied a Last Supper Passover narrative: Jesus' table-sharing became retold as a Noble Death tradition, transmitted to Corinth by Paul, and woven into a Passover narrative by Mark.
- A resolution of the discussion whether 1 Corinthians 11 and 1 Corinthians 14 represent the same or different events. The answer is both. The similar language owes to both events being Corinthian table-sharing; the differences owe to one having the Jesus ritual as its symposium (1 Cor. 11) and the other having an ecstatic, tongue-speaking, "séance" as its symposium (1 Cor. 14).
- A resolution of the discussion whether Augustine was realistic or symbolic, by noting that binary categories are insufficient. A more adequate parsing requires realistic (metabolic), realistic (nonmetabolic), and symbolic categories. Augustine was realistic (nonmetabolic).
- A renaming of the principal medieval, reforming, eucharistic positions:
  - Medieval catholic eucharistic theology—Erasmus
  - Medieval catholic, evangelical eucharistic theology—Luther
  - Patristic catholic, evangelical eucharistic theology—Zwingli, Bucer, Calvin, Bullinger
- A rethinking of the categories proposed by B. A. Gerrish, in his seminal essay on the Supper in the Reformed tradition. This study argues for four categories, therein agreeing with, and supporting with further study, the Swiss argument that Zwingli was not a "mere memorialist":
  - Symbolic instrumentalism (Calvin)
  - Symbolic parallelism (Bullinger)
  - Symbolic anamnesis (Zwingli)
  - Symbolic memorialism (Zwinglianism)
- A correction of an overcorrection made by Thomas Davis in his superb study on Calvin's eucharistic theology, a study with which I frequently agree and follow. Davis follows the great Dutch scholar G. P. Hartvelt, who took a comment by Calvin about medieval baptism out of context and applied it

to Calvin's sacramental theology in general. Both Davis and Hartvelt are mistaken that in 1536 Calvin did not argue for sacramental efficacy, even if Calvin's arguments were still developing.

- A suggestion (p. 233, n. 141) about the theological poverty of preaching textbooks currently available to Reformed graduate students. The suggestion arises from the (chap. 5) discussion between John Williamson Nevin and Charles Hodge, and the observation by Gerrish that for Calvin preaching, like the sacraments, brings the real presence of Christ.

- An extension of Willy Rordorf's point that the origin of Sunday is the postcrucifixion celebration of the "Lord's Supper"—hence, the "Lord's Day." The final chapter points out that the entire church year, therefore, is grounded not in a resurrection as such but in Jesus' table-sharing.

- An application of an insight from Willi Marxsen's book *The New Testament as the Church's Book*. This study argues that the Jesus-kerygma that proclaims Jesus' table-sharing is apostolically normative for both Protestant and Roman Catholic traditions about the Supper/Eucharist. This means that the Reformed/Roman Catholic debate, whether the normative origin for the Supper is "scriptural warrant" or "priestly inception," is answered with "Yes—the table-sharing of the Jesus-kerygma."

- A careful explication, in the final chapter, of an insight that Marxsen makes in passing. The eucharistic tradition handed on, and embodied again and again in new ways, is not Jesus' table-sharing as such but "the Jesus-business" (*Die Sache Jesu*). This "Jesus-business" was embodied as table-sharing in Jesus' ministry, and it was embodied as divine food offered in the Eucharist in some patristic traditions.

- A suggestion in the final chapter of how Barth's Reformation insight—and that of Charles Hodge as well—that grace is personal, not material, can be understood as the mystical true presence of the Divine, given in and to each moment and then re-presented in the Supper.

- A brief sketching of a nonsubstantialist view of the Supper as a triune event (pp. 235–36, n. 17).

A few words about citations and translations: Unless otherwise noted, all translations are my own, with the note giving both the original source as well as an English source. The original source citations typically give volume number, followed by page number, and in some cases then follows the standard convention of line number(s). In a few rare cases, where the original source was not available, I have quoted the English and the note gives only the English source.

The people to whom my deepest thanks are owed are many and by naming some I fear that I will leave out others. First, my thanks to the editorial board of the Columbia Series in Reformed Theology (CSRT), and through them to all who have supported this series, which is a remarkable series for its many high-level and diverse contributions to Reformed theology. I am honored that the CSRT would make this the second book that I have authored in this series; and I hope that the baptism book and this Supper book serve as benchmarks for conversation in the Reformed traditions about sacramental theology.

My Reformed colleagues in the Catholic/Reformed dialogue deserve much credit because with them, and in dialogue with our Roman Catholic brothers and sisters, many features of this Supper study have either come to fruition or been sharpened. The Reformed theologians were Lydia Veliko, Sid Fowler, Richard Mouw (Reformed chair), Martha Moore-Keish, Robina Winbush, Doug Fromm, Renee House, John Paarlberg, Lyle Bierma, Ron Feenstra, Sue Rozeboom, David Engelhard[†], and George Vandervelde[†]. It was my immense pleasure to get to know these Reformed colleagues and to see their living theology. In particular I want to thank Ron Feenstra for his crucial suggestion not to name the Reformed eucharistic position with the language from Roman Catholic liturgical scholars "nonmetabolic" (Geiselmann) or "nonsomatic" (Kilmartin). As Ron rightly pointed out, this would have made the Reformed position derivative from another. And so for a number of reasons, outlined at the start of chapter 2 of this study, once the study came to Protestant theology I abandoned the terms "nonmetabolic" and "nonsomatic," and chose instead the words "mystical true presence." Occasionally I retain the Roman Catholic terms in parentheses for the sake of continuity and clarification. Among the Protestants who participated in the dialogue, I also want to thank Scott Ickert, our Lutheran observer throughout the dialogue, whom I thought of frequently as I wrote the complicated chapter on Luther's eucharistic theology.

Among the Roman Catholic scholars were Bishop Patrick Cooney (Roman Catholic chair), Thomas Weinandy, Dennis McManus, Dennis Tamburello, Ralph Del Colle, Joyce Zimmerman, Francis Tiso, and Leo Walsh. I want to thank Bishop Cooney for his ever-gracious insights and personal support. Dennis Tamburello was a help with his insights on Calvin. I leaned on Dennis McManus for numerous issues in liturgical theology and history, as well as his support of the baptism book and its claims about Roman Catholic and Reformed views on baptism. Dennis also helped immensely with some very obscure language in Bucer about "shadow-boxing," which most likely concerned priestly gesticulations during Mass, while light cast their shadows. Ralph Del Colle was a constant partner with me in theological discussion and helped sharpen my focus. And Joyce Zimmerman offered much help from liturgical history. The mention of Roman Catholic colleagues reminds me that I owe a great debt to Edward Foley and Joanne Pierce for help with Aquinas and with late medieval baptismal theology.

Finally, a special thanks to a former graduate student of mine whose help with this manuscript has been invaluable, Kara Reagan Windler.

Among my teachers I would be remiss not to mention again Edward Kilmartin, as well as my doctoral adviser James F. White, both of whom are now dead, and to whom I now belatedly say (if I might borrow the words of Ezra Pound),

I make a pact with you Walt Whitman—
I have detested you long enough.
I come to you as a grown child
Who has had a pig-headed father;
I am old enough now to make friends.
It was you that broke the new wood,
Now is a time for carving.
We have one sap and one root—
Let there be commerce between us.[3]

I would also be most remiss in not thanking particularly four scholars whose work has influenced my life, not merely my scholarship (but that very much also): Schubert Ogden, Brian Gerrish, Chris Gamwell, and most especially Philip Devenish.

Let me also thank a number of new teachers as life spirals progressively outward, embracing the hymn of the universe: Sharon Kist, James Harris, Jack Pennington, Teresa Hamra, Angela McConachie, Judy Smith, Holly Diesel, Jennifer Williams, Nancy Van Aman, Martha Hoffman, Deirdre Schweiss, Kathy Dawson, Anne Vigil, Karen Bess, Katie Jett, and Kathleen Jay. A great thanks to Patty Williams.

There have been many friends and colleagues who have been *lucis fenestrae divinae* amid the *animi tenebrae mei*: Kim Schlichting, Andrew Schlichting, Ben Ivanowski, Susan Ivanowski, Nick Franke, Beth Lewandowski, Terry Cooper, Bill Utke, Kathy Gloff, Shira Krause, Bill Perman, Deborah Krause, Philip Devenish, Steve Patterson, Billy Arraj, Mark Weisshaar, Marilyn Sonne, Mary Paré, Jerry Paré, Betsy Happel, Jean Roth Jacobs, and Tony Jacobs. A very special thanks to Chris Frey. And all my love to Andrew and Abigail.

1

FROM JESUS' TABLE-SHARING
TO THE PROTESTANT REFORMATION

Fifteen centuries of eucharistic faith and practice preceded the Protestant Reformation. Since the Reformation, scholars have debated, often along partisan lines, how well the Reformers understood and interpreted this tradition. To understand the Reformed tradition adequately, this chapter summarizes the Western eucharistic tradition that the Protestant Reformers inherited. The origins of the Lord's Supper, and the development from table-sharing to sacred food, begin this chapter. The patristic and early medieval periods follow, and a summary of high and late medieval eucharistic theology concludes this historical introduction.

THE LORD'S SUPPER THROUGH
THE LATE NEW TESTAMENT PERIOD

To organize the studies in a helpful way, I want to say a few words about method. Broadly speaking, the studies on the Lord's Supper can be divided into three approaches. Some studies primarily focus on the historical Jesus and what he did or did not actually institute during his ministry.[1] A second approach primarily studies the development of the eucharistic prayers and actions, tracing the lineage between the earliest records and subsequent liturgical traditions.[2] Finally, a history-of-religions approach primarily studies meal traditions in the ancient world, seeking parallel material that will help parse the meal descriptions and Last Supper scenes in the Gospels and other New Testament material.[3]

That this division is somewhat artificial, and that material overlaps, I readily admit. For example, in a classic study Hans Lietzmann worked backwards from liturgical texts themselves and argued historically for two types of early church practice. One practice traced back to the Pauline tradition and the death of Jesus; the other traced back to the *Didache* and preserved the tradition of Jesus' meal-sharing with his disciples.[4] So too the influential work of Gregory Dix worked from liturgical texts and argued for a fourfold action of Jesus, historically rooted in Jewish fellowship meals.[5] Or, again, Dennis Smith's thorough study of the banquet tradition in the ancient world would fall into a broad history-of-religions approach. Yet Smith has an excellent chapter on the banquet in the Gospel

1

material, in which he denies any direct historical connection between the Gospel meal scenes and Jesus' own ministry, arguing instead for histori- cal characteristics of Jesus' ministry proclaimed through the meal genre, so that all the Gospel meal scenes were constructed by the early church during table-sharing.[6]

These observations do not make the division of the material inappro- priate. However much overlap there may be, the three approaches are distinctly different, and this difference can affect how secondary material is appraised. As a brief example, take the work of Willi Marxsen, which was crucial among twentieth-century historical-critical scholarship.[7] When a history-of-religions approach is taken, Marxsen's 1960 essay on the Lord's Supper can be classified with that of Lietzmann. Klauck, for example, gives little attention to Marxsen's essay and essentially sees it as epigenous to Lietzmann's work.[8] By contrast, if one arranges the material from an historical-critical standpoint, asking historically what did Jesus do, and asking historically and theologically what Jesus' witness meant for the church, then Marxsen's essay takes on a new importance.[9]

This first section takes an historical-critical approach and arranges the material accordingly. Why? Historical theology asks the question of what the Christian witness has meant in specific historical contexts in order more adequately to understand what the Christian witness might look like in our contexts.[10] For Protestants, this has also meant a normative status given to Jesus' witness of faith as found through the apostolic tes- timonies we call Scriptures. Thus, for example, in accord with the Protes- tant Reformation, the Reformed tradition originally sought and still seeks dominical warrant for the sacramental practices of its churches, however such practices might be embodied today.[11] An historical-critical approach, therefore, suits this particular study of the Lord's Supper in the Reformed tradition. This approach also, I might add, appropriately fits the interest, explicit or implicit, of many influential scholars who have written on the Supper, from Bultmann to Jeremias to Marxsen and others.

As twentieth-century scholars looked critically at early Christianity and New Testament–era texts, they came to understand the Lord's Sup- per in new ways. In his *History of the Synoptic Tradition* Rudolf Bultmann opened his discussion of the Last Supper narrative with the simple asser- tion that "[a]fter the work of Eichhorn and Heitmueller I do not need to prove that a cult legend lies behind Mk. 14:22–25."[12] The Last Sup- per narrative gave a legendary origin to a practice already established in the Christian community that produced that narrative. That Jesus did not institute a "Last Supper," and that the Supper scenes, as well as the various forms of institution narrative, are etiological and catechetical in nature, remains a well-argued point.[13]

The view typified by Bultmann produced responses from various scholars who argued that the Last Supper somehow had dominical institution. For example, some argued that the Last Supper was a "kiddush" meal—a meal of blessing within Judaism. Others varied this by arguing for a Sabbath kiddush—a blessing meal connected with the Sabbath. Still others argued for a "chaburah" meal—a fellowship meal within Judaism. Others argued for a farewell meal such as appeared in the Old Testament (Gen. 27) and developed during the intertestamental period.[14] Over the course of several decades, Joachim Jeremias argued influentially that the Last Supper began as a Passover meal celebrated by Jesus.[15] This position was itself overturned within a decade by Eduard Schweizer, who showed that the New Testament material cannot yield a Passover setting for the Lord's Supper.[16]

In the middle of the twentieth century Willi Marxsen published a short, groundbreaking essay.[17] Marxsen first argued that the Supper tradition developed from pre-Pauline and Pauline forms into the later Markan account. He then argued that the New Testament Supper material itself does not support the idea of any actual *last* Supper instituted by Jesus. Next, Marxsen made a simple yet remarkably important suggestion: that the Last Supper scene is pure etiology and that Jesus actually instituted *the* Last Supper are not the only alternatives. As a middle ground, Marxsen argued that Jesus' ministry was characterized by a meal-sharing in which God's eschatological reign was experienced. The *Last* Supper tradition within the early church therefore continued and interpreted this earlier tradition of the *Lord's* Supper that *was* dominically practiced.[18]

Marxsen's thesis that the "Lord's Supper" began the early church's traditions about Jesus' "Last Supper" came to dominate the late-twentieth-century view of the Supper. In the English-speaking world, Norman Perrin's *Rediscovering the Teaching of Jesus* brought Jesus' table-sharing into bold relief. At table with "tax collectors and sinners" Jesus shared meals, and such practice not only contributed to his death but continued on in the early church through its Supper traditions.[19] Significant scholarship has developed this perspective so that it has become a dominant position today.[20]

In short, the internal, textual, historical-critical evidence from the New Testament permits neither a Passover setting for the Last Supper scene nor a dominically instituted Last Supper itself. This view finds support from the external manuscript witnesses. The earliest Christian witnesses that we have, found within the *Gospel of Thomas* and the *Q Gospel*, as well as the prayers in *Didache* 9 and 10, know no Last Supper of Jesus. As Crossan puts the matter,

I cannot believe that those specific Christians knew all about those elements and yet studiously avoided them. I can only presume those elements were not there for everyone from the beginning—that is, from solemn, formal, and final institution by Jesus himself. What Jesus created and left behind was the tradition of open commensality seen so often earlier, and what happened was that, after his death, certain Christian groups created the Last Supper as a ritual that combined commensality from his life with a commemoration of his death.[21]

Crossan and a consensus of scholars take up Marxsen's essential point that Jesus' table-sharing historically grounds the Supper scenes, grounding as well the many table-sharing references that appear throughout the Gospels.[22]

One more contribution from late-twentieth-century scholarship needs mention because it helps clarify these many table-sharing scenes in the Gospels and Epistles. Two major studies examine the banquet tradition in the ancient Mediterranean world at the time of Jesus.[23] These two independent studies show a common meal tradition, with meal structure and well-known ethical expectations for communal upbuilding, that was basic to social formation across peoples, cultures, and socioeconomic issues. This meal tradition not only formed the basis for all meals, so that one ought to think of a common tradition with variations, rather than different types of meals (mystery meals, festival meals, Jewish family meals, Christian agape, sacrificial meals, Eucharist, and so on).[24] This meal tradition also produced, and was produced by, a well-known literary meal genre.

In basic structure, all meals had two courses, the meal proper (*deipnon*) and the subsequent communal sharing designed for community upbuilding (*symposion*). This commonly structured, foundational form of community formation lies behind the many meal scenes in the New Testament material, including the Last Supper scenes of the Gospels. A recent study by Taussig that works with and develops his previous work, as well as the insights of Smith and Klinghardt, shows how the Hellenistic age saw a blossoming of the inherited meal pattern throughout all classes of people. The Roman Empire, and its spread of Hellenism, brought forth the disruption of stable cultures. It also brought meal-sharing that tried to engage new ways of social interaction that experimented and innovated new boundaries within a ritual setting that was manageable.[25]

Given this summary of secondary scholarship, the question naturally arises: if Jesus did not formally and consciously institute the Christian ritual of the Last Supper, how did the cultic practice come to be?[26] As Jesus traveled through the countryside, he would have come to towns where people invited him to share table, share wisdom, and perform healings. This would have happened within a commonly known meal pattern. During Jesus' table-sharing, customary boundaries of clean and unclean, class, status, ethnicity, and gender would have been broken, only to have a new community formed that has been characterized by Elisabeth Schüssler Fiorenza as having a "praxis of inclusive wholeness."[27] Above all, such healing and table-sharing were, as Crossan puts the matter, "the heart of Jesus' original vision and program."[28] Three comments are needed here, given the work of Smith, Klinghardt, and Taussig.

First, this table-sharing is not something that Jesus instituted as such, but was a common feature of Mediterranean life during the Augustan age. Likewise, as Taussig has shown, social experimentation across boundaries such as honor/shame, male/female, and Jew/Gentile was itself not instituted by Jesus, but was also a feature of the same context. Finally, for some people, such table-sharing of Jesus was the divine presence itself, although people had and expressed their table-sharing experience in differing ways. For example, some people experienced this table-sharing as God's imperial rule; others experienced these events as an encounter with *Sophia*, God's wisdom incarnate (see Matt. 11:19).

As this table-sharing tradition continued after Jesus' death, Jesus himself and his meal-sharing were understood and proclaimed within the Hellenistic-Jewish martyrdom tradition that was familiar with the Noble Death tradition. Here one suffered abuse and death for honor and for obedience to a noble cause, thus serving as a sacrificial model that empowered those disciples who followed.[29] Antioch, where Paul spent formative time in his early Christian ministry, was steeped in the Hellenistic-Jewish Noble Death tradition of Fourth Maccabees, a Jewish martyrological work from the time of Christian origins.[30] The Supper tradition that Paul cited to the Corinthian church (1 Cor. 11:23–26), which he likely learned at Antioch, was expressed through the Noble Death tradition.

The Passover motif was a Markan redaction that came when Mark borrowed the Noble Death Supper tradition (from the Christ cult), linked it with Jesus traditions, including wisdom traditions about the killing of the prophets, and produced a Last Supper scene. His composition proclaimed that Second Temple Judaism had brought judgment on itself, resulting in the destruction of the temple. Out of this Judaism arose the "true Israel," with its true "paschal lamb," Jesus.[31] Furthermore, a Passover motif would have made sense to those people for whom Jesus' ministry with table-sharing already had been experienced as a type of Passover event.[32]

As for the actual practice of the Lord's Supper in the years subsequent to Jesus' table-sharing, the most detailed information that we have comes from the tradition in Corinth (1 Cor. 11), which shows the standard meal-sharing pattern of the meal proper (*deipnon*) followed by the symposium (*symposion*).[33] In this case, the meal was followed by a symposium whose content was the Jesus ritual of bread and cup that Paul had handed down to them.[34] The Corinthians themselves had something amiss during the eating part of the table-sharing. Gerd Theissen has given a widely influential social analysis that argues for a basic division in the Corinthian church between those who were well-to-do and those who were not. At the communal meal this produced problems when some had food to eat while others were lacking.[35] This analysis does, however, make Paul's solution to the problem a little perplexing, because he says to those at Corinth to *wait for* one another (not *share with* one another) and to eat first at home if really hungry (1 Cor. 11:33–34). Smith has suggested instead a situation that might include perceived differences in food amounts, in which everyone ate their own food, in their own manner, and thus produced a cluster of individual meals rather than the intended communal meal that should instead have produced upbuilding community and been Christ's body (*sōma*).[36]

Whatever the issue that divided the meal tradition at Corinth, the likely pattern to the Corinthian table-sharing would have been typical and would have begun with a time of food-sharing together. Paul urged the Corinthians to work together for the upbuilding of the community when they ate, and here Paul showed common banquet social ethics taken up into christological formation.[37] After the meal sharing came the symposium, which the Corinthian text and context suggest was the bread-and-cup ritual recited within the Noble Death tradition about Jesus' Last Supper.[38] People should discern the communal body (*sōma*) of Christ during the meal, so that during the symposium they do not "eat the bread" and "drink the cup" of "the Lord in an unworthy manner" (1 Cor. 11:27–29).

Some scholars have also argued that the community gathering described in 1 Corinthians 14 was part of this same meal gathering, and more recent scholarship has argued that this would have functioned as the second course, the symposium part of the meal.[39] The most compelling evidence is the similarity in language for gathering together as a church and as a body.[40] Yet such linguistic parallels themselves indicate only that Paul viewed the community and its meal gatherings in a consistent manner. Paul makes no specific remarks about the Supper in 1 Corinthians 14, and in 1 Corinthians 11 he makes no remarks about the activities described in 1 Corinthians 14. Further, the communal ethos to the gatherings seems to differ. First Corinthians 11 has the problem of private meals with some uneven distribution of food and drink that offends people; 1 Corinthians 14 describes events wild and exotic by the developing Western liturgical practices. At the very least there were ecstatic, spirit-filled utterances, often at the same time; and a careful argument has been made that "speaking in tongues" was most likely the spirits of the dead speaking through the mouths of the living—an event sometimes described today as "channeling," with the supremely powerful spirit of Jesus himself speaking through Paul.[41]

Perhaps a reason that scholars have differed as to whether 1 Corinthians 11 and 14 represent different events or one single event is that the question itself has been put in these two alternatives, which surely are not the only options. Given what we now know about meal-sharing and community formation, does it not make more sense to think of a single meal tradition, taken over by Corinthian Christians, in which there were different symposia, one a predominately spirit-filled time of speech, another the Jesus ritual of bread and cup with narrative? This would explain the great similarity of language used to describe the gatherings, yet allow for the differences between the descriptions that have already been noted.

Further, if we imagine that in 1 Corinthians 11 the symposium was a narrative telling of Jesus' Noble Death tradition with a bread-and-cup ritual, we need not imagine a secular meal that was followed by a religious ceremony.[42] Rather, the meal itself, with two courses, formed an integrated religious event in which the first course, the meal proper (*deipnon*), needed to reflect authentically the communal ethos demanded by the second course, the bread and cup with Noble Death narrative (*symposion*).[43] As such, this Corinthian meal tradition would represent *a middle stage* between the actual table-sharing of Jesus and the complete separation of the bread-and-cup ritual from the meal context, a pattern we first see in the writings of Justin Martyr.[44]

A final historical comment about early Christian meal-sharing deserves mention, prior to this chapter turning to the post–New Testament period. What can be said about the Jesus groups—Christians connected to the Jesus movement (and oriented to the Jesus-kerygma)[45]—as distinct from the Christ groups that we see in Paul's ministry, and whose table-sharing can be found in 1 Corinthians? If the early followers of Jesus participated in the common practice of meal-sharing, with its experimental and boundary-bending ethos aimed a true community, but did so as people shaped by the encounter with Jesus, what did their symposia look like? Whereas Christians such as those in Paul's churches had symposia such as we see in 1 Corinthians, the Jesus groups likely told parables (think of Luke 15:11–32) or may even have performed healings (see Luke 10:7–9).

In the one hundred years between 1 Corinthians (ca. 50–55 CE) and Justin's *First Apology*, the Lord's Supper underwent two changes whose historical and theological significance have gone somewhat underdeveloped in the literature of liturgical scholarship.[46] The first change was that the bread-and-cup ritual, with the Jesus narrative, became a rite separated from a communal meal and located in a Word service that included the reading of texts, preaching, offering, and prayer.[47] Second, the elements of this bread-and-cup ritual came to be experienced as, and proclaimed as, divine food. The prayers found in *Didache* chapters 9 and 10 show evidence of exactly these two changes.[48] The second of these two changes, the elements as divine food, became a dominant theme of the medieval and Reformation periods.

By the late first century, Christian communities already began to experience and express the Supper in terms of divine food. The redaction to the sixth chapter of John's Gospel shows this development. In a scene that echoes the Synoptic Gospels, Jesus blesses and distributes bread; but then, unlike the Synoptics and much like the Fourth Gospel, Jesus launches into a long discourse, typically known as the Bread from Heaven discourse.[49] Scholars have agreed, with little dissent, that the original discourse ended at 6:51a and that verses 51b–57 are a later redactional addition.[50] Where originally Jesus talked symbolically about being the "bread of life," which had "come down from heaven" as the true manna, in the redactional addition Jesus proclaims that one must "eat my flesh" and "drink my blood" (John 6:54, 56). The word for flesh is not the Synoptic word for "body" (*sōma*), which has a wide range of connotations from corpse to human body, to person, to gathered community. Instead, the redaction uses a word that has a more literal, concrete meaning of flesh or meat (*sarx*). Analogously the redaction uses a verb that means to munch, or to chew, with the teeth (*trōgein*), rather than the more general word for eating (*esthiō/phagein*). The redaction then pairs this "munching flesh" with the command to "drink my blood," likewise a graphic portrayal, and proclaims that those who chew flesh and drink blood abide in Jesus and Jesus in them (John 6:56).

The traditionally given historical setting for the Gospel, as well as for the redaction in verses 51b–57, was the separation between Christianity and Judaism, with its resultant competition and hostility.[51] By proclaiming that followers of Jesus were to chew flesh and drink blood, the Christian community clearly separated its table from that of Judaism.[52]

But also visible is a different sensibility about how the Divine comes to be within community. Marxsen first drew careful attention to this issue in several important essays,[53] and the care with which Marxsen made the point must not be overlooked. Within the table-sharing tradition, the divine reality was experienced as present, and proclaimed as present, in and through the language of sharing and remembering together. In another context this same divine reality was experienced as present, and proclaimed as present, in and through the language of divine food that was to be consumed. There was a "translation," to be sure, from table-sharing to divine food, but what was translated was not table-sharing into divine food, but the total reality known through table-sharing, which could be experienced and expressed only through new ways, namely, divine food.[54]

Why this change? Marxsen consistently argued that it reflected a fundamental transition from the more Jewish setting of table and memory to the more Hellenistic setting where divine beings took human flesh and the Stoics thought that all things including spirit were material. The force of Marxsen's argument cannot be entirely gainsaid, but neither is it all that can be said, because the historical situation was more complicated. Judaism was already thoroughly Hellenized,[55] and Hellenistic meal traditions could show Noble Death and martyrdom traditions as ways of experiencing the ongoing reality of the one who has died.[56]

Further, gender politics and fixed offices may have contributed to the shift from table-sharing to divine food. This transition happened at the same time as fixed offices were replacing wandering charismatic leadership, as Christians debated issues of gender roles and leadership, and as the church was slowly accommodating itself to its context. Just as patrons controlled the means of life, including banquets, for their clients, so also male, ecclesial leadership was fencing the once-open commensality of the table and controlling the divine means of life.[57]

The transition from table-sharing to divine food should probably best be conceived as complex and not entirely clear. The experience and proclamation of the Supper as divine food was, however, clear by the late first century and early second century. Roughly contemporaneous with John 6:51b–57 are the writings of Ignatius of Antioch that display the theme of divine food, as well as that of fixed offices. For Ignatius the eucharistic elements were the "flesh of our Savior Jesus Christ,"[58] and thus the "medicine of immortality" and the "antidote that wards off death."[59]

By the end of the New Testament period, Justin Martyr's *First Apology* shows the fundamental shift from table-sharing, in which the divine reality was present in and through the meal sharing, to a cultic rite with bread and cup, attached to a Word service, in which the divine experience was present in and through divine food.[60] For Justin, just as the Word became flesh in the incarnation, so also the eucharistic elements no longer were ordinary food but became the very body and blood of Jesus Christ.[61]

PATRISTIC AND EARLY MEDIEVAL PERIODS

From the first century of the common era to the beginning of the early medieval period (476 CE),[62] the church grew exponentially. From about 50,000 Christians in roughly fifty locations in 100 CE, the church grew to 5,000,000 by the year 300 CE and to 30,000,000 by the year 400 CE.[63] The sacramental life of the church may well have had an implicit missionary draw on Hellenized people who desired to enter the mysteries of the Christian faith and be nourished by consuming the divine food provided by the church.[64] How did the theologians of the patristic and early medieval periods conceive that the divine reality was present?[65]

We have seen already that the New Testament period itself showed two main cultural-linguistic modes for experiencing and expressing the divine reality during the Lord's Supper. Some communities were grounded in table-sharing, and the divine presence was known in the gathered community as it shared table, remembering who God is and thus living in God's presence. We saw this in the table-sharing of Jesus and in the meal tradition at Corinth. There were also those communities for whom the divine presence was experienced and expressed in the gathered community through the presence of divine food, a somatic presence, if you will. As a broad observation, these two communal, cultural-linguistic contexts continued for centuries to follow.

As Justin's *First Apology* and the final redactions to *Didache* 9 and 10 show,[66] by the mid- to late second century different Christian communities not only took the Last Supper scenes as normative for their eucharistic celebrations; they also experienced and proclaimed that Jesus' own body and blood were truly present. This continued into the next century, so that "[i]n the third century the early Christian identification of the eucharistic bread and wine with the Lord's body and blood continued unchanged." Explanations for *how* this was so, however, differed.[67]

Almost a century ago, Darwell Stone gave an organization to these explanations that has remained astute.[68] Stone argued that in the ante-Nicene church "the presence and gift of the Eucharist" was expressed by "three different kinds of phraseology." First, the eucharistic gift was "a spiritual gift without defining its specific nature." This was the case, as we have seen, in Justin and in the *Didache*. Others discussed the eucharistic gift as a "figure" or "symbol" that could "make present" the body and blood of Christ. Here Tertullian is a notable example. Finally, for some "the bread and wine of the Eucharist are described as the body and blood of Christ."[69]

As Stone argued, and as later scholarship has confirmed, the language in Tertullian of "figure" and "symbol" are not to be taken anachronistically, as though Tertullian meant "merely a symbol," in some memorialist sense.[70] The pre-Montanist Tertullian worked from the Greek concept of image and prototype, in which the holy reality participated in and through the image.

In sum, of these "three different kinds of phraseology," the first clearly pertained to a stage of early and emerging eucharistic reflection. The other two types of language that Stone described—the more symbolic and the more realistic—both asserted the eucharistic gift to be the body and blood of Christ, although authors differed on how the gift was the body and blood.[71]

Two decades after Stone's work, Josef Rupert Geiselmann, in his influential study of prescholastic eucharistic thought, *Die Eucharistielehre der Vorscholastik*, conceived these categories similarly when he argued that the ninth century inherited two distinct strands of eucharistic theology from the early church. Significantly developing directions already established by both Protestant and Roman Catholic scholars, Geiselmann argued for a metabolic tradition that traced back to Ambrose of Milan (ca. 340–397) and a less realistic, nonmetabolic tradition that traced back to Augustine of Hippo (354–430).[72] Both traditions are found through early medieval theology and liturgical traditions, with the Gallican liturgical tradition preferring Ambrosian language that proclaimed a change in the eucharistic elements, and the Roman liturgical tradition preferring Augustinian language that proclaimed the saving presence of Christ for believers through the symbols of bread and wine. The well-known introduction of the Roman liturgy into the Carolingian territory under the leadership of Alcuin, and the seeking for liturgical uniformity, brought these two views into contrast with each other.[73] Both traditions continued through the Carolingian period,[74] and led into the eucharistic controversies of the ninth and eleventh centuries.[75]

Although subsequent scholarship has debated the eucharistic theology of particular thinkers within these two traditions, and shown the diverse ways these themes could be held together, the basic categorization inherited and developed by Geiselmann has stood the test of scholarship.[76] Modern Roman Catholic liturgical scholarship has argued that a clear summary of "the history of eucharistic theology of the first millennium" shows that what was "seriously debated" was the manner of conceiving the eucharistic sacraments of body and blood. This oscillated between the more realistic theology of somatic presence characteristic of the fourth-century school of Antioch, exemplified by John Chrysostom, and the more symbolic theology of Augustine, whose Neoplatonic philosophy prevented him from interpreting the sacraments as more than signs pointing to a spiritual reality.[77]

A brief comment on the theology of eucharistic sacrifice, which "did not prove to be a subject of serious debate," is needed prior to describing these two interpretations of eucharistic presence.[78] While strongly repudiating in supersessionist manner the animal sacrifices of Judaism, the tradition largely upheld the sacrificial life and death of Jesus as one with his ascended heavenly life and reign as glorified Lord.[79] The earthly church, whose life and worship is a living, spiritual sacrifice, has communion with this crucified and risen Christ, who is the foundation of the church, which is the body of Christ. The liturgical life of the church is thus realized participation in Christ's paschal "mystery" (*mysterion* [Greek] or *sacramentum* [Latin]).[80] Leo the Great (pope, 440–61) would summarize this most notably in his homily for Ascension Day: "And so the sight of our Redeemer today passes into mystery (*sacramentum*)," which meant that what Jesus had done in history had passed into "sacrament" or "mystery" celebrated by the church each day in the liturgy.[81] Understandings of how the eucharistic celebration related to both the eschatological reign of Christ and the church, which was the body of Christ, varied and will be taken up later.

The somatic eucharistic theology of Antioch found notable expression in the homilies and catechetical instructions of John Chrysostom (ca. 347–407), the great preacher in Antioch (386–98), who later was ordained bishop of Constantinople (398). Chrysostom was "the classical teacher of the somatic real presence and the most expressive witness of the identity of the eucharistic and historical body of Jesus. . . . No one called it so emphatically and urgently to the consciousness of the believer, no one made it so fruitful for the pious life as he."[82]

Early in his priesthood Chrysostom composed his famous "On the Priesthood," where in chapter 6 he described what it meant to be a priest who "invokes the Holy Spirit, and offers the most awe-filled sacrifice, and continually handles the Lord common to all people." Chrysostom writes that "[a]t such a time, angels stand by the Priest; and the whole sanctuary, and the space around the altar, is filled with the powers of heaven, in honor of Him who lies there." Chrysostom agreed with a vision that someone had in which the angels clothed in shining robes encircle the altar like soldiers who bow down before their king.[83] Such reverential imagery was demanded because Jesus' very body and blood not only were present at the altar but were touched by the hands,[84] and taken into the mouth.[85] For Chrysostom the elements became the very body and blood of Jesus Christ, now transfigured, who gives himself personally to the one receiving the eucharistic elements.[86] The "flesh of Christ is a means of union with the Risen Lord."[87]

The eucharistic theology of Chrysostom was essentially taken up by fellow theologian Theodore of Mopsuestia (ca. 350–428), often regarded as the best Antiochene thinker.[88] In a passage that eerily foreshadows later Reformation discussions, Theodore argued that Jesus did not refer to the bread as a symbol but, using the verb "to be," told followers that the bread and wine *are* body and blood that are set before us.[89]

For Theodore, as for the Greek East in general, this change came through anamnesis, a Greek term that lacks any good English translation.[90] Anamnesis essentially meant making effectively present from the past, through cultic activity, both the christological events of salvation history and the personal presence of the Savior himself.

The somatic tradition of the older Antioch thinkers such as John Chrysostom and Theodore of Mopsuestia did not continue among the Antiochenes of the next century. The great christological debates of the century changed matters.[91] In an interesting move of piety and theology, Nestorius (ca. 381–451), patriarch of Constantinople, and his friend and defender Theodoret of Cyrus (393–ca. 460), argued Christology against monophysite opponents by appealing to the Eucharist. For Nestorius the bread and wine, through the celebration of the Eucharist, became the body and blood of Jesus Christ for the gathered believers. How exactly Nestorius conceived this to happen is not entirely clear, but Nestorius was quite clear that the nature of the elements did not change and that the eucharistic bread remained bread.[92] Theodoret continued this theology in more development by arguing that indeed there was no change in the nature of the elements. Rather grace (χαρις) was added to their nature (φυσις), thereby completing their change through a process of elevation, so that gathered believers receive Christ himself.[93]

The eucharistic traditions of Antioch can be seen in the Latin West as well, notably in Hilary of Poitiers (ca. 315–67) and Ambrose of Milan.[94] In particular, Ambrose studied Greek eucharistic theology and represented a Latin voice upholding the somatic presence of Jesus Christ, borrowed from Antioch and the Greek East.[95] The bread and wine in their nature are changed into the somatic real presence, and this change happens "by the blessing" (benedictio).[96] However one takes Ambrose's assertion about the blessing, it remains clear that the change ultimately results from the word of Christ that is as creative now as it was in the creation itself:

> For that sacrament which you receive is by the word of Christ. But if the word of Elijah was so greatly effective that it could bring down fire from heaven, will not the word of Christ be effective so that it changes the form of the elements? You read about the making of the whole world: "He spoke and they were made, He commanded and they were created." Therefore, is the word of Christ, which was able to make out of nothing that which was not, not able to change things that are into what they were not?[97]

For Ambrose the effected, somatic presence of Christ in the Eucharist was a personal encounter, not by way of shadow (umbra) or symbol (figura) or image (typo), but face to face (facie ad faciem). "I find you," says Ambrose, "in your sacraments" (in tuis te invenio sacramentis).[98]

While Greek eucharistic theology influenced Ambrose's thinking on the somatic presence of Christ and on the word of Christ as effecting that presence, the Greek concept of anamnesis was lacking. Like Cyprian before him, Ambrose rejected the idea that Christ's sacrifice, as a constitutive part of salvation history, was actualized with that saving history and Savior through commemoration.[99] Rather, argued Ambrose, Christ is the one true high priest, whose Old Testament type was Melchizedek, and whose sacrifice is offered during the Eucharist as the church's believers participate with him.[100]

This more realistic, somatic eucharistic theology, which typified the fourth-century Antiochene theologians and Ambrose, contrasts with a more symbolic eucharistic theology typified by Augustine and carried on by Pope Gelasius I (pope 492–96) and Fulgentius of Ruspe (462–527).[101] Here the Eucharist was seen as dependent on the church, the true body of Christ (*verum corpus Christi*), and was a means of furthering the unity of the church. The church was not primarily a fruit of the Eucharist.

Prior to discussing Augustine's eucharistic thought as such, perhaps some introductory comments are needed, since, in the words of Pierre Batiffol, "[t]he doctrine of St. Augustine on the Eucharist has been considered by theologians and critics who studied it as one of the difficult chapters in the history of dogma."[102] Since the Protestant Reformation of the sixteenth century, in which Protestants and Roman Catholic scholars both appealed to Augustine's teaching on the Eucharist, the discussion has typically revolved around the question of whether Augustine's teachings were "realistic" or "symbolic." Even though the better and more influential essays of the twentieth century readily admit this approach to be anachronistic, almost all recent essays still raise the question in something like this binary manner.

On one side, there are passages in Augustine that discuss sacramental and eucharistic signs as pointing to, while participating in, spiritual realities; passages where Augustine says that the bread and cup are the body and blood of Christ in "a certain fashion" (*quodam modo*); and passages where Augustine says that the appropriation of the Eucharist is to be spiritual. Augustine's commentaries on the Fourth Gospel are especially notable for comments such as these. By contrast, Augustine has passages in which he talks about holding Christ when the elements are held; or, communicants being offered Christ's body, or being able to recognize the body of Christ in the bread and the blood that flowed from Christ's side in the cup.[103]

As some scholars have carefully pointed out, although Augustine never denies a "realist" position, even the passages in which he sounds "realistic" never specifically *affirm* a metabolic presence such as Ambrose clearly gave.[104] Most scholars acknowledge the two different types of passages in Augustine and try to find ways to account for both: realistic and symbolic positions are both present, but not as moderns so conceive the issue;[105] or Augustine's teaching on signs cannot be fit into the later realistic/symbolic binary categories, because Augustine is "neither realistic nor symbolic but sacramental";[106] or with reference to the signs Augustine would be "symbolic," but with reference to the realities signified he would be "realistic";[107] or the issue of realistic or symbolic misses the larger ecclesial context of sacrifice and community, wherein believers together, as the body of Christ, are united to God;[108] or tensions simply exist in Augustine's eucharistic thought.[109]

On the trajectory outlined by Geiselmann and Kilmartin, and undergirded by the work of Betz—all three notable Roman Catholic scholars—these two options are not sufficiently adequate to describe Augustine, who insisted that believers do indeed participate in Christ's true body, although for Augustine "we do not so much receive Christ; rather, he receives us and engrafts us more deeply into his body."[110] Furthermore, once one assumes the (inadequate) alternatives of symbolic or realistic, Augustine can seem symbolic because he does not affirm a localized metabolic or somatic presence, and yet he can seem realistic because he affirms a real communion with Christ.[111] Put slightly differently, the alternatives are not realistic or symbolic, but realistic (metabolic presence), realistic (nonmetabolic presence), and symbolic. Later chapters of this study will argue that because the false alternatives of realistic or symbolic have been applied to Reformed eucharistic theology, centuries of mistakes have been made about Zwingli, Calvin, and the Reformed tradition, even mistakes from within the Reformed tradition in its own self-understanding.

Turning to Augustine now, the essential, internal dilemma for his eucharistic thought came from his combination of Christian faith and Neoplatonic metaphysics. By faith Augustine believed what otherwise would seem incredulous to a Neoplatonist: Christ's bodily presence, formed from the sensible world, had ascended and was glorified in the spiritual realm; what came from "below" was literally present "above." Because Augustine refused to conceive that this glorified body received the divine quality of immensity, what remained was the alternative that the glorified, historical body remained in heaven. As Henri de Lubac put the matter, in his study on the Eucharist in the Middle Ages, "among many Augustinians the localizing of the body of Christ would constitute, for centuries to come, the principal obstacle to sacramental realism."[112]

For Augustine himself the issue of where the glorified risen body was situated did not arise as it did in later medieval debates, partly because of the materialism of the later period, and partly because of how Augustine held together ecclesiology, Christology, and sacrament. According to Augustine in *The City of God*, Christians live out the true Christian sacrifice and as a community become united in, and as, Christ's body. Exegeting the meaning of Romans 12:1–3, Augustine begins the sixth chapter of the tenth book by asserting that "a true sacrifice is every work that is done that we may be united to God as a holy union" (*ut sancta societate inhaereamus Deo*).[113] This unity of the church in Christ is then offered to God as its sacrifice through Christ who is "the great High Priest" (*sacerdotum magnum*), and who offers himself to God as priest and sacrifice. The church as Christ's body participates, offering "itself through him."[114] So Augustine can conclude chapter 6 by intimately connecting the sacrificial lives of believers, who live the love of Christ (*caritas Christi*), to Christ himself as his body, to the Eucharist that itself is this body of Christ:

This is the sacrifice of Christians: the many, the one body in Christ. And this likewise is the sacrifice that the church repeatedly celebrates by the sacrament of the altar, noted by the faithful, in which she shows that she herself is offered in the offering that she makes to God.[115]

As such, the body of Christ is the foundation for, not merely the result of, the Eucharist itself. Kilmartin puts this succinctly by saying that for Augustine

[t]he core of the eucharistic liturgy is love: unity of Christians in Christ and with one another in the Spirit of Christ who is the soul of the church. This unity is the essential presupposition of the possibility of authentic eucharistic celebration and not merely an effect of the reception of the eucharistic flesh and blood.[116]

How, then, did the Eucharist convey the body of Christ? The eucharistic elements themselves were for Augustine signs that pointed beyond themselves to their ultimate reality and by so doing can be said to participate in that reality. The bread and wine were thus images of Christ's body and blood, and they were the means by which the believers came to be more deeply abiding in Christ and the church, which is Christ's true body.[117] For Augustine the Eucharist does not afford, precisely, an "encounter" with Christ, as in the case of Ambrose's teaching, but a deepening of one's being in Christ. In the Eucharist we do not so much receive Christ; rather, he receives us and grafts us more deeply into his body.[118]

There is a nonmetabolic quality that unmistakably separates Augustine's treatment of the Eucharist from the more metabolic Western tradition of Ambrose,[119] and this nonmetabolic trajectory continues into Gelasius and Fulgentius of Ruspe.

Gelasius continued and de facto ratified this nonsomatic tradition in the West that can be seen in Augustine, but did so not by borrowing from Augustine, but from the later Antiochene thinkers Nestorius and Theodoret of Cyrus, who, as noted earlier, departed from the classical Antiochene somatic tradition exemplified by Chrysostom and Theodore of Mopsuestia.[120] Following the tradition of Augustine, and preceding him Cyprian,[121] Gelasius understood the unity of the church not primarily as a result of the Eucharist but as its presupposition. Fulgentius of Ruspe continued this Roman trajectory and supplied the connection of baptism that Gelasius did not discuss. From the moment of baptism onward, Christians were members of Christ's body, a "living victim" (*viva hostia*), and so the Eucharist signified to Christians the gifts received, as members of Christ's body, when the Eucharist is received.[122]

These two strains of eucharistic theology concerning the real presence of Christ, one more symbolic and oriented to deepening the reality in which the gathered community already existed, the other more realistic and oriented to a metabolic presence of Christ in the elements themselves, were inherited by the early medieval period in the Latin West. The context of this era helped shape and blend these two traditions in a new way.

The worldview of the early medieval Latin West was oriented to the concrete, material world in a way that the patristic thinkers were not. For the patristic world, from Augustine in the West to the Greek theologians of the East, Neoplatonism generally undergirded the prevalent worldview. What was at hand, by senses and conception, were signs that participated in, however imperfectly, the abiding realities to which they pointed. This tradition was largely lost to the early medieval West, where generations of tribal migrations and social changes produced "a kind of practical positivism, or practical materialism" to what lay at hand. It was a worldview of "thingly realism."[123] In this worldview, signs pointed to realities that existed completely outside themselves. This differing orientation in the West led, for example, to the inability of Frankish theologians to appreciate the iconoclastic debates of the East—from the Synod of Hiereia (754) to the Second Council of Nicaea (787) to the Synod of Constantinople (842)—and to insist that icons lacked any spiritual quality. The distinction between veneration and worship, dependent as it was on partial participation of the spiritual through the material, was lost on the Frankish thinkers of the ninth century.[124]

The great eucharistic debates of this period were conducted in this more materialistic context, as were early scholastic philosophical distinctions that were to have significant effect on Western eucharistic theology. Paschasius Radbertus (786–ca. 860), who was abbot of the Benedictine monastery at Corbie, composed the first extant essay devoted to the Eucharist, "On the Body and Blood of the Lord" (De corpore et sanguine Domini), written in 831 for the monks of Corbie, and sent in 844 to Emperor Charles the Bald.[125] The treatise occasioned questions from the emperor, who sought a scholarly response from Ratramnus of Corbie (d. ca. 868), whose essay bore the same title as that of Paschasius.[126] The assessment of these two works has been controversial from the start, made all the more difficult because their thought world was neither that of the later scholastics nor fully that of patristic Neoplatonism.[127]

Paschasius based his eucharistic realism on a fundamental principle that owed much to the material character of his century. Because the Eucharist offers the spiritual nourishment of Christ's body and blood, that body and blood must be contained in the Eucharist, because something cannot offer what it does not have:

> It must, therefore, be that this sacrament which confers life, itself possesses what it gives to those who receive it rightly. If life is in this sacrament, the sacrament is the flesh of the true living being, it is the blood in which is, in very truth, to be found the life which exists forever.[128]

According to Paschasius, the senses perceive the eucharistic elements, which are the image (*figura*), while *faith receives* the reality within that image, "the true flesh of Christ which was crucified and buried."[129] Where the older Greek thought world saw the reality giving itself through the image, so that, by participating in the reality, the image was a special type of its presence, for Paschasius the image has become the merely visible, to be grasped by the senses, that *contains something distinct from it*, which was to be *grasped by faith*. Paschasius also simply identified the historical body of Christ and the eucharistic body of Christ. The result was the tendency to identify univocally what was material (bread and wine) with the historical Jesus that it contained, so that, as Paschasius wrote to Frudegard, "we receive in the bread what hung on the cross."[130]

Not all theologians were convinced by Paschasius's arguments. Hrabanus Maurus (ca. 776–856), abbot of Fulda and archbishop of Mainz, complained that some have not "thought correctly about this sacrament of the body and blood of the Lord," by asserting that the body born of Mary and crucified on the cross "is the same that is received on the altar."[131] From within Corbie itself came the strongest and most articulate responses, that by Ratramnus, who firmly upheld the Augustinian tradition.[132]

Ratramnus could not agree that the resurrected body of Christ, which left this space for the heavenly space, could be locally present in corruptible elements. This would contradict the resurrection itself. Yet the pious life of faith demanded the present body and blood of Christ on the altar. How to reconcile this problem?

For Ratramnus the bread and wine were "figures" (*figurae*) that also were "true" (*veritas*). The difference between figure and reality was not between sign and signified, between what is symbolic and what is real. Rather a figure was a *veiled* presence of something, while truth was a *manifest* presence. The difference between figure and truth was thus between a veiled manner of being revealed and a clear manner of being revealed. So the eucharistic elements were "truly" what they were, bread and wine, and could not "truly" be Christ's body and blood. The elements were "figuratively" Christ's body and blood, by which Ratramnus meant they presented Christ's real presence but did so in a veiled manner.[133]

Here arises another aspect of Ratramnus's eucharistic teaching, one that had a heritage stretching back to Jerome (ca. 347–ca. 420): Jerome clearly posed the distinction between the historical body of Christ, crucified, dead, and risen into glory, and the eucharistic body of Christ present on the altar.[134] This distinction between the historical and glorified body of Christ and the eucharistic body of Christ was to continue through the medieval period and, as we shall see, be given a distinctive shape by early scholastic theologians, particularly Lombard (ca. 1100–ca. 1160).[135]

Ratramnus was aware of this passage from Jerome and commented upon it,[136] and stood at the delta of Carolingian reflection on just this distinction.[137] Exactly how Ratramnus conceived that the eucharistic body would participate in the historical, glorified body is not explicitly clear from his treatise, although a strong case has been made that Augustine's Neoplatonism lies behind Ratramnus's argument.[138] In a special way the prototype participated in the image, bestowing its presence there.

HIGH AND LATE MEDIEVAL PERIODS

Theologians made significant developments in eucharistic theology during the period from the eleventh through the thirteenth century. Theology increasingly focused upon the metabolic presence, representing the Antiochene tradition, to the expense of the nonmetabolic Augustinian tradition of nourishing the faithful ever more deeply in Christ their head, a tradition that was vital during the early scholastic period in both a mystical form and an ecclesial form.[139] In the high and late medieval periods, the consecration became conceived as centering around the conversion of the elements into Christ's body and blood; the priestly activity was seen to center on the words of institution and the moment of consecration; and a primary means of lay participation was watching.[140]

Berengar of Tours (ca. 1000–ca. 1088), head of the cathedral school at Tours, marked a transition from the eucharistic debates of the prescholastics during the early medieval period to the scholasticism of the high and late medieval periods.[141] Berengar represented a logical extension, in some ways, of the Augustinian effort to reconcile the historic, glorified body of Christ and the eucharistic body. Berengar partly used concepts and passages borrowed from Ratramnus that he wrongly attributed to the Irish theologian John Scotus Erigena (ca. 810–ca. 877).

Ratramnus had contrasted figure (*figura*) and truth (*veritas*). Berengar also contrasted figure and truth, but did so in a different fashion, arguing that the bread and wine are only images or signs of the body and blood of Christ. The substance of the bread and wine remain, and Christ imparts his real spiritual presence, through the symbols, to believers. Where Ratramnus held to the real presence of Christ's body and blood, bestowed by its Neoplatonic participation in the eucharistic body of Christ, which itself was communicated in a true but veiled manner to the believer, Berengar made a non-Augustinian appeal through a concept of substance (*substantia*). Since substance referred to the sensible properties of something, the substance of Jesus' body and blood clearly were not given in the sacrament. In this regard, Berengar contributed to the eucharistic discussion the issue of exactly *how* the bread and wine became the body of Christ.[142]

His argument extended even further the medieval "thingly" orientation regarding the Eucharist.

Berengar was forced to recant his eucharistic theology. His first oath, and perhaps the one best known, was required by the Council of Rome of 1059. It partly read that the bread and wine, once consecrated on the altar, "are not only the sacrament, but also the true body and blood of our Lord Jesus Christ, and sensually, not only by sacrament, but in truth, are touched and broken by the hands of the priests, and are torn apart by the teeth of the faithful."[143] At the Council of Rome of 1079 Berengar was forced to confess a more sophisticated oath that reflected a medieval tradition in which the eucharistic body and blood were elevated to heaven, united with the glorified body of the risen Lord, and thus became for the believer the presence of that historical, glorified body of Christ.[144]

As Kilmartin notes, by the beginning of the eleventh century the scholastic theologians had three eucharistic themes with which to work. From Augustine they learned that eucharistic grace was the unity of the church as the one body of Christ that nourished believers. From Ambrose they received the metabolic (or somatic) tradition, strengthened at the beginning of high Middle Ages by the materialistic orientation of the Carolingian theologians and the eucharistic debates from Radbertus, Ratramnus, and Berengar. Finally, from Jerome came the distinction between the eucharistic body and the historical, glorified body of the risen Christ.[145] Using the basic Augustinian dyad of sign and reality (*sacramentum et res*) as a building block, the early scholastics grasped these three themes (Ambrose—eucharistic realism; Jerome—eucharistic body distinguished from historical, glorified body; Augustine—unity of the church as the specific grace of the eucharist) and linked them together by developing a new, *threefold* pattern that went beyond the older, Augustinian *twofold* (sign and reality/*sacramentum et res*) pattern.[146]

There was, first, the bread and wine. This was the sign itself (*sacramentum tantum*) that signified its reality (*res*), the eucharistic body and blood, that participated in that sign of bread and wine.

The eucharistic body and blood was itself then a sign that signified, and thus was called a *sacramentum et res*. This eucharistic body and blood signified the historical, glorified body that participated in that sign of bread and wine.

This eucharistic body and blood, as the glorified body of Christ, also signified the ultimate and sanctifying grace of the sacrament, the unity of the church as the body of Christ (*res tantum*). The structure might be laid out like this:

- *sacramentum tantum* (the sign itself):
    bread and wine that signify the invisible, eucharistic body
    and blood that participate in this sign

- *sacramentum et res* (the sign and reality)
    the invisible, eucharistic body and blood that signify the
        historical, glorified body of Christ
    that participates in this sign and effects as present the
        unity of the Church
- *res* (the reality itself)
    the grace of the sacrament as the unity of the Church[147]

A significant change was first added to this scheme by Peter Lombard (ca. 1100–ca. 1160) when he conceived of the threefold structure as:

- *sacramentum* (sign)
    the bread and wine (species)
- *res contenta et significata* (the reality contained and signified)
    the eucharistic body and blood (*caro et sanguis*)
- *res significata et non contenta* (the reality signified and not contained)
    the unity of the church (*unitas ecclesiae*)

With this adaptation to the threefold pattern, Lombard situated the ultimate grace of the sacrament *outside* the sacrament itself, though still available to the believer. This highlighted the somatic presence and the grace "radiating from the eucharistic body," but this also obscured the eschatological dimension of the heavenly Christ in glory now "in the midst of the heavenly church" with whom one also is in communion.[148]

An interesting corollary to this threefold structure was that the early scholastics also conceived of a double consecration: from the elements to the eucharistic body and blood, and from the eucharistic body and blood to the glorified body. The purpose of this double consecration was "the integration of the liturgical community into this single *transitus* of Christ from suffering to glory in virtue of its self-offering made in union with Christ in the power of the Holy Spirit."[149] These early scholastics held to a broad and encompassing meaning to the word "consecration."

With the metabolic presence highlighted by the eucharistic controversies, and by the threefold structure as posed by Lombard, the problem to solve became *exactly how the eucharistic body was actualized*. The early scholastics conceived of transubstantiation as one of several answers, with annihilation and consubstantiation as alternative explanations. Once Lanfranc (d. 1089) distinguished between the essence of something (*substantia*) and its appearances (*species*), the way was open to better explain the process of eucharistic change. The outward appearances of bread and wine remained, but the underlying substance changed to the body and blood of Christ (so-called transubstantiation). Early scholastics also conceived that consubstantiation was a possibility—to the substance of the bread and

wine was added the substance of the body and blood. So also annihilation (or succession) was conceived as possible—through the consecration
the substance of bread and wine were destroyed by, or succeeded by, the
body and blood present under the appearance of bread and wine.[150]

While the eleventh- and twelfth-century scholastics constructed the
basic eucharistic structure that would dominate the high and late medieval period, the scholastics of the thirteenth and fourteenth centuries
gave the inherited teachings some new and, as history has shown, influential features that persisted to the Protestant Reformation and beyond.
Where the early scholastics tended to see the priestly activity as that of
whole church, the thirteenth-century scholastics focused on the presiding
priest, acting as Christ himself, effecting the conversion of the elements.
Where the early scholastics conceived of consecration in a broad sense,
encompassing a twofold movement (from bread and wine to eucharistic
body, and from eucharistic body to glorified body), the thirteenth-century
scholastics conceived of a single consecratory moment. Finally, following a trend begun among certain early scholastics, the thirteenth- and
fourteenth-century thinkers argued for the words of Christ, as contained
in the institution narrative, as the essential form needed for the consecration.[151] The result was, on the practical theology level, that the high point
of the liturgy was the priestly words of consecration and the elevation of
the host, with gazing upon the elevation as the key activity that was done
by believers.[152] Miracle stories associated with the elevations, indulgences
given to farmers working in the field who turned to look at the church
when the bells signaled the elevation, lawsuits in order to gain a better
view of the altar, and laity racing from church to church in the cities to see
as many elevations as possible, were soon to follow.[153] At this point, seeing (not eating) became eucharistic participation.[154]

Why this emphasis on the visual? The overwhelming sense of sinfulness
and thus unworthiness that the laity experienced was a major contributor,
so that even those who were thought to be most pious still preferred confession to actually receiving the Eucharist.[155] The sense of unworthiness
extended even to the seeing itself, so that serious theological debate asked
whether sinners would commit a mortal sin by *watching* the elevation.[156]
People did not want to receive the Eucharist physically, out of awe and
unworthiness, and the medieval church at the Fourth Lateran Council
(1215) *mandated* yearly eucharistic participation.[157]

Thomas Aquinas (1224–74) was part of the medieval eucharistic world
that assumed votive masses for living and dead, multiple side altars
in the churches, communion in only one kind, the priestly practice of
silently saying parts of the mass, adoration of the sacrament, and infre-
quent lay communion. In this setting, he gave a thorough, and later to
be taken as classical, exposition of eucharistic theology and sacrifice that

was a feature of an entire theological worldview that was, so to speak, eucharistic.[158] The whole world was related to and dependent upon the grace of God, known in creation, proclaimed in salvation history, and present once and still in Jesus Christ, Word made flesh, the one mediator, who has united believers into his reign, the body of Christ.[159] Into this triune God one was baptized, and by the very being of this God one was nourished during life's spiritual journey. Any study of Thomas's eucharistic theology must be set in the context of someone who composed the following liturgical verses:

> O most precious and wondrous banquet, bringing us salvation and filled with goodness! What can be more precious than this feast in which, not the flesh of calves and kids, as in the Old Law, but Christ, the true God, is set before us to be eaten![160]

Christ instituted the Eucharist, argued Thomas, because he desired to remain present in the church, in a sacramental manner available to faith, unlike a mere corporeal presence available to the senses. The whole economy of salvation, which comes to the individual as spiritual nourishment through faith in Christ's passion, is thus effectively realized now in the sacrament that is Christ's activity in the church itself.[161]

For Thomas, in this sacramental commemoration of the passion the entire Christ is present through divinely given signs, not through mere outward appearances. Appearances only show something, but signs communicate the reality itself, and the words of Christ show that Christ himself is given.[162] This means that Christ's substantial presence is not to be conceived as many Protestants (and Roman Catholics?) ordinarily conceive it: The commonplace says that the external appearances remain bread and wine, but beneath these sensory appearances a miracle has happened locally, and in a hidden manner, that turned the stuff of bread and wine into Christ's body and blood, as one might chemically change one substance into another. This mistakenly takes the sacramental signs of consecrated bread and wine to be mere accidental appearances, available to the senses, under which a material change has taken place that went with appearances.

This also mistakes the underlying event to be some kind of natural change. Rather, argued Thomas, no natural change has taken place at all, since natural change means readjustment of worldly matter. Any natural change, that resulted in locally moving from place to place, for example, or coming to be through decay and generation, was rejected by Thomas as inappropriate for understanding Christ's presence. Once such natural substantial change is rejected, then the idea of substantial change can be properly appropriated. What happens, argued Thomas, is that a total substantial change has taken place that defies imagination and transcends the natural order: a miracle, on the order of creation, or incarnation, not on the order of chemical transformation. In this sense, "from the outset of his explanation Aquinas saw this [i.e., the substantial presence of Christ] as an essentially spiritual presence."[163] This is why the truly personal presence of the entire Christ, body and blood, soul and divinity, can finally be known only, in some fashion, to the intellect itself in a spiritual manner:

> [T]he body of Christ is in this sacrament as if it were just substance. But substance as such cannot be seen by the bodily eye, nor is it the object of any sense, nor can it be imagined; it is only open to the intellect, the object of which is the essence of things, as Aristotle says. Hence, properly speaking, the body of Christ, according to the mode of existence which it has in this sacrament, can be reached neither by sense nor by imagination; it is open only to the intellect which may be called a spiritual eye.[164]

Transubstantiation as explained by Thomas was an elegant proposal that generally solved several long-standing theological problems. First, it steered a sensible path between the Scylla of a "merely" symbolic eucharistic presence of Christ and the Charybdis of a crassly materialistic presence, alternatives that might be presented by a reading of Berengar and his oath of 1059 respectively.[165] Second, an answer was found to the question originally raised by Jerome and puzzled over by medieval theologians: What is the relationship between the glorified historical body of Christ and the eucharistic body offered, and how can the one glorified body be present during the many Eucharists that are celebrated? Quantity is an accidental property, not properly predicated of substance, nor applicable to the total substantial change during the Eucharist; the substance of Christ's body can be present anywhere. Finally, the issue of unworthy reception was addressed. An unworthy recipient received not the substance totally transformed, but merely the outward accidents of the signs.[166]

The question of unworthy reception deserves more attention, because it brought to discussion the relationship between the sign (sacramentum) character of the Eucharist and the metaphysics attached. This issue looked back both to the teacher of Thomas, Albert the Great (1193/1206–1280), and to the teacher of Bonaventure (1221–74), Alexander of Hales (d. 1245). The discussion continued into Thomas and beyond.[167] As a general observation, the Franciscan tradition, beginning with Alexander, emphasized the sign function of the Eucharist so that unbelievers, or even a mouse, might consume the Eucharist but, having no faith in the sign, would receive only bread and wine. As the later Franciscan theologian Duns Scotus (1266–1308) put the matter, these people (or animals) receive the sacrament but do not receive sacramentally.[168]

By contrast, the Dominican perspective, beginning with Albert the Great and continuing through Thomas, held closely to the metaphysics over and against the sign value of the Eucharist and the intention of the recipient. How could substance and accidents become attached and detached so easily? The body and blood are received along with the sign into both the mouth and the stomach; but Thomas distinguished between what was received and the reception by the one receiving. In the latter case, only when the receiver understood the sign and its spiritual reality was there reception as such.

Bringing the medieval section to a close requires two more comments. First, the medieval period, up to and including the Council of Trent, showed variety on the issue of the transformation of the eucharistic elements.[169] Not until Duns Scotus (1266–1308) did anyone take the teaching on transubstantiation given by the Fourth Lateran Council, originally aimed at the Cathars, to be normative;[170] but Scotus, as well as William of Ockham (1285–1349) and Gabriel Biel (ca. 1425–95), taught so-called annihilation, or succession, as a form of transubstantiation, and all three thought such a view was included by Lateran IV.[171] Although consubstantiation lost favor by the fourteenth century, some theologians, including John of Paris (d. 1306), continued to find it an option as a form of transubstantiation.[172] Pierre d'Ailly (1350–1420) mentions all three options, preferring the annihilation (or succession) argument, and noting that consubstantiation remained an alternative.[173] Furthermore, the options between annihilation and transubstantiation (strictly speaking) remained disputed by Franciscan and Dominican theologians so that the Council of Trent (1545–47, 1551–52, 1562–63) likely left these two options open.[174]

Second, as ought to be clear so far, the medieval period generally showed plurality about the Eucharist in many ways.[175] The metabolic tradition from Ambrose, with its physical consumption of divine food, and the nonmetabolic tradition from Augustine, with its more spiritual and mystical development, both continued. Also, the sign function of the eucharistic elements remained important within medieval thought, and when brought to bear on scholastic metaphysics, it helped produce a wide variety of interpretations about what happened to the body of Christ during and after consecration.[176] Connected to this issue was the ongoing medieval divergence between the Neoplatonic sign function of the Eucharist, looking back to Augustine, and the scholastic metaphysics that had borrowed instead from Aristotle. Finally, the mode of eucharistic transformation was widely discussed, with three options at hand: transubstantiation; annihilation (succession), which was taken by some to be a form of transubstantiation, and thus authorized by Lateran IV; and consubstantiation, which fell somewhat out of favor by the fourteenth century but remained an option into the fifteenth century. From within these complex traditions, and looking to Scripture, the Protestant Reformers fashioned their eucharistic theologies. Before turning to the Protestant Reformation, however, one more addition needs to be made: the history of *sacramentum*.

EXCURSUS: HISTORICAL OVERVIEW ON JESUS AND "SACRAMENT"

The Reformed tradition shares a common tradition about sacrament that begins with the apostle Paul and the Greek word *mysterion* ("mystery") as found in Paul's letters (e.g., 1 Cor. 2:1; 4:1; Rom. 16:25).[177] There the word referred to God's hidden plan for salvation. The developing deuteropauline tradition (e.g., Eph. 1:9; 3:3, 4, 9; Col. 1:26–27; 2:2) took up this theme and proclaimed that this "mystery" is embodied in Christ, in whose sufferings we share (e.g., Col. 1:24–2:3).[178] From there, early North African, Latin translations of the Greek New Testament translated *mysterion* with the word *sacramentum*. In this context, *sacramentum* referred to the redeeming work of God that was known through Jesus.

The writings of the North African theologian Tertullian (ca. 160–ca. 230), including what may be the earliest work on sacramental theology (*De baptismo*), continued the connection between *mysterion* and *sacramentum*.[179] In *De spectaculis* Tertullian calls the Eucharist a sacrament (3:10), and in *Adversus Marcionem* he calls baptism a sacrament several times, as he also does in *De baptismo*. Furthermore, Tertullian does not limit his understanding of sacrament simply to baptism and Eucharist; he calls charity "the highest sacrament of the faith" (*De patientia* 12:133–34), and he uses *sacramentum* in relation to martyrdom (*Scorpiace*, chap. 9).

The word "sacrament" carried two principal meanings by the early third century. It referred to Jesus, because God's redeeming presence was known through the man Jesus. Sacrament also referred to certain rituals of the church, because likewise God's redeeming presence was known through something physical. The much-beloved biblical passage that symbolically connected Jesus as sacrament to the church's sacraments was the scene of blood (symbolizing the Eucharist) and water (symbolizing baptism) flowing from the wounded side of Christ (John 19:34). Many of the early church theologians allegorically interpreted this scene as referring to the birth of the church through the issuance of Christ's blood and water, that is, through the sacraments of baptism and Eucharist.[180]

By the fourth century the words *mysterion* and *sacramentum* gained prominence as the rite of Christian initiation, and the catechetical teachings about baptism and Eucharist flourished in the post-Constantinian period. The writings of Ambrose (339–97), Cyril of Jerusalem (ca. 315–86), Theodore of Mopsuestia (ca. 350–428), and other patristic theologians speak about baptism and Eucharist from a Neoplatonic perspective in which the physical sign of the sacrament could be distinguished from the spiritual reality signified in it, yet truly participative in that same spiritual reality.

Perhaps the most influential among these theologians, however, stands the North African bishop Augustine of Hippo (354–430), for whom physical realities were the windows through which the spiritual realities reach us.[181] As this chapter has just discussed, Augustine also has a notable chapter in the tenth book of *The City of God* that essentially exegetes the meaning of Romans 12:1–3. There he argues that the communion of Christian lives given in love is offered to God as its sacrifice through Christ "the great High Priest (*sacerdotum magnum*) who offered himself to God in His passion for us." Augustine then closes the chapter by asserting that "[t]his is the sacrifice of Christians: the many, the one body in Christ. And this likewise is the sacrifice that the church repeatedly celebrates by the sacrament of the altar, noted by the faithful, in which she shows that she herself is offered in the offering that she makes to God."[182]

The two senses of sacrament, as Jesus himself and as the sacraments of the church, continued into the medieval period, and Latin theologians gradually synthesized the two ideas of sacrament into an integrated theology. The basic medieval concept was that the church is the mystical body of the crucified, resurrected, and glorified Lord, and God's grace continues to come to us through Christ, just as it did in the incarnation. Only now the grace that comes through Christ comes through the sacraments, most especially the Eucharist, by which Jesus Christ continues to be present in the church. As we have seen above, Aquinas gave a thorough exposition of eucharistic theology and sacrifice (*Summa Theologica*, III, 73–83) that was a feature of an ecclesial worldview.[183] All creation was dependent upon the God of salvation history, the Word, who united believers into the body of Christ and sustains them with the divine presence effectively realized now in the sacrament that is Christ's activity in the church itself.

The late medieval period, and particularly the various reforming efforts in the late fifteenth and early sixteenth century, inherited the traditions that connected sacrament to Christ himself and to the rites that constituted the church and existed through the church. The Protestant reformers of the Reformed tradition continued to affirm that the true church was ultimately the body of Christ, just as they continued to affirm the sacraments that Jesus Christ instituted. The theological arguments by which they connected sacrament, church, and Jesus Christ constructed the tradition differently, however, than did the late medieval church as it moved into the Council of Trent.

From within the long-standing Western tradition where "sacrament" referred both to the body of Christ and to the sacraments constituting the church, the Reformed tradition asserted that the true church, invisible to human eyes but visible to God's eyes, is comprised of God's faithful people gathered as the body of Christ. So the Westminster Confession (IX.4) says, "By the indwelling of the Holy Spirit all believers being vitally united to Christ, who is the Head, are thus united one to another in the Church, which is his body."[184] Reformed theology, however, calls neither the visible nor the invisible church a sacrament.

Reformed theology applies the word "sacrament" to the two divinely instituted signs, baptism and Lord's Supper, to which God attaches the promise of grace.[185] In a loose sense, the true *visible* church might be called "sacramental" because its two principal marks, the preaching of the gospel and the right administration of the sacraments, both communicate God's real self-giving in Jesus Christ, but such language would be historically foreign to the Reformed tradition. Likewise, although some church rites, such as ordination, penance, and marriage, are God-given and useful;[186] and although some simple church rites that are not contrary to the Word of God might be useful ceremonies;[187] the Reformed tradition has never considered such rituals to be "sacramentals," in the way that the sign of the cross, palms, ashes, incense, or candles were a means of grace within the medieval church.

By contrast, the Reformed tradition has considered the created order to be "sacramental," insofar as that word connotes God's self-communication, even if Reformed theology typically has refrained from such language. For example, Calvin believed that God accommodates God's self in order that we might know who God is. God desires to span the distance between Creator and creation and meets us where we are, communicating to us as we so need, because we otherwise are incapable of knowing God (e.g., Com. Exod. 3:2; Com. Rom. 1:19; Com. 1 Cor. 2:7).[188] The essence of God, of course, we can never know (*Inst.* 1.13.21), but God's activity and will, however, can be seen in creation itself:

> Consequently we know the most perfect way of seeking God, and the most suitable order, is not for us to attempt with bold curiosity to penetrate to the investigation of his essence, which we ought more to adore than to search out meticulously, but for us to contemplate him in his works whereby he renders himself near and familiar to us, and in some manner communicates himself to us.[189]

Creation can clearly be a means by which God communicates to us, because God

> daily discloses himself in the entire working of the universe, so that we cannot open our eyes without being compelled to see him . . . on each of

his works he has engraved sure marks of his glory, so clear and prominent that even uncultured and dim-witted people cannot plead ignorance as an excuse.[190]

The universe has become, says Calvin, "a kind of mirror (*speculi*) in
which we are able to see him, so far as it concerns us to know him."[191]

Furthermore, human culture also reflects God's beneficent glory so that
the human mind, even though "fallen and perverted from its wholeness, is
nevertheless clothed and ornamented with God's excellent gifts."[192] Thus
Calvin acknowledges that law, philosophy, rhetoric, medicine, and math-
ematics were true and glorious achievements of ancient cultures because
God's grace was at work in the ancients and through these achievements
God's beneficence can be seen.[193] Likewise, through every age moral people have existed whose upright character can be contrasted with those
less moral. The moral qualities exemplified are "special graces of God"
(*speciales Dei gratias*) that show forth divine beneficence.[194] The Canons of
Dort (III/IV, art. 4) put the issue this way:

> There is, to be sure, a certain light of nature remaining in man after
> the fall, by virtue of which he retains some notions about God, natu-
> ral things, and the difference between what is moral and immoral,
> and demonstrates a certain eagerness for virtue and for good outward
> behavior. But this light of nature is far from enabling man to come to a
> saving knowledge of God and conversion to him—so far, in fact, that
> man does not use it rightly even in matters of nature and society.

Human moral achievements, both individually and culturally, count
not to our glory but to our condemnation, because, as Calvin saw the matter, they are done not from thanksgiving that glorifies God, who was the
source of such special graces, but were done from our own self-interest.[195]
Thus the Canons of Dort say straightforwardly that we "suppress" this
light of God in "unrighteousness" and in so doing we render ourselves
"without excuse before God."[196]

Finally, the Reformed tradition also understands that within the created order God has given certain signs that enable our confidence in
God's promises. Calvin says that such signs can be through natural elements, or even through miracles, and he calls such signs "sacraments"
(*sacramenti nomen*).[197] Among natural signs, God used "the tree of life
as a guarantee of immortality" to Adam and Eve. So too God gave the
rainbow to Noah as a pledge of grace toward the earth. Although both
tree and rainbow began as natural objects, when they were "inscribed
by the Word of God" (*inscripta fuerunt verbo Dei*), they "began to be what
previously they were not" (*inciperent esse quod prius non erant*). Among
the miracles that were divinely given signs, Calvin notes the light in the
smoking firepot (Gen. 15:17), the fleece with dew (Judg. 6:37–38), and

the shadow of the sundial going backwards (2 Kgs. 20:9–11).[198] These signs were not humanly invented but were given by God, and Calvin differentiates these from the "ordinary" sacraments that God instituted among God's people, both of the old law and those instituted by Christ in the new law.[199]

The Reformed tradition historically argued at the time of the Protestant Reformation, and still theologically maintains, that worship ought to be done according to Scripture. For some of the tradition, only those practices could be done that Scripture warranted:

> But the acceptable way of worshipping the true God is instituted by himself, and so limited by his own revealed will, that he may not be worshipped according to the imaginations and devices of men, or the suggestions of Satan, under any visible representation or any other way not prescribed in the Holy Scripture.[200]

For other parts of the tradition, rites not prescribed by Scripture could still be celebrated for our benefit so long as they did not go against Scripture. As the Second Helvetic Confession (XXVII) pastorally puts the matter, "a few moderate and simple rites, that are not contrary to the Word of God, are sufficient for the godly."

The Reformed tradition thus counts the dominically instituted sacraments as two, baptism and the Lord's Supper.[201] To these sacraments the Reformed tradition applies the long-standing dyad of *signum–res* to explain what a sacrament is. To the outer sign God attaches an inner reality; and the Reformed tradition typically understands that the inner reality that inheres to the sign is ultimately Christ himself.[202] As the Second Helvetic Confession says,

> [T]he principal thing which God promises in all sacraments and to which all the godly in all ages direct their attention (some call it the substance [*substantiam*] and matter [*materiam*] of the sacraments) is Christ the Savior.[203]

Some Reformed voices express the object signified with a proximate description, such as "holy signs and seals of the covenant of grace, immediately instituted by God, to represent Christ and his benefits, and to confirm our interest in him."[204] When one reaches the actual discussion of baptism and Supper, however, one typically finds there the description of a person's baptismal "ingrafting in Christ,"[205] or that in the Supper those who partake "really and indeed . . . receive and feed upon Christ crucified, and all the benefits of his death."[206]

Reformed theology distinguishes between the validity and the efficacy of the sacraments. The sacraments are to be administered by duly ordained ministers of the church,[207] and when so administered, with the proper sign and divine promise of grace, as the church intentionally follows the mandate of Scripture, the sacrament validly offers what the sign signifies:

> Two things are necessary for the right administration of the sacraments. The first is that they should be ministered by lawful ministers . . . and the second is that they should be ministered in the elements and manner which God has appointed. Otherwise they cease to be the sacraments of Christ Jesus.[208]

In a long discussion, the Second Helvetic Confession contrasts validly offered sacraments with the efficacy that includes "the condition of those who receive them."

> For we know that the value [i.e., fruitfulness] of the sacraments depends on faith and upon the truthfulness and pure goodness of God. For as the Word of God remains the true Word of God, in which, when it is preached, not only bare words are repeated, but at the same time the things signified or announced in words are offered by God, even if the ungodly and unbelievers hear and understand the words yet do not enjoy the things signified, because they do not receive them by true faith; so the sacraments, which by the Word consist of signs and the things signified, remain true and inviolate sacraments, signifying not only sacred things, but, by God offering, the things signified, even if unbelievers do not receive the things offered.[209]

Thus, while under right administration sacraments validly offer the divine reality that the signs signify, the efficacy applies only to those who receive the sacraments in faith. Calvin's 1545 Geneva Catechism (no. 329) simply asserts that when the sacraments are offered "[m]any do close the way by their perverseness and so make it worthless for themselves. Thus its fruit reaches only the faithful. Yet from that nothing of the nature of the sacrament disappears (*nihil sacramenti naturae decedit*)."[210]

As a last remark about Reformed sacramental theology, the Reformed tradition holds that baptism and the Lord's Supper are not strictly speaking the first sacraments that God gave to God's people. God granted sacraments in the old dispensation, and the "sacraments of the ancient people were circumcision, and the Paschal Lamb, which was offered up."[211] The Reformed tradition generally ascribes to these sacraments the same ultimate reality signified as those signified by the sacraments instituted by Jesus Christ,[212] for in each case Christ "is the chief thing and very substance of the sacraments in both."[213] The Reformed tradition argues that there is an ultimate unity of covenant between old and new. As Calvin put the matter, "The covenant with all the patriarchs is so much not different from ours in substance and reality (*substantia et re*) that it is utterly one and the same thing."[214]

This covenant unity exists because the patriarchs "had and knew Christ the mediator, through whom they were joined (*coniungerentur*) to God and were partakers of his promises."[215] Thus Calvin rejected "that scholastic dogma (to mention this in passing) which notes so great a difference between the sacraments of the old and new law, as though the old did nothing but foreshadow the grace of God, but the latter truly conferred it as a present reality."[216]

At the same time, some Reformed confessions also try to distinguish the sacraments that were given "under the Law" from those given under the new dispensation.[217] The Second Helvetic Confession asserts that "a great difference" exists between the signs. The new signs are "more firm and lasting," "more simple and less laborious," and "belong to a more numerous people." Further, "both the substance and promise" (*et rem et promissionem*) have been "fulfilled or perfected" in Christ, and "a greater abundance of the Spirit" follows.[218]

Finally, although this excursus chronologically now leaps several centuries, it would be lacking without a brief comment about the twentieth century, which itself ties closely to the concluding chapter of this study: In the twentieth century, the ancient and medieval perspective, that sacrament can be conceived in two related but distinguishable ways—as Jesus himself and as the sacraments of the church—came to be argued articulately by both Roman Catholic and Protestant scholars.

Roman Catholic theologians such as Otto Semmelroth, Eduard Schillebeeckx, and Karl Rahner made significant advances in the idea of Jesus as sacrament and, by extension, the church as sacrament, as they theologically prepared for the advent of the Second Vatican Council.[219] While there are differences between these thinkers that ought not be overlooked, there remains a general perspective that can be fairly summarized.[220] God's redemptive work toward the world was inseparable from God's Word, and God's Word and work encountered us as Jesus, who, in the words of Schillebeeckx, is "the norm and the source of every encounter with God."[221] The sacraments of the church continue this activity of Jesus so that "a sacrament is simply the outwardly perceivable glance of God's generosity towards a particular person ["man"]; the sacrament is this generosity."[222] The sacraments themselves, in the words of Rahner, "make concrete and real, for the life of the individual, the symbolic activity of the Church as the primary sacrament and therefore constitute at once, in keeping with the nature of the Church, a symbolic activity."[223]

In sum, Jesus was the *primal* sacrament. When people were encountered by Jesus, they were encountered by the "face of redemption turned visibly towards us."[224] The church that continues this encounter is the *primary* sacrament by which the same divine face of redemption still encounters us today. In more recent years, this distinction between Jesus as the *primal* sacrament and the church as the *primary* sacrament has been appropriated by the eminent American theologian Schubert Ogden.[225]

Ogden puts the matter quite straightforwardly. The possibility of salvation is constituted solely by the eternal redeeming love of God, who is our Alpha and Omega. In the encounter with the man Jesus people were decisively encountered by this divine, redeeming love, and so Jesus was, to borrow from our description of Augustine's theology, the physical window through which came the spiritual reality of redemption. He was the *primal* sacrament.[226] The church that continues his witness of faith, and takes its character from the character of Jesus' witness of faith, itself becomes a window through which comes redemption, and thus is the *primary* sacrament to the world, not constituting the possibility of salvation as such, but re-presenting that ever-present possibility yet again, here and now.[227] Ogden recognizes the general connection of his perspective to modern Roman Catholic theology and says that "[t]he language here is the language of recent Roman Catholic theology, which commonly distinguishes between the church as the *primary* Christian sacrament and Christ himself as the *primal* sacrament."[228]

2

THE FIRST GENERATION

Martin Luther

Chapter 1 traced the development of the Lord's Supper from the table-sharing of Jesus through the eve of the Protestant Reformation during the sixteenth century. The first chapter pursued an historical-critical approach to the topic of Jesus' presence in the Supper. More than a century ago scholars began to trace two distinct trajectories of the Supper though the ages: a metabolic tradition that passed to the West through Ambrose, in which Jesus' real presence somehow abided in or as the elements themselves; and, a nonmetabolic tradition that moved through Augustine to the West, in which the real presence of Jesus also was available, and into whose presence believers were engrafted yet more deeply, thus nourished directly by his body and blood. During the medieval period scholastic theologians synthesized these two strands into a single theological perspective, although variations in how these were combined were creatively present, particularly in the early scholastic period. The manner in which the bread and wine became the body and blood of Christ also admitted several explanations (annihilation, consubstantiation, transubstantiation), two of which (annihilation and transubstantiation) fell within the teachings from the Council of Trent.

Chapter 1 argued that categorizing the Supper according to "realistic" or "symbolic" failed to account for all the options, and that the historical material sorts out more adequately into general categories of realistic (metabolic presence), realistic (nonmetabolic presence), and symbolic.[1] At this point a constructive issue must be raised that could have been addressed earlier, but that seems better raised here. Any categorization that works from a scheme of "X/non-X" cannot do justice to the second term, which will always be merely derivative from the first term.[2] In the pairs of metabolic/nonmetabolic (Geiselmann) and somatic/nonsomatic (Kilmartin), terms used by two preeminent Roman Catholic scholars, one from the first half of the twentieth century, the other from the second half, the nonmetabolic (nonsomatic) must stand derivative from, and thus in some sense less than, that which is metabolic (somatic).

For several reasons, I continued with these pairs in chapter 1. These pairs refer to two distinct traditions, bearing *equally ancient* patristic pedigrees, and this historical observation about the traditions has occasionally been at odds with Roman Catholic teaching, as can be seen by the placing of Batiffol's 1905 edition of *L'Eucharistie* on the *Index Librorum Prohibitorum*.[3] A revised edition later appeared that so thoroughly downplayed the Augustinian/Ambrosian contrast of traditions that basically the Ambrosian (metabolic) tradition remained. It therefore seemed better to stay with terms used by Roman Catholic historians, lest someone think that I have imposed on the historical material a Protestant category of interpretation of the Supper that traces back to Augustine.

Once the study turns to the Protestant Reformation, however, describing Protestant theology by the terms of metabolic/nonmetabolic, or somatic/nonsomatic, would imply that Protestant eucharistic views that did not concern a metabolic presence were somehow deficient. Changing the terms "nonmetabolic" or "nonsomatic" raises the question of what terms to use,[4] and the phrase that I will here propose is a beginning. From this point onward, the study will call the nonmetabolic/nonsomatic tradition the "mystical true presence," in contrast to the "metabolic real presence."

The adjective "mystical" may seem problematic, since it carries a variety of technical definitions and includes a rich history of scholarship into Christian mystical traditions, which themselves have been quite varied.[5] Even if we adapt Troeltsch's basic definition and say that mysticism is a "direct inward and present religious experience of God,"[6] the question of mediation arises. How do Christians who assert the mediation of Jesus Christ hold to an immediate experience of God? This question has appeared throughout the history of Christian mysticism, sometimes more directly focused around some people (e.g., Meister Eckhart) than others.[7] Systematic theology must also ask the constructive question what *ought* the relationship to be between immediate experience of God and mediation through Jesus Christ. Of course, this systematic question and its answer assume, explicitly or implicitly, answers to the questions whether immediate (nonmediated) experience can be had and, if so, how does *immediate* experience relate to *mediated* awareness. These issues obviously cannot be dealt with here, although the second and third part of the final chapter will suggest a direction to be taken for sacramental theology.

For the moment, let me merely follow Tamburello and use a definition of mysticism given by the medieval theologian Jean Gerson (1363–1429), a French scholar and chancellor of the University of Paris, who himself wrote on mystical theology: "Mystical theology is experiential knowledge of God through the embrace of unitive love."[8] While this definition may seem to beg the issue toward a christocentric mysticism based on a "conformation of the will" (*conformitas voluntatis*),[9] it bears the great merit of defining mysticism according to the fifteenth century, within reach of the Protestant Reformation.

Why, then, use this phrase ("mystical true presence") for the sacramental tradition described so far as "'nonsomatic' real presence"? As we
shall see, some scholars, both Protestant and Roman Catholic, have used
the term "mystical" to describe the Augustinian (i.e., nonsomatic) tradition as it appeared in Luther.[10] Recent Finnish scholarship has also made
clear the role that union with Christ plays in Luther's theology.[11] Further,
Walter Köhler applied the word "mystical" to a certain (Erasmian) stage
in the development of Zwingli's eucharistic theology.[12] Finally, union
with Christ is certainly a major theme in Calvin and his sacramental
theology.[13]

What then of the term "true" as used in the phrase "mystical true presence"? The word "true" here contrasts neither with "untrue" nor with
"false," but with the word "real," so that "true presence" contrasts with
"real presence." Nearly a half-century ago, the Jesuit Calvin scholar Joseph
Tylenda noted how important it was for Calvin to talk about Christ's "true
presence" in the Supper, rather than the "real presence."[14] As Calvin says,
in his commentary on 1 Corinthians 11:24,

> Christ does not offer us the mere benefit of his death and resurrection,
> but the very body in which he suffered and rose again. I conclude that
> really [*realiter*] (as they commonly say)—that is, truly [*vere*]—Christ's
> body is given to us in the Supper that it might be salutary food [*cibum
> salutarem*] for our souls. I speak by common usage, but I understand
> that our souls are fed by the substance of the body [*substantia corporis*]
> so truly [*vere*] we may be made one with him; or, what effectively is
> the same, that a life-giving force from Christ's flesh is poured into us
> by the Spirit, though it is greatly different from us, and is not mixed
> with us.[15]

By replacing the phrase "nonmetabolic (nonsomatic) real presence"
with the phrase "mystical true presence," I intend to speak in a broad
way, which is constructive and not merely derivative, of a mystical
union with Christ, who truly offers himself in the Supper. As the first
chapter argued, this general tradition stands as apostolic as any in the
church, tracing back to Augustine (and Tertullian), forward through creative combinations in the early scholastics, and forward into a creative
merger with the metabolic real presence in the high and late medieval
periods. This tradition was part of the eucharistic theology of the Protestant Reformers of the sixteenth century, becoming dominant with the
Reformed theologians who, being humanist scholars, returned to the
original texts of the patristic era, where they found the voice of Augustine to be particularly helpful. We can hardly be surprised that in 1527
Luther complained that the Swiss Reformed theologians "regard Augustine as their own."[16]

MARTIN LUTHER

Born November 10, 1483, in Eisleben, Martin Luther grew up a few miles away in Mansfeld, where his father mined copper and later managed and owned several mines and gradually became one of the town's leading citizens.[17] Luther's life was aimed at his becoming a lawyer, a family desire that was sidetracked when he was caught in a thunderstorm on his way to law studies at Erfurt. In a famous scene, Luther cried out to St. Anne, the patron saint of minors and those threatened by storms, "Help me, St. Anne, and I will become a monk." Luther exhibited not neurosis but a typical reaction for someone of his setting.[18]

Luther became an Observant Augustinian Friar at Erfurt and progressed in his studies, receiving his doctorate in 1512. Johann von Staupitz, overwhelmed by his duties as vicar-general of Luther's order, soon handpicked young Martin to take over his chair in biblical theology at the University of Wittenberg. Over the next few years at Wittenberg, Luther taught on the Psalms twice (1513–15 and 1518–21), as well as Romans (1515–16), Galatians (1516–17), and Hebrews (1517–18), and in the process of teaching his "beloved holy Scriptures," said Luther, "the papacy fell to the wayside" for him.[19] Exactly how and when Luther had his "breakthrough" remains a matter of discussion,[20] although the wide-ranging discussion of when, and in what area, Luther had his breakthrough suggests that the process happened gradually—not as some moment on the "road to Damascus"—as it worked its way through various areas of Luther's thought.[21]

As the prior chapter suggested, the sacraments, especially the Lord's Supper, were so thoroughly entwined in the life of the medieval church that "the eucharist was the central symbol and reality for late medieval culture. The eucharist was presented by the church as the foremost sacrament which supported the whole sacramental system and clerical power."[22] Deeply aware of this and of the problems that arose for piety, as well as for church structure, from the medieval abuses of such a sacramental church, Luther wrote his 1520 *Babylonian Captivity* to show that God's people had once again been taken into exile. This time the exile came through the sacramental abuse that vitiated everything from theological construction through lay piety.[23]

Luther's criticism of the medieval Mass and his reform of eucharistic theology have produced a long history of Luther study that essentially began in the early 1520s in the eucharistic controversies between Zwingli and Luther.[24] These studies have concentrated on a number of issues that often intertwined: What was Luther's view on sacrifice? What was his view on the presence of Christ in the Supper? What was the structure of his sacramental theology? Can his views on sacrament and the Supper be categorized into different periods, and do these periods show development or mere unfolding? Are the (supposed) variations in Luther's thought merely the results of the well-known two-front problem that Luther addressed (first Rome, then the Enthusiasts)? What was Luther's relationship to late medieval, especially nominalist, eucharistic thought? How does Luther's eucharistic theology work as a whole? What was the nature of the debate between Luther and Zwingli, and the Reformed position more generally? How do we evaluate the Marburg Colloquy of 1529; or the Wittenberg Concord of 1536? How does the eucharistic teaching of Melanchthon relate to that of Luther? Luther studies typically enter through one or more of these questions and then address some of the other questions along the way, insofar as these other questions contribute to the discussion originally engaged. Because Luther's writings were themselves always context bound, and because I think Luther's eucharistic theology clearly is different in different periods, though by no means contradictory and perhaps even remarkably cohesive, this section moves chronologically. A few comments on chronological division help preface the material.

One of the early studies that chronologically parsed Luther's eucharistic theology according to several periods—indeed the earliest study that I know—was done in the early twentieth century by Friedrich Graebke,[25] whose work was then developed by J. A. Faulkner.[26] A somewhat similar division appeared in Paul Althaus's 1962 study on Luther's theology, although Althaus mentions neither the Graebke study nor the Faulkner study.[27] In 1969 Susi Hausamann intentionally took an historical approach, citing Althaus among others, and criticizing nondevelopmental approaches.[28] About twenty years after Hausamann, about twenty years ago, the American scholar Ralph Quere took up this same approach and suggested numerous subphases in various periods of Luther's thought.[29] All these studies stand in some contrast to those that simply take a nondifferentiated historical approach,[30] or those that specifically argue that Luther had a unified and consistent eucharistic theology.[31]

This section takes a slightly wider perspective on these studies, and the question of historical development of Luther's eucharistic teaching, by using a (Graebke-Faulkner-Althaus-Hausamann-Quere) historical approach and seeing Luther in the trajectories that he inherited of the metabolic real presence and the mystical true presence. Viewed in this way, the fundamental turn that Luther made in 1526, when he moved from discussing the right use of the sacrament through faith to the object of that faith, which was being assailed by many (*von vilen angefochten wird*),[32] can be seen *as the receding emphasis on the mystical true presence and the increasing emphasis on the metabolic real presence*. The integration of these two into a whole, and done in a way different than the scholastic integration that chapter 1 described, remains a testimony to Luther the reformer as well as the articulate doctor of the medieval church.

After the indulgence controversy of late 1517 and its aftermath, and the debates with Cajetan at Augsburg (August 1518) and Eck at Leipzig (July 1519), Luther in late 1519 turned to pastoral issues. In September Luther completed his work *Fourteen Consolations*, designed as comfort to the ailing Fredrick the Wise (1463–1525), originally written in Latin, then translated into German for Fredrick's benefit, and eventually published in 1520 for wider dissemination.[33] During November and December of that same year, Luther wrote a trilogy that comprised the sacraments of penance,[34] baptism,[35] and the Lord's Supper,[36] with the hope to make clear for people the grace of God freely offered them in the sacraments.[37] In all three essays, Luther applied the traditional Augustinian structure that we have already seen, sign and reality, and to these Luther added a third feature, faith.

"The sacrament or external sign," says Luther, "consists in the form and shape (*der form und gestalt*) of bread and wine, just as baptism finds its sign in the water."[38] Luther acknowledges that people may only receive the bread, but allows that the clergy receiving both bread and cup, and the people's desire for daily celebration, will suffice. Luther then goes on to assert that the reality signified by the sign is the communion of all the saints (*gemeinschaft aller heiligen*):

> Christ with all his saints are one spiritual body, just as the people of a city are one community and body, each citizen a member of the other and the whole city. So all the saints are members of Christ and the church, which is the spiritual, eternal city of God. Whoever is received into this city is said to be received into the community of the saints and incorporated into Christ's spiritual body and made a member of him.[39]

By receiving this sacrament, the believer is given a "sure sign" that she or he is united with Christ and his saints, having all things in common.[40] Reflecting ancient imagery first seen in Christian literature in *Didache* 9, a document not yet discovered in Luther's time, Luther talks about the grains mixed together and becoming one bread, each grain losing its own form and taking on the common form of the bread, just as the drops of wine lose their form and take on a common form. So too "Christ with all his saints, through his love, takes up our form."[41]

The duty for the Christian life is fellowship with others, sharing both joys and sufferings, just as in a city, where a citizen shares the benefits of citizenry, such as support and protection, but also shares its downfalls, such as floods, enemies, and taxes. To share in the profits is also to share in the costs.[42] If overburdened, lay your cares on the altar and seek help from the gathered community that is Christ's spiritual body.[43]

The Blessed Sacrament (1519) has typically been taken to concern right living amidst community, blessed by the love of Christ with hope and forbearance for neighbor.[44] The sacramental understanding is "essentially spiritual," and Luther shows himself at this time "no less a Spiritualist than perhaps Erasmus or the early Zwingli."[45] On this view, even though Luther clearly allows for the presence of Christ, the mode of presence remaining mysterious,[46] the "real presence" as such has little theological function in Luther's thought prior to 1526.[47]

The issue would be better put, it seems to me, that in the early 1520s the *metabolic* real presence had little theological function. If the alternatives of symbolic (spiritual) and realistic are widened, as we saw necessary in the first chapter, then in 1519 Luther conceived of a *mystical true presence*, which conveys intimately through the signs, thus (in his own way) restoring Augustine's dyad of sign-reality that had become weakened in Western Augustinianism.[48] In the citation given above, the unnamed but clear reference to Augustine's *City of God* recalls the mystical true presence in which believers, engrafted into Christ himself and enlivened by the Spirit, lead lives of sacrifice for neighbor. Luther went on to say that

> He [Christ] appointed these two forms of bread and wine, rather than any other, to show further the very union and community which is the sacrament. For there is no more intimate, deep, and indivisible union than the union of the food with him who is fed. For the food enters into and is changed into his very nature, and becomes one substance with the person who is fed. Other unions, achieved by such things as nails, glue, cords, and the like, do not make one indivisible nature of the objects joined together. Thus in the sacrament we too become united with Christ, and are made one body with all the saints, so that Christ cares for us and acts in our behalf.[49]

The mystical quality to such passages in *The Blessed Sacrament* has not gone unnoticed by some Roman Catholic and Protestant scholars,[50] and they reflect the scholarship that Krodel offered on Luther's view of the sacrament present in his first lectures on the Psalms (1513–15). Leaning on the writings of the so-called church fathers, Luther oriented himself to God's self-revelation in Jesus Christ, which was for Luther a *sacramentum* in which God's miraculous and mysterious salvation took flesh for us.[51] This salvation effectively continues in the church through Word and sacrament, and the Supper "manifests God in Jesus Christ through the power of the Spirit." Thus the Supper brought the true presence of Christ, and the reality of the sacrament was the "mystical body of Christ, of which the individual becomes a member by his spiritual participation in the Lord's Supper."[52]

As odd as this may sound to those accustomed to hearing Luther's forensic view of justification by faith, this view finds support in, and stands as mutually confirming of, basic arguments from the Finnish interpretation of Luther, which has developed since the mid-1970s under the leadership of Tuomo Mannermaa at the University of Helsinki. Central to this view is Luther's idea that "Christ is *really present* in faith itself" (*in ipsa fide Christus adest*).[53]

Luther continued the theme of Christ's presence in his 1520 *Babylonian Captivity of the Church*,[54] and he once again made the connection between incarnation and the sacrament, this time arguing against the scholastic doctrine of transubstantiation. Just as it was not necessary for the human nature of Christ to transubstantiate at the incarnation in order for the Divine to be present with human accidents, so also there is no need to posit transubstantiation during the Supper. "Both natures simply are there in their entirety, and it is truly said: 'This man is God; this God is man.'"[55] Jesus Christ is truly there, although transubstantiation is rejected by Luther on several counts.[56]

What comes to the forefront in the *Babylonian Captivity* and in the *Treatise on the New Testament, that is, The Holy Mass* (1520)[57]—recognized long ago as a significant shift in Luther's eucharistic theology[58]—is the divine presence as a *speaking* presence that offers the divine promise of forgiveness,[59] which naturally correlates with the human faith that trusts that personal promise:

> You see, therefore, that what we call the Mass is a promise of forgiveness of sins made to us by God, and such a promise as has been confirmed by the death of the Son of God. . . . If the mass is a promise, as has been said, then access to it is to be gained, not with any works, or powers, or merit's of one's own, but by faith alone. For where there is the Word of the promising God, there must necessarily be the faith of the accepting person.[60]

God's word of promise and the real presence of Christ stand together in these two works, but seem somewhat disconnected. Oddly, the body and blood of Christ are "signs" that point us to the promise of God's forgiveness,[61] and such signs are "external" (*äußerlich*).[62] But how can the body and blood of Christ be an external sign as such? In a similar, seemingly unconnected juxtaposition of sign and promise, Luther can say that words are more important than the signs and that one can be saved by the words without the sacrament, but not by the sacrament without the words.[63]

The contrast between grace as something material and grace as the personal, speaking reality that is God is an issue noted by Althaus and other "liberal" Luther scholars.[64] For the moment, I want simply to cite at length the eminent Reformed historical theologian of the early twentieth century, A. C. McGiffert, in order to clarify the issue at hand:

> In substituting an ethical for the traditional physical conception of salvation, and in maintaining that salvation consists in divine forgiveness, not in the transformation of human nature, Luther repudiated the basis upon which the sacramental theory of the Catholic church was built; but unfortunately he retained the sacraments themselves, or at any rate two of them, because he believed they were commanded by Christ. It became necessary therefore to reinterpret them, and this he did when he asserted that they are merely signs or testimonies of God's forgiving love in Christ and that they have exactly the same sort of efficacy that the spoken word of the gospel has; that they are in fact merely the word made visible. This interpretation was in line with his reinterpretation of the word grace, which he took to mean not something to be given or conveyed to man but simply God's gracious attitude or forgiving love. Our word graciousness expresses better than our word grace the meaning of grace as Luther wished to have it understood. This view of grace was entirely consistent with his notion of salvation and of course with such a view it was impossible to think of the sacrament as conveying grace. Strictly speaking there was not grace to be conveyed. They *could* be nothing more than signs of God's graciousness.[65]

Regardless of how one assesses McGiffert's (historically one-sided) assessment of Luther, this view does point to a development in Luther's theology of the sacraments. Luther's 1520 writings such as the *Babylonian Captivity* and the *Treatise on the New Testament* reflected Luther's emerged evangelical perspective that God is a personal God who speaks the word of promise; that faith comes from hearing;[66] and that the promises of God inhere to the sacraments, which are to nourish our faith ("all sacraments were instituted to feed faith").[67] In these ways Luther synced the divine activity in the sacrament with a view of faith that had developed by 1518.[68]

Because Luther had rejected the historically inherited sacrificial character of the Mass,[69] had rejected withholding the cup from the laity, and had rejected the idea of transubstantiation, practical questions arose about what Luther's views might be. By January 1523 people in Bohemia wondered whether Luther opposed the adoration of the sacrament. During the course of that year, in a series of letters and meetings, Luther attempted to ascertain the Bohemian views and to reply to their concerns.[70] In January 1523 Luther preached a sermon on the adoration of the sacrament that was the basis of the published treatise *The Adoration of the Sacrament of the Holy Body of Christ*.[71]

Luther continued the evangelical theme that he argued so strongly in the *Babylonian Captivity* and the *Treatise on the New Testament*. The Word is not something merely to be considered, but rather it is a "living, eternal, all-powerful Word" (*lebendig ewig almechtig wort*) that makes us "alive and free from sin and death."[72] The Word thus deserves all adoration and should be kept in the "real golden monstrance" that is the heart.[73] Luther also reiterated what he had said previously, that the Word should be esteemed higher than the sacrament because life and salvation can come without the sacrament but not without the Word.[74]

Because the treatise aimed at the Bohemian question of adoration of the sacrament, Luther naturally discussed at some length the metabolic real presence. Much of Luther's argument was directed at a view of the Supper that was known to Luther—a view that Luther says held some appeal to him when he was younger[75]—put forth by the Dutch humanist Cornelius Hoen and apparently presented to Luther in 1521.[76] Although Hoen's epistle has been known primarily for one argument—that the word "is" ("This *is* my body") really means "signifies"—Hoen made many different points when he argued against the doctrine of transubstantiation.[77] Luther fundamentally directed his criticisms at two key ideas: (1) that in the words of institution (*Verba*) the word "is" really means "signifies"; and (2) that when faith receives Christ in the Supper a person receives the spiritual presence but not the bodily presence of Christ.[78]

Luther spent quite some time arguing against the first point, as he later would when arguing with Zwingli, who himself was influenced by Hoen's epistle: Such a view would reduce the Supper, and baptism as well, to mere symbols of what God otherwise does. The word "is" remains clear in the text, and to change its meaning here would open the way to changing the meaning to "is" anywhere one wanted, thus voiding Scripture of any real content. Further, one cannot interpret the words of institution by means of Paul's comments in 1 Corinthians 10, where he says that those of old drank from the same spiritual Rock, namely, Christ; rather, the *Verba* must stand on their own and interpret 1 Corinthians 10.

As for the second argument, Luther argues that "participation in Christ" is different from being offered the body of Christ: "For who in good conscience can allow the word that Christ speaks, 'This is my body, which is given for you,' should be taken to mean, 'This is the communion in my body, which is given for you'?"[79] By contrast the words of Christ make abundantly clear that Christ gives his body, not mere participation in Christ.[80] Luther does not deny the participation in Christ's mystical body; in fact he reasserts this idea that was so present in his 1519 essay *The Blessed Sacrament*. Speaking about the theme of union with Christ and his saints, Luther says,

> So it is true that we Christians are the spiritual body of Christ and all together are one bread, one drink, one spirit. Christ does all this, *who through his own body makes us all one spiritual body* so that we all partake

equally of his body and thus are equal and one with one another. Likewise, that we consume one bread and drink makes us to be one bread and drink. Just as one member serves another in such a common body, so each eats and drinks the other; that is, each consumes the other in all things and is food and drink for the other, that we are simply food and drink for one another, as Christ is simply food and drink for us.[81]

By 1523 Luther has significantly developed his comments on the metabolic real presence and has linked this real presence with the mystical true presence. By faithfully receiving the body and blood of Christ that are the elements, Christians are made one in Christ's spiritual body.

In sum, during the period from 1520 through 1523 Luther showed more features of his eucharistic theology than were present in 1519. To the mystical union with Christ present in *The Blessed Sacrament* (1519), Luther added the evangelical insistence on a personal God whose promise of forgiveness is attached to the outward sign. Arguments for the metabolic real presence also emerged, rather than merely assuming such a presence or merely arguing against transubstantiation, and Luther linked the mystical presence to this metabolic presence.

This middle, evangelical stage of Luther has yet one more work that needs comment, *Against the Heavenly Prophets* (1525),[82] a work that signals a transition to the eucharistic theology of the later Luther that would emerge a year later.

The struggles between Luther and Andreas (Bodenstein von) Karlstadt (ca. 1480–1541) are generally known and now easily accessible in some detail.[83] Andreas Bodenstein, called Karlstadt after his place of birth, Karlstadt on the Main, received his doctorate in theology and taught at Wittenberg, where he was a colleague of Luther's. A Thomist with humanist leanings, he opposed Luther at first but later became convinced by Luther's views. Karlstadt seemed to waver between academia and parish, between technical theology and parish theology, and by 1523 he was ambiguously positioned between the parish at Orlamünde, which supplied a substantial portion of his support, and the university, where he was not upholding his duties. Further, for a half dozen years he had been influenced by German mysticism and was supported by Thomas Müntzer (1489?–1525) although Karlstadt rejected violence as unbiblical. Despite their differences, common elements between Karlstadt and Müntzer—such as mysticism, lay piety, denial of infant baptism, memorialist (and mystic) interpretation of the Lord's Supper, and rejection of images—led by mid-1524 to Karlstadt being viewed as Müntzer's ally. An attempted reconciliation between Luther and Karlstadt's congregation at Orlamünde only made matters worse, as did a meeting between Luther and Karlstadt at Jena. By the end of 1524 Luther felt both personally attacked by Karlstadt's supporters and dismayed by the spread of Karlstadt's ideas. The evangelical pastors in Strasbourg had read Karlstadt's writings, and some in the city found the arguments convincing; so the pastors (Bucer and Capito among them) wrote Luther, asking his views on infant baptism, the Lord's Supper, and images. In December Luther replied with his *Letter to the Christians at Strasbourg in Opposition to the Fanatical Spirit*.[84]

By later December Luther had finished the first part of his reply to Karlstadt, *Against the Heavenly Prophets*, and by January 1525 he had finished part 2 of the rather lengthy treatise. After a short introduction in the first part, Luther then took up the issues of images, of Karlstadt's expulsion from Saxony, and of Karlstadt's attacks on the Mass. The second part of the treatise has two main sections; the first treats Karlstadt's exegesis and the second Karlstadt's use of reason in his arguments about the Supper. These latter two sections, which comprise part 2 of the treatise, provide two overall observations.

First, Luther takes Karlstadt to task for his creative, if not odd, exegesis of the *Verba*. Karlstadt had argued that when Jesus said, "Take, eat, this is my body given for you," the first part of the sentence ("Take, eat") referred to the bread; but when Jesus said the word "this" (*touto*) in the second part, he was referring not to the bread but was pointing to his own body that would be given on the cross. After some opening comments aimed to refute Karlstadt on biblical language and on the Mass, Luther takes up his main argument in this section of part 2:[85] Because one ought not deviate from what Scripture says unless a specific warrant is given,[86] the scriptural words mean what they say and say what they mean. The words of institution form a unified sentence, giving a single clear witness: Jesus refers to the bread as his body.

Second, in the middle of the second section of part 2, Luther says that since he desires that his ideas be understood better, he will "talk about them clearly and broadly" (*will ich deutlich und groß davon reden*).[87] Luther begins by distinguishing the achievement of forgiveness of sins by Christ's death on the cross from the distributing and giving of the forgiveness of sins, which has happened through the Word from the world's beginning all the way to its end.

Luther goes on to say that one can find in "the sacrament or the gospel the word which distributes, grants, offers and gives to me that forgiveness that was won on the cross."[88] Thus Luther can even say that "even if only bread and wine were present," so long as the words of institution are present, then through that word the forgiveness of sins is also present. It is just like baptism, says Luther, where only water is present, but the Word of God connects to it and it becomes the bath of regeneration. "Everything," says Luther, "is due to the Word" (*Es ligt alles am wort*). [89]

In the very next paragraph Luther goes on to criticize Karlstadt, saying that Karlstadt would abolish the sacrament completely, both the bodily

Christ—body and blood—and the spiritual occurrence of the forgiveness of sin. Neither the sacrament nor its fruits would remain—only the human efforts of remembering and knowing.[90]

As with Luther's other major writings on the Supper between 1520 and 1525, *Against the Heavenly Prophets* shows the prominent evangelical theme of the Word proclaimed and received in faith as foundational. There is also an increased emphasis on the metabolic real presence, which one would expect, given the views on the Supper that Karlstadt held and against which Luther argued. At the same time, however much Luther indeed insisted on a metabolic real presence, such a real presence would not be *strictly necessary* for the Supper, since the forgiveness of sins, distributed through the Word from the beginning of creation, would suffice, as Luther himself asserted. Everything depends on the Word.

Finally in this treatise, the mystical true presence, in which we are taken into Christ and his saints, receives less attention and appears to be a social fruit of the sacrament, rather than the mystical reality of which the sacrament is a sign. Since Luther was concerned with Karlstadt's emphasis on the human inner efforts to receive the Supper, and thus the works righteousness that connected to mysticism itself,[91] his lack of emphasis on the mystical aspect of union is readily understandable.

This connection between the "fanatics," mysticism, and the Supper as fundamentally an activity of remembering—all without a metabolic real presence—was subsequently deepened for Luther by contact and conversation with Caspar Schwenckfeld (1489–1561).[92] A result was that *communio*, in which the early Luther argued that believers were mystically one with Christ, becomes increasingly a social aspect to the sacrament, as can be seen from Luther's 1526 *The Sacrament—Against the Fanatics*.[93] As we shall see, Luther eventually embraced the mystical true presence only within the metabolic real presence.

During the course of 1525 a number of events eventually forced Luther to preach against the position of the Swiss (and others) during Holy Week of 1526. John Bugenhagen (1485–1558), who was a pastor in Wittenberg and a colleague of Luther's on the faculty of Wittenberg, had engaged Zwingli on the Lord's Supper, and the people of Reutlingen desired to hear Luther's view. Luther replied in early January 1526. Also, fourteen pastors from Swabia had put together a small treatise on the Lord's Supper (*Syngramma Suevicum*, or Swabian Syngramma) that took to task the position of the Basel Reformer John Oecolampadius (1482–1531). Luther found the tract agreeable and added a preface to the German translation that appeared in June 1526.[94]

On Wednesday and Thursday of Holy Week 1526, Luther preached three sermons, two on the Lord's Supper and one on penance. Not originally intended for publication, they nevertheless came to press in 1526 with some apparent additions that can be seen when comparing notes taken from the sermons with the printed form.[95] In the first sermon, Luther begins his argument with the same point upon which he wrote a great deal in *Against the Heavenly Prophets*. The words of Scripture are plain and so simple that any ordinary person would know what they mean. Would someone not understand if a glass were put before them and they were told, "Take the glass and drink; this is Wittenberg beer"?[96] Likewise the words of Christ are clear: his body and blood are given.

Luther then takes up the two principal arguments from his opponents, the reasonableness that Christ's body and blood should be in the bread and wine, and the necessity for their presence there. Luther's response to the first argument particularly concerns our discussion. Luther discusses God's miraculous (and not reasonable) activity from the incarnation and crucifixion to the miracles of creation itself—the soul, grains of wheat, and the very speaking of words to communicate. This last example leads Luther to preaching:

> Likewise, I preach the gospel of Christ, and with my bodily voice I bring Christ into your heart, so that you may mold him in yourself. If now you truly believe, so that your heart grasps the word and clings fast to that voice within, tell me, what have you in your heart? You must say that you have the true Christ, not that he sits in there, as one sits on a chair, but as he is at the right hand of the Father. How that happens you cannot know, but your heart fully feels him—he undoubtedly is there—through the experience of faith.[97]

Just as Christ can come into the heart and dwell there, so also he "distributes himself in the bread."[98]

Luther then broaches the subject of ubiquity. Being seated at the right hand of God means that Christ himself is present "in all creatures" and can be found in stone or fire or water or a rope.[99] But just so no one would burn in the fire, or drown in the water, or be hanged by the rope, in seeking Christ, we must look where the Word directs us, because the Word shows us where to find him: "with the Word he binds his body and blood so that they may be received bodily (*leiblich*) in the bread and wine."[100]

Furthermore, the words of institution that bind the body and blood to the elements also do so "for you." Unlike preaching, which is generally directed to the congregation, Christ's body and blood are the direct gift from God given directly to each person so that those who received the sacrament "should believe and be assured, not only that they are receiving the true body and blood of Christ in it, but also that it is there given to them and is their own."[101] With this gift of Christ himself comes the great treasure, the forgiveness of sins.[102]

In sum, Christ's ubiquitous presence "is the ground-beneath-the-ground—a sort of ontological substratum."[103] It is the condition for the possibility that through the Word Christ himself both *truly dwells* in our hearts and, in like manner, comes to us in the bread and wine, so that in Christ we have forgiveness of sins. Luther concludes his two sermons on the Supper by talking about *communio*. Luther has already attached the mystical true presence of Christ directly to the Word, which through faith makes Christ himself to dwell in our hearts. What remains for the "communion" aspect is right believing and living in love within Christendom itself.[104]

The continued discussion of Luther's views on the Supper, including dozens of published tracts criticizing his eucharistic theology,[105] prompted friends and foes alike to urge Luther to respond. During the winter and early spring of 1527 Luther worked in a most concentrated and careful manner, producing what has been called "the most systematic work of his writings on the Lord's Supper,"[106] *This Is My Body*.[107] After beginning the discussion over the role of the devil in the debate over the Supper—a procedure about which Oecolampadius complained, with Luther later acknowledging that complaint[108]—and naming the issue as that of the words of institution, Luther discusses the views of Zwingli, the Swiss exegesis of John 6:63, the views of Oecolampadius, and whether bodily presence made sense. He ends with some comments about Bucer, whose translation into German of Bugenhagen's Psalm commentary was altered by Bucer with Swiss eucharistic perspectives.[109]

In the section on Zwingli's view of the ascension that begins the criticism of his opponents,[110] Luther makes in more detail the point that he made against Karlstadt a year earlier. According to Scripture, "the right hand of God is not a specific place where a body must be or may be, like a golden throne, but is God's almighty power, which simultaneously can be nowhere and yet must be everywhere."[111] Because Christ sits at the right hand of God, his presence also can be nowhere and yet must be everywhere, an assertion that would be true regardless of the words of institution:

> Even if Christ had never spoken nor set forth these words at the Supper, "This is my body," still the words, "Christ sits at the right hand of God," would demand that his body and blood may be there as in all other places, and that although there need be no transubstantiation or transformation of the bread into his body, it nevertheless can well be present there, just as the right hand of God is not necessarily changed into all things even though it is surely present there and in them.[112]

Naturally, says Luther, just because Christ's humanity sits at God's right hand and thus dwells in all things, we should not think that we can "eat him or drink him like the cabbage and the soup" that sit on our table.[113] Why? "Because it is one thing if God is there, and another if he is there *for you*. He is there for you when he adds his Word and binds himself and says, 'Here you can find me.'"[114]

A word should be said here about nominalist distinctions concerning presence, which Luther uses here in *This Is My Body* and a year later (1528) in his *Confession Concerning Christ's Supper*.[115] "There are three modes of being present in a given place: locally or circumscriptively, definitively, repletively."[116] Circumscriptive presence occurs when the object and its space fit together with exact correspondence; the part exists where the part exists and the whole exists where the whole exists: The coffee mug is circumscriptively present on the table.[117] Next, definitive presence means that a whole thing is present in the whole, but could also be entirely present only in a part: The soul is descriptively present in the body.[118] Third, to be repletively present is to be present everywhere at the same time, occupying all places but not measured according to any space occupied: God (only) has repletive presence.[119]

Luther used these concepts, sometimes explicitly giving their definitions, other times simply using the terms or concepts involved in the terms.[120] When he used these explanations, he was not grounding his position on Christ's presence in a logical argument. Luther was abundantly clear that he believed Christ to be bodily (*leiblich*) present because of the words of institution, as the very title of his 1526 essay showed, *That These Words of Christ, "This Is My Body," Still Stand Firm against the Fanatics*. Luther used these arguments to show that, contrary to his opponents, it was not absurd to argue for the bodily presence of Christ in the Supper.[121] This would be in keeping with his view that reason has its good and necessary place within the realm of faith.[122] As Luther had put the matter almost ten years earlier, in philosophical thesis 29 from the *Heidelberg Disputation*, "If you wish to philosophize using Aristotle without danger, you must first become utterly foolish in Christ."[123]

After discussing the issue of "Christ at the right hand of God," Luther continued by taking up the "cardinal point" or "cornerstone" upon which the Swiss built their arguments[124]—exegesis of John 6, particularly John 6:63.[125] The Swiss, says Luther, are unable to show that the saying "the flesh is of no avail" pertains to Christ's flesh. Unless they can, which Luther believes impossible, then the institution narrative must stand primary and not be interpreted in terms of the Johannine passage. As for his own view on John 6:63, Luther believes that it connotes the "old Adam" that contrasts with life in the Spirit. Finally, to challenge what he apparently sees as an incorrect dualism in the Swiss view, Luther draws on numerous Old Testament people, as well as Mary, to argue for the value of the body in God's economy of salvation.

In the last major section that concerns the central Swiss thinkers, such as Zwingli and Oecolampadius, Luther turns to Oecolampadius's patristic references.[126] Augustine, says Luther, is regarded by the Swiss "as their own."[127] This is a significant comment, regardless of how one assesses Luther's assessment of the Swiss arguments, which will be taken up shortly. As we saw in chapter 1, Augustine was the major (though not only) source of the mystical true presence that can be found in Western eucharistic traditions. Among the several passages that Luther treats from Augustine is Augustine's Psalm commentary that, as we saw in chapter 1, actually admits not a metabolic but a mystical reading.[128] Luther goes on to discuss a number of passages from Tertullian, another author to whom Oecolampadius has appealed, and another North African theologian who, as we saw in chapter 1, held to a mystical true presence.

Prior to taking up Luther's 1528 *Confession concerning Christ's Supper*, and prior to drawing the theological points from that essay and from *This Is My Body*, I want to note that Luther understands that the Swiss appealed not only to John 6, but to Augustine and his commentary on John 6, as well as to Tertullian. The rhetorical question that presently arises is whether Luther really understood what the Swiss, perhaps including Zwingli, were trying to say about Christ's presence and the ancient tradition to which they appealed.

By late February 1527 Zwingli had authored a rebuttal to Luther's doctrine of the Supper and his own critical reading of the institution narratives, *Friendly Exegesis, that is, Exposition of the Eucharist Affair to Martin Luther*.[129] Luther desired to reply and to put the eucharistic controversy to bed once and for all, at least so far as his efforts were concerned, but 1527 was a difficult year for him: his bodily health was poor; Katie was pregnant; their son Hans was quite ill; political concerns took up time; pastoral concerns mounted (the plague struck Wittenberg, and Luther and Bugenhagen stayed to minister); issues with Karlstadt pressed; Anabaptist questions about baptism arose; and his mental health was suffering.[130]

Luther envisioned *Confession concerning Christ's Supper* (1528) as a three-part essay that was to be his final major effort on the subject.[131] The first section would warn people about the "enthusiasts" and address the errors that Zwingli, Oecolampadius, and others had put forth about the Supper. The second part would exegete the four biblical texts on the Supper, a process that Zwingli had followed in his *Friendly Exegesis*. Since eucharistic theology was part of Christian theology as a whole, and the Swiss had corrupted theology overall;[132] and since Luther thought the *fides historica* could demand something other than a plain reading of the text;[133] part 3 of the *Confession concerning Christ's Supper* gave Luther's confession of the articles of faith.

In the section dealing with Zwingli,[134] Luther took up Zwingli's exegetical methods and again found them wanting. No basis exists for a purely spiritual interpretation. No figurative language or linguistic hair-splitting (e.g., Zwingli's distinction between "command words" and "action words") is appropriate. One of the most interesting parts of this first section is Luther's discussion of the words of institution as God's own, creative Word. God spoke the words at creation, such as "Let there be sun and moon," and the sun and moon came to be, because God's Word is a word of power (*machtwort*). If anyone else says these words, no sun or moon comes into being. Likewise, said Luther in a wordplay, Jesus Christ, true God and true man, spoke not a mere word that we should imitate (*nachwort*), but rather a word of power (*machtwort*), when he said, "Take, eat, this is my body." Thus Christ gave himself to the first disciples at the Last Supper, and when we, speaking Christ's word of power as he has commanded us so to do, likewise say, "Take, eat. This is my body given for you," his presence is in the elements.[135]

Luther warned against Zwingli's approach of "alloiosis"—a rhetorical term that Zwingli used to describe the predication or exchange of divine and human properties in the person of Christ—because he believed it overly separated the divine and human natures.[136] On Luther's view, this was part of "Satan's poison" that ultimately threatened the very idea of redemption, illicitly splitting the human from the divine.[137] To show that it is not unreasonable that Christ can be bodily present, Luther then went on to discuss the three types of presence (circumscriptive, definitive, and repletive). Since Christ, fully incarnate and resurrected, sits at God's right hand, even his flesh and blood share the divine repletive presence.

When Luther then took on the views of Oecolampadius,[138] to whom his tone here, as will be the case in Marburg, was less strident than it was toward Zwingli, he rejected Oecolampadius as a poor logician, whose arguments simply do not overturn the clear meaning of the institution narratives.[139] Neither an appeal to rhetorical devices nor direct appeal to ancient authors—both approaches signaling the humanist method in Oecolampadius—can make sufficient case for a spiritual body and spiritual eating rather than a bodily eating:

> Thus Oecolampadius stands out in the cold over this principal point: He cannot prove that Christ is only in heaven in a particular place; and he will never find an answer how the two are contradictory, that Christ is in heaven and simultaneously his body is in the Supper, a point I have pressed in my little book. They cannot make it happen—it is impossible—and they fully feel it.[140]

Luther began section 2, his discussion of the four biblical texts on the Last Supper (Paul and the Synoptic narratives), by summing up his main points against the Swiss: (1) they admit he takes the texts for their plain reading; they just cannot read the texts plainly; (2) the words of institution are not humanly derived but are from God; (3) the Swiss cannot themselves produce one sure and defendable text; (4) they themselves disagree upon the texts to defend and disagree on their interpretations; and (5) "Even if one assumes that our text and interpretation were uncertain or obscure (it is not)," says Luther, from God's own lips we have a text to believe and God does not deceive.[141] This last point Luther later put more dramatically at Marburg, when he replied to Oecolampadius, "Even if He ordered me to eat dung I would do it, since I know with contentment that it is salutary (*heilsam*) for me. The servant does not ponder over the will of his lord. You must close your eyes [and eat!]."[142]

Once again Luther holds to a plain reading of the text, as compared to his opponents, but now synthesizes his evangelical insight, about the personal, speaking God who awakens our faith, with the metabolic real presence:

> For the new testament is gospel, spirit, forgiveness of sins in and through the blood of Christ, and whatever more, for it is all one thing, gathered together into one mass or substance, all in the blood, all in the cup. Where the one is, there the other also is. Whoever names or points to the one, meets them all.[143]

Through the elements that are the bodily presence of Christ, one encounters the whole of the good news, and does so *in a certain direction*, even though "one sacramental reality" (*ein sacramentlich wesen*) is encountered.[144] The institution narrative begins, then the elements, then Christ's body and blood, then the new testament, then the forgiveness of sins, and then eternal life and salvation:

> The words are the first thing, for without the words the cup and the bread would be nothing. Further, without bread and cup, the body and blood of Christ would not be there. Without the body and blood of Christ, the new testament would not be there. Without the new testament, forgiveness of sins would not be there. Without forgiveness of sins, life and salvation would not be there. Thus the words first connect the bread and cup to the sacrament; bread and cup embrace the body and blood of Christ; body and blood of Christ embrace the new testament; the new testament embraces the forgiveness of sins; forgiveness of sins embraces eternal life and salvation.[145]

Together a single sacramental reality exists, so that one can say of each part that it is Jesus' body and blood, the forgiveness of sins, and life and salvation. It is just like pointing at Jesus and saying, "This is God. This is the truth, the life, salvation, and so on."[146]

Luther makes one more important development in his *Confession concerning Christ's Supper*. He has an extended exegesis of Paul's passage from 1 Corinthians 10:16–17: "The cup of blessing that we bless, is it not a sharing in the blood of Christ? The bread that we break, is it not a sharing in the body of Christ? Because there is one bread, we who are many are one body, for we all partake of the one bread."[147] Against the Swiss opponents (as Luther reads them), who take this to be a spiritual participation by the community in the spiritual body of Christ, Luther argues that the text plainly says that body of Christ is given in the elements and that the community shares in the elements. Not just the worthy receive the body and blood of Christ when they receive the elements; even Judas does as well. The unworthy partake but, lacking faith, eat to their own condemnation. By their thus sharing the elements together, the Supper forms them into a gathered community—wheat and tares to be sure, but a community of which Paul can say, "We are one body." This common partaking of the same reality Luther designates as communion, fellowship, or participation.[148]

What then of the mystical union of believers in Christ himself, occurring in the Supper, of which Luther wrote so elegantly a decade earlier? Over time, as Luther addressed the mysticism of the enthusiasts, and the sacramental ideas of the Swiss (and others), often and fatefully conflating these people and ideas,[149] he detached the mystical union with Christ aspect of *communio* from the Supper gathering so that what remained of communion was not only the confessing visible church (see *Against the Heavenly Prophets* and *The Sacrament—Against the Fanatics*), but finally the visible church, both wheat and tares. Did anything of the mystical true presence found in the early Luther still remain?

Indeed it did, and Luther united this mystical true presence with the metabolic real presence of Christ. In *This Is My Body* Luther asserts that the eucharistic food "transforms the person who eats it into what it is itself, and makes that person like itself, spiritual, alive, and eternal."[150] And so a mystical process engages, which becomes clear on the last day, that "when we eat Christ's flesh physically and spiritually, the food is so powerful that it changes us into itself and out of fleshly, sinful, mortal people makes spiritual, holy, living people."[151]

To sum, over the course of *This Is My Body* (1527) and *Confession concerning Christ's Supper* (1528), Luther developed several themes while retaining points upon which he continually insisted. He continued to assert the importance of the words of institution, in their clear and simple meaning, against any attempt to understand them otherwise. They were likewise not to be interpreted in terms of other passages, such as John 6, but stood coherently with 1 Corinthians 10 as a witness to the metabolic presence of

Christ. But, even more, Luther came to argue that words themselves were God's word of power that brought about what they declared, just as God made creation.

The mystical true presence of Christ into which we are united when receiving the sacrament in faith, and which Luther had emphasized as the reality of the sacrament in his early years, becomes united with the metabolic presence. One receives both, bodily and spiritual Christ, just as we are both body and spirit and as Christ was the incarnate Word. Luther stood against what he took to be a Swiss dualism that threatened salvation itself.

By 1528 Luther had also come to an integrated eucharistic theology that was both evangelical and Augustinian in its own way. The evangelical emphasis on the personal, speaking God, whose word awakened our trust, was the first aspect of "one sacramental reality" that included, in order, eucharistic elements, body and blood of Christ, new testament, forgiveness of sins, life and salvation. Word, sign, and reality were held as closely together as possible, while still distinguishing them as features of a single thing. This is strikingly Augustinian, with Luther's own evangelical emphasis on the word.[152] Where Luther differs from Augustine concerns his insistence on a metabolic real presence.

This suggests also that Luther's mature eucharistic theology was not only evangelical, and (formally) Augustinian, but was also medieval and catholic. Just as the scholastics of the early and high medieval periods had found a way to synthesize the metabolic and nonmetabolic views inherited ultimately from Ambrose and Augustine, so Luther synthesized both positions in his mature eucharistic theology, but did so as part of his evangelical insistence on God's Word.

Finally, the presence of Christ, both metabolic and mystical, was for Luther God's sheer gift to humankind, not dependent upon our works, which included our faithful reception. Luther here fused his works-righteousness criticism of the mystical traditions, which he saw in the inner spirituality and contemplation of Karlstadt's position, and a rejection of a spirit-matter dualism, in an attack on all the Swiss positions on the Supper: The mystical true presence may be given, but God gives that only in and through the metabolic real presence, all dependent on the Word of the personal God.

3

THE FIRST GENERATION

Huldrych Zwingli and Martin Bucer

Luther's eucharistic theology shows the gradual development of the metabolic real presence from the inherited view of transubstantiation (and annihilation), in which the substance of the elements was changed from bread and wine to the body and blood of Christ, to a view in which Jesus was corporeally (*leiblich*) given "under the bread and wine."[1] As we have seen, this metabolic real presence gradually enclosed within it the inherited view of the mystical true presence, and Luther subsumed both under the Word.

Although the Protestant Reformers unanimously rejected transubstantiation, not all agreed with Luther that a metabolic real presence should be retained, although rejecting such a presence by no means meant rejecting a true presence of Christ in the Supper. Mere memorialism was not the only alternative to a metabolic real presence. Among the diversity of early sixteenth-century reformers were some theologians who actively emphasized the mystical true presence and who would later be seen as the headwaters of the Reformed tradition.

HULDRYCH ZWINGLI

Born on New Year's Day in 1484 in the village of Wildhaus, Zwingli's early education came from an uncle.[2] Formal education continued with Heinrich Wöfflin, a local humanist, and then at the Universities of Vienna and Basel. At Basel he was trained in the *via antiqua*, which was the (realist) tradition of early and high scholasticism, not the *via moderna*, which was the tradition of late medieval nominalism that was influential on Luther at Erfurt.

In his first parish at Glarus, Zwingli developed his interest in the Fathers and humanism, interests that really went hand in hand, since humanism was primarily a method that returned to the original texts, in the original languages, in their historical setting.[3] By 1516 Zwingli had taken a call at Einsiedeln and had read more deeply in the Fathers. His humanism had driven him to a close reading of the Greek New Testament, especially the letters of Paul. The all-sufficiency of the work of Christ, our only mediator, had become clear to Zwingli.[4]

Zwingli was called to Zurich in 1519, and over the next three years he began to question a number of late medieval worship practices, such as penance and indulgences, fasting, veneration of the saints, clerical celibacy, and pilgrimages. January 1523 brought a public disputation, ordered by the town council, to be held in German and to be done according to the one norm of God's Word. The bishop of Constance sent representatives, who appealed to procedure—such issues were not matters for a Zurich discussion without the doctors of the church present—and Zwingli appealed to Scripture. The council agreed that Zwingli and the Zurich preachers should preach according to the Word of God.

Zwingli began to reform the Mass that year, rejecting transubstantiation and editing the canon, or eucharistic prayer proper, with his own prayer, the fourth section of which ended by praying: "Draw our hearts, O Lord, by the grace of your light that worthily—by faith—it may be fitting that we approach this most holy banquet of your Son, of which he himself is both host and sumptuous meal."[5] What shall we make of this prayer, given its realistic Supper language, and assuming for the moment that Zwingli the reformer and humanist was quite capable of saying what he meant and meaning what he said?

The debate over Zwingli's eucharistic teaching began almost five hundred years ago, and over time the epithet "Zwinglian" has become synonymous with a "merely" memorialist view of the Supper:[6] A Christian community gathers for the Lord's Supper and recalls together the once-for-all sacrifice of Jesus Christ, thereby recommitting themselves individually and corporately to his service.[7] The view that Zwingli was memorialist, which found typical expression in authors such as Baur, Staehelin, and Seeberg,[8] found an early modern challenge in a thesis by Miéville and was thoroughly challenged by Köhler's important 1924 work, which argued that the early Zwingli was not memorialist, but that Zwingli became so beginning in 1524, as a variety of religious and social issues affected him, among them Hoen's letter and the struggles with Karlstadt, Luther, and Erasmus.[9]

Köhler was answered by Bauer, who (1) questioned when Zwingli first held a symbolic view—given Zwingli's letter to Matthew Alber (November 1524);[10] (2) questioned how to interpret Zwingli's July 1523 explanation of his eighteenth article presented in the *Sixty-seven Articles* that he prepared for the First Zurich Disputation in late January 1523;[11] (3) questioned how the variations in Zwingli's thought connected to the older literature (e.g., Sigwart and Dieckhoff); and (4) questioned Köhler's "real motive," which was to preserve Zwingli's theological integrity.[12]

Köhler replied that Bauer had missed the principal point of his magisterial work, which was to show how dogmatic development and sociopolitical context worked together. Köhler argued that Bauer had misinterpreted

Zwingli's letter to Alber; had not really grasped the category ("spiritual-mystical") that Köhler used for Zwingli; did not understand the context of Zwingli's explanation of the eighteenth article or the medieval German dative that Zwingli used; and that rehabilitating Zwingli's character was not his main goal.[13]

Bauer replied by giving a longer explanation of Köhler's inadequate appraisal of the older secondary literature; reviewing chronological issues—including bringing forth his own expert scholar to testify about datives in medieval German—and challenging Köhler's consistency of method; and questioning Köhler's overall view of Zwingli.[14]

Köhler next responded with an interesting and (on my view) quite insightful categorization of eucharistic options that argued for Zwingli's cautious change from 1523–24, indicating a more subtle trajectory of eucharistic influence in the Reformed tradition than Bauer's view of Zwingli as "the predecessor of Bucer and Calvin."[15] More recently, Neuser supported Köhler's reading of Zwingli's 1523 letter to Thomas Wyttenbach, about which Köhler had written that no symbolic view was present.[16]

Discussion has also occurred about the "later" eucharistic views of Zwingli that came after the controversy with Luther, a time when Zwingli could reflect purely constructively rather than reacting against other points of view. Do Zwingli's later writings show a relatively uniform position with earlier periods (Miéville); a similar position to his earliest writings that was interrupted by the conflicts with Luther (Barclay); a more positive attitude toward the sacrament that appeared at least implicitly, if not occasionally explicitly, in the early period (Stephens); a real emphasis on the objective character of the sacrament and God's presence for us that balanced his earlier emphasis on the subjective character (Blanke); or, despite an acknowledgment of the objective character to which the sacrament points, an essential continuity of eucharistic view that remained oriented toward human faith toward God, not God's activity toward us (Niesel)?[17]

In more recent years, a Swiss defense of Zwingli was made through a series of studies by Courvoisier, Schweizer, and Locher, who argued that Zwingli saw the real presence of Christ as the mystically transformed community that was his body, a liturgical event (Courvoisier, Schweizer) realized through an active "remembering" (or anamnesis) that reflected Zwingli's Neoplatonic epistemology (Locher).[18] This Swiss view of Zwingli has been criticized in several essays by Gerrish; although this Swiss view is generally supported (perhaps more than he knows) by Jenny's careful work on liturgical forms, liturgical history, and architecture.[19] Among other British and American scholarship, Barclay seems influenced by the work of Köhler,[20] as does Stephens.[21] Barclay himself was later criticized sharply by Richardson, who accused Barclay of "trying to show that

Zwingli was not a Zwinglian," thereby introducing "a good deal of confusion into the issue," assertions that seem to me to beg the question.[22]

A general summary of secondary scholarship on Zwingli's eucharistic theology would be that no one should assume that Zwingli was merely a "memorialist." He may have been, but the detailed scholarship on this topic, going back to the mid-nineteenth century, indicates a wide range of views. Characterizing Zwingli as memorialist must be carefully shown and not merely assumed.

Scholarship has generally accepted an approach to Zwingli's eucharistic theology that divides his work into three periods: his early writings (up to 1524), prior to the controversies with Luther; a middle period running from Zwingli's letter to Alber (1524) up to (or, for some scholars, through) the Colloquy at Marburg (1529); and a final period from Marburg through Zwingli's death (1529–31). This division has been followed by scholars who hold a range of views on Zwingli's eucharistic teaching, from those who find a relative uniformity of nonmemorialism (Miéville); to those who find nuanced changes within Zwingli's memorialism (Blanke, Bosshard); to those who see differences but think they are relatively external (Niesel) and thus agree with the older scholarship (Baur, Staehelin) that takes Zwingli as memorialistic; to those who think Zwingli went from a "virtual real presence" to memorialism (Köhler); to those who take the middle period to be an interlude between relatively similar early and late periods (Barclay).

In his (July) 1523 *Exposition of the Sixty-seven Articles*, Zwingli discusses the articles that he had presented at the First Zurich Disputation in January that same year. The eighteenth article takes up the attack on the sacrifice of the Mass, insisting that the Mass is a memorial of Christ's one true sacrifice that was efficacious for our redemption: "So it follows," says Zwingli, in language that seems familiar to us, "that the Mass is not a sacrifice but a memorial (*widergedächtnus*) of a sacrifice." Zwingli then continues by saying that people must believe

> that Christ has paid on the cross for their sin, and in such faith eat and drink his flesh and blood, and recognize that it has been given them as a seal that their sins are forgiven, just as Christ first died on the cross. So powerful and present to all times is Christ, for he is an eternal God. So also his suffering is eternally effective, as Paul says (Heb. 9), "How much more will the blood of Christ, who has offered himself spotless through the eternal spirit to God, make pure our conscience etc."[23]

Two features of this striking passage stand out. First, the Mass does not make Christ be present, because he already is present as the eternal God. Second, Christ is effectively present now for our redemption that is realized in "memorial." Locher has rightly insisted that for the Platonized,

Augustinian Zwingli, "memorial" was no mere retrospection but an effective "re-presentation" of the suffering of Christ.[24]

We can recall that for Plato the mind already had knowledge of eternal forms of all things because of its preexistence in the eternal realm.[25] Attaining knowledge was then a matter of realizing within someone what she or he already deeply knew, just as Socrates awakened the rules of geometry from within a slave. All learning was fundamentally remembering (*anamnesis*). For Augustine such anamnesis was the product of divine illumination, in which Christ, the eternal Word (*logos*), directly illumines the mind with the eternal truths present in the mind of God. All learning comes from the presently effective grace of God.[26] Thus Locher can say of Zwingli's idea of "memorial" that "[i]n this act of remembrance, the congregation does not transport itself back 1500 or 2,000 years to the place of the historical event, but rather, the one who was crucified for us comes to us in the present."[27] Even though the sacrifice on the cross was once forever, yet that sacrificial death of Christ remains "eternally effective" and present now, because Christ is eternal God.[28]

That the ever-present Christ is effectively present through anamnesis may lie behind one of the more debated aspects of Zwingli's exposition of the eighteenth article. In a section dealing with criticism of the Mass as sacrifice, Zwingli says that "here simple folk should learn that one ought not quarrel whether the body and blood of Christ are eaten and drunk (*no Christian doubts this*), but whether it is a sacrifice or only a memorial."[29] The disputed phrase—"no Christian doubts this" (*dann daran zwyflet dheinem Christen*)—has been taken to mean either (1) "the real issue is sacrifice not Christ's presence, and ordinary folk typically think one eats the body and drinks the blood of Christ"; or (2) "the real issue is sacrifice, no one doubts that you eat and drink the body and blood, nor do I [Zwingli] doubt that."[30] The phrase itself does not specify a metabolic presence as such, and in his discussion of the eighteenth article Zwingli was able to understand memorial (*anamnesis, widergedächtnus*) to mean "eating and drinking of the body and blood of Christ."[31]

In a letter to his former teacher, Thomas Wyttenbach, written about the same time as the *Exposition of the Sixty-seven Articles*, Zwingli specifically takes up this issue of eucharistic presence.[32] For the first time, Zwingli expressly rejects the doctrine of transubstantiation, although he does so by comparing the change of water to wine at the wedding at Cana and arguing for the inconsistency of scholastic arguments: the wine at Cana is "changed water" for which one need posit only a change in accidents, not a change in substance.[33] Zwingli goes on to say that whatever happens in the Supper happens through divine power, although we are ignorant of the mode, and God is let into the soul (*illabatur animae*).[34] Curiosity over the mode of divine presence ultimately signals doubt, says Zwingli, because anyone who truly has the bread that feeds the soul—the faith that Christ died for us—would not then worry about how we "eat him who sits at the right hand of God."[35] What Zwingli rules out is an ongoing physical transformation of the bread, such as would be preserved, since the only true preservation occurs in the human soul.[36] Nevertheless, just as there is fire in the flint only when it is struck, so Christ is to be found under the bread only through faith, and eaten in a miraculous way that the faithful do not worry about.[37]

These reflections to Wyttenbach about eucharistic presence support the second of the two readings from the *Exposition*: no Christian, not even Zwingli, doubts that one eats the body and blood of Christ during the Supper, although a metabolic real presence is not demanded by the comment in the *Exposition* and is rejected in the letter. Zwingli's *Canon of the Mass*—dated August 29, 1523, or ten weeks after the letter to Wyttenbach, and finished hurriedly—continues this same trajectory of thought.[38]

"Christ called [the Eucharist] his body and blood, not the 'Mass,'" says Zwingli. As such the name Eucharist "proclaims nothing other than this food and drink are the freely given and good gift and grace of God."[39] Continuing the argument found in the letter to Wyttenbach, Zwingli comments on the section of the eucharistic prayer "that it may become to us the body and the blood of your most beloved Son, our Lord Jesus Christ":[40]

> Nevertheless, there is nothing impious said if we pray that the bread might become the body and the blood of the most beloved Son of God; provided that you take the expression "become" not for the "transubstantiation" of our theologians, but rather you discern that with faithful eating the bread and wine become the body and blood of Jesus Christ, in whatever manner it finally happens.[41]

In keeping with his denial of a metabolic presence somehow localized in the elements, and with his comment to Wyttenbach that where there is faith, there Christ is present, Zwingli insists that the feeding on Christ happens through the Word, the Spirit, and the presence of faith that someone brings:

> For that [Word] is the bread that gives life to the world; we shall eat the flesh and drink the blood of your Son without effect unless by faith in your Word we firmly believe, prior to all things, that this same Son of yours, our Lord Jesus Christ, nailed to the cross for us, atones for the transgressions of the whole world. For he himself said that the flesh profits nothing, but it is the Spirit who vivifies.[42]

This earliest period of Zwingli shows several key features. First, Zwingli clearly asserted that believers are fed by the body and blood of Christ himself in the Supper. There is no reason to doubt that he included himself when he commented in the *Exposition* that no Christian doubted that one fed on Christ's body and blood. Second, Zwingli explicitly denied transubstantiation and with it the idea of a changed substance independent of a faith that trusts through the power of the Spirit. The image in the letter to Wyttenbach is significant: just as there is fire in the flint only when struck, so the presence of Christ is there only when faith is there. Zwingli's point was not some kind of works righteousness, or conditioning God upon human faith. His significant point might be put like this: ontology is not religion, and elements that can be preserved are not faith in Christ. The Christ who is eternal God and already present is realized in the soul through the event of faith and the Spirit. Third, a means by which the divine Christ nourishes the soul is the Supper, which is a memorial (*widergedächtnus*) or anamnesis, but not mere retrospection.

In these perspectives held by Zwingli, and in others such as the ethical dimension of the Supper, Köhler argued for Erasmus as the principle source ("Hauptquelle").[43] Bauer, however, criticized Köhler's view that Zwingli began with the Erasmian mystical (or mystical-spiritual) presence, because, argued Bauer, this portrays Zwingli as too personalistic rather than communal oriented.[44] Courvoisier renewed this criticism, particularly relating to the Supper,[45] as did Schweizer, who argued that Zwingli's liturgy from early 1525 (*Action or Use of the Lord's Supper*) indicated the transformation of the community, through the Word, into the very body of Christ.[46]

The influence of Erasmus, and also the need to account for the communal nature of Zwingli's eucharistic thought, lead to a final comment: The eucharistic teaching of Zwingli traces back not merely to Erasmus (and Luther and the mystics—so, Köhler), but to the Augustinian tradition of the mystical true presence. This needs to be said strongly: The connection between Erasmus, Zwingli, and John Oecolampadius (1482–1531) is not so much that of the great humanist and then disciples influenced by him, but rather a family-type of related positions, all influenced by the humanist study of the original sources, particularly Augustine.[47] Erasmus found the position of the Basel Reformer Oecolampadius persuasive, yet he continued to maintain the metabolic tradition upheld by church authority.[48] Zwingli carefully read Augustine's tractates on the Gospel of John, as his many margin notes demonstrate.[49] In his notes on Augustine's tractates (25–27) on the Bread from Heaven discourse—a *locus classicus* for Augustine's nonmetabolic views, as we have seen—we find Zwingli oriented toward the communal character of the sacrament as the body of Christ himself, members united in Christ in love and through faith.[50] As we saw in the first chapter, Augustine's nonmetabolic view presupposed the mystical body of Christ, in which believers were fed by Christ's real presence and more deeply taken into him.[51]

Zwingli's second period is typically taken to begin with the letter to Matthew Alber that is dated November 16, 1524, and was published in March 1525.[52] In the letter Zwingli deals appreciatively with Karlstadt, whose five tracts on the Supper had appeared. Zwingli applauds Karlstadt's courage and theological forthrightness but not his clarity.[53] Zwingli spends a good deal of time on John 6 and how the flesh profits nothing, but faith in Christ counts for everything; eating means nothing other than believing.[54] He then moves to what is "most difficult," the words of institution. In the course of the discussion, he takes up the argument from Hoen's letter, certainly known to Zwingli, that *est* means "signifies": the bread signifies or symbolizes the body of Christ that was given on the cross.[55] Tertullian and Augustine are cited as corroborating views that uphold a figurative, nonliteral meaning to the words of institution. Even before them, the apostle Paul wrote to the Corinthians that the Supper showed a confessing and professing community of believers. In short, Christ wished "to leave us a rite of memorial that he was horribly slain for us."[56]

When viewed as a whole, it is easy to see how the letter to Alber has been understood to reflect a merely memorialist view of the Supper, especially when Zwingli says:

> I do not think that there has been anyone who believed that he or she ate Christ bodily and essentially in this sacrament. . . . [Y]ou, along with me, have not believed, or have diverted your mind lest it cry out against this, or you have been powerfully anxious about the way that the truth would freely be made known at last.[57]

On further reflection, however, the case for the mere memorialism of the letter to Alber is not so clear. On the deconstructive side, what Zwingli rejects is eating the "corporeal and essential body" of Christ, a point that he clearly made also to Wyttenbach.[58] The scriptural texts to which Zwingli appeals come from John 6, particularly John 6:63 ("The flesh profits nothing"), and he makes an often misunderstood or, at the least, underappreciated point. The perception that comes through the senses is by nature contingent, and it cannot be the ultimate source of redemption that comes from the one strictly necessary reality, God alone. The redemption that comes from God in Christ can be seen, says Zwingli, but it must be perceived with a different sense—with the "eyes of faith."[59] It is perception, but not sensationist perception.

The rejection of a "corporeal and essential body" lies behind the exegetical point and the scriptural examples, taken from Hoen. If in the words of institution, "This is my body," the word "is" (*est*) really means "signifies," then what Zwingli rules out is a localized presence that would need to be preserved somewhere other than in the soul. (See his comments to Wyttenbach.) The exegetical approach that understands *est* to mean "signifies" does not mean that Zwingli holds a memorialist view; it simply means that he denies a metabolic real presence.

The alternatives that remain are memorialist or mystical true presence, and, on the constructive side, Zwingli speaks for this mystical true presence. Locher's point that for Zwingli *memoria* was a re-presentation (*Vergegenwärtigung*) of the saving presence of Christ, the eternal God, helps interpret the many references that Zwingli makes to "memorial" in his letter to Alber, and it allows them to be seen coherently with Zwingli's remark that

> [i]f we eat his flesh—that is, we believe he died for us—and drink his blood—that is, we believe firmly that his blood was poured out for us—then Christ is in us and we are in him. But is Christ in anybody physically (*corporaliter*)? By no means![60]

The mystical true presence continues to underlie Zwingli's understanding of the Supper, and it can come as no surprise that he cites in support both Tertullian and Augustine, both of whom stand in the ancient non-metabolic tradition that chapter 1 traced.

These themes continue in his *Commentary on True and False Religion*, which was written at roughly the same time, published in March 1525, and which was, like Calvin's first edition of the *Institutes*, dedicated to Francis I. Zwingli for the first time wrote at length about the Supper and began the eucharistic material (section 18) by giving an apologia for speaking pastorally, with concern for the lay people, rather than with full openness when he had written his *Exposition*. A careful pastor plows the earth and sows seed in the springtime, when reception is possible, not in the dead of winter, and people were so deeply embedded in the winter of late medieval piety that he "did not wish to give food at the wrong time."[61]

Zwingli then moves to a long discussion of John 6 that he introduces by saying, "Therefore this is the food that he orders us to seek—to trust (*fidere*) the Son. Faith (*fides*), then, is the food about which he talks so deeply through all this chapter."[62] When he renews the argument that in the institution narratives the word "is" (*est*) means "signifies," so that the Supper is a "reminding of the Lord's death,"[63] Zwingli surely seems "memorialistic."[64]

But further reading of this section requires a different judgment. First, throughout the section on John 6, and then into the material on the institution narratives, Zwingli specifically criticizes the idea that what is present in the Supper is the "bodily flesh"; the "essential or bodily flesh"; the "true, that is, bodily and essential" body and blood of Christ; the "actual, bodily, or essential" body of Christ; "the essential body or the bodily and sense-related body"; "bodily flesh"; the "bodily and sense-related flesh of Christ"; "bodily flesh or sense-related body"; and "the bodily flesh of Christ."[65]

Zwingli historically connects this sense-related, bodily flesh to the tradition of the medieval church, commenting for instance on Berengar's confession.[66] He epistemologically relates this idea of real presence to the five human senses, which supply him with the phrase the "sense-related" ("sensible") flesh.[67] The senses perceive that which is bodily, and that which is created has no power to save and ought not be worshiped.[68] As Zwingli already has laid out, "true religion or piety is that which clings to the one and only God," and by contrast "false religion or piety" occurs "when anything other than God is trusted."[69] At the beginning of section 18 on the Supper, Zwingli not surprisingly gives a long list of created things that have been wrongly worshiped, of which the eucharistic stands foremost.[70]

But if one rejects the sense-related, bodily flesh as being present, and which has been wrongly worshiped, one need not go to the other extreme, as did Karlstadt, when he became only a memorialist and argued that Jesus meant his own body when he said the word "this" (*touto*):

> They have emerged in our time who have said that a symbolic meaning is to be discovered in the word "this." I commend their faith, if only it is not false. For God looks into the heart, we wretched people judge from the face. I very greatly commend their faith, therefore, but not because they too imprudently dared to treat these words, but because they see it not possible to take the position that we understand bodily flesh here. I will not, however, speak now of the Charybdis the fear of which drove them upon this Scylla, for it has no bearing upon this matter.[71]

Zwingli's interesting comment on Karlstadt needs some interpretation, because its precise meaning is not self-evident. In the context of the discussion about the "sense-related" bodily presence, Zwingli claims that Karlstadt opposed this view, although whose view and exactly what view Karlstadt opposed Zwingli passes over. However, claims Zwingli, avoiding the whirlpools of Charybdis caused Karlstadt (like the ship of Odysseus) to be snared by Scylla; but, what is the danger that Scylla represented? Was it a (merely) symbolic interpretation? Was it the exegetical discussion of "this" (*touto*) in the institution narrative? Or was it the exegetical discussion that produced a merely symbolic view?

Since the goal is to steer midway between two monstrous alternatives, the image itself suggests that Zwingli had in mind an error by Karlstadt that went beyond formal procedure to material content, so that a safe middle path would (like that of the Argonauts) avoid both a sense-related, essential presence and a merely symbolic and memorialist view of the Supper. Does the material in the *Commentary on True and False Religion* support this reading of his comments on Karlstadt?

Zwingli allows for a view of "spiritual manducation" (*de spirituali manducatione*), provided that it is according to Christ (*modo Christi*), not on one's own beliefs.[72] Now it may be, as we have seen, that this food is nothing other than when "we trust Christ" (*Christo fidamus*),[73] but such language is for Zwingli no mere forensic talk. This is the "mystical discourse" (*mysticum sermonem*) that comprises John 6.[74] Faith itself is a gift from God, existing "in our hearts through the Spirit of God, and we *perceive* it" (*Fides constat per spiritum dei in cordibus, quam sentimus*).[75] In this event of faith, the Spirit draws the human spirit to itself, unites with the human spirit, and transforms it into itself. This is the "food of the soul" (*animae cibus*).[76] God, therefore, truly dwells in that person whom God inwardly teaches, "and at the same time, whoever abides in Christ, in him Christ also abides."[77] The mystical true presence.

We can hardly be surprised, then, when Zwingli draws on Augustine's tractates on the Gospel of John, especially tractates 26 (John 6:41–59) and 27 (John 6:60–72),[78] which, as we have seen, comprise an articulate expression of the mystical true presence (nonmetabolic real presence). Zwingli quotes Augustine on John 6:

> Moreover, he [Jesus] explained the mode of the bestowal and his gift, how he would give his flesh to eat, saying, "Whoever eats my flesh and drinks my blood remains in me and I in them." This is the sign that one has eaten and drunk: if one abides and is abided in, if one dwells and is dwelled in, if one clings and is not abandoned. He therefore taught this and reminds us of this in mystical language, that we may be in his body, in his members under himself as head, eating his body and not giving up unity with him.[79]

For Zwingli, those who through the Spirit are renewed and dwell in Christ, and he in them, are fed by his divine presence. This is the Augustinian tradition of believers being fed as they are taken by Christ even deeper into union with himself. This seems to me exactly what Schweizer and, following him, Schmidt-Clausing were pointing to when they argued that for Zwingli through the Spirit the congregation itself is "transubstantiated," and this is realized during the Supper.[80]

Zwingli's liturgical sensitivity has been as caricatured as his eucharistic teaching. In a careful study of Zwingli's attitude toward church music, Jenny has shown that what Zwingli opposed were the late medieval musical practices that retarded congregational devotion. Instead, Zwingli encouraged evangelical hymns, wanting lively music that promoted congregational attention and participation.[81] In liturgical practices, commented Schmidt-Clausing, "Luther cleansed, Zwingli created."[82]

In the liturgy that Zwingli designed for Easter 1525 and that was presented to the council of Zurich on Tuesday of Holy Week, the chancel altar became a table present in the congregation.[83] The men, gathered on the right side of the church, and the women, gathered on the left side, then antiphonally recited the *Gloria in excelsis* and the Apostles' Creed, a practice that was rejected by the council. Either during the Word service, or prior to the Word service itself, the bread and wine were placed on the table.[84] People received the Supper where they were and in their hands, from wooden plates and cups carried by the ministers.[85] Where the canon of the Mass once had been, Zwingli had an invitation to the congregation, followed by the Lord's Prayer, and then, where the consecratory prayers and actions traditionally had occurred, Zwingli had the following prayer:

> O Lord, Almighty God who, through the Spirit in unity of faith, has made us into your one body (*zů einem dinem lyb gemacht hast*), which body you have commanded to give you praise and thanks for your goodness and free gift of your only-begotten Son, our Lord, Jesus Christ, whom you have given into death for sins:
> Grant that we may do the same so faithfully that we, with no hypocrisy or falseness, may not provoke [you who are] the truth that cannot be deceived;
> Grant also that we may live so innocently, as befits your body, and your family and children, so that even those who do not trust may learn to recognize your name and honor.
> Look after us, O Lord, that your name and honor may never be reviled because of our lives.
> O Lord, always increase our faith—which is trust in you—you who lives and reigns, God in eternity!
> Amen![86]

This remarkable consecratory prayer does not call for God now to make the gathered people one body, nor does it necessarily mean that through the Word they have been "transubstantiated" from that which they were (a collectivity of gathered people) into that which they have become (the single, mystical body of Christ).[87] Rather, it seems to me, this prayer precisely signifies the Augustinian idea that those who are believers—for Zwingli this means those who actually trust God, and who are already engrafted into Christ—anamnetically realize their union in Christ and thus are fed, through the Spirit, by Christ himself. Two implications arise.

First, if Christ feeds us because we truly are engrafted into his body, he feeds us with his body, so long as that is a spiritual (not "essential") matter. Thus Zwingli would say to Luther two years later, "[I]f this presence of Christ's body is of a spiritual nature" (*Si spiritualis est ista corporis praesentia*), so that it is a question of trust and presence in the heart rather than being present "naturally or essentially" (*naturaliter sive essentialiter*), then there "now will remain no disagreement between us" (*iam nihil dissidii inter nos manebit*).[88]

Second, on this trajectory from Augustine, the Supper does not make something to be present that is not already present; and we already saw that for Augustine the mystical union of believers in the body of Christ is a presupposition of, not an outcome of, the Eucharist. As Zwingli would put the matter to Luther in August 1528, "No sacrament has ever been which made present that which it signified." Zwingli goes on to give circumcision, Passover, and baptism as examples illustrating his point, and then, regarding the Supper, he concludes that

> likewise the Supper of Christ, or the bread and wine, do not make present the body or the death of Christ; but those who, acknowledging the death of Christ, who suffered once, to be their life, bring this to the Supper in their thankful hearts; and there, together with their co-members, they receive the sign that Christ instituted, in order that it should be accepted by them who confess his death and signify [their faith].[89]

This raises a question, to anticipate an issue that will arise shortly, concerning the value or function of the signs themselves, a criticism crisply made by Gerrish,[90] and an issue that Calvin and Bullinger clarified in the next generation of Reformed theologians. At this stage of Zwingli's thought, the issue remains unclear, and what we shall see in the third stage of Zwingli's eucharistic teaching is not a move from "memorialistic" to some kind of realism, but an emphasis on the objective nature of the signs themselves.[91]

Six months after his *Commentary on True and False Religion*, Zwingli published (August 1525) his *Subsidiary Essay on the Eucharist*, complaining that he so often was pressed into writing that he never had enough time to think and prepare. "All my writings," lamented Zwingli, "you might more rightly name as impulsive thoughts than books."[92] Zwingli wanted to correct that problem by adding some more reflective thoughts to his earlier *Commentary on True and False Religion*. Also, the spring of that same year had seen the Zurich council ban the Mass and approve the new Supper liturgy and, during the course of the debates, Zwingli had been reflecting on the comments of a council member, Joachim Am Grüt, who had questioned Zwingli's argument about figurative language.

In the *Subsidiary Essay*, Zwingli begins by spending a good deal of effort explaining issues of allegory, grammar, and vocabulary in the Greek New Testament, as well as the Hebrew writings and the Vulgate. He displays a keen humanist interest in text and contexts. Along the way two discussions are worth more comment. First, while vexed by Am Grüt's challenge that his examples of figurative language came from the parables, Zwingli had a now-famous dream during Holy Week 1525. A figure, "either black or white, I cannot remember because I am talking about a dream," chastening him for being a "slacker" (*ignave*) and pointing him to the text of

Exodus 12:11: "It is the Passover; the passing over (*transitus*) of the Lord." Zwingli says that he awoke, studied the text carefully, and then preached on the topic in a way that clarified for people the meaning of the Supper.[93]

Second, Zwingli continued to specify that not all perception came from the five outer senses—not all sensation was "sensationist"—because we had an inner sense that belongs to faith:

> There is something else about which the unskilled make a mistake: the meaning of the word 'sense.' They think that this word is to be taken for the organs of sense, or for the perceptions of the flesh, when it is said 'this is inconsistent with sense,' . . . When 'sense' is here understood for 'mind' and 'judgment,' acquired not from flesh and blood, but from the Spirit of God and is held in our hearts.[94]

Faith, says Zwingli, is a "sure experience" (*certa experientia*) in which we are conscious of ourselves and confident in God, primarily "trust" (*fiducia*) not "credulity" (*credulitate*).[95] Faith is therefore "a reality, not knowledge or opinion or imagination," but something that a person "*perceives* within, in the heart."[96] As we have seen above, this experience that is faith, which is Spirit-given and whereby Christ dwells in us, allows us to be fed by Christ, even his body, so long as we consider the matter "spiritually."[97] Now it becomes clearer how Zwingli could write to Wyttenbach that Christ was present only where there is faith, just as there is a spark only when the flint is struck.

During the remainder of this middle period, Zwingli continued to make these same points and then to contrast the position that he held with that held by Luther, who in his 1526 preface to the Swabian Syngramma found Zwingli's views to be demonic.[98] Zwingli's 1526 *Clear Teaching on the Lord's Supper*, which was written in German, aimed to defend his eucharistic teaching by giving it a public hearing. There Zwingli added one last and lasting feature to his eucharistic theology, a discussion of the ascension.[99]

Zwingli divided his treatise into four parts: three principal misinterpretations of the Supper (Rome, Erasmus, and Luther); an appeal to Scriptures and creed to show the falsity of these positions; the correct understanding of the Supper, based on Scripture; and possible objections to the position just presented. In the second section, Zwingli raised the issue of Jesus' ascension and thus also the issue of Jesus' "two-natures."[100] Zwingli carefully distinguished the human and divine natures, asserting that they had unity in the "person" of Christ, which, as Locher points out, "is identical with his divinity" and makes his Christology fit "effortlessly into the doctrine of the Trinity."[101] Within the person of Christ, one could attribute, by means of alloiosis—a figure of speech borrowed from Plutarch—the properties of one nature to the other, but the "property of each nature should remain intact" (*die eigenschaft yeder natur unversert bliben*).[102] Therefore, says Zwingli, Christ sits at the right hand of God, although the ascension into heaven properly refers only to the human nature, and he will return only at the last day and not before.[103]

Over the next three years, the eucharistic discussions between Zwingli and Luther intensified and culminated with the 1529 Marburg Colloquy. Zwingli wrote four tracts that addressed Luther, who, according to Zwingli's (fairly accurate, it seems to me) claim, "was utterly ignorant of my views" (*adparet nostra tibi esse ignotissima*):[104] *Friendly Exegesis* (February 1527), *Friendly Reply* (March 1527),[105] *Zwingli's Christian Reply* (June 1527),[106] and *Two Replies to Luther's Book* (August 1528). These tracts take up arguments that we have seen Zwingli develop through 1526, and the arguments against Luther can be grouped into three categories.

First, Scriptures offer ample evidence of allegorical language, including the parallels that we have seen between Exodus 12 and the Lord's Supper.[107] In a very interesting argument Zwingli correctly challenges Luther over logically begging the question (*quod principii petitionem incurritis*) when it comes to interpreting the language in the Supper account. The fundamental disagreement, says Zwingli, is whether the flesh is (bodily) eaten or not bodily eaten, and the two positions logically are contradictories: if one is correct, the other is false. Luther, however, says the alternatives are Christ speaking literally ("this *is* my body") or Christ lying to us, since the words really mean something figurative. Zwingli argues that Luther has already assumed his own (literal and bodily) position to be correct—the alternative is the impossibility that Christ is a liar—but *exactly that position* (a bodily meaning to the words of institution) is what must be proved, not already assumed.[108]

This precise point against Luther, and Luther's anticipation of it, would later provide the dramatic scene from the Marburg Colloquy (as reported by Osiander and "Anonymous," with some variation) in which Luther and Zwingli had been arguing over the words of institution.[109] Zwingli (and Oecolampadius) demanded that Luther prove from Scripture that Christ meant a bodily presence. Luther argued that he needed to give no proof, but rather Zwingli needed to prove from Scripture that Christ *was not* present. Zwingli retorted to Luther that "it would be a shame" not to prove such an important point from Scripture. At that point, Luther pulled off the table cloth to reveal what he had written beneath it: "This is my body." Zwingli jumped to his feet and reminded Luther that he was *assuming* the point that needed to be proved (i.e., "begging the question"). Luther replied that he was merely quoting Scripture, to which Zwingli replied, "Must everything, then, go according to your will?"[110]

The second argument that Zwingli has developed that he used against Luther was the exegesis of John 6, particularly but not exclusively John 6:63, along with the attendant concept of faith. As we already have seen, according to Zwingli the "flesh profits nothing," because bodily flesh is what the outer senses experience. These outer senses that perceive only the "sense-related" flesh cannot perceive the Spirit that "draws the wretched spirit of a person to itself, and unites and binds it to itself, and wholly transforms it into itself."[111] So, says Zwingli to Luther, "It must be that the Spirit makes the heart (mentem) alive, and who enters into it; it shrinks from feeding on flesh."[112]

The (nonsensationist) sense whereby the Spirit is *perceived*, and through which the Spirit renovates the wretched soul of a person, is the "eye of faith" (fidei contemplatione), not the outer, sense-related eye.[113] Zwingli has come to the heart of the issue: Taking up the Reformation insistence on justification by grace through faith, Zwingli says to Luther that

> we deny that applying a physical body to the soul does anything towards justification; not only because the soul cannot be fed with physical flesh, but also because Christ himself has most clearly discussed that it must be the Spirit who justifies, whereas the flesh profits nothing at all.[114]

Zwingli knew well what late medieval piety was like. At the beginning of the eucharistic section of his *Commentary on True and False Religion*, Zwingli decries the false worship practices of the his era, most of all concerning the Supper. People falsely adore and worship

> wood, stones, earth, dust, shoes, vestments, rings, hats, swords, belts, bones, teeth, hair, milk, bread, eucharistic loaves (quadras), tablets, wine, knives, jars . . . and most blockheaded of all we reckon ourselves plainly blessed if we have caught sight of anything of that kind. We promise ourselves remission of sins, prosperous fortune and the whole world.[115]

This trust in good works was all too easily longed for and visited again, because it embodied long-standing pious practices of late medieval Christians.

Zwingli thought that Luther's insistence on a "sense-related," bodily presence only encouraged this false religion of old, with its eucharistic adorations and the concentration on viewing elevations of the host, sometimes as often as possible on Sunday morning.[116] In a reference to Numbers 11, Zwingli said that Luther's words "begin to reek of the garlic and onions of Egypt":[117] Rather than put their faith in God and the food that comes from heaven (manna), the people of God are longing for merely earthly food that once sustained them. By contrast, Zwingli's stand on the real Bread from Heaven (John 6) insisted on the primacy of justification only through faith. "Are there two ways to justification?" Zwingli asked Luther. "One is by faith, the other by bodily eating? Where are we going?"[118] Against any attempt at outer justification that occurs through the outer bodily senses, Zwingli upholds *sola fide*.[119]

Zwingli did not deny that the whole Christ was present to believers in the Supper, including his body; but, he insisted to Luther, this happened in a spiritual manner:

> Second, the word "presence" is taken naturally or essentially, because the body of Christ becomes present by faith. But how? In the Spirit and the heart (*mente*)? Or in itself and by nature? If this presence of the body is spiritual—for instance, if it means that we trust in our hearts (*mente*) that Christ has died for us—then no disagreement will remain between us. For we also assert this very presence, for we know that it is the one thing that makes sufficient what we are dueling over.[120]

By saying that the body is present "spiritually," not of itself and by its own nature, Zwingli rules out the "sense-related," bodily flesh that he always has rejected.[121] In his humanity Jesus is not present as he was in Galilee, or as he will be at his second coming. The ascension and session of Jesus, and the doctrine of the two natures, ground Zwingli's view and form the third main argument against Luther.

Zwingli spends considerable effort differentiating his view of Christ's two natures from that of Luther, whom he believes has not been careful enough about their particularity and who therefore tends to "confuse the natures in Christ—now, not as an exchange of natures (*per alloeosim natu-rarumque*) and a change of proper qualities (*idiomatum commutationem*)—but truly wanting to proclaim of the human what only is of the divine, and of the divine what is merely of the human."[122] The issue for Zwingli went to the heart of the gospel, because it concerned our very redemption by God. Only by being human as such could the divine truly suffer on our behalf; only by being divine as such could redemption be effected through the suffering; and these two natures exchange their properties in the person of Christ, but must not be confused with each other.[123] The issue is not what the meaning might be to sitting "at the right hand of God." Luther poked fun at Zwingli and the Swiss for thinking that the ascension and session were like going up a ladder into a tree house, from which one could then descend. Zwingli was clear that "no one denies that the right hand of the Father is infinite (*non esse circumscriptam*), but it is necessary that the human nature of Christ be finite (*humanam Christi naturam circum-scriptam esse*)."[124] And so Zwingli pointedly says to Luther,

> But now since Christ by his own word . . . cannot bodily be anywhere except where he has prescribed, it is impossible for him to be eaten in the bread. He is at the right hand; he has said that he is going to sit there continuously until he returns as the judge of all things. "He can be in only one place," as far as referring to the human nature.[125]

The meeting at Marburg produced no new theological formulations from Zwingli and the Swiss Reformed. What did become clear, it seems to me, was exactly how foundational the christological differences were between the two sides. In a now-famous exchange, recorded in only two of the sources, and often cited by Lutherans as a wonderful and concise statement of theology by Luther, Oecolampadius urged Luther to move from "the humanity and flesh of Christ" (in the Supper) and focus rather on the divinity. Luther replied, "I know of no God except the one who was made flesh, and so I want to have no other."[126] On one side, the Swiss carefully distinguished the two natures without separating them (no "Nestorianism"), with Zwingli preferring the literary and humanist term "alloiosis" to the term *communicatio idiomatum*; on the other side, Luther held the two natures together as carefully as possible without confusing them (no "Eutychianism"). Here Locher's speculation seems sound, that the Protestant Reformation might have turned out differently from the start, had there been recognition of the christological differences prior to the eucharistic debates.[127] Once Marburg began, and political alliances and public prestige were at stake, it was hard to find substantive, univocal eucharistic agreement.[128] This was all the more so because, like the Nestorian challenge of the liturgical phrase Θεοτόκος (*theotokos*, "god-bearer"), a worship practice and encounter with the Divine was under discussion, and people on all sides had existential involvement.

In the two years that Zwingli lived after Marburg, his eucharistic teaching gradually became less controversial and more constructively oriented. When Martin Bucer, along with Wolfgang Capito and Caspar Hedio, composed a Reformed confession for the Diet of Augsburg (1530) in the name of the four imperial cities (Strasbourg, Constance, Memmingen, and Lindau),[129] Reformed voices called for Zwingli also to respond to the Confession of Augsburg (the so-called Augustana, taken from the Latin *Confessio Augustana*). From Augsburg, Jacob Sturm sent Zwingli a copy of the Augustana and asked Zwingli to submit a confession of faith "as pious and as inoffensive to anyone as possible."[130] Zwingli replied with his *An Account of the Faith*, which went unread by Charles V, and to which John Eck, who headed the Roman Catholic theologians at Augsburg, responded.[131]

The eighth section concerns the Eucharist. Zwingli begins with his distinction between the "body of Christ in essence and reality" that is available to the outer senses and able to be "chewed" with the teeth, and "the true body of Christ" that is perceived by the inner sense, "the eye of faith."[132] The ascension and Jesus' true human nature prohibit his earthly body from being present. Furthermore, that which is of the outer senses is nourished by the merely physical; that which is of faith is nourished in the soul by the Spirit, as Augustine, among other ancient authors, made perfectly clear. Nothing new about the Supper appears in this apologetic work written to a Roman Catholic and Lutheran audience.

Zwingli refused to reply to Eck's response to his *An Account of the Faith*,[133] but he did address important eucharistic arguments raised by Eck. In his *Letter to the Princes of Germany* (August 1530) gathered at Augsburg,[134] Zwingli defended the idea that the "whole Christ" (*totus Christus*) is present in visible form to the senses when the bread and wine are consecrated and distributed in the gathered community.[135] The sacrament is presented to the outer senses and the whole Christ—although not "the body as such" that is naturally touched by the hands and the mouth (*corpus ipsum naturale manibus et palato tractandum*)—is simultaneously presented to the inner sense for contemplation.[136] Zwingli goes on to say that

> I have never denied that Christ's body is present in the Supper sacramentally and mysteriously, both because of the eye of faith and (as I have said) of the whole action of the symbol. . . . Since, therefore, this presence would be nothing without the eye of faith, it is through faith that the things are present or become present, and not through the sacraments.[137]

Not only Terullian, says Zwingli, but especially Augustine repeatedly distinguished between the external elements that are converted into the sacramental body of Christ, to be neither "neglected nor despised," and the inner justification brought by the Spirit that is the "spiritual body which we eat."[138] The relationship between the outer sacramental body and the inner spiritual body can be seen by thinking about a precious ring that a paterfamilias gives his wife when leaving on a long journey. In the ring itself is engraved the image of the husband (*imago sua*) so that, as often as the wife looks at it, she will "have him just as if present" (*me velut praesentem habeas*). The *imago* present to the outer senses "awakens" (*excitetis*) the inner "remembrance" (*memoriam*) of Christ when (as Zwingli's marginal notes indicate) the words of institution are said.[139] "Therefore," says Zwingli, "we have the Supper of the Lord, glistening spotlessly with the presence of Christ. But in all this—as I have always said—is not the sum of the whole issue that the body of Christ is present sacramentally and to the *eye of faith*?"[140]

Zwingli makes another point, both supple and Augustinian in its own way. Responding to the idea that sacraments themselves cause what they signify, Zwingli says that "the sacraments do not confer grace" (*sacramenta non conferre gratiam dicimus*). Rather they "make effective and testify to the conferring" (*sed collatum exercere ac testari*) of grace.[141] The true mystical presence of Christ is already present to believers through the Spirit and faith, he dwelling in them and they in him.[142] This presence is anamnetically realized again when the outer symbol (*imago*) awakens the inner remembering (*memoria*).[143] As the noted Jesuit sacramental theologian

Kilmartin said of Augustine's nonmetabolic real presence, in the Supper "we do not so much receive Christ; rather, he receives us and grafts us more deeply into his body."[144]

At this point we can clearly see Zwingli's dilemma. Charged with not believing Christ to be truly present at the Supper, Zwingli continued to defend the mystical true presence to which he believed the Scriptures attested, as did the patristic thinkers, especially Augustine. Zwingli indeed stood in the ancient tradition, tracing back to Augustine (and earlier) a mystical true presence ("nonmetabolic real presence") of Christ; and he rejected the idea of a "metabolic real presence," which he expressed as the natural or sense-related bodily presence of Christ. But how to defend that view without reinforcing what he believed to be idolatrous medieval piety that focused on the external five senses?[145]

In late February 1531, six months after his *Letter to the Princes of Germany* and eight months prior to his death, Zwingli wrote to Bucer. The real issue between himself and Luther, wrote Zwingli, was over neither Christ's presence nor Christ's ubiquity as such, but that Christ's body is truly (not naturally or corporeally but sacramentally) in the meal. For the pious soul, the "eye of faith" (*fidei contemplatione*) perceives this presence; the outer senses could see only the natural substantial body, which is located in one place.[146] On this point the Lutherans stood with the papists.[147] Yet the conciliatory language of the *Tetrapolitan Confession*, penned by Bucer and Capito, went too far, because it covered over what was truly intended. Christ did not truly give, and does not truly give, his true body in the meal (*corpus suum verum vere dedit Christus in coena, et etiamnum dat, in cibum animae*), because that body, which was begotten on earth, was nailed to a cross and was given as food for the soul only by way of a sign (*quum in terra nasceretur, praebendique quum crastino cruci adfigeretur, in cibum animae symbolum dedit*).[148] It was the task of Bucer, and particularly Calvin and Bullinger, to clarify the Reformed position of the mystical true presence that lay between the alternatives of metabolic real presence and mere memorialism, and to do so in a positive way that included the instrumentality of the signs.

MARTIN BUCER

Born in the Alsace in 1491 and educated in the Latin school there, Martin Bucer joined the Dominican order.[149] He studied theology and humanism at the University of Heidelberg, after which he was laicized and married. Reformation efforts at Wissembourg led to his excommunication, and in 1523 he moved to Strasbourg. He became the pastor at St. Aurelien a year later. Over the next twenty-five years he labored on behalf of the Refor-

mation in Strasbourg, helping to organize the evangelical churches there
and becoming a leading Protestant theologian and statesman. In 1549
Bucer left for England when Charles V imposed the Augsburg Interim on
the city of Strasbourg. Bucer became professor of theology at Cambridge,
was influential with Cranmer and Ridley, worked on the *Book of Common Prayer*, and authored his *On the Kingdom of Christ*, which outlined
religious and social change.[150] The blossoming of Bucer research during
the second half of the twentieth century has generally seen his theological approach as mediating, pragmatic, more or less irenic,[151] aimed at
the edification of the church, and oriented toward a true ecumenical and
catholic church.[152]

Bucer's churchmanship thoroughly occupied him with eucharistic
issues, and his first essay on the Supper as such appeared in the summer
of 1524.[153] Although Bucer's eucharistic teachings show change over the
years, secondary scholarship has generally viewed these changes as developments or fuller explanations of "an inner consistency" (Stephens) or
as clarifications and deepenings with "very little alteration in the expression" of his views on the Supper (Eells).[154] Hazlett's careful study of all
Bucer's Supper writings essentially shows the same, although he makes
clear that the various contexts in which Bucer wrote make summarizing
Bucer's work a difficult task.[155]

The most significant development for Bucer was in 1524, not long after
he began his Strasbourg pastorate. His early eucharistic ideas show the
influence of both Luther and Erasmus,[156] although this depends upon
how Luther is read, and whether Luther is seen as leaving behind his
early period (1519–20) for an emphasis on corporeal presence. In that case,
the Erasmian influence on Bucer might be seen as gaining prominence,
as Bucer rejected Luther's insistence on such a presence.[157] As we have
seen, however, Luther's development was subtle. Beginning with a primary emphasis on the mystical true presence even through 1523, while
never denying the metabolic real presence (although repudiating how
that presence was conceived to come about—transubstantiation), Luther
gradually subsumed this aspect within the metabolic real presence and
subordinated them both to the Word.

Bucer himself, in a letter from late 1525 and so looking back on this
period of change from only a short distance, wrote that he never had
really been convinced of a bodily presence of Christ (*prasentiam carnalem
Christi in pane eucharistia*). He held that position because of Luther's own
authority, only to come to the idea of "a spiritual eating of Christ" because
of Luther's teaching on John 6.[158] Bucer was most likely referring to a
sermon that Luther had preached in 1522, which was published a year
later in Strasbourg.[159] Referring to John 6:54, 63, Luther said that "eating and drinking is nothing other than believing."[160] Although Luther

characteristically said that John 6 does not specifically treat the Supper, Bucer would soon apply the lesson directly to the Supper.

The eucharistic developments in Luther and Bucer thus show inherently contrasting movements. Both received the Western tradition of metabolic real presence and mystical true presence, woven together in various fashion over the centuries and given a scholastic integration in the triadic structure of *sacramentum tantum–res et sacramentum–res tantum*. As Luther developed, especially in reaction to Karlstadt and the other spiritual "enthusiasts," the mystical true presence receded from the foreground that it held early in his writings. By contrast, for Bucer the metabolic real presence receded from the foreground—to whatever extent he really did hold to the doctrine—and the mystical true presence remained more visible, supported by Bucer's understanding of John 6.

Bucer was also influenced in 1524 both by the writings of Karlstadt, which had appeared in Strasbourg and caused a stir among the pastors, and by a visit from the Dutchman Hinne Rode, who bore the eucharistic letter by Hoen.[161] These forces helped produce what is typically considered to be a fundamental change in Bucer's thought, as he moved from a more corporeal mode of Christ's presence toward a more spiritual mode of presence.[162]

By December 1524, only six months after Bucer's arrival in Strasbourg, his *Grund und Ursach* appeared, in which the Strasbourg evangelicals gave the "foundation and cause" of the Reformation changes that appeared in liturgical matters, not least of all at Bucer's church, St. Aurelien.[163] Of the twelve sections, Bucer wrote seven on eucharistic matters, and much in these sections reads like a primer in Reformation eucharistic changes:[164] The Supper should be celebrated according to Scripture; the Supper is not a present sacrifice but a memorial and thanksgiving of Christ's one sacrifice; a Christian life of love is the true sacrifice that the Supper calls for; the elevation should be abolished, because it reinforces the idea of a present sacrifice and encourages idolatrous worship; ultimately the Spirit and the faith evoked by the Spirit bring the life that is salvation; the canon and priestly gestures encourage false ideas of sacrifice and merely external (and thus hypocritical) worship; the sacrificial altar must become the table of the Lord; private masses and feast days should be abolished, and the Supper should be celebrated only in community and on Sunday.

Several distinctive features stand out in Bucer's eucharistic teaching in late 1524. At precisely the same time that Zwingli wrote to Matthew Alber and extensively discussed John 6, Bucer also appealed to John 6: the Spirit brings life, the flesh profits nothing. As with Zwingli, the issue did not reflect some deep-seated dualism but rather the pious life of faith. Talking about the elevation, which as we have seen became the visual center and miraculous moment of the medieval eucharistic rite, producing so many putative miracles that people worried about unworthy observation, Bucer says that

> when this bread and cup were elevated, the people worshipped them as their God and Christ—indeed present bodily—with some odd little prayers, which then were supposed to be far more powerful than at other times, since the true, saving presence of God and Christ is known invisibly only through true faith.[165]

For this reason, says Bucer, citing John 6:63, the Spirit gives life and the flesh profits nothing, because salvation comes not from seeing what is elevated but from trusting that Christ was sacrificed for our sins.[166] Bucer had taken to heart Luther's teaching on faith and John 6 and was applying the lesson to the Supper in a way that Luther did not do.[167]

Bucer repeatedly says that the Supper is a memorial meal, but such comments are typically contrasted with what the Supper is not.[168] He takes up the presence of Christ when he discusses Karlstadt's writings, which he criticizes heavily, not so much for Karlstadt's theological views but for raising a church-dividing issue.[169] Bucer entirely agrees that the people should be led "from the flesh, from physical elements, to the Spirit and spiritual practices,"[170] but causing a quarrel about the elements themselves only distracts people from the saving faith that trusts the death of Christ given for their salvation. It compares to a father who gives a golden cup to his children so that they can drink from it, but they proceed instead to argue about its material construction rather than being thankful for the one who gave them such goodness. What should have been a sign of unity unto eternal life has become a sign of disunity unto death.[171] Whatever someone's precise views might be on the presence of Christ during the Supper—and Bucer said little on this precise topic in his *Grund und Ursach*—the foundation remains the good news preached and received in faith through the Spirit. What is secondary must serve the good news, which is primary, and not the other way around. In his ending to an extended analogy that connected the apostle Paul to Strasbourg, Bucer says that "the Word frees me from external things and commands me to use them for the edification of neighbor and therefore although I am not subject to anyone, yet have I made myself everyone's slave in order to win many of them."[172]

In these early and extended arguments on the Supper, we see three related themes that will remain and develop more fully: a cautious rejection of localizing the divine presence to any particular physical entity, because idolatry easily arises; the application of John 6 to the Supper; and a pastoral sensitivity to local congregations in making changes that these two themes suggested. What Bucer has not yet developed is a more constructive way to express the presence of Christ in the Supper. To say that he was "Zwinglian" begs the question toward memorialism, because the word often and thereby wrongly attributes mere memorialism to Zwingli. Furthermore, in a letter from the pastors of Strasbourg to the imperial Reichsregiment, Bucer argued in February 1525 that "they did not uphold that the true sacrament was not present under the form of bread and wine, nor did they uphold anything Karlstadt-like."[173] What Bucer does uphold he clarifies over the next three years.

Beginning as early as late 1525, in the discussion with the Swabians that began with the controversy between Bucer and his former teacher Johannes Brenz,[174] and extending through 1528, including his commentaries on Matthew and John, Bucer developed the idea of outer and inner eating.[175] What we outwardly do through the elements also happens inwardly through the power of the Spirit and faith, thus producing a "double manducation." In his commentary on the Gospels, the second volume of which includes commentary on Matthew,[176] Bucer paraphrases Jesus at the Last Supper:

> In the same way, then, that I hand over to you the bread for eating by the mouth of the body, so I give you my body for eating by the soul, for now it will be given unto death for your life—this is a sign of my body—so that just as the bread taken up by me you eat by the mouth, and you carry into the stomach, that thereafter your life is sustained and made strong for work, so you believe in your heart that I hand over my body for you, that in this way trust may be fed and strengthened in the God who undoubtedly recognizes you as sons and heirs, for whom I will hand my body unto death.[177]

Bucer continued the theme of outer and inner eating through his 1528 *Commentary on the Gospel of John*,[178] where in typical Reformed fashion he links the presence of Christ not to a metabolic real presence in the elements but to the mystical true presence in which the believer is engrafted into Christ himself:

> "He who eats my flesh and drinks my blood remains in me" (John 6:57). Indeed it is altogether necessary that he be taken into and transformed into Christ, he who will have acknowledged [him] by faith alone and will have carefully weighed how enormously he lovingly embraced us, while he endured to die for our sake. Again, Christ works and lives in this one, perfecting all things in him by his Spirit, and so it is that "Christ remains in him" (John 6:57).[179]

Over the next few years, running roughly from the Marburg Colloquy (1529) through the Wittenberg Concord (1536), Bucer worked to reach a public rapprochement with the Lutherans, to the consternation of the Swiss, especially Zwingli, who thought he had compromised too much.[180] Bucer's clarification of the Wittenberg Concord to his colleagues (June 22,

1536) shows both his interest in eucharistic agreement and why the Swiss might have been nervous about his position. "The body and blood of Christ himself," wrote Bucer,

> are truly present not merely effectively (*effective*), powerfully, effectively (*würklich*), and spiritually, but truly (*vere*), substantially (*substantialiter*), essentially (*essentialiter*), essentially and truly (*wesentlich unnd warhafftig*), and they are given and received with the bread and wine. For one has to distinguish the *sacramentum* and the *rem sacramenti*, namely that the body and blood of Christ (altogether the *res sacramenti*) are given and received with the bread and wine in the Supper.[181]

To say that the body and blood of Christ were "substantially" (*substantialiter*) given represents a language of concord toward the Lutherans, and is a word that Bucer first employed in 1534 when defending his Supper teaching against the "Sorbonnist" Bishop Ceneau.[182] In his clarification of Wittenberg, Bucer clearly says that such a presence is given *with* the bread and wine, not in any way *under* or *in* the bread and wine. Two key issues arise.

First, this represents language that went beyond Zwingli, because such "substance" language made Zwingli nervous, since it made Christ present to the outer senses—his "sense-related" body—and this view, thought Zwingli, easily led to idolatrous practices. Zwingli rejected that Christ was present "really, corporally, or essentially" (*realiter, corporaliter, aut essentialiter*).[183] Yet Zwingli himself, when writing to Luther, said clearly that the issue between them was not whether the whole Christ, body included, was present to believers, but whether the body was present "spiritually" or "in itself and by nature."[184] Given what we have seen of Zwingli's view of the mystical true presence, Bucer's clarification to his colleagues is not so distant from Zwingli's comment to Luther in his *Friendly Exegesis*, especially since Bucer argued the body of Christ was given "with" the bread and that this was the work of the Spirit.

Further, we have already seen that by 1528 Bucer had clearly grounded the eucharistic presence of Christ in the mystical union that believers have with him. By 1534 Bucer defended his eucharistic position by comfortably speaking about the "mystery of the true and natural union" between Christ and the believer,[185] so that "our savior, God, and Lord, who is love itself, lives in us" and "we are united in true divine love with all our co-members, one body, one loaf, which has communion as one bread." Bucer continued by saying that "all words and sacraments . . . are first directed to this that for us—in whom is communion of our Lord Jesus—for us he may not only intercede with the Father, but that he may also live in us . . . ."[186]

Related to this arises the second issue: that the eucharistic gift of Christ is not only offered to, but also received by, the communicant. The body and blood of Christ "are given and received with the bread and wine," said Bucer. This was a key issue for concord with the Lutherans and, as with the language of *substantialiter*, Bucer developed his concept of "eating by the unworthy" (*manducatio indignorum*) in his dialogue with Ceneau.[187] Borrowing from Bernard and ultimately from Augustine, Bucer distinguished "eating by the godless" (*manducatio impiorum*) from "eating by the unworthy" (*manducatio indignorum*). The godless received the sign only; however, the unworthy were Christians who had faith, who were gathered at the table, but who were weak or failing in their faith at the particular moment of communion. To them Christ himself truly was offered and received, although he was received in temporary and ultimately therapeutic judgment. Speaking of 1 Corinthians 10, Bucer said of the apostle Paul that

> he himself recognizes no other eating of the Lord than a true eating, than that which is always saving, as much as indeed it is an eating of the Lord, and if the same might sometimes happen from an unworthy approach a judgment would be brought on someone.[188]

In this way unworthy believers, engrafted in Christ, not only would have Christ truly offered them, but also truly receive him, yet receive him both to judgment as a means of discipline and also unto their ultimate salvation.

With the concession of substantial language and the nuance between "unworthy eating" and "ungodly eating," both finally rooted in a long-standing eucharistic doctrine of mystical union in Christ, which Bucer found in John 6,[189] Bucer's teaching on the Supper came to its "more or less final form" by the mid-1530s.[190] Bucer's thought, like that of Zwingli, shows features that would characterize Reformed eucharistic theology: a mystical true presence of the whole Christ, that is both individual and corporate; an inner and outer eating; an appeal to John 6; and the assertion that the true feeding on Christ that belongs to the Supper is the work of the Spirit. The next generation, particularly Calvin, developed these themes as the connection between sign and reality was made clearer, as was the instrumentality of the signs, and the work of the Spirit in bringing about the mystical true presence.

4

THE SECOND GENERATION

John Calvin and Heinrich Bullinger

The broad traditions of the metabolic real presence and the mystical true (i.e., nonmetabolic) presence, with their variations and combinations, formed the patristic and medieval context within which the sixteenth-century Reformers read the Scriptures and argued over the character of the Supper. Although attracted to the patristic and humanist scholarship from Oecolampadius that argued for the mystical true presence, and critical of transubstantiation as such, Erasmus deferred to the consensus of the church and its authority about the metabolic real presence. Because Erasmus found both the metabolic and nonmetabolic positions adequate to some degree, and because he rejected scholastic arguments explaining the metabolic real presence but still upheld the primacy of the metabolic position on account of church authority, Erasmus can be said to have had a medieval catholic eucharistic theology.

By contrast, Martin Luther eventually folded the mystical true presence into the metabolic real presence, and then subsumed and grounded them both within the Word of God. When pressed, he could defend the credible character of the metabolic real presence, using carefully argued yet traditional medieval technical arguments about bodies and space. By holding together both ancient traditions, yet ultimately orienting both traditions to the Word of God, Luther can be said to have had a *medieval* catholic, evangelical eucharistic theology. (Note the order of adverbs, adjective, and substantive.)

Zwingli flatly rejected that the "bodily and sense-related flesh of Christ" was present in the eucharistic elements, but he upheld that the body of Christ becomes present by faith, through the "Spirit and the heart," not "in itself and by nature." He thus attempted to avoid the idolatrous worship of creatural things, available to the outer senses, while retaining mystical union with Christ, who was fully present through Spirit and faith. Zwingli appealed carefully to Scripture, arguing for the use of figurative language in the Supper accounts; taking up the Fourth Gospel, especially John 6, as necessary to be read alongside the institution narratives; and insisting upon the scriptural accounts of Jesus' ascension and second coming. As we saw, Zwingli also appealed to Augustine, and he appealed to those very tractates in Augustine that modern scholarship has argued display most clearly the nonmetabolic real presence. In comparison to Erasmus and Luther, Zwingli can be said to have had a *patristic* catholic, evangelical eucharistic theology.

Martin Bucer shared a fundamental orientation with Zwingli that would become characteristic for Reformed eucharistic theology. Through the work of the Spirit and faith, which itself is a gift of the Spirit, believers are mystically engrafted into Christ both personally and communally. During the Supper there is an outer and an inner eating so that inwardly believers are fed with the whole Christ in whom they are engrafted. Bucer appeals to the Bread from Heaven discourse in John 6; and he appeals to the catholic tradition, especially Augustine, with perhaps this distinction between Zwingli and Bucer: Where Zwingli came to his teaching on the Supper in part through reading and commenting on Augustine and his tractates on John 6, Bucer's appeal to Augustine, as well as the wider catholic tradition, grew from defending a Supper theology already held. As with Zwingli, Bucer's theology of the Supper can be called a patristic catholic, evangelical eucharistic theology.

Among the second-generation Reformed theologians, Calvin and Bullinger took up this nascent Reformed position and principally answered two key questions whose answers were left underdeveloped in the thought of Zwingli and Bucer: What does it really mean to be bodily present but only in a spiritual manner? And an issue upon which Zwingli began to work late in life: How do the God-given eucharistic signs function as a means of grace?

JOHN CALVIN

Born July 10, 1509, in Noyon, France, John Calvin spent his early life within the patronal system that was the way of the West from ancient times onward. Calvin's father, Gérard, worked his way to a responsible position within the cathedral chapter, assuming several duties under the patronage of the bishop. The diocese itself was under the influence of the de Hangest family, which had wider connections in French civil and ecclesiastical politics, and Gérard Calvin had his son John taken into the noble house of the Montmors, whose father was a de Hangest. There he received his initial education and tutelage into a class of society well above his own paternal roots. Through his father and the patronage of the bishop, Calvin also received an ecclesiastical benefice that helped sustain him until he renounced it in May 1534.[1]

At the Collège de la Marche in Paris, Calvin studied the basic liberal arts and most importantly mastered Latin under the tutelage of Mathurin Cordier, whose Latin textbook was a standard for centuries and whose piety was that of the *devotio moderna*. At the University of Paris, Calvin then studied at the Collège de Montaigu, which had been founded in 1314. By history its ethos was that of the *devotio moderna*, and the spirituality was that of Gérard de Groote and Thomas à Kempis, although by Calvin's time sheer discipline seemed dominant.[2] At Paris Calvin studied the basic liberal arts, lived and breathed the scholastic milieu,[3] and was engaged by the evangelical humanism of Erasmus and its French developments. He finished his licentiate and master's at Paris perhaps as early as 1525 or 1526, but instead of proceeding to theology he studied law at both Orléans and Bourges, likely finishing at Orléans as early as 1531. We know that Calvin was licensed in law by 1532.[4]

At Orléans or perhaps Bourges he learned Greek from the classicist and Reformer Melchior Wolmar, who seems to have had some influence on Calvin toward the evangelical faith. Calvin continued his study of Greek and classics in Paris after his father's death in 1531 and, influenced by the scholarship of the great humanists of his day such as Erasmus and Guillaume Budé, wrote his first book, a commentary on Seneca's *De clementia*. Both humanist and inherently evangelical through its appeal to Francis I to be gracious toward those of the evangelical faith in France, the book was not the success for which Calvin had hoped.[5]

A tipping point in Calvin's life was All Saints' Day 1533. Nicholas Cop, who was the rector of the University of Paris and a friend of Calvin's, preached a reforming sermon much on the lines of Erasmian thought. Cop was forced to flee Paris, and Calvin as well, although exactly where Calvin went (probably Noyon) is not clear. We know that he renounced his benefice in Noyon in May 1534. Later that year, in the Affair of the Placards, posters attacking the Mass were posted throughout France. Hundreds of arrests were made and twenty people executed, among them a friend of Calvin's. In February 1535 Calvin fled to Basel; there he completed the first edition of his *Institutes of the Christian Religion*, which was published in March 1536 by the Basel printers Thomas Platter and Balthasar Lasius.[6]

During that year, after a brief sojourn in Italy and completing family business in Paris, Calvin attempted to travel from Paris to Strasbourg, accompanied by his brother and his half sister. Armed conflict forced them to detour south and around through Geneva. The energetic French evangelical Guillaume Farel (1489–1565) visited Calvin in Geneva during what was supposed to be a short layover. Farel prophetically called Calvin to ministry in Geneva, and Calvin stayed until he and Farel were forced out in April 1538, when they rejected interference in the Geneva church, over relatively minor issues, by the city of Bern and its ministers.

Calvin finally finished his journey to Strasbourg, where he found a mentor in Martin Bucer. In Strasbourg Calvin married, wrote, taught, and, perhaps most importantly for his theological development, served a church as its pastor. While in Strasbourg Calvin completely revised his *Institutes* to be an educational resource for training clergy, rather than a catechism for French evangelicals and an apologia to Francis I concerning the evangelical faith.

In September 1541 Calvin returned to Geneva, at Genevan request, and ministered there until his death in 1564. Two overall areas of conflict, not unrelated to each other, plagued Calvin's second term of ministry in Geneva. People objected to the discipline of the ministers, and French refugees came to the city, taxing its economy and changing its demographics. Lying beneath these issues was the fundamental concern, especially among the traditional power centers of Geneva, that the city was transforming beyond them. They were right. Geneva was becoming a major international center for the evangelical faith and its Reformed expression.[7]

The young Calvin first took up the issue of the Lord's Supper in his 1536 *Institutes*; he returned frequently to the topic, not only in the subsequent editions of the *Institutes*, but in his Scripture commentaries, treatises, letters, and liturgies. Scholarly study of Calvin's eucharistic theology has been extensive,[8] beginning in modern scholarship with Ebrard's influential section on Calvin in his 1845 two-volume study on the Supper. Calvin, says Ebrard, developed a eucharistic theology independent from Luther and Zwingli that yet mediated between them by arguing for Christ truly communicating himself from heaven while yet bodily remaining at God's right hand. By a "deeper" concept of corporeality (*Leiblichkeit*) and a focus on the activity of Christ's self-communication that nourishes believers, Calvin gave a "sharper grounding" to his Supper teaching than had Reformation predecessors.[9] Beginning with the first edition of the *Institutes*, and seen clearly in the 1537 *Confession of Faith concerning the Eucharist*,[10] Calvin clearly rejected prior scholastic notions of substance and understood that the Supper offered a "real renewing and furthering of that continual living unity" that believers have by virtue of their mystical engrafting in Christ.[11] The chart that ends section 36 then essentially illustrates Ebrard's key thesis that Calvin's unique eucharistic theology, which finds concord with Melanchthon (sect. 37), navigates between extreme forms of both Zwinglianism and Lutheranism.[12]

At virtually the same time Ebrard wrote, the American theologian John Williamson Nevin argued that Calvin's doctrine of the Supper was grounded in the mystical union of believers in Christ himself, so that participation in the Supper was a deepened participation in Christ through the nourishment of Christ that the Supper brings. Protests erupted among German Reformed theologians in America, and in 1846 Nevin published his work *The Mystical Presence: A Vindication of the Reformed or Calvinistic Doctrine of the Holy Eucharist*, a work inherently about ecclesiology as much as sacramental theology.[13] Nevin replied to criticisms from his former teacher, Charles Hodge, with his extended essay "Doctrine of the Reformed Church on the Lord's Supper."[14]

Nevin's two works on Calvin's eucharistic theology have remained a benchmark,[15] although recent work (Davis, Janse) has shown developmental features of Calvin's thought as his historical contexts unfolded.[16] Nevin's work, along with that of Ebrard, has effectively shown the grounding of Calvin's eucharistic theology in mystical union with Christ, and the centrality of Calvin's developed position for Reformed theology.

In the early twentieth century, after Batiffol's eucharistic study but prior to Geiselmann's study of the early scholastics,[17] Joachim Beckmann's study on the eucharistic teaching of Augustine and Calvin showed "total identity" in their "basic constitutive ideas,"[18] a point later Roman Catholic scholarship was to reaffirm.[19] Beckmann's study falls short, in its tendency to overspiritualize the presence of Christ and to emphasize insufficiently the real nourishment of Christ's true body and blood that come from a true yet nonmetabolic feeding.[20] Here the study lacks the historical context of the mystical true presence tradition that ran through the Latin West and that can be seen in various ways in first-generation Protestant Reformers. Beckmann's study could be criticized as a mere typological analysis abstracted from the Reformation context and influences; and in his published dissertation Wilhelm Niesel criticized Beckmann for a study that may have shown connections to Augustine, but did so at the cost of being too ahistorical.[21]

Niesel argued that, against the background of Roman eucharistic teaching, which was for Calvin the greatest of errors that robbed Christians of salvation, Calvin developed a theology of the Supper that avoided both the memorialism of Zwingli and the christological error of Lutheranism, which threatened Christian soteriology by losing the character of Jesus' real humanity.[22] As the subtitle to the original dissertation makes clear, Niesel read Calvin primarily through the discussion with Westphal and the last edition of the *Institutes*, which represent for Niesel what Calvin wished to hand on to his followers when he was near death.[23]

At roughly the same time as Niesel's dissertation appeared in print, Barclay's study on the Supper in Protestantism appeared.[24] As with the Zwingli material, which was covered in the last chapter, Barclay moves historically through Calvin's teachings on the Supper, dealing with both secondary and primary sources. Just as he seemed to lean on Köhler's work for progressing through Zwingli's eucharistic teaching, so Barclay leans on Ebrard's work on Calvin and the Supper, perhaps more closely than might be expected.[25] Overall, Barclay's work presents a solid view on Calvin because he takes up Nevin's central point, also found in Ebrard, that mystical union in Christ grounds both the true presence of Christ and the nourishment from his body and blood that are the gifts of the Supper. At times, however, the argument becomes somewhat strained, particularly in Barclay's discussion of how the Consensus Tigurinus faithfully represented Calvin's position, which, in its creative independence, stood as the best of the Swiss eucharistic theology.[26]

The postwar ecumenical efforts and modern liturgical renewal movement were the background for two significant studies on Calvin's eucharistic theology.[27] G. P. Hartvelt's 1960 study *Verum Corpus* argues that, to the surprise of Hartvelt ("tot onze eigen verrassing"), not only do the benefits of Christ accrue through community with him, but those in community with him have communion in his life-giving (*vivifica*) flesh as the source of these benefits.[28] Hartvelt not only frequently finds this idea in Calvin's writings, but he notes Calvin's comments on John 6, where Calvin echoes Augustine, even if the Johannine passage itself does not directly concern the Last Supper.[29] While such a view represents Calvin's mature eucharistic theology—his commentary on John appeared in 1553, for example—Hartvelt also argues that the ability of the sacrament to be a means of grace effecting the presence of the life-giving flesh (the "instrumental character of the sacrament") develops in Calvin's thought between 1536 and 1539.[30]

Just a few years later, the Benedictine scholar Kilian McDonnell published his *John Calvin, the Church and the Eucharist*, done in an earlier version as a doctoral thesis at Trier.[31] McDonnell worked to balance Calvin's eucharistic teaching in the context of Roman Catholic thought and practice, while also acknowledging Calvin's primary task of constructing a biblical eucharistic theology that has union with Christ at its center.[32] While recognizing Calvin's insistence on the real presence,[33] McDonnell also raises a question that remains central for Roman Catholics: if mystical union with Christ is central to Calvin's theology and eucharistic theology, what, if anything, can be said to be the distinctive eucharistic gift as such?[34] By way of anticipating an answer, for the mature Calvin, the Supper itself brings a particular, mystical knowledge of the Christ in whom the believer is already engrafted, thus bringing about a deepened engrafting by Christ.[35] As we have seen, this perspective strongly reflects the eucharistic theology of Augustine,[36] and McDonnell himself notes the well-observed use of Augustine by Calvin.[37]

McDonnell's study, unlike that of Hartvelt, works primarily from Calvin's 1559 *Institutes*, since on McDonnell's view "[t]he 1559 edition of the *Institutes* gives the definitive form of Calvin's doctrine. This book limits itself to Calvin's doctrine as found in this edition. His other works are cited to throw light upon the doctrine as found in the 1559 edition, the last before his death in 1559."[38] Just as an opening observation, the Latin 1559 edition of the *Institutes* was not Calvin's last edition. One year later his

1560 French edition appeared, which showed changes, some of whose sacramental changes prove interesting and challenge McDonnell's method straightforwardly.[39] Further, McDonnell's approach ironically ignores the historical contexts in which Calvin actually wrote, while attempting to put Calvin's work into the historical context of his late-medieval thought world. This method problem was decisively solved by Thomas Davis in his 1995 study of Calvin's eucharistic theology.[40]

In *The Clearest Promises of God: The Development of Calvin's Eucharistic Teaching*, originally done as a dissertation at the University of Chicago, Davis begins by reviewing scholarship. He then takes up the Consensus Tigurinus as a test case for showing the difficulty of assuming a single eucharistic position in Calvin and reading his mature eucharistic theology back into an earlier period.[41] Then, working through Calvin's eucharistic theology from 1536 forward, Davis argues that Calvin develops the sacramental instrumentality of the Supper, the substantial presence of the Christ's true body and blood, the special eucharistic gift that the Supper brings, the role of the Spirit, and the Supper as a form of divine accommodation to human capabilities.[42] Davis's book sets new boundaries for the study of Calvin's eucharistic teaching. Although I will disagree on some major points about Calvin's early work, and although I find the work of some prior scholars (especially Tylenda) more adequate at times, I do so acknowledging a debt to Davis, within whose reappraisal I work and whose work I here follow. His careful historical and contextual study of Calvin's developing eucharistic teaching reflects the approach that I took in my studies, done at about the same time, on Calvin's baptismal theology.[43]

Taking up the historical approach of Davis's study, which he calls "epoch-making,"[44] Wim Janse begins his study of Calvin's eucharistic doctrine by saying that to speak of the "existence of *the* eucharistic doctrine of Calvin" is to speak a "fiction." What we find in Calvin's eucharistic development are "Zwinglianizing (1536–37), Lutheranizing (1537–48), and again spiritualizing tendencies (1549–1550s)."[45] Janse's careful historical study provides important contextual arguments that advance our understanding of Calvin, but, in the end, his essay represents such a departure from the ahistorical approach typified by McDonnell that one wonders whether he has not finally lost the forest while carefully noting each tree.

An important feature of Hartvelt's argument, which has been decisively followed by both Davis and Janse, is that Calvin's 1536 *Institutes* showed a lack of sacramental instrumentality for the Supper and that by 1539 Calvin had moved from this original position.[46] Revisiting Calvin's argument in its original context proves valuable for reappraising this Hartvelt appraisal, and thus for reappraising both Davis and Janse.

The oft-cited passage from Calvin's 1536 *Institutes*, which supposedly bespeaks the lack of sacramental instrumentality in Calvin's theology, says,

> Not because such graces are tied to and included in the sacrament, or because the sacrament is an organ or instrument by which they are conferred upon us, but merely because, by this sign, the Lord testifies to us his good will; namely, that he wants to lavish these things upon us.[47]

The actual context in which Calvin makes this remark, however, does not support a global claim that in 1536 he had not yet developed the concept of sacramental instrumentality that would appear in 1539 and develop thereafter. Beginning several paragraphs earlier, Calvin had taken up a long discussion of *baptism*, which is the context at hand.[48]

Calvin begins his 1536 section on baptism with his unwavering insistence that baptism, as with all sacraments, is primarily a present gift from God intended to evoke and nourish our faith and, following that, a sign by which we testify to our faith before others.[49] This is precisely the prioritizing that he had just made clear when, in his discussion of sacraments in general, he criticized the view (of Zwingli) that *sacramentum* was primarily a fealty oath that a soldier makes to his commander.[50] After establishing this priority for baptism, Calvin gives basic scriptural support for his view. He next criticizes what he believes to be the mistaken view of baptism held by the late medieval church, which is where the given citation occurs.

The scholastics held a view of original sin that may be summarized like this. In the original, graced state of humankind, Adam and Eve had, first, the natural state of original righteousness, by which their natural powers were organized, and that lacked that internal desire for a good lesser than God that brings disharmony to the natural powers (*concupiscence*). Second, Adam and Eve were also gifted with a supernatural grace (*donum superadditum*), which generally was taken to be the ground of the original righteous state itself. More particularly, said Thomas, this additional grace gave Adam (and Eve), as the head of the human race as such, knowledge that he could order his life according to knowledge of God and of the world, and teach such knowledge to others. Third, and chief among these graces from God, was the indwelling of God, an infused love that directed passion to the love of God (*supernaturale complementum*), molding the human person in all human efforts and powers to the final telos, which is God, thus sanctifying the person unto eternal life. According to Thomas, this third of the divine ways of gracing Adam and Eve was given at creation itself together with the original righteousness itself. The reason for this grace was simply that humankind could not attain to a good beyond its natural state, and attainment to a supernatural end required grace to be infused and forming of human activity.

Through the fall, Adam and Eve lost their original righteousness—here following the original Augustinian trajectory that evil, and thus sin, are strictly speaking the absence of the good—and this loss of original righteousness that is transmitted from generation to generation is what we call original sin. The result of original sin is the concupiscence that followed. In this sense, says Thomas, "original sin is materially indeed concupiscence; but formally also a defect of original righteousness."[51] As Thomas himself suggests, original sin is something like a bodily sickness, only attaching to the soul itself: There is a lack of original health (formal aspect) as well as unhealthy activity itself in which the soul is unregulated and "ignorance, malice, infirmity, and concupiscence" now dwell (material aspect).

For late medieval scholastics, the sacrament of baptism *restores a person from the state of original sin*, though its effect (concupiscence) remains. Baptism brings the fruit of justification whereby the child receives sanctifying grace and becomes a "new creature" that is, a child of God and heir of heaven.[52] In Protestant terms, at baptism the child is not merely pronounced just, but *is ontologically made just*, and thereby baptism *literally brings forth a new creature* capacitated for faith. By his or her becoming just, a new and real sanctified *state* is created in the child. This represents exactly what Calvin speaks against in his 1536 *Institutes*:

> Now, it is clear how false is that which some teach, that because of baptism we are released and freed from original sin, and from that corruption that was propagated from Adam into all his posterity, and that we are brought back into that same righteousness and purity of nature which Adam would have maintained, had he remained sound in the way that he had been first created.[53]

Calvin then goes on to give his own view of baptism, summarizing with the passage cited above, which says that God's graces are not "tied to and included in the sacrament," nor is the sacrament "an organ or instrument by which they are conferred upon us." He then follows this comment with the example of Cornelius the centurion (Acts 10) and says explicitly:

> Besides, *we obtain* from this sacrament nothing except whatever much we receive *by faith*. If this faith is absent it will be a witness of our being accused toward God because we were unbelieving of the promise given there.[54]

Care must be taken here. Calvin *does not say* that the sacrament of baptism, which is what is under discussion here, does not work instrumentally. Calvin says that baptism is not an instrumental means of grace *in the way that late medieval theology believed it to be* a means of grace. Even as early as the 1536 *Institutes*, for Calvin baptism *is* a means of grace because it does exactly that which it says it does: it is the means by which God presently offers the divine grace that can be realized in baptism. Baptism is God's very presence doing and offering who God is and what God does. But such doing and offering, as personal divine activities, require faith to become *fruitful* for the person (cf. Cornelius)—"we obtain . . . by faith." This can hardly be said clearly and strongly enough. What Calvin objects to is the late medieval idea that *baptism makes the child just and ontologically confers a new sanctified state.* According to Calvin, such sanctification would be the fruit of God's grace offered to us, and it occurs where and when faith exists, as with Cornelius; but the divine presence as, and offer of, grace as such, which is what baptism instrumentally does, does not itself instrumentally confer that sanctified state, as the medieval theologians mistakenly thought. Study done on Calvin's early baptismal theology, and its relation to his sacramental structure, has shown this in detail.[55] The sacraments, says Calvin in 1536, "have the same office as the Word of God: to offer and present Christ to us."[56]

Over the years Calvin strengthened this position on the sacramental instrumentality of baptism;[57] specifically concerning the point of baptismal instrumentality, already by 1539 Calvin *was defending his earlier insistence* on the instrumentality of baptism in the case of infants who could not hear the promise that God was speaking through the sign. By 1559 he would attempt to strengthen the 1539 defense of sacramental instrumentality in the case of infants by adding the metaphor of a seed: the seed of future repentance and faith is planted during baptism.[58]

Not only do the 1536 *Institutes* speak for sacramental instrumentality—to offer and present Christ—but Calvin is clear that the Supper can directly nourish us with Christ himself. In the opening paragraph on the Supper, Calvin tells us that the Supper is "to confirm to us that the Lord's body was once for all so handed over to us, as now to be ours, and also forever to be so."[59] This happens, as Calvin then clarifies, because we already have mystical union with Christ: "We recognize Christ to have been thus engrafted in us as we, likewise, have been engrafted in him, so that whatever is his we are permitted to call ours, and whatever is ours is counted as his."[60] Even by 1536 Calvin gives the classic Augustinian (nonmetabolic) mystical true presence. Already engrafted into Christ we are deepened in that true presence through the Supper.

The second paragraph on the Supper connects this mystical union both backward and forward, so to speak. "The present distribution of the body and the blood of the Lord" brings benefit only because they have already been given for our "redemption and salvation." Likewise this present distribution of the body and blood brings benefits to us that Calvin describes analogically: as bread nourishes, so Christ's body is the "food and protection of our spiritual life," and as wine brings benefits to the body, so Christ's blood is "spiritually imparted."[61]

Calvin then, and I think significantly, cites John 6:56 in the third paragraph and strongly asserts that "his flesh is food indeed and his blood is drink." This section of John's Gospel is *precisely* the classical Augustinian locus for the mystical true presence (nonmetabolic presence) wherein believers, already engrafted into Christ himself, receive Christ directly in the Supper and are deepened into him. Therefore, further along in this paragraph, Calvin notes "the sacrament therefore does not make Christ to be the bread of life"; rather, it "calls back into memory that he was made the bread by which we continually feed."[62]

Tylenda notes, on my view with some accuracy, that while Calvin "may not give the idea of spiritual nourishment an extended treatment . . . he does bring it to the forefront so as to make it a cornerstone of his eucharistic theology."[63] Davis takes exception to Tylenda's assertion by arguing that the "term is present but the content is not," because Calvin has not yet developed his idea of the life-giving flesh that is given in the Supper.[64] Davis's argument, however, does not seem as careful as Tylenda's, which speaks to the sequence and points to Calvin's eucharistic argument in the 1536 *Institutes*.[65] Tylenda's argument also is quite strengthened, on my view, by understanding the Augustinian nonmetabolic tradition of engrafting into Christ's body.

Calvin wrote in the aftermath of Marburg and argued that a return to the fundamental "force of the sacrament," wherein we scripturally hear that Christ instituted the Supper to nourish believers with his body and blood, would have avoided the "frightful contentions" that trouble the church when people "endeavor *to define how* Christ's body is present in the bread."[66] Calvin then criticizes, without specifically naming people, the eucharistic positions of the late medieval church, Luther, and Zwingli.[67]

Rather than focus on the "how" of Christ's presence, Calvin is content to say that Christ himself is *exhibitum* ("communicated" or "truly shown") in a way that the soul "knows Christ again" (*agnoscat*), since "to receive any fruits from the sacrament is to have received him."[68] This description by Calvin, coming as it does several paragraphs after his discussion of mystical union and his citing of Augustine, speaks quite clearly about the mystical true presence (nonmetabolic presence), whereby believers are engrafted through the Supper yet more deeply into the Christ in whom they are united and who possesses them.

Tylenda may be right that Calvin intended this as an ecumenical middle ground between overrealism and mere memorialism, but, as this study has argued, what Calvin historically represents in the 1536 *Institutes* is a young scholar's appropriation of the mystical true presence studied by the humanist scholars of his era and taken up in Zwingli and Bucer. Given this Augustinian background, it is not the case that Calvin's concept of "spiritual nourishment" has no content, although, as we shall see, Davis is certainly correct that Calvin has not yet connected this nourishment to Christ's life-giving flesh. The issue here does not resolve into a binary—*either* Calvin has no real meaning to "spiritual nourishment" and his eucharistic teaching is "ambiguous,"[69] *or* he has a fully developed concept of "spiritual nourishment" that includes the life-giving flesh of Christ that we receive.[70] Given the long-standing tradition of the mystical true presence within which, and from which, the young humanist Calvin worked in 1536, there is real content to his theological claim of "spiritual nourishment," even if significant developments occur later—a point on which Davis is undoubtedly correct—developments that, on my view, actually help clarify the entire Augustinian tradition from which Calvin was working.

One of the first key developments concerns the role of the Holy Spirit during the Supper, an issue that Davis rightly notes was somewhat ambiguous to Calvin in 1535 as he finished his first edition of the *Institutes*.[71] A year or more later, Calvin contributed significantly to the 1536 Lausanne Disputation by commenting on Christ's true presence in the Supper.[72] Calvin cited Tertullian, Chrysostom, and most notably Augustine to support his position that we are "truly participant of his body and his blood."[73] In light of what we have seen concerning the mystical true presence, and its roots in North Africa, especially in Augustine, Ganoczy's view that Calvin showed more rhetoric than theology cannot stand. From his earliest years, Calvin appealed to precisely that catholic tradition that the Reformed tradition found as home for its eucharistic teachings.

With that eucharistic teaching went the already established (see Zwingli and Bucer) classical Reformed assertion (also found in Augustine) that because Christ had a true human body, it had to be located in only one place. Calvin took up this issue at Lausanne, and he explained how Christ's body, present dimensively in only one place—heaven—could be communicated to believers.[74] In the disputation session of October 5, 1536, Calvin asserted that "it is a spiritual communication by which he makes us truly participants of his body and his blood, but wholly spiritually, that is by the bond of his Spirit."[75] By the word "spiritually," as Calvin makes clear, he did not intend to say that something other than Christ's true body and blood were communicated, but simply that such communication happened by the Spirit.

The next year Calvin reiterates and strengthens these themes. The 1537 *Confession of Faith concerning the Eucharist* begins with the assertion of mystical participation in Christ, by which the faithful "communicate not less in his body and blood than in his Spirit, so that thus they possess the whole Christ (*totum Christum*)."[76] Likewise, "the apostle" teaches that believers are flesh of Christ's flesh and bone of his bone in the "great mystery of our communion with his body, whose sublimity no one is able to explain adequately in words."[77]

After beginning with the mystical union that believers have in Christ, the *Confession* then asserts that this union exists even though Christ dimensively dwells in heaven, because the "Spirit is the bond of our participation in him," so that we are truly fed "with the substance of the body and the blood of the Lord."[78] Finally the *Confession* then says that Christ offers this "communion of his body and blood under the symbols of bread and wine (*sub panis et vini symbolis*)."[79]

Here we find not only Calvin's already-held Augustinian position of mystical true presence, in which believers engrafted into Christ are fed by him in the Supper, but also the clear assertions that Christ offers the "substance" of his body and blood (*carnis et sanguinis Domini substantia*) and that this flesh of Christ is communicated through the Spirit. As Davis rightly points out,[80] these last two assertions by Calvin are explicit advances from his prior eucharistic position—Calvin has begun to argue that the mystical true presence that feeds us brings Christ's very flesh and that such union happens through the Spirit—and these advances can also be seen in the *Geneva Catechism* and its section on the Supper.[81]

Calvin's 1539 reworking of the *Institutes* represents a significant development of that work, as Calvin moved it from an educational and confessional document, based on Luther's Small Catechism,[82] to a theological resource for students, to be read alongside Scripture and Scripture commentaries.[83] The content of the *Institutes* expands considerably, and the sacramental material moves toward a shape that Calvin will finalize by the 1559 edition: a chapter on the sacraments in general; a chapter on baptism; a chapter on infant baptism, drawn from a separate French tract that he had written; and a chapter on the Supper. For 1559, and reflecting a history of sacramental controversies, Calvin added a fourth chapter on the false sacraments. Davis sums the 1539 *Institutes* well when he says,

> Much of the new data in 1539 has to do with the work of the Holy Spirit in the sacraments in general and the Eucharist in particular. There are also new sections on the concept of the life-giving flesh of Christ and how that flesh is truly communicated to the believer. There is also a greatly expanded section on the idea of the Eucharist as a "sacrifice of praise." . . . Finally, there is a new emphasis in the 1539 *Institutes* that relates the concept of the Eucharist as an instrument of God.[84]

Particularly important for this study is that Calvin lectured on the Gospel of John for the benefit of the Strasbourg clergy soon after his arrival there.[85] We already have seen in the 1536 *Institutes* that Calvin cited the Bread from Heaven discourse, especially John 6:56, when he linked the mystical union that believers have in Christ to the Supper. Calvin appeals even more strongly in the 1539 *Institutes* to the mystical engrafting into Christ and the Augustinian idea that the Supper nourishes us through that mystical union.

So, for instance, Calvin authors two new, important paragraphs near the beginning of the chapter on the Supper.[86] In the tenth paragraph, Calvin criticizes the argument that for some people communion with Christ means merely "partakers of the Spirit only, without mentioning flesh and blood. As if all this were said uselessly: that his flesh is true food and his blood is truly drink; that none have life except those who eat his flesh and drink his blood."[87] Calvin makes clear reference to John 6:55 and then follows that with a reference to John 6:53, two Johannine passages that we have seen dead center in Augustine's argument for a mystical true presence (nonmetabolic presence). Calvin confesses that his mind cannot grasp how such feeding can occur, but he confesses "admiration for this mystery" (*in eius mysterii admirationem*).[88]

Calvin then provides in the next paragraph the fundamental ground for such mystical feeding during the Supper: "from the beginning the life-giving Word of the Father" is the font whence all things are themselves alive.[89] When this "font of life begins to abide in our flesh, he no longer lies hidden from us far away, but shows us that we ought to partake of him."[90] Hence, says Calvin, slightly conflating John 6:48 and 6:51, Jesus says "I am . . . the bread of life come down from heaven. And the bread which I shall give is my flesh, which I shall give for the life of the world."[91] Thus, says Calvin in the following paragraph, "the flesh of Christ is the icon of a rich and bottomless font that pours into us the life gushing from divinity into itself. Now who does not see that communion of the body and blood of Christ is necessary for all who aspire to heavenly life?"[92] After citing Ephesians and then the apostle Paul (1 Cor. 6:15: "Do you not know your bodies are members of Christ?"), Calvin says that such influx of life happens because Christ "cleaves to us" (*adhaereat*) completely in "body and spirit" (*spiritu et corpore*).[93]

Calvin then naturally proceeds to distinguish this view of the true body of Christ from the errors of the late medieval church, including both a discussion of technical issues of eucharistic presence and the character of the body of Christ, born of a virgin and crucified and raised into heaven.[94] He follows this with material from the 1536 *Institutes* concerning the purposes for which the Supper was instituted and the communal nature of the sacrament that truly feeds us with spiritual food.[95] By this progression of argument, Calvin essentially repeats his point from the beginning of the 1536 *Institutes*: when all the technical discussions from the medieval church have had their hearing, the best recourse is to return to why Christ instituted the Supper, which is to nourish believers who already are engrafted into his mystical body. As Davis rightly observes, "Thus, there is a presence of Christ in the Lord's Supper, but it is not a special kind of presence, in the sense of joining the Christian to Christ in a manner separate from daily Christian life."[96]

Davis's keen observation would profit in two ways if it were set in the context of the Augustinian tradition of true mystical presence that Calvin, as well as Zwingli and Bucer, has taken over. First, Davis's description of what Calvin thinks that the Supper brings would read as less cognitive and more, if I may use the word as described in chapter 2, mystical.[97] Rather than merely "a clearer understanding," which undoubtedly happens, it might be more adequate to say something like "a fuller realization," in which "to realize" indicates not only something cognitive but also a new mode of existing that has come to be: to *realize* one's union in Christ is to experience that mystical union more deeply and fully yet again. This would seem more adequate to Calvin's use, already in 1536, of *exhibere*.[98]

Also, what Calvin has developed from 1536 to 1539 is neither sacramental instrumentality nor being fed by true mystical union with Christ, both of which were present in 1536, as we have seen. By 1539 Calvin has added a much fuller grounding of this mystical feeding in the Johannine tradition of mystical union,[99] to go along with his developed view on the activity of the Spirit as the agent of such mystical feeding.

One further point that Davis makes must be mentioned. Calvin has become clear that God is "the efficient cause of all mercy, which includes the mercy of knowledge of him and his disposition toward humanity." Christ, word, faith, and sacraments are all instruments by which God works divine mercy in and through all God's creation. As Davis rightly observes, this description of God refutes the sometimes (usually Roman Catholic) complaint that Calvin is not fully "incarnational" in his sacramental theology, showing Nestorian tendencies along the way.[100]

Calvin's 1541 *Short Treatise on the Holy Supper* stands as an integrated summary of much of what we have seen him develop from his Augustinian mystical true presence beginnings in 1536.[101] As will be seen, without understanding the Augustinian tradition of the mystical true presence, which forms the background for Calvin's entire eucharistic theology, the integration and advances in the *Short Treatise* cannot be fully understood.

Calvin opens with a précis of his five points: the telos of the sacrament; its fruit; the proper use of the Supper; the most pernicious errors; and the source of the dispute, particularly among the Reformers. When he discusses his first point, which treats the goal for instituting the Supper, Calvin makes a simple argument, drawn from the Augustinian mystical true presence and its roots in John 6. God provides a physical food that gives bodily nourishment, yet also provides a spiritual food that gives spiritual nourishment. "Now all scripture tells us," says Calvin, alluding predominantly to John 6, "that the spiritual bread (*le pain spirituel*) by which our souls are maintained is the same Word by which the Lord has regenerated us; but it often adds the reason, that in it Jesus Christ, our only life, is given and administered to us."[102] We thus have "communion with the body and blood of Jesus Christ" (*communication au corps et au sang de Jesus Christ*), yet we cannot understand this because of our impoverished understanding. God, however, accommodates the divine self to our need and "therefore the Lord instituted for us his Supper, in order to sign and seal in our consciences the promises contained in the gospel concerning our being made partakers of his body and blood."[103]

The second section of the treatise, which treats the second of Calvin's five points, the benefits of the Supper, contains the clearest and most remarkable assertions about the true mystical presence of Christ ("nonmetabolic real presence") that Calvin had yet made. He begins his description of the Supper by using the image of a mirror in which we can contemplate the saving work of Jesus that rescues us from damnation and brings us to eternal life.[104] Borrowing an image present throughout medieval literature, and tracing to Augustine and Plato, Calvin uses the image of a mirror to reflect not only what is but also what ought to be:[105] The "what is" is the gift of Christ and his benefits, and the "what ought to be" concerns the gradual ascent of the believer into the very image of Christ, who, as must be the case for such transformation to occur, must iconically be present in the Supper itself, both as its origin and its telos.[106] Calvin therefore follows the opening mirror image with the remarkably clear assertions that "the matter and the substance of the sacraments is the Lord Jesus."[107] In the Supper we therefore both "communicate in his body and blood" (*communiqué à son corps et à son sang*) and receive the fruits of the sacrament, the latter unable to occur without the former being given. So Calvin can say that we must partake of Jesus' humanity in the Supper and that "to deny that the true communication of Jesus Christ is presented us in the Supper is to render this holy sacrament frivolous and useless—a blasphemy execrable and not to be listened to."[108]

This does not mean, as Calvin asserts, that this substantial presence of Christ is to be located somehow "in" the bread and the wine, but rather the bread and wine are signs that Christ uses as instruments by which the body and blood are distributed to us.[109] In this way the bread and the wine, and the body and blood of Christ, are to be held together but not confused, distinguished but not separated: "the sacraments of the Lord should not and cannot be separated from their reality and substance. To distinguish them, so that they are not confused, is not only good and reasonable but entirely necessary. But to divide them, so as to construct them one without the other, is absurd."[110]

With this relatively brief discussion of the substance of Jesus Christ, and the relationship between sign and reality, Calvin eloquently lays his position so as to avoid the errors committed by both Luther and Zwingli (and Oecolampadius), while also crediting what they wanted to credit.[111] With Luther, Calvin credits that the substance of Jesus Christ, including his very humanity, are communicated to believers in the Supper. Yet, by holding sign and reality together without confusing them, he avoids the mistakes that Luther made when he spoke less carefully than he might have. With Zwingli, Calvin is clear that the Supper is an event that cannot be perceived by either the eyes or the natural senses as such,[112] so that sign and reality must be distinguished, lest idolatry occur. Yet, by distinguishing sign and reality without separating them, he avoids thinking of merely empty symbols and can give positive content to the divine presence that is communicated. All that needs to be added to this development in section 2 is what Calvin gives in the final section, a development that we have seen in Calvin between 1536 and 1541: that the humanity of Christ, ascended into heaven and thus located neither here (Rome) nor everywhere (Luther), is communicated to us through the work of the Holy Spirit.[113]

Written in French during Calvin's Strasbourg years,[114] the *Short Treatise* was aimed at a general audience—Calvin notes that it was not written for a learned audience in Latin—and thus ultimately aimed at providing a middle ground between Protestant positions that ordinary folk ("unlearned") would understand.[115] In that regard, it is interesting that although the largest section of the treatise deals with the errors of Roman eucharistic teaching about real presence, Calvin says nothing substantial about his disagreements with Luther, crediting Luther where he can and criticizing only Luther's excesses.[116] Within about a year of the *Short Treatise*, Calvin found himself at Worms, upholding the Lutheran position of the Augsburg Confession as presented there by Melanchthon (the so-called "variata"), a position that Calvin certainly thought faithful to the *Confession*,[117] and may well have been where he thought Luther's own thought intended to go.[118]

With the *Short Treatise* Calvin's eucharistic teaching was completely realized in structure, although it continued to develop through enrichment. As Davis rightly says, "[T]he foundation for Calvin's mature thought is in place. However, . . . [t]he walls and the roof of Calvin's eucharistic theology must still be built before the final 'structure' of Calvin's eucharistic teaching can be discussed."[119] Two key developments can be noticed that, historically speaking, go together. Calvin continued to emphasize the way that the Supper functioned as a distinct means of grace by which one realizes one's participation in the body and blood of Christ. This led partly— and in some ways perhaps necessarily—to his debate with Westphal, who could not comprehend Calvin's Augustinian insistence on the mystical true presence (nonmetabolic presence) as an authentic Reformation way of expressing the communication of Jesus' very body and blood.

Calvin's 1546 *Commentary on 1 Corinthians* contains a remarkably insightful connection between knowledge and revelation.[120] We can see in Calvin's commentary on the Supper scene in 1 Corinthians 11:23–29 that, for Calvin, the knowledge given during the Supper has a cognitive aspect, in which the Supper serves as a memorial that Christ has given himself, body and blood, for us. The very words of 11:24, "do this in remembrance of me" (*hoc facite in mei memoriam*), indicate for Calvin that just as "Christ gives thanks" to God for the divine mercy toward humankind, so also we too should remember God's boundless love for us, responding to God's grace with our gratitude.[121] The knowledge that the Supper brings, however, involves something deeper and more foundational than the natural knowledge that God acted toward us with grace. The knowledge depends on the work of the Spirit and is not a natural knowledge as such.[122] As Davis puts the matter,

> knowledge is not natural knowledge; Calvin is no rationalist. He makes it clear that what takes place with the eucharistic celebration is a heavenly act. Thus, both the substantial partaking and the knowledge thereof take place through the power of the Spirit . . . What is more, the knowledge of union with Christ that the Supper gives serves a twofold purpose. The first has been treated extensively here: knowledge serves to heighten the sense of union with Christ, in fact, makes the union more real, increases its depths, and leads to growth in the Christian life.[123]

This bespeaks precisely the Augustinian tradition of mystical true presence (nonmetabolic real presence) in which, as we have seen repeatedly, believers are said to be nourished directly by the real body and blood of Christ by being engrafted more deeply into Christ. This involves a cognition, *which at the same time is a re-cognition, and thus a realization*, of what was already true and yet is now truly given again and anew for this particular moment. The subtlety of Calvin's point seems striking, and perhaps a mundane example, here meaning "of this world," will help clarify.

When I say these words—"we see with our eyes"—we now know something that brings with it a re-cognition that we always are seeing with our eyes. At the very same time, when we immediately experience that we "see with our eyes," the only thing *in that moment* of which we are aware is *that very experience itself*. Thus, the cognition is also a re-cognition, which also is a *realization*, by which I mean that the reality itself is realized in us. This, finally, is the subtle answer to McDonnell's question about what distinctive eucharistic gift is present according to Calvin's (and Luther's) eucharistic teaching:[124] Christ himself is present, not just again but *anew*, in and to the experience of believers in this particular moment.[125]

The 1549 Consensus Tigurinus, which through eucharistic consensus served to bind the Reformed churches of Switzerland, French- and German-speaking alike, ironically served also to sharpen the eucharistic differences between some Lutherans and Calvin. Calvin believed that his eucharistic teaching would have found essential agreement from Luther.[126] However, ultra-Lutherans thought Calvin had shown himself to be a mere sacramentarian; notable among them was Joachim Westphal, a Lutheran pastor in Hamburg. Westphal took exception, among other things, to Article 24 of the Consensus:

> In this way are refuted not only the fiction of the Papists concerning transubstantiation, but all the gross figments and futile quibbles which either derogate from his celestial glory or are in some degree repugnant to the reality of his human nature. For we deem it no less absurd to place Christ under the bread or couple him with the bread, than to transubstantiate the bread into his body.[127]

Calvin's first response to Westphal, first published in 1555, consisted of a 1554 letter to the Swiss pastors, the 1551 published version of the Consensus, and an exposition of the agreement.[128] Davis has a very good discussion of the Consensus and Calvin's reply to Westphal,[129] and I want here to disagree not so much with what Davis found but with how he interpreted what was found. As we have seen, the Reformed tradition clearly relied upon and developed the mystical true presence tradition of Augustine, and this perspective makes a difference in seeing the Consensus and in Calvin's replies to Westphal. For example, articles 5 and 23 were not in the original agreement, which totaled twenty-four articles, not twenty-six. Article 5 asserts that,

> [m]oreover, that Christ may thus exhibit himself to us and produce these effects in us, he must be made one with us, and we must be ingrafted into his body. He does not infuse his life into us unless he is our head, and from him the whole body, fitly joined together through every joint of supply, according to his working, maketh increase of the body in the proportion of each member.[130]

Davis comments that "this article speaks to Calvin's concept of union with Christ,"[131] and Davis follows that by citing article 23, and then Calvin's letter to Bucer in June 1549, all as showing these additions to an agreement that was all too "Zwinglian" appearing and something of a mere political compromise by Calvin. But the issue seems to me more subtle.

The addition of article 5 near the beginning of the document precisely structures the subsequent discussion according to the mystical true presence, whereby through the Supper believers are engrafted yet more deeply into the body of Christ and thus fed by his body and blood. Not only have we traced this theme through *both* Zwingli and Bucer, but this precisely parallels the 1537 Confession of Faith concerning the Eucharist that reflected Reformed views from both Geneva and Strasburg.[132] Not surprisingly, since we have seen this perspective in Zwingli's works, and since it represents the backbone, if you will, of the mystical true presence tradition, this article found ultimate support in the final form of the Consensus. It reflects not merely Calvin's perspective on the Supper but that of the larger Reformed tradition that had already developed.[133] In light of the mystical true presence trajectory that we have traced here, Calvin's comments on mystical union in his first reply to Westphal are striking. He asserts simply and strongly that "[t]here is no other way of infusing his life into us than by being our head, from which the whole body, joined together and connected by every joint of supply, according to his operation in the measure of every part, maketh increase of the body."[134]

Likewise, later in his discussion, Calvin says that "[w]e acknowledge that the sacred union which we have with Christ is incomprehensible to carnal sense. His joining us with him so as not only to instill his life into us, but to make us one with himself, we grant to be a mystery too sublime for our comprehension, except in so far as his words reveal it."[135] In between these two passages, in which Calvin treats several issues, he relies repeatedly on Augustine, particularly Augustine's homilies on the Gospel of John, which, as we have seen, were central places that scholars have identified the nonmetabolic real presence in Augustine's thought.[136]

In similar light we should view the addition of article 23:

> When it is said that Christ, by our eating of his flesh and drinking of his blood, which are here figured, feeds our souls through faith by the agency of the Holy Spirit, we are not to understand it as if any mingling or transfusion of substance took place, but that we draw life from the flesh once offered in sacrifice and the blood shed in expiation.[137]

Here we see precisely the assertion of the mystical true presence as it stands starkly over and against the tradition of the metabolic real presence, which, as we have seen, traced back to the early Antiochenes, through Ambrose, and into the medieval church. Within the later medieval church, we saw this position in Erasmus, whom I have described as having a "medieval catholic eucharistic theology," and also in Luther, whom I have characterized as having a "medieval catholic, evangelical eucharistic theology."[138]

While scholars have rightly lifted up Calvin's responses to Westphal,[139] which also include (in the third letter) responses to other Lutheran voices, as clearly asserting that Christ feeds believers in the Supper with his flesh and blood, something else is also quite striking. Calvin repeatedly distinguishes the mystical true presence, which he repeatedly finds in Augustine, from the metabolic real presence. So, for instance, in his second reply to Westphal, using his favorite word *exhibere*, Calvin says, "I said that the body of Christ is exhibited in the Supper effectually, not naturally, in respect of virtue, not substance. In this last term I referred to a local infusion of substance."[140] Calvin says to Westphal that the issue at hand is not whether Christ feeds believers in the Supper with his body and blood, but the "mode" of such feeding, since, for Calvin, such feeding is not about that which enters the "mouth and stomach" (*in os et ventrem*).[141] Thus, says Calvin, Westphal's fifth point concerns "the transfusion of substance" (*de transfusione substantiae*), and Calvin asks Westphal "whether we ought to dream that the substance of Christ is transfused into us and thereby defiled by our impurities?"[142]

So, also, in the last reply to Westphal, Calvin begins by narrating the course of events that has led him to this final response (*ultima admonitio*). Along the way of this historical introduction, Calvin subscribes to the Augsburg Confession, likely the Variata, which he says contains not a word that runs counter to his teaching (*verbulum in ea . . . non exstare doctrinae nostrae contrarium*).[143] Calvin claims Philip Melanchthon as his ally because, when it comes to the Supper, "in this matter Philip can no more be torn from me than he can from his own bowels."[144]

Calvin next turns to a lengthy discussion of Augustine.[145] He criticizes Westphal's use of Augustine and discusses many passages from Augustine, first concerning the mystical true presence and then concerning the ascension.[146] Instructive is a discussion that rejects any "gross mode of eager swallowing" (*crassum vorandi modum*),[147] and instead takes up the position of Augustine, citing his tractates on John, a position that contrasts visible appearance with true spiritual union:[148] "The whole reality of the sacred Supper," says Calvin, "consists in this—Christ, by ingrafting us into his body, not only makes us partakers of his body and blood, but infuses into us the life whose fullness resides in himself."[149]

Such passages, repeating throughout Calvin's replies to Westphal, not only reiterate the ancient and differing Supper trajectories about how the flesh and blood of Christ truly nourish believers, they also reflect precisely the Reformed position that we have seen in Zwingli, Bucer, and Reformed documents such as the 1537 Confession of Faith concerning the Eucharist, which begins with the mystical union with Christ, prior to taking up the matter of the Supper as such.[150] These passages also reflect the continued use of the Fourth Gospel, particularly the Bread from Heaven discourse in John 6, as well as Augustine's use of John, where we have seen him lay out his teaching on the nonmetabolic real presence. Calvin's commentary on the Gospel of John, published simultaneously in French and Latin, was written during the period of his replies to Westphal;[151] and the commentary deserves to be taken up now, even if only briefly, because Calvin so clearly summarizes what we have seen to be the Reformed teaching on the mystical true presence, a teaching that these humanist Reformed scholars saw clearly in Augustine.

Commenting on John 6, which contains the heart of Augustine's teaching on the mystical true (nonmetabolic real) presence, Calvin begins by asserting, near the start of the Bread from Heaven discourse, that

> those who infer from this passage that the eating of Christ is nothing but faith, do not reason carefully enough. I certainly acknowledge that we eat Christ in no other way than by believing. But the eating is the effect and fruit of faith rather than faith itself. *For faith does not look at Christ merely from afar, but embraces Him, that He may become ours and dwell in us. It causes us to be united in His body, to have life in common with Him and, in short, to be one with him.*[152]

Notice how thoroughly this view reflects the catholic tradition of the mystical true presence. We have seen time and again that Reformed eucharistic theology at the time of the Protestant Reformation began with the mystical union with Christ, so that, through the work of the Spirit, when Christ feeds believers at the table with his very body and blood, then believers realize, here and now in this or that context, the literal feeding by which Christ nourishes them. We can hardly be surprised when Calvin, commenting on the words "the one who eats my flesh," says this about the Bread from Heaven discourse:

> [I]t is certain that He is now treating of the perpetual eating of faith. At the same time, I confess that there is nothing said here that is not figured and actually presented to believers in the Lord's Supper. Indeed, we might say that Christ intended the holy Supper to be a seal of this discourse. This is also therefore why John makes no mention of the Lord's Supper. And therefore Augustine follows the proper order when, in expounding this chapter, he does not touch on the Lord's Supper until he comes to the end. And then he shows that this mystery is represented in a symbol whenever the Churches celebrate the sacred Supper, in some places daily, in others only on the Lord's Day.[153]

To sum what we have seen about Calvin's teaching on the Supper, we noted first that Calvin, from the first edition of the *Institutio* onward, teaches both the instrumentality of the Supper and that believers are nourished by the very body and blood of Christ. This is the Augustinian tradition of the mystical true presence which he, like the Reformed tradition that preceded him, believed to be both scriptural (rooted particularly in the Fourth Gospel) and catholic. Asserting that Calvin began his eucharistic teaching by asserting a true mystical presence, instrumentally offered through the signs of bread and cup, by no means indicates that he had a mature, selfsame eucharistic theology throughout his career as pastor and doctor of the church. He indeed developed and integrated, but he developed and integrated from within the Augustinian tradition of the mystical true presence.

We have also seen, following the work of Davis, that Calvin developed both the teaching that Christ's very flesh is communicated and that such communication happens through the work of the Spirit. We have also seen that Calvin increasingly followed the Fourth Gospel, both in good Reformed tradition and bespeaking his catholic, Augustinian tradition, when grounding these eucharistic issues in mystical union with Christ himself. Through the late 1540s and into the next decade, several additional themes appeared: Calvin maintained his agreement with Lutheranism as represented by the Variata and the teaching of Melanchthon.[154] He also, as Davis shows, developed the teaching that the Supper brought a new religious knowledge, a "spiritual knowledge," or, as I put the matter, a new and fully context-laden "realization" of one's union with Christ and the deepening of that union through the Supper. Thus as Davis shows, Calvin also developed the theme of divine accommodation and the importance of the eucharistic signs. With these developments, especially the latter two, it seems to me, Calvin has developed the Reformed position along the lines that in his *Short Treatise* he had developed when criticizing both Oecolampadius and Zwingli. Now the real flesh of Christ is offered through the signs, and the signs themselves, through the divine process of accommodation, intimately convey such true presence, yet do not convey that presence, as we have seen Calvin repeatedly say to Westphal and the Lutherans, in a way that concerns "the transfusion of substance" (*de transfusione substantiae*). In short, Calvin developed the catholic, Augustinian tradition in the late medieval context of the Protestant Reformation, and did so in a way that overcame the difficulties presented by the first generation of Reformed theologians, while still distinguishing the Reformed position from the catholic tradition of a metabolic real presence.

HEINRICH BULLINGER

Living between the years of 1504 and 1575, Heinrich Bullinger has typically been seen as a second-generation, Reformed contemporary of John Calvin (1509–64), a description that is chronologically accurate but, as we shall see, needs some nuance for the eucharistic material. Bullinger was born to Heinrich Bullinger, a priest in Bremgarten (just west of Zurich), and Anna Wiederkehr, the daughter of Bremgarten's miller.[155] The younger Heinrich received both his bachelor's (1519) and master's (1522) degrees from the University of Cologne, where he read actively in patristic material, as well as reading both Luther and Melanchthon. After graduation, Bullinger took a call in Kappel, teaching New Testament at a Cistercian monastery. Within two years the monastery had abolished the Mass, and in 1526 the Supper was celebrated in a Reformed manner.[156] Zwingli and Bullinger met in 1523, and Bullinger worked with Zwingli, first attending, and then clerking, at the Zurich disputations. With Zwingli's death in 1531 at the battle of Kappel, Bullinger directed the religious life of Zurich for the next four decades as its central theologian and pastor. Bullinger scholarship over the last half of the twentieth century established Bullinger's place as a key Reformed theologian, with some discussion about his stance at the headwaters of the Reformed covenant tradition, representing an alternative to a more predestinarian theology.[157]

The young Bullinger was influenced in his Supper theology by Luther's *Babylonian Captivity* and Luther's use of testament as a means to describe the Supper.[158] We also see language from the mid-1520s that sounds very much like Zwingli's *De vera et falsa religione*.[159] Finally, Hans-Georg vom Berg has shown that the young Bullinger learned from and adapted late medieval sources on the Supper. Rather than merely taking a symbolic and memorialist position, such as we have seen presented in Hoen, in which the remembering community is the active participant, for Bullinger "the community in faith re-presents the gracious offering of Christ," resulting in a "sacramental act of dedication and re-presentation" wherein the community was passive and the self-bestowing Christ (*der sich schenkende Christus*) was active.[160]

Bullinger's writings on the Supper from 1525–26 show no real attempt by Bullinger to connect this divine active participation ("re-presentation") through the community with mystical union with Christ, with the Bread from Heaven discourse in John 6,[161] and with the writings of Augustine, themes we have seen in the Reformed tradition.[162] In his July 1525 essay against the idolatry concerning the eucharistic bread (*Wider das Götzenbrot*), we find only a passing reference to Augustine and a sloughing off of the realistic language found in the redaction occurring in John 6:51b and following.[163] In December of the same year, writing on the institution of the Supper (*De institutione eucharistiae*), Bullinger provides more references to Augustine, though they concern the use of trope in Scripture;[164] the spiritual eating of the flesh;[165] the relation of the law and the eucharistic cup(s), noting the two cups of Luke's narrative;[166] and, finally, a standard reference that eating is nothing other than believing (*edere aliud nihil esse quam credere*), where he mentions not only John 6 but Augustine's brief words to "believe and eat" (*crede et manducasti*).[167] Finally, Bullinger's March 1526 four lectures on the Supper at the monastery at Kappel (*De pane eucharistiae declamationes*) deal with specific eucharistic issues, and the second of these concerned John 6 and the theme that eating meant spiritual eating.[168]

By the mid-1540s, however, we again see something more than mere memorialism in Bullinger's thought. The 1545 *Warhaffte Bekanntnuss* (*True Confession*) was done by Bullinger and the Zurich clergy, at the urging of Zurich officials, in order to present their views in contrast to the teachings of Luther.[169] The action (*Actio*) of breaking the bread and eating it, and the pouring of the cup and drinking the wine, bring the faithful to faith again, so that "[s]uch remembrance neither may nor can happen correctly, and happen as the Lord commanded, without true faith. That's why the remembrance (*gedächtnus*) in the Supper is not an empty dream (*lär gedicht*)—because faith is no vain dream (*kein ytel gedicht*)." True faith consists in believing that the Son of God was crucified, dead, broken, and given for our salvation;[170] yet such faith, in Bullinger's wordplay, brings a real remembrance, which is something quite different than mere thoughts in the mind such as in a dream.

If this looks somewhat familiar to the Augustinian anamnesis that we have seen in Zwingli—perceiving not with our physical eyes but real perceiving with the eyes of faith—then Bullinger's sermon on the Supper, from the *Decades*, dating later in the 1540s, traces the perspective more fully.[171] Bullinger says straightforwardly that he wants to "distinctly confess" (*diserte profiteor*) that he neither "simply condemns nor attacks all presence of Christ in the church as well as in the very action of the Supper," but that he "distinctively attacks that bodily presence of Christ in the bread" (*oppugno enim significanter corporalem illam prasentiam Christi in pane*) that the "papists" hold and enforce.[172]

We have, says Bullinger, a "fellowship, union, or participation in the Lord Christ" (*societatem, coniunctionem vel participationem Christi domini*), through his spirit (*per spiritum suum*) and our faith, so that "he may live in us and be wholly ours, just as we are wholly his" (*ac ipse vivat in nobis ac totus noster sit, quemadmodum ipsi sumus eius toti*).[173] "This promise and communion of Christ," says Bullinger, "is now first conveyed to us not in the Supper or by the Supper."[174] It was a promise given to our forebears in the faith, given to the apostles, conveyed by baptism and preaching, and received by faith, "through which we are joined to Christ, and made his members" (*per quam Christo coniungimur membraque eius efficimur*).[175] Bullinger continues that

> through this very action or celebration of the Supper the promise is retrieved in us, and we spiritually revive and continue, by the body and blood of Christ, that communion that we have in Christ, and in which we exist, truly participating in his life and all his good gifts through faith; and so, by this means, we eat the Lord's body and drink his blood.[176]

Nothing, it seems to me, could read more in the Reformed tradition of the mystical true presence, present again (*anamnesis*) during the action of the Supper. Later in the sermon Bullinger continues his discussion of what it means to "eat" and "drink" the body and blood of Christ when he takes up John 6, and there he refers to Augustine at the same places where we have seen Augustine's nonmetabolic view of Christ's real presence.[177] The question then becomes, as we saw in the last chapter with Zwingli, and as Rorem so carefully documents,[178] the relationship between this nourishment in Christ and *the signs* of the Supper themselves. Near the beginning of his sermon on the Supper, Bullinger says, in a somewhat convoluted argument, that

> the Lord himself visibly confirms and seals that spiritual communion and promise of life through Christ, by visible symbols, the banquet (I say) of bread and wine, joined to his word or promise; namely, that he is the life-giving bread and drink; and that we, having received the symbols by faith and obedience, and being sealed, sustain in us that promise and communion of Christ, by the imprint or transfer into our bodies the seal or sacrament of the body and blood of Christ.[179]

We might think, it seems to me, of a divine signet ring sealing into the hot wax (*impresso/sigillo*) of our souls the very presence of the one Lord who speaks, and who thereby joins himself inwardly to us. Toward the end of the discussion on eating the body and blood of Christ, and prior to turning to the reasons for the Supper, Bullinger sums up his position by saying that "the bread and the mystical cup are a sacrament and sign and sealing" of the body and blood of Christ.[180]

It is not entirely clear to me that at this point Bullinger is entirely clear about the role of the signs during the Supper. Opitz assigns this sermon to the same theological period of development (stage three) in Bullinger to which the Zurich Agreement belongs and, therefore, the same period in which the Bullinger and Calvin discussed the function of the signs just prior to the Zurich Agreement.[181] In discussions late in 1548 and early in 1549, prior to the Zurich Agreement, where Calvin wanted the preposition "through" (*per*) as in "through the sacraments" (*per sacramenta*), Bullinger thought this ascribed too much to things and not enough to the power of the Spirit; and where Calvin liked the word *instrumentum*, Bullinger sharply rejected such a word, rejecting even the word (later to be used in the Zurich Agreement) *organum* (implement). In some seeming frustration, Calvin wrote to Bullinger that he (Bullinger) seemed to make the argument that "only God acts and therefore instruments cease."[182] Further, as Rorem details, a curious exchange happened between Calvin and Bullinger when they discussed the word *simul* as concerns the temporality of divine activity and sacramental activity.[183] Bullinger objected to the idea of divine action given any temporal restriction, and Calvin nuanced for Bullinger than he meant *similiter*, so that just as the eyes see the sign, so also we participate in the signified. On Rorem's view, in these discussions prior to the Zurich Agreement, we see that "when Calvin spoke of the sacraments as testimonies of grace rather than as instruments of grace, agreement flourished, for this was Bullinger's theme throughout the exchange and indeed throughout his entire corpus."[184]

Seen from this perspective, the Zurich Agreement shows not so much compromise by Calvin, who already had shown himself flexible in order to work toward agreement with Zurich,[185] but more of a balance between Calvin and Bullinger.[186] First and foremost, Calvin had article 5 added to the agreement, which gave the basis for the mystical feeding through the Supper, and did so by using in the christological context Calvin's favorite eucharistic word for the actual making-present of Christ (*exhibere*).

By way of secondary scholarship, since the work done on the metabolic and nonmetabolic ("mystical true presence") traditions by Roman Catholic scholars, mostly in older German literature, remains largely unknown to Protestant scholarship, and along with it the Augustinian mystical tradition to the Supper, Protestant scholars often pass too quickly over article 5 and the beginning of article 6 of the Zurich Agreement. For example, Rorem says that

> [a]lthough this article [i.e., article 5] states clearly that "we are made one with him, and are engrafted into his body," it does so as part of the Christological introduction, before the sacraments themselves are introduced, thus apparently honouring Bullinger's aversion to binding this spiritual process of grace too closely to the external sacrament. . . . Article 6 makes the transition from communion with Christ to the sacraments by saying that preaching was instituted and the sacraments commended to us "for the sake of testifying to this" communion.[187]

We would do well not to view the "Christological introduction" as mere prolegomenon to a balance between "memorialist" and "instrumentalist" views of the sacrament of the Supper. Article 5, which was proposed by Calvin and accepted by the Zurich theologians, was *precisely* the point to the Augustinian tradition already present in Zwingli, Bucer, and the 1537 Reformed Supper confession. In the Zurich Agreement this article connected into a unified whole the christological material that preceded with the sacramental material that followed. The Christ who nourishes believers by their ingrafting into him continues to feed them in the Supper. Was this not precisely Bullinger's point, which we have just seen, that such feeding does not begin with the Supper; but the Supper does bring about in us the retrieval of the divine promise and the spiritual revival and communion that we have Christ, "by the body and blood of Christ" (*corpore et sanguine Christi*)?[188] What ultimately needed resolution, it seems to me, was not so much an impasse between the Zurich (and Bern) memorialist view of the Supper and Calvin's more "realistic" view of the Supper, but how precisely to connect the nourishment that God gives through the Supper with the nourishment given through the mystical union with Christ.[189] That is a slightly different question.

The articles following 5 and 6 again show a balance of Bullinger's noninstrumental view of the signs and Calvin's instrumentalist view.[190] Article 7 goes beyond the signs as "marks and badges" to say that they also "testify, represent, and seal" God's grace to us. Article 8 may have lost Calvin's reference (from his March 1549 propositions sent to Bern) to the sacraments as figuring for us what is truly represented, but the sacraments are said to figure outwardly what God does inwardly (*intus*). Article 9 weakens Calvin's (Bern) phrasing about the faithful receiving the Christ who is offered with the sacraments; yet article 13 uses the word "implement/s" (*organo/a*) for the sacraments, which Bullinger earlier rejected, although this was a change from Calvin's original word "instrument." Similarly, article 12 speaks about the "ministry" of the sacraments and uses the word "aids" for the sacraments, a word disliked by Bullinger; but the article then couples these phrases with the insistence that all the work is ascribed to God alone. Articles 14 talks about the inward (*intus*) baptism by Christ and then immediately says that Christ "in the Supper (*in coena*) makes us partakers of himself" (*nos in coena facit sui participes*), which certainly leans toward an instrumental view of the sacraments. This same Supper phrasing appears again in article 19, where it is said that "in the Supper Christ communicates himself to us" (*in coena se nobis communicat Christus*). One could think, as Rorem suggests as conceivably possible, that perhaps Bullinger himself read the preposition "in" temporally ("during") rather than having any instrumental sense ("by means of"); but even in that case, which itself is complete conjecture, Bullinger has still acceded to a more instrumental phrase.[191]

The point here is simply that while the Zurich Agreement would seem to be a balance of the more instrumentalist view of the sacraments held by Calvin and a more testifying view of the sacraments—and it may well be that this balance reflects agreement between Calvin and the more moderate "Zwinglians" in Zurich, over and against the more extreme "Zwinglians" in Bern[192]—this balance represents *a modest but perceptible shift toward* the instrumentalist view of Calvin, when compared to the discussions between Calvin and Bullinger in later 1548 and early 1549, where Calvin seemed to be the more accommodating. This is worth mentioning, because when Bullinger wrote the Second Helvetic Confession (1561), he said of the Supper,

And this is visibly represented by this sacrament outwardly through the ministers, and, as it were, presented to our eyes to be seen, which is invisibly wrought by the Holy Spirit inwardly in the soul. Bread is outwardly offered by the minister, and the words of the Lord are heard: "Take, eat; this is my body"; and, "Take and divide among you. Drink of it, all of you; this is my blood." Therefore the faithful receive what is given by the ministers of the Lord, and they eat the bread of the Lord and drink of the Lord's cup. At the same time by the work of Christ through the Holy Spirit they also inwardly receive the flesh and blood of the Lord, and are thereby nourished unto life eternal. For the flesh and blood of Christ is the true food and drink unto life eternal; and Christ himself, since he was given for us and is our Savior, is the principal thing in the Supper, and we do not permit anything else to be substituted in his place.[193]

Here we see both the idea that the believing communicant receives both the sign and that which is signified; and, furthermore, that sign and reality are temporally linked, so that what happens outwardly (*foris*) happens at the same time, in parallel fashion, inwardly (*intus interim*).[194] Given the conversation between Calvin and Bullinger from 1548 and into 1549, where Calvin can be seen to be more accommodating than Bullinger, and given the Zurich Agreement of 1549, where there seems to be a balance between Geneva and Zurich, it appears that Calvin has had a slow but steady influence on Bullinger, a point that Rorem suggests very cautiously, but which seems to me clearer.[195]

A CLOSING OBSERVATION ON SIXTEENTH-CENTURY REFORMED SUPPER THEOLOGY: SIGN AND REALITY

This chapter, and the two that preceded it, have argued that the Augustinian tradition of the mystical true presence (nonmetabolic) of Christ in the Supper emerged during the Protestant Reformation, and emerged most clearly in the Reformed tradition, with its heritage of humanist Christianity that returned *ad fontes*. With Zwingli and Bucer we saw the insistence on the ascension and session of Christ; the mystical union with Christ through faith; and the nourishment of this union with Christ during the Supper, often focusing on John 6 and the very passages that notable Roman Catholic scholars have argued best represent the nonmetabolic position of Augustine.

The religious struggle was how to connect this divine nourishment in the Supper with the elements, when, at the same time, the Protestant Reformers and especially the Reformed Reformers, were so concerned with the late medieval abuses of the elements. Recall, for a moment, how the Protestant Reformers clashed among themselves over the elevation of the host, emblematic as it was of such idolatry. I have come to believe what I was unsure about when beginning these chapters: in the end, it was indeed Calvin who solved the issue and stamped the Reformed Supper tradition with a powerful sign-theology.

Calvin's instrumentalism carefully walked the keen edge between too closely identifying sign and reality and too distantly separating sign and reality. By viewing the signs as divinely appointed instruments that communicate what they represent, and by understanding such divine use of the sacraments to be one of many gracious acts of divine accommodation, Calvin not only gave language to Zwingli's theology that it needed in order to overcome a dualism that left the signs without much ministry; Calvin also influenced Bullinger toward his mature position in the Second Helvetic Confession. According to Calvin, through the signs of bread and cup, and by the work of the Spirit, Christ himself takes us yet deeper into mystical communion with himself, feeding us with his life-giving body and blood. This brings *new* religious knowledge, because it is an *experienced* ac-*knowledg*-ment *in this moment*—*hic et nunc*—of our ever-new life in Christ.

Reformed Supper theology thus had several options for thinking about the reality of Christ's true presence (*res*) and its relationship to the signs (*signa*) of bread and cup. In his now classic, and in many ways still unsurpassed, essay on the Lord's Supper in the Reformed confessions,[196] B. A. Gerrish distinguishes three options within Reformed theology for the relationship between *signum* and *res*:

- Symbolic instrumentalism (Calvin)
- Symbolic parallelism (Bullinger)
- Symbolic memorialism (Zwingli)

Chapter 3 of this study, building on the work of several Swiss scholars, argued that Zwingli thought of an anamnestic re-presentation of Christ himself, in whom believers were mystically engrafted. The influence of Augustine, both as historical source and theological resource, was very evident. The problem for Zwingli was not memorialism as such, but a dualism that hindered connecting the anamnestic event of mystical union in Christ with the physical signs, a problem that Zwingli slowly began to solve later in his career, once he was freed from arguing against the positions of others, so that he could devote more discussion to constructing the relationship between sign and reality.

On this view, then, Zwingli's position might best be renamed "symbolic anamnesis," and the category of "symbolic memorialism" left as an option for, shall we say, "Zwinglianism," perhaps as represented by Bern during the discussions over the Zurich Agreement. This would then result in four Reformed categories, by which the Reformed confessions might be considered in the next chapter:

- Symbolic instrumentalism (Calvin)
- Symbolic parallelism (Bullinger)
- Symbolic anamnesis (Zwingli)
- Symbolic memorialism (Zwinglianism)

5

THE REFORMED TRAJECTORY

The Reformed eucharistic tradition emerged as the Reformed scholars of the emergent Protestant tradition, steeped in humanist methods, returned to the original sources in Greek and Latin (*ad fontes*) and there discovered a eucharistic tradition as catholic as could be found, tracing back to Augustine of Hippo and, through him, even earlier. They found support in Scripture, particularly but not solely in John 6, exegeting the same Johannine passages as did Augustine. On the basis of Scripture, and following the Augustinian tradition, they argued for a mystical (nonmetabolic) true presence of Christ in the Supper. Chapter 3 noted this was true even for Zwingli; following certain Swiss scholars, I argued that Zwingli was far from a "memorialist." He did, however, struggle to connect the mystical true presence to the elements themselves, perhaps displaying something of what Calvin noted long ago, in his *Short Treatise on the Lord's Supper*. Calvin observed that Zwingli (and Oecolampadius) were so opposed to "the superstitious and fanatical opinion of the Papists, touching the local presence of Jesus Christ within the sacrament, and the perverse adoration consequent upon it, that they labored more to pull down what was evil than to build up what was good."[1] Chapter 4 showed the efforts of Calvin and Bullinger to connect the mystical true presence, upon which the Reformed tradition was insistent, with the divinely appointed ministry of the elements as such.

This chapter now moves from key Reformed theologians of the first two generations to the Reformed confessions. From there the discussion moves to Friedrich Schleiermacher, who proves himself a disciple of the mystical true presence; to the nineteenth-century discussion in America between John Williamson Nevin and Charles Hodge, each of whom was partly correct about Calvin, but with Nevin quite close to the classic Reformed position; and then to the twentieth century and the Swiss theologian Karl Barth and the Scottish theologian Donald Baillie, who also, in his own way, captured the mystical true presence of the Reformed tradition.

THE REFORMED CONFESSIONS

The Reformed confessions themselves overlap some of the very Reformers whom prior chapters have discussed, since these Reformers were themselves instrumental in composing confessions of faith.[2] As is well-known, the Reformed tradition has neither a central teaching office nor an official document such as the *Book of Concord* (1580) by which a unified doctrinal tradition can be affirmed. It relies instead on a confessional heritage whose content varies in several ways.[3] The confessions come from a variety of contexts, both historically and geographically; they reflect different types of documents, such as catechisms, confessions, and pronouncements (e.g., Barmen); and they show diversity theologically, which can be seen by comparing, for example, the Synod of Dort, the Heidelberg Catechism, and the Presbyterian Church (U.S.A.) Confession of 1967.[4]

In what remains the single most insightful essay written on the Supper in the Reformed confessions, Gerrish devotes the first three sections of the study to the confessional work of Zwingli (I), Calvin (II), and Bullinger (III).[5] From these sections, Gerrish discerns types of Reformed eucharistic doctrine: "symbolic memorialism," as typified by Zwingli; "symbolic instrumentalism," which was Calvin's position; and "symbolic parallelism," as seen in Bullinger.[6] As chapters 3 and 4 of this study have argued, Gerrish remains quite on track but with this important alteration: Zwingli was insistent on the mystical true presence, however much he spoke negatively, particularly early in his career, about the elements because of what he experienced as gross eucharistic idolatry. The evidence seems quite convincing, and chapter 3 argued extensively that Zwingli had in mind an Augustinian notion of anamnesis. So, to repeat my suggestion, as we turn to the confessions after Zwingli, Calvin, and Bullinger, we might more adequately consider not three but four categories:

- Symbolic *anamnesis* (Zwingli)—Zwingli-like
- Symbolic *instrumentalism* (Calvin)—Calvinist
- Symbolic *parallelism* (Bullinger)—Bullinger-like
- Symbolic *memorialism* (Zwinglianism)—Zwinglian[7]

In this classification, the word "symbolic" simply indicates that for Reformed theology God has accommodated the divine self to human capacities by self-communicating through signs. Within the categories, the first three indicate that the Supper provides direct nourishment of the body and blood of Christ through the realization of mystical union with his true presence, while the fourth category indicates that the Supper signifies the divine grace given through the one means of grace, Jesus Christ, and the human pledge of obedience in faith to Jesus Christ. Among the first three categories, "instrumentalism" indicates that the nourishment happens because of the signs themselves—through the signs—because God has given them this ministry. "Parallelism" indicates that the nourishment happens simultaneously with the taking of the elements, because

God alone directly causes such nourishment to happen. "Anamnesis," which the second chapter applied to Zwingli, indicates that mystical union with the true presence feeds the believers when through faith they remember, but the connection to the signs as such is left underspecified.

Because chapters 3 and 4 have looked carefully at the Supper theology of Zwingli, Bucer, Calvin, and Bullinger, this section turns to the Swiss confessions: the First Helvetic Confession (1536), the Geneva Instruction in Faith (1537) and the Geneva Confession of Faith (1537), the Geneva Catechism (1545), and, briefly, The Second Helvetic Confession (1566). The following section will take up the continental confessions: the French Confession (1559), the Belgic Confession (1561), and the Heidelberg Catechism (1563). Finally, the section on the British Reformed confessions will take up the Scots Confession (1560), the Articles of Religion (1563), the Anglican Catechism (1647), and the Westminster Confession and Westminster Catechisms (1647).

Swiss Confessions

From January 31 through February 4, 1536, Swiss theologians from the churches of Zurich, Basel, Bern, Biel, Schaffhusen, St. Gall, and Mühlhasen gathered in the Augustinian monastery in Basel in order to compose a confession of faith that might represent all the Swiss cantons. The First Helvetic Confession (also called the Second Confession of Basel) was primarily the work of Heinrich Bullinger, Oswald Myconius, Leo Jud, Simon Grynaeus, and Caspar Megander, with numerous council representatives present from the various cities.[8] The original was in Latin, and Jud provided a longer German version.[9]

Article 20, "Concerning the Power and Efficacy of the Sacraments," opens by saying that the sacraments are not merely empty signs (*non nudis signis/nit bloße und läre*) but at the same moment consist—using the classic Augustinian terms (*signum et res*)—of sign and reality.[10] Given the later discussion between Calvin and Bullinger over words such as *simul* (at the same time, together), one can suppose that Leo Jud's German version, which lacks this adverb when connecting sign and reality, represented for the general audience a loosening of the connection between sign and reality.[11] So the article goes on to say that the sacraments are not only outward signs of Christian fellowship (*societatis christianae/christlicher gsellschafft*) but also signs of divine grace (*gratiae divinae symbola/zeichen göttlicher gnaden*), although all power is to be ascribed to God alone.[12]

Article 22, "The Eucharist," begins thoroughly Reformed with a strong statement of the mystical true presence wherein the Lord "truly offers to his own" his "body and blood," so that "more and more he lives in them and they live in him."[13] The intentional realism of this opening sentence is highlighted by the denial that follows, when the confession says that "it is not because the body and blood of the Lord are united to the bread and wine, whether naturally, or locally enclosed here, or any presence of the fleshly is here established."[14] It happens, rather, because the bread and wine are signs by which the "true imparting of his body and blood" (*vera corporis et sanguinis eius communicatio*) is "held forth" (*exhibeatur*). This raises the question about the relationship between this mystical true presence and the signs.

The signs themselves "hold forth the things signified" (*exhibeo*—Calvin's favorite word, as we have seen); they "offer testimony to the things witnessed" (*praebeo*); they "show" or "represent the difficult matters" (*repraesento*); they "bear light (*lucem affero*) upon these mysteries";[15] and, finally, they are an "aid" (*auxilium*) to our faith and an "oath" (*iusiurandi*) by which we bind ourselves to Christ the head and to the church.[16]

On the one hand, the signs "hold forth" for us the "true imparting of the body and blood." Furthermore, this true imparting of Christ's body and blood happens not only by Christ's activity but also "through the ministry of the church" (*per ecclesiae ministerium*), which celebrates the sacraments with its signs. This sounds something like Calvin in his mature development. By contrast, what the "eyes of faith" (*fide oculis*) perceive are the death of the crucified Christ and the heaven that awaits us with its foretaste now. These would be the "things that have happened" to which the sacrament testifies. So too the signs are a social pledge that believers give both to the Christ who has won salvation and given a foretaste of heaven, and to the church that is his.

In sum, the confession stands thoroughly Reformed (and Augustinian) in its insistence on mystical participation in Christ's body and blood, through his ever-increasing living in us and our living in him. The relationship between this gift of grace and the signs themselves, however, is described variously. The sign function in this confession sounds like differing assertions that come from a committee, so that assertions are strung together, some of them more instrumental, and some more testifying and pledge-oriented. This should not surprise us, because Bucer had a strong hand in the confession, particularly in the Supper article (article 22); the young Bullinger himself, as we have seen, was no mere epigone of Zwingli; and Leo Jud brought his own influence of Zwingli, particularly in his German translation.[17]

As a guide to the Reformation process in Geneva, William Farel and John Calvin offered the Articles Concerning the Organization of the Church and of Worship at Geneva (1537), along with Instruction and Confession of Faith (1537), which was a catechism for children adapted from the *Institutes*, and The Confession of Faith (1537), which was a shortened version of the Instruction and Confession, done in twenty-one articles and designed to be subscribed to first by the council and then by the citizens of Geneva.[18] The Genevan Instruction and Confession of Faith, and the Confession of Faith, show the theology of William Farel, the young Calvin, and the theological pulse of the French Swiss, dating from about the same time as the German Swiss First Helvetic Confession that we have just looked at.

The Instruction and Confession of Faith begins its sacramental discussion with exactly the twofold definition that developed between the 1536 and 1539 editions of the *Institutes*, where Calvin augments his original Augustinian definition: sacraments are signs that embody the divine promise that they might nourish our faith before God, *and also attest our faith before others*.[19] The promise embodied in the signs of bread and wine is that "the Lord presents to us the true communication of his body and blood" (*le Seigneur nous presente la vraye communication de son corps et du son sang*). Even though this is done "spiritually" (*spirituelle*), which means "by the bond of his Spirit" (*du lien de son Esperit*), so that Christ does not have to be "enclosed" in the elements—the body under the bread and the blood under the wine (*ne requiert point une presence enclose, ou de la chair soubz le pain, or du sang soubz le vin*)—yet Christ is "presented to us there not less than if he could be put in the presence of our eyes and touched by our hands" (*nous y est presenté non pas moins que s'il estoit mis en la presence de noz yeulx et estoit touché de noz mains*).[20] By analogy (*similitude*), what we outwardly see as bread and wine nourishing our bodies precisely happens inwardly with Christ nourishing us with his body and blood.[21]

This is the Reformed (Augustinian) mystical true presence as clearly stated as could be, as early as 1537, which should not surprise us, given what we have seen of Calvin in the previous chapter. Likewise, as we saw in chapter 4, there are yet no specifics on the (instrumental) ministry of the signs and no precise specification (although it certainly is implied) that the work of the Spirit is to bridge the gap between heaven and earth.[22] While in no way differing from these assertions about the Supper, article 16 of the Confession of Faith merely says that the Supper of the Lord is a sign "by which he represents to us the true spiritual communication, under the bread and the wine, which we have in his body and blood."[23] Thereafter, the remainder of the article mostly rails against the diabolical mass of the pope, which was material perhaps useful for political subscription by the citizens of Geneva, but was hardly edifying for children, and thus was not present in the Instruction and Confession.

Five years after these first confessional Genevan documents, Calvin revised his early instruction for children into his well-known Geneva Catechism, originally in French (1542) and later translated by Calvin into Latin (1545).[24] The section on the sacraments opens with a standard Calvin assertion that we have seen so often, that the sacrament is an outer sign of an inner grace that confirms the truth to our hearts (Q. 310).[25] Only two questions later (Q. 312) the Catechism provides what was specifically lacking in the earlier Swiss confessions that we have looked at: while all the power of the sacraments is to be ascribed to the work of the Spirit, yet God uses the sacraments as subordinate instruments (*instrumens inferieurs*) or secondary implements (*secunda organis*), according to the divine good pleasure, without detracting from the work of the Spirit.[26] A similar assertion then occurs in Q. 313.[27]

When we turn to the section on the Supper, we find the Reformed (and Augustinian) teaching on nourishment through the mystical union with Christ: Q. 340 (French 1542) begins the section with the straightforward assertion that the Lord has instituted the Supper because the "communication of his body and blood nourishes our souls";[28] while the Latin (1545) text says that by "the communication of his body and blood he might teach us and assure us that our souls are educated in the hope of eternal life."[29] We truly eat (*vescimur*) or communicate in (*communiquer*) the body and blood of Christ (Q. 342) because the benefits of Christ can be imputed unto us (*nous est imputée; nobis feratur*) only if he possesses us. He communicates his blessing to us only when he makes us his.[30] It is by faith that we receive Christ, thus making his life efficacious for us (Q. 343), and this reception through faith is one in which "he dwells in us" (*il habite en nous; in nobis quoque habitare*) and "we are united to him as members are to their head" (*est conioinct avec nous en telle union, que le chef avec ses membres; nosque illi coniunctos esse eo unitatis genere, quo membra cum capite suo cohaerent*) (Q. 344).[31] The following question (Q. 345) asks whether this union with its benefits is present only in the Supper. The answer cites not only 1 Corinthians 1 and Ephesians 5, but also the Reformed and Augustinian standard of John 6, and it replies that we always are "flesh of his flesh and bone of his bones."[32] In the Supper this mystical communion is "confirmed and increased" (*confirmatur et augetur*) in us (Q. 346).[33] Although Christ is in heaven, through the miraculous activity of the Spirit that broaches space (Q. 354), we are made "participants of his very substance" (*nous face participans de sa proper substance; suae nos substantiae participes faciat*: Q. 353).[34]

The last chapter already took up the Second Helvetic Confession in the course of discussing Bullinger's development of the Supper and his growth, apparently under the influence of Calvin, toward linking the mystical union with Christ to the sign activity itself.[35] As we saw, Bullinger's key struggle was to connect the mystical nourishment that believers have in Christ, and which they realize yet again in the Supper, with the signs themselves. In the discussion between Calvin and Bullinger in the late 1540s, prior to the Zurich Agreement, Bullinger disliked Calvin's instrumental sense that the nourishment of the Supper happened "through the sacrament" (*per sacramentum*), and he rejected not only Calvin's description of the sacrament as an "instrument" (*instrumentum*), but also as an "implement" (*organum*), even though article 12 of the Zurich Agreement changed Calvin's word *instrumenta* ("instruments") for the sacraments to the word *organa* ("implements").[36] In the exchange of careful and detailed letters between Bullinger and Calvin during the second half of 1548 and into 1549,[37] Calvin eventually showed some exasperation with Bullinger's reluctance to credit secondary agencies appointed by God, and he wrote to Bullinger, "Yet, consider what kind of argument yours is: 'God alone acts; therefore instruments cease.' Really?"[38]

By the time he wrote the Second Helvetic Confession (probably in 1561),[39] Bullinger had developed a cautious yet careful means of connecting sign and reality signified. Article XIX opens the discussion of the sacraments by making clear the crucial importance of the personal relationship between God and humankind: God self-communicates through the Word, and faith receives that Word.[40] Then in a careful explanation of how a sacrament works, the Confession says that "faith rests only upon the Word of God; and the Word of God is like papers or letters, and the sacraments are like seals which only God appends to letters."[41] The sense here, I suspect, can be lost upon modern ears; even with the advent of the printing press, the sixteenth century was an oral culture, and oral cultures depend on speaking from the interior of one person to the interior of another. The written document is an external way to communicate this speaking and hearing over a distance, and the seal signifies not so much the authenticity of the document as it signifies that the sender is actually and literally speaking to the hearing recipient.[42] The point here is that the sacraments directly connect the divine to the human, in an immediate Thou-I relationship, in which the very heart of God speaks directly to the human heart.[43]

Thus the confession can say that the substance (*substantia*) of the sacrament that God promises to us is Christ the Savior, which is what "some" call "the substance and matter of the sacrament."[44] This substance and matter (*materia*), however, are not present so "as to say that the bread itself is the body of Christ, except in a sacramental way; or that the body of Christ is hidden corporally under the bread, so that it ought to be worshipped under the form of the bread; or yet that whoever receives the sign, receives the things itself."[45] The confession naturally condemns the decree against Berengarius, asserting that "neither did godly antiquity believe, nor do we believe, that the body of Christ is to be eaten corporally and essentially with a bodily mouth."[46] As we have seen throughout the first two generations of Reformed theologians, "the body of Christ is in heaven at the right hand of the Father."[47]

Despite the ascension and session of Christ, we are still fed by him in the Supper, for when believers outwardly receive the bread and cup, then inwardly "by the work of Christ through the Holy Spirit they also receive the flesh and blood of the Lord, and are thereby nourished unto life eternal. For the flesh and blood of Christ is the true food and drink unto life eternal; and Christ himself, since he was given for us and is our Savior, is the principal thing in the Supper."[48] This is a "spiritual eating" (*spiritualis manducatio*), which is the confession's way to distinguish the merely corporal eating with the teeth from the direct nourishment of "the flesh and blood of Christ" (*caro et sanguis Christi*) that comes through the work of the Spirit.[49] This "spiritual eating" is precisely what the Fourth Gospel discusses in the Bread from Heaven discourse, and the Confession cites the passages from John 6 that we have seen discussed from Augustine onward, into the Reformed tradition, when upholding the mystical (nonmetabolic) true presence of Christ.[50]

The relationship between the signs and this mystical, spiritual nourishment by the flesh and blood of Christ—the connection between sign (*signum*) and reality (*res*)—is precisely outer and inner at the same time: "Bread is outwardly (*foris*) offered by the minister, and the words of the Lord are heard: 'Take, eat . . .' At the same time (*interim*) by the work of Christ through the Spirit they also inwardly (*intus*) receive the flesh and blood of the Lord."[51] The confession clearly displays the "symbolic parallelism" that Gerrish described.[52]

To sum these Swiss confessions, we see that all stand squarely in the Reformed (and Augustinian) tradition of the mystical true presence, in which believers already engrafted into the mystical body of Christ are fed immediately by Christ (through the Spirit) during the Supper.[53] The confessions also show development, both in the French and the German lineages, from only vaguely (1537 Instruction and Confession of Faith, 1537 Confession of Faith) or diversely (1536 First Helvetic Confession) connecting sign to reality, to clearly connecting sign and reality either instrumentally (1542/5 Geneva Confession) or by parallelism (1566 Second Helvetic Confession). These confessions are Zwingli-like, Calvinist, and Bullinger-like.

Continental Confessions

The French Confession (1559) was produced by the first National Synod held by French Protestants in Paris.[54] Usually seen as the work of Calvin, the Confession itself, which indeed represents Calvin's teachings, was a joint effort by Genevan theologians based on prior confessional material.[55]

Article XXXV (baptism) asserts that by baptism we are engrafted into Christ. Following this article, and with utter clarity, the article on the Supper (XXXVI) begins by asserting the Reformed position of the mystical true presence:

We confess that the Supper (which is the second sacrament) is a witness of the union which we have with Christ, inasmuch as once he not only died and rose, but also feeds and nourishes us truly with his flesh and blood, so that we may be one with him, and that our life may be in common. But even though he may be in heaven until he comes to judge the whole world, nevertheless we believe that by the secret and incompressible power of his Spirit he feeds and vivifies us with the substance of his body and of his blood.[56]

The confession goes on to say that God gives us "really and actually that which he figures there,"[57] and that "those who bring to the sacred table of Christ a pure faith, like a vessel, truly receive that which the signs witness to them: that the body and blood of Jesus Christ serve as food and drink for the soul no less than bread and wine do for the body."[58]

The Belgic Confession (1561) had as its principal author Guy de Brès, a Protestant reformer and martyr in the Netherlands who worked for toleration of the new evangelical faith in the Low Countries. The Belgic Confession, modeled on the French Confession, became the confessional standard in the Netherlands, linking the Dutch Reformed church to the Reformed tradition.[59]

The sacraments are given by God, in accommodation to our crudeness and weakness (*rudesse et infirmité*), in order to seal (*pour seller*) God's promises in us, pledge (*ester gages de*) divine grace, and nourish and sustain (*nourrir et soustenir*) our faith (Article XXXIII).[60] As such they "represent better to our external senses" that which God "does inwardly in our hearts" (*representer à nos sens exterieurs . . . ce qui'il fait intrérieurement en nos coeurs*).[61]

The section on the Supper (Article XXXV) runs almost twice as long as the Supper material in the French Confession and begins, curiously enough, by missing the usual Reformed mark for its start: rather than beginning with our engrafting into Christ (cf. the French Confession), the Belgic Confession begins by asserting that we are already born again and "engrafted into his family: his church," which seems to describe what was mystical (union with Christ) as something more social (familial).[62] The confession then compares at some length the physical, earthly life with the spiritual, heavenly life as a prelude to distinguishing the outer eating with the inner eating. "Just as truly" (*aussi veritablement*) as the elements are held by our hands and consumed through our mouths, "so truly (*aussi vraiement*) we receive into our souls for our spiritual life, the true body and true blood of Christ (*le vray corps et le vray sang de Christ*), our only Savior."[63] Christ "communicates himself to us" and so he cares for "our poor desolate souls by the eating of his flesh," and he "relieves and renews them by the drinking of his blood."[64] In Reformed fashion, the Bread from Heaven discourse in John 6 is one of the principal sources for the description of the outer/inner, earthly/heavenly, spiritual feeding on Christ's true body and blood; and, in similar Reformed fashion, all this happens through the incomprehensible work of the Spirit, who unites us with Christ who remains in heaven.

Following this material about the true (spiritual) nourishment from the true body and blood of Christ, the confession describes coming to the table in faith and the personal and social commitment that follows from such nourishment. The Christian social life, which lives out gratitude to God for the grace given, echoes the social aspect that began this Supper section with engrafting into the church family.[65]

As this section takes up the Heidelberg Catechism (1563), it would be worth noting again that these Reformed confessions usually were composed amid social struggles within European politics as well as amid religious struggles, for both went together. The Palatinate, where the Heidelberg Catechism was birthed, was a territory whose ruler was one of the seven electors of the Holy Roman Emperor. The Reformation began there in 1546 under Fredrick II, and continued briefly (1556–59) under Elector Ottheinrich (nephew of Fredrick II) whose reforming efforts were Lutheran. The Reformed direction was then taken up by Fredrick III, and a catechism was composed that reflected the dual reforming tradition of the area.[66]

Gerrish makes the important observation that the "Heidelberg Catechism (1563) shows a subtle variation from Calvin's Geneva Catechism at the very beginning of its presentation on the sacraments: It asks, not how does Christ communicate himself to us (cf. Geneva Cat., Q. 309)? but how do we obtain faith (Heidelberg Cat., Q. 65)?"[67] Gerrish describes the catechism as more didactic here. Thus the sacraments confirm faith (Q. 65); they are a means of understanding more clearly the gospel promises and they seal the gospel (Q. 66); they assure us about our salvation (Q. 67); and they orient us toward the cross (Q. 66–67). This does not indicate that the sacraments are merely memorialistic, but it does indicate that the catechism is "apparently shy about the notion of sacramental means,"[68] and so orients more toward Bullinger (or Zwingli) than Calvin.

The Supper questions themselves are thoroughly Reformed in their assertion of union with Christ and nourishment truly by his body and blood. The opening question (Q. 75) asks how the Supper reminds and assures of the cross and Christ's gift, and then replies "as surely . . . so surely" (*so gewiß . . . so gewiß*): as surely as the eyes see the elements, so surely the body and blood were offered on the cross; as surely as the elements are received in the hand and tasted by the mouth, so surely the soul is nourished unto life eternal by the "crucified body and poured-out blood."[69] The outer-inner parallelism familiar from Bullinger's Second Helvetic Confession appears here, although this could mean a merely

"Zwinglian" outer-is-seeing and inner-is-believing structure. So, is this *merely* memorialistic believing? The next question therefore addresses that possibility by elegantly saying, Yes, "it means to accept with a believing heart," but immediately adds the very Reformed assertion of the mystical true presence by saying,

> But it means more.

> Through the Holy Spirit, who lives both in Christ and in us,
> we are united more and more to Christ's blessed body.
>   And so, although he is in heaven and we are on earth,
>   we are flesh of his flesh and bone of his bone.
>   And we forever live and are governed by one Spirit,
>   as members of our body are by one soul.[70]

Question 77 then adds that in the institution narrative believers are promised to be nourished by Christ's body and blood "as surely as" (*so gewiß also*) they eat the broken bread and drink the cup, citing not only 1 Corinthians 11, but also 1 Corinthians 10, where Paul speaks of the unity of the body of Christ. Questions 78–80 then continue by addressing the issues of the transformation of the elements and the Roman Catholic Mass.[71]

British Reformed Confessions

On August 24, 1560, the Scottish parliament adopted the Scots Confession (1560), which a committee of six people, including John Knox, had composed in four days.[72] In what today seems like efficient committee work, probably due to the size of the committee and the influence of Knox, the committee produced a striking confession that Dowey calls "as craggy, irregular, powerful, and unforgettable as the hills of north Scotland."[73]

The chapter on the sacraments (XXI) says clearly, in full Reformed fashion, that just as through baptism we are "engrafted into Christ Jesus and in relation to the ongoing mystical union with Christ that is realized and deepened in the Supper,

> [t]hus we confess and believe without doubt that so in "the Supper rightly used, Jesus Christ is so joined with us that he becomes the very nourishment of our souls."[74] This happens not at all because of transubstantiation, but it is a "union and conjunction" that we have with the "body and blood of Christ Jesus" when in right use of the sacraments it is "wrought by the Holy Spirit."[75]

The confession then expresses the entire issue, and the Augustinian [nonmetabolic] tradition, of the mystical true presence concisely when it asserts that the faithful, in the right use of the Lord's Table, do so eat the body and drink the blood of the Lord Jesus that he remains in them and they in him; they are so made flesh of his flesh and bone of his bone that as the eternal Godhood has given to the flesh of Christ Jesus, which by nature was corruptible and mortal, life and immortality, so the eating and drinking of the flesh and blood of Christ Jesus does the like for us. We grant that this is neither given to us merely at the time nor by the power and virtue of the sacrament alone, but we affirm that the faithful, in the right use of the Lord's Table, have such union with Christ Jesus as the natural man cannot apprehend. Further we affirm that although the faithful, hindered by negligence and human weakness, do not profit as much as they ought in the actual moment of the Supper, yet afterwards it shall bring forth fruit, being living seed sown in good ground; for the Holy Spirit, who can never be separated from the right institution of the Lord Jesus, will not deprive the faithful of the fruit of that mystical action. Yet all this, we say again, comes of that true faith which apprehends Christ Jesus, who alone makes the sacrament effective in us. Therefore, if anyone slanders us by saying that we affirm or believe the sacraments to be symbols and nothing more, they are libelous and speak against the plain facts.[76]

Finally, the confession takes up Calvin's classic *via media* for sacramental signs; that the signs should not be so held together with the reality that they signify as to confuse the two; nor should they be so distinguished from their reality as to be separated from it. So, says the Confession, "we neither worship the elements, in place of that which they signify, nor yet do we despise them or undervalue them, but we use them with great reverence."[77] Overall, one cannot imagine the Scots Confession being any more Calvinist ("symbolic instrumentalism") in its theology of the Supper.

With roots reaching back to the Ten Articles of Henry VIII, the Articles of Religion of the Church of England, more commonly referred to as the Thirty-Nine Articles, helped form the basis of the Church of England.[78] As Gerrish notes about the Supper material, "Zwinglianism is plainly ruled out."[79] Article XXVIII says that "[t]he Body of Christ is given, taken, and eaten, in the Supper, only after an heavenly and spiritual manner."[80] Perhaps by way of an unspoken *via media*, neither here, nor in the article on the sacraments (XXV), nor in the article on baptism (XXVII), do the Articles discuss the relationship between the sign and that which is signified. The sacraments article does say, however, that the signs are "sure witnesses" (*certa testimonia*) and "effectual signs of grace" (*efficacia signa gratiae*) by which God "doth work invisibly in us" (*per quae invisibiliter ipse in nobis operator*). There may here be a nod toward Calvin (*per quae*), a reading that seems confirmed by the 1662 Anglican Catechism, which dates from 1549 but which had significant changes between then and 1662:[81] The definition of a sacrament is there given as "an outward and visible sign of an inward and spiritual grace given unto us, ordained by Christ himself, as a means whereby we receive the same, and a pledge to assure us thereof."[82]

The Long Parliament of 1643 gathered 121 Puritan ministers, 30 members of Parliament, and 6 Scottish Presbyterian advisors and gave them the task of reforming worship, discipline, and organization of the Church of England.[83] Within three months the English and Scottish Parliaments approved the Solemn League and Covenant, pledging to reform faith, polity, worship, and catechism. The Westminster Assembly finished the Westminster Confession in November 1646, and the catechisms were presented to Parliament in their final form in April 1648. That same year Parliament approved the Westminster Confession, and the Larger and Shorter Westminster Catechisms.[84]

Of the Westminster Confession, Gerrish notes that its

> teaching on the sacraments (1647) is not so plainly Calvinistic as the teaching of the Anglican Catechism; and the confession comes as close to symbolic parallelism as do the Thirty-Nine Articles. Since the aim of the Westminster divines was to produce a more strictly Calvinistic confession than the Thirty-Nine Articles, their lack of clarity in the teaching of a sacrament is surprising.[85]

To read the article on the Lord's Supper, in fact, is to read something that truly appears Bullinger-like, which (pace Gerrish) seems not so surprising to me when we consider that the sovereignty of God above all earthly entities, though by no means disconnected to them, was a generally shared outlook between Zwingli (whose God was the most predestinarian of all the early Protestant Reformers) and the Westminster divines. The desire to maintain divine sovereignty, even when it concerns the sacramental elements that God appointed, was a concern for Bullinger and seems to show here, in the Confession, which indeed reflects Bullinger's symbolic parallelism:

> Worthy receivers, outwardly partaking of the visible elements in this sacrament, do then also inwardly by faith, really and indeed, yet not carnally and corporally, but spiritually, receive and feed upon Christ crucified, and all the benefits of his death: the body and blood of Christ being then not corporally or carnally in, with, or under the bread and wine; yet as really, but spiritually, present to the faith of believers in that ordinance, as the elements themselves are to their outward senses.[86]

Bullinger could not have expressed his own view any more clearly than that. The Larger Catechism simply echoes this when it takes up sacramental means and says that Christ self-communicates to his church using "all his ordinances, especially the Word, sacraments, and prayer."[87] A sacrament is thus "an holy ordinance instituted by Christ in his church, to signify, seal and exhibit unto those that are within the covenant of grace, the benefits of his mediation."[88] For those already engrafted into Christ himself (the elect), the sacrament reminds them of that reality in which they already exist, so that those "that worthily communicate, feed upon his body and blood to their spiritual nourishment and growth in grace; have their union and communion with him confirmed; testify and renew their thankfulness and engagement to God, and their mutual love and fellowship with each other, as members of the same mystical body."[89] The confession shows a parallelism, almost Second Helvetic–like, when it next describes the mode of this communication:

> As the body and the blood of Christ are not corporally or carnally present in, with or under the bread and wine in the Lord's Supper; and yet are spiritually present to the faith of the receiver, no less truly and really than the elements themselves are to their outward senses; so they that communicate in the sacrament of the Lord's Supper, do therein feed upon the body and blood of Christ, not after a corporal or carnal, but in a spiritual manner; yet truly and really, while by faith they receive and apply unto themselves Christ crucified, and all the benefits of his death.[90]

FRIEDRICH SCHLEIERMACHER

In 1768 the person who was to become the great Reformed theologian and eminent churchman, Friedrich Schleiermacher, was born to an army chaplain (Gottleib) and his wife (Katharina-Maria).[91] Because of his father's own religious sensibilities, Schleiermacher was raised in a pietist household and was sent to study at Moravian schools and seminary. His unique blend of Reformed theological formation, born-again religious heart, and Enlightenment mind brought him to challenge and then rethink old teachings for a new context. He went on to study at the University of Halle and became a private tutor to a noble family, an assistant pastor, and then a chaplain at the still-existing Charité Hospital in Berlin (1796).

While in Berlin Schleiermacher became friends with Friedrich Schlegel, with whom he began, and without whom he finished, the translation of Plato into German. His best known work during this early period was *On Religion: Speeches to Its Cultured Despisers* (1799), intended not to conform Christianity to humanism, but quite the opposite: Because religion was at the heart of being human, and organized religion fundamentally concerned the religious association that people had, since the human person was fundamentally social, to be humanist without being religious was to have a truncated humanism. Schleiermacher taught briefly at the University of Halle (1806–8) and then at the new University of Berlin until his death in 1834. There he wrote and revised his great work *Christian Faith* (*Der christliche Glaube*), while reading and writing widely in theology, as well as preaching and actively helping lead the German church under Fredrick III.[92]

To understand Schleiermacher's teachings on the Supper, a brief summary of his theology and his teaching on baptism needs to come first.[93] Schleiermacher asserted that all people have, upon reflection, a "feeling of absolute dependence," a term that meant not some concrete emotion—"I feel this way or that way today"—but rather an intuition, or sense, or awareness, beneath any and every moment of selfhood, that self and world were both intimately related and absolutely dependent. This "feeling of absolute dependence" was the awareness of being immediately related to God, and this original revelation lies behind all religions. In Christianity it was called forth, named, and then given formation by the decisive revelation of God in Jesus Christ, our Redeemer: "If it be the essence of redemption that the God-consciousness already present in human nature, though feeble and repressed, becomes stimulated and made dominant by the entrance of the living influence of Christ, the individual on whom this influence is exercised attains a religious personality not his before."[94]

Early in his life Schleiermacher had rejected the classical doctrine of the two natures of Christ, and he came to argue that Christ had perfect "God-consciousness" that he both "expressed" through his words and deeds and "impressed" onto others, thus giving their religious life the shape of the Redeemer's. Christ's very God-consciousness therefore lives on in the church, and just as it occurred decisively in the physical existence of the Redeemer, so also it lives on in the physical existence of his believers who are the church:

> On the one hand, as the organism of Christ, which is what Scripture means by calling it [the Christian Church] His body, it is related to Christ as the outward to the inward, so that in its essential activities it must also be a reflection of the activities of Christ. And since the effects produced by it are simply the gradual realization of redemption in the world, its activities must likewise be a continuation of the activities of Christ Himself.[95]

Here we see precisely a blend of born-again Christian, the Scripture scholar from the University of Berlin whose favorite Gospel was that of John, and the Enlightenment thinker. The church truly is the body of Christ, into which we are engrafted when we are born again in the Redeemer, whose influence is upon us and who lives in us. So it was, for instance, that Schleiermacher wrote *The Christian Faith*, which is a reflection upon the ongoing event of faith from within, and addressed to, the Christian community.

On Schleiermacher's view the preaching of the Word, and its acknowl-edgment by the hearer, precede entrance to this Christian community,[96] so that faith is a precondition to baptism,[97] and "[b]aptism is received wrongly if it be received without faith, and it is wrongly given so."[98] Ide-ally conversion (changed form of life) and justification (changed relation-ship to God), which are aspects of "regeneration,"[99] should coincide and be present at baptism, which is "the channel of divine justifying activ-ity."[100] But this would be the case only where individuals were baptized whose conversion was mature in its faith. In actual practice, however, this is hardly the case, for there are "baptized persons who are not yet regener-ate but in the most active way are being commended to divine grace for regeneration by the prayers of the Church."[101] Likewise, infant baptism, which is an "ecclesiastical custom," really is a subset of this issue, so that Schleiermacher can argue that "infant baptism is the same as any other baptism which has erroneously been imparted prior to the full faith of the person baptized and yet is valid; only its proper efficacy is suspended until the person baptized has really become a believer."[102]

In *Christian Faith* Schleiermacher begins his discussion of the Supper at precisely this point, and he starts the discussion by observing that

> [t]o keep touch with the previous Doctrine [i.e., baptism], the subject of the present one would be utterly devoid of content if the salvation beginning with rightly administered baptism were so conferred that automatically it sustained itself unimpaired and adequately secured its own growth. The analogy of all life, however, argues the contrary; and it lies in the indissoluble bond between entrance rite into the living fellow-ship of Christ [*Lebensgemeinschaft Christi*] and entrance into the fellow-ship of believers that each of these two must be supported by the other. But just for this reason the mode in which the church coexists in the world, as well as the hampering influence of the world on the church, demands that this fellowship should be nourished and strengthened; and it is the satisfaction of this need that believers seek in the sacrament of the altar.[103]

Because the church is the living body of Christ in the world, and is comprised of individual members who continue their journey of regen-eration into the fullness of Christ, there is a single process, which can be viewed from either or both of two sides, the individual and the commu-nal: "the two kinds of fellowship unite—that of believers with each other and that of each soul with Christ; and hence it is clear that everything that takes place here must have effects on both." The area where these two spheres meet is "public worship," and here is where "the Lord's Sup-per too belongs; for Christ instituted it as a communal act, which, while it is a presenting of himself (*eine Vergegenwärtigung seiner*), is certainly a strengthening of both kinds of fellowship."[104] One might think of the

analogy of a wagon wheel in which all the spokes (believers) are fully connected to the hub (Christ), yet work together to form one entity (church
as the body of Christ). The closer the spokes become to each other, the
closer they are to the hub; and the closer they are to the hub, the closer
they are to each other. The mutual deepening of the God-consciousness
that is Christ's, individually and corporately, happens in the Supper in a
way unique to the Supper because

> [i]t is simply the whole redeeming love of Christ to which we are pointed
> there; and as the distributing minister is nothing more than the organ
> of Christ's institution, the receivers uniformly find themselves simply
> in a state of completely open receptivity for Christ's influence. With-
> out the special interposition of any individual, therefore, every effect
> flows directly and undividedly from the Word of institution in which
> the redeeming and fellowship-transforming love of Christ is not only
> represented but made newly active, and in trustful obedience to which
> the sacramental action is ever anew performed. It is in this undivided
> and exclusive immediacy and in the resulting freedom of its effects from
> the dependence on changing personal moods and circumstances, that
> the Supper differs from all other elements of public worship.[105]

To put this simply, the living ("organism") body of Christ, and the lives
of the believers that comprise it, are sustained by the presence of Christ,
through the Supper. This is not an issue of materialism and the "eating
of His flesh and drinking of His blood," but rather (citing John 6:52, 56),
this concerns "in how profound a sense He Himself must become our
being and well-being" (*er selbst uns warden und gedeihen muß*).[106] It hardly
needs saying how very Reformed a eucharistic theology Schleiermacher
expresses, even if it has found reexpression in a new time and place. Actually engrafted into the body of Christ, believers are deepened and sustained by the nourishment of Christ's true presence.

When Schleiermacher then turns in the next section to the relationship
between "the bread and wine and the body and blood of Christ in the
Lord's Supper," he asserts that "the Evangelical [Protestant] Church" finds
its home in the wide and historically speaking diverse middle ground that
"takes up an attitude of definite opposition only, on the one hand, to those
who regard this connexion as independent of the act of participation, and,
on the other hand, to those who, regardless of this connexion, would not
admit any conjunction between participation in the bread and wine and
spiritual participation in the flesh and blood of Christ."[107]

To the former group, Schleiermacher assigns the Roman Catholic
Church, not because of its doctrine of transubstantiation as such, but
because of the underlying assertion that the metaphysics of transubstantiation tries to explain: that there is a change in the elements themselves
that "persists even apart from the act of reception, or that even what is not

partaken of in the Supper undergoes the same change as the rest of the elements."[108] So the main ground for rejecting this perspective, apart from its
exegetical unsoundness (says Schleiermacher the New Testament scholar
in a remark seemingly given because it is so obvious),[109] is that "it seeks by
its so conceived union of the elements with the body and blood of Christ
to attain quite different ends, and to attach magical spiritual effects to an
effect that is bodily."[110]

To the latter group, Schleiermacher assigns the name of "Sacramentar-
ians," a group that Schleiermacher makes clear is not what Luther meant
by the word but, rather, those who flat-out reject the sacrament. The term
refers to those who "assert that partaking of the bread and wine indicated
by the phrase 'body and blood' is only a shadowy emblem (*ein Schatten-
bild*) of that spiritual participation in the body and blood of Christ that is in
no sense bound up with any such sacramental action, and that as soon as
we have the assurance of this spiritual reality, the merely figurative action
is better given up."[111]

In between these two groups, says Schleiermacher, lie the historical positions represented by the teachings of Luther, Zwingli, and Calvin, whose positions Schleiermacher accurately describes, if however
briefly.[112] Schleiermacher judges each of these positions to have its own
inadequacy, and he hopes for "yet another view to emerge which will not
make shipwreck on any of these rocks."[113]

Given the then-present impossibility of common agreement on the
Supper within the Evangelical church, says Schleiermacher, we ought
to state only two basic ideas: that participation in the body and blood of
Christ confirms Christians both in their union with each other and thus
also in their union in Christ, since these two must go together;[114] and, second, that "unworthy participation in the Lord's Supper conduces to judgment for the partaker." In a paragraph Schleiermacher references some
Reformed confessions about unworthy participation and judgment on
such action, and he then immediately says that "[i]t is not easy to explain
to oneself clearly how this paragraph is to be applied."[115] Schleiermacher
ventures an historical guess that when the Supper was instituted by the
church as a common action, it was supposed that some people came to the
table without proper introspection, and so "[i]n its origin such participation is unworthy, for it has no connexion with the purpose of its institution."[116] On the other hand, if "the judgment described as a consequence
of this unworthiness be taken as meaning consignment to eternal damnation, then it seems impossible to establish any connexion between the two
things."[117] In sum, says Schleiermacher, "fit and worthy participation"
promotes the "living fellowship with Christ," while unworthy participation falls short of what can happen in the Supper, "and thereby is always
enhancing the power of hindrances."[118]

JOHN WILLIAMSON NEVIN AND CHARLES HODGE

After reading the key sixteenth-century Reformed theologians, and after examining the more central Reformed confessions, to read the eucharistic writings of John Williamson Nevin (1803–86) is to be astounded at the accuracy, completeness, and vision of his enterprise.[119] Since almost 175 years have passed, and eucharistic scholarship and the study of church history and historical theology have changed and maybe advanced, we do see some issues more clearly. Few would want to divide historical groups into Reformed and Puritan, or make sweeping assertions about the whole history of (authentic) Christianity being centered in an incarnational church. The "Biblical Argument" stands hopelessly out of date and holds historical interest only, although Nevin's extended discussion of John 6:51–58 stands out, given what we have seen of the trajectory of the mystical true (nonmetabolic) presence from Augustine through the Reformed theologians of the sixteenth century.[120] Reading the Reformation material, I hardly recognize Luther, so I assume Lutherans would feel much the same, even more so. Not only would the characterization of Luther's teaching on Christ's presence not be accurately given as "consubstantiation," but the contrast of bodily incarnation (Luther) versus sacrificial death (Zwingli) would hardly pass the *theologia crucis* test. Finally, as we have already seen, primarily thanks to the work of Davis, Calvin's eucharistic theology cannot be read as a single mature entity, springing from the 1559 *Institutes* like Athena from the head of Zeus. Yet, as we also have seen, perhaps Nevin can be given slack here, since in some areas, such as asserting that the young Calvin did not consider the sacraments to be means of grace, more of the mature Calvin can be found in the young Calvin than Davis allows.

Beyond these areas and maybe some others, such as his own constructive ideas about presence, Nevin seems quite on target, especially given his change in perspective on Zwingli that the work of Ebrard brought about.[121] Nevin's reading of Bucer, Calvin, and Bullinger is good; as well as his pointing out the importance of the theologically often-overlooked 1537 confession on the Supper; and then his being spot-on for the other major Reformed confessions. Commenting on Nevin's *The Mystical Presence*, Gerrish rightly comments, "One wonders, indeed, what there is to rival it in English even at the present day."[122]

Nevin was raised in a "Scotch-Irish" Presbyterian home, where his parents "were both conscientious and exemplary professors of religion," so that he was religiously formed "according to the Presbyterian faith as it then stood."[123] When he went away to school, however, at Union College in upstate New York, Nevin had his "very first contact with the genius of New-England Puritanism, in its contradiction to the old *Reformed* faith" in which he had been raised. At the college "a 'revival of religion,' as it was called, made its appearance" and Nevin underwent a revival experience that he later found not to his liking, with its standard techniques and its coaching unto new spiritual birth:

> Our college awakening was no part of the proper college order as such; Dr. Nott had nothing to do with it; it formed a sort of temporary outside episode, conducted by our mathematics professor Rev. Dr. Macauley (on whose name a sad cloud fell afterwards), and certain "pious students," previously Christianized, *secundum artem*, who now all at once, were found competent to assist him in bringing souls to new birth. Miserable obstetricians the whole of them, as I now only too well remember! For I, along with others, came into their hands in anxious meetings, and underwent the torture of their mechanical counsel and talk. One after another, however, the anxious obtained "hope;" with each new case, as it were, stimulating another; and finally, among the last, I struggled into something of the sort myself, a feeble trembling sense of comfort—my spiritual advisers, then, had no difficulty in accepting as all that was required. In this way I was converted and brought into the Church—as if I had been altogether out of it before—about the close of the seventeenth year of age.[124]

In contrast, Nevin longed for a church that would be the seat of spiritual nurture and health, a place where the anxieties of the heart would not be increased by all-too-frequent introspection but by the presence of grace itself, embodied in the life of the church. This he found, or perhaps it found him, through the writings of August Neander, Schleiermacher's colleague at the University of Berlin: "How much I owe him in the way of excitement, impulse, suggestion, knowledge, both history and religious, reaching onward into all my later life, is more than I can pretend to explain; or it is in truth more than I have power to understand."[125] It was, so to speak, as though Nevin indeed had a true born-again experience that embraced his whole being and led him to a new vision of the church that left behind his "Puritanical Presbyterianism." Nevin says of Neander's views on history that they "were for me an actual awakening of the soul, which went far beyond any direct and outward instruction involved in it, and the force of which was by no means confined to the theological sphere with which it was immediately concerned, but made itself profoundly felt also in the end on my whole theological and religious life."[126]

Of this new mother church that birthed him and nourished him, and of its sacrament of the Lord's Supper, Nevin would say in *The Mystical Presence* that "Christianity is grounded in the living union of the believer with the person of Christ; and this great fact is emphatically concentrated in the mystery of the Lord's Supper; which has always been clothed on this very account, to the consciousness of the Church, with a character of sanctity and solemnity surpassing that of any other Christian institution." For this reason, Nevin tells us, the sixteenth-century sacramental controversy was not mere theological jousting but rather "belonged to the innermost sanctuary of theology and was intertwined particularly with all the arteries of the Christian life. This was *felt* by the spiritual heroes of the Reformation." Sadly, says Nevin, both the Lutheran and Reformed churches "have receded, to no inconsiderable extent, from the ground on which they stood in the sixteenth century."[127]

Calvin was the central figure for Nevin, who gives long and numerous Calvin citations. Nevin shows quite carefully that for Calvin, as we have seen, believers dwell in mystical union with Christ, who, through the Supper, nourishes them and thus deepens them in their well-being in him.[128] According to Nevin, Calvin has written extensively on the Lord's Supper and

> he tells us that Christ's body is indeed locally in heaven only and in no sense included in the elements; that he can be apprehended by faith only and not at all by the hands or lips; that nothing is to be imagined like a transfusion or intromission of the particles of his body, materially considered, into our persons, And yet that our communion with him notwithstanding, by the power of the Holy Ghost, involves a real participation—not in his doctrine merely—not in his promises merely—not in the sensible manifestations of his love merely—not in his righteousness and merit merely—not in the gifts and endowments of his Spirit merely; but in his own true substantial life itself; and this not as comprehended in his divine nature merely, but most immediately and peculiarly as embodied in his humanity itself for us men and our salvation. . . . The flesh of Christ, then, or his humanity, forms the medium and the *only* medium by which it is possible for us to be inserted into his life.[129]

This accurately describes the mature Calvin and, mutatis mutandis, describes the Reformed confessions that this chapter has already discussed. However much that might be, Nevin's description of Reformed eucharistic theology, and the view of church that it entailed, did not sit well with Charles Hodge (1797–1878), who opens his review of Nevin's *Mystical Presence* with the dismissive remark, "We have had Dr. Nevin's work on the 'Mystical Presence' on our table since its publication, some two years ago, but have never really read it, until within a fortnight. We do not suppose other people are quite as bad, in this respect, as ourselves. Our experience, however, has been that it requires the stimulus of a special necessity to carry us through such a book."[130]

As to the true Reformed position on the Supper, asserts Hodge, "It is confessedly a very difficult matter to obtain clear views," a difficulty that "arises from various sources." The Supper itself is a mystery; the union of believers with Christ is a mystery; there exists a diversity of Reformed views on what is received when we receive the body and blood of Christ; "all the Reformed confessions were framed for the express purpose of compromise"; it is hard to tell where to look authoritatively—private writings or public confessions.[131] Of particular difficulty is the split that occurs within Reformed theology:

> But as Christ speaks of eating his flesh and drinking his blood, and we are said to have communion in them, the question is in what way this is to be understood? All the Reformed answered, that by receiving the body and blood of Christ, is meant receiving their virtue or efficacy. Some of them said it was their virtue as broken and shed, i.e., their sacrificial virtue; others said, it was a mysterious, supernatural efficacy flowing from the glorified body of Christ in heaven; and that this last idea, therefore, is to be taken into the account, in determining the nature of the union between Christ and his people.[132]

Hodge goes on to ask, "[W]hich of these two views above stated is entitled to be regarded as the real doctrine of the Reformed church?" Would it be that some received the "sacrificial efficacy" that his body and blood brought us? Or would it be that "there was a mysterious virtue in the body of Christ due to its union with the divine nature, which virtue was by the Holy Spirit conveyed to the believer"? While Hodge says that the "fairest answer" is "neither to the exclusion of the other," yet he straightforwardly asserts "the higher authority is certainly due to the doctrine of the sacrificial efficacy first mentioned." Not only does it have "high symbolical authority in its favour," but "of more real consequence, the sacrificial view, is the only one that harmonizes with the other doctrines of the church." The former view, says Hodge, is an "incongruity" and not "a genuine portion of the faith," an assessment that becomes confirmed when Reformed thinkers such as Hodge's hero in systematics, François Turretin, "expressly discard it."[133] In the process, Hodge relegates Calvin's view to that of merely a "private authority" that is "outweighed" by the key Reformed confessions.[134]

Of such analysis Nevin will have none, accusing Hodge (rightly, it seems to me) of historical eisegesis; and with some pointed humor Nevin says of Hodge that "[h]e proposes simply to take up the whole subject in an ex-cathedra general way, lumping the authorities to suit his own mind, and ruling their testimony thus to such results as the investigation in his judgment is felt to require."[135] Nevin replies that Hodge's binary is false because there "is no inward contradiction between the two views of the Christian salvation which are here taken to stand in such relation. The life of Christ is the true and real basis of his sacrifice, and so the natural and necessary medium of communion with it for the remission of sins." Both elements—as Hodge himself has acknowledged—not only occur together, but the "two sides in question entered organically into the contents of the old doctrine." Nevin then goes on to reply to Hodge with an historical analysis, including a long section on Calvin, which he then follows by taking the argument to Hodge's supposed home field, the Reformed confessions themselves.[136]

As Gerrish points out, Hodge's critique of Nevin's *Mystical Presence* continues with an attack that is "much more damaging" and, in its focus on the Word in Calvin's teaching, "does expose a weakness in Nevin's case."[137] It should be added, however, that Hodge's criticism of Nevin is a two-edge sword that also exposes a weakness in Hodge's case. As a further criticism of Nevin, Hodge points out that "[a]ccording to the Reformed church, Christ is present in the sacraments in no other sense than he is present in the word."[138] Gerrish gives ample examples showing that "Calvin uses 'eucharistic' language of a real presence even when speaking of the oral proclamation of the gospel."[139] As Gerrish says elsewhere of Calvin, "[I]f the sacraments confer no more than the Word, it is equally clear to Calvin that they confer no less. The sacraments have the *same* function as the Word of God: to offer and present to us Jesus Christ. In other words, the sacraments, like preaching, are the vehicle of Christ's self-communication, of the real presence."[140]

The fascinating lesson to learn is that Calvin can use the same language for the work of the Word that he can use about the Supper, that it engrafts us into the very body of Christ, and yet Hodge fails to notice (or at least mention) the mystical engrafting that goes with the Word. But Nevin fares no better, because, as Hodge makes clear, he fails to notice (or at least mention) that what happens through the Supper also happens through the Word. One can only suspect that by the mid-nineteenth century in America, preaching had so commonly devolved from its "eucharistic" ministry that neither Nevin or Hodge could see what, according to Calvin, preaching was really supposed to be, a devolution still prevalent in early-twenty-first-century America.[141]

TWO TWENTIETH-CENTURY VOICES:
KARL BARTH AND DONALD M. BAILLIE

Finally, this chapter turns to two Reformed theologians who wrote a century after Schleiermacher, Nevin, and Hodge: the Swiss Reformed theologian Karl Barth (1886–1968) and his Scottish contemporary Donald M. Baillie (1887–1954).

By contrast to Nevin's work on the church and the Supper, Karl Barth's massive *Church Dogmatics* at first glance seems to say very little about the Lord's Supper or the sacraments in general. In one section of only fourteen pages, the first volume explicitly addresses preaching and sacrament as the twofold form of proclamation by the church;[142] and the final volume deals entirely with baptism.[143] Yet, in a broad way, all of the *Church Dogmatics* bears upon the sacraments, because "[d]ogmatics is the self-examination of the Christian Church in respect of the content of its distinctive talk about God";[144] and such talk about God "seeks to be proclamation to the extent that in the form of preaching and sacrament it is directed to man [sic] with the claim and expectation that in accordance with its commission it has to speak to him [sic] the Word of God to be heard in faith."[145] So sacrament, as a feature or form of proclamation, connects to dogmatics, which reflects on the church's proclamation.

What then is a sacrament, according to Barth?

For the Reformers and Roman Catholics alike, grace lies "at the heart of the Church's life." Barth makes clear that for the Reformers, the grace that comes through proclamation "must mean repetition of the divine promise" that calls us to obedience found only in faith. Grace is the strictly personal summons from God whose human correlate is faith—an asymmetrical personal relationship, established by God, between the God who speaks and the human person who hears.[146] By contrast Roman Catholic dogmatics also

> describe[s] the event at the heart of the Church's life as grace. But it understands by grace, not the connexion between the Word and faith, but connexion between a divine being as cause and a divine-creaturely being as effect. It sees the presence of Jesus Christ in his Church, the mystical unity of the Head with the whole body, in the fact that under certain conditions there flows forth from Jesus Christ a steady and unbroken stream or influence of divine-human being on his people.[147]

But, says Barth, "proclamation" cannot be the appropriate term for such a sacramental event, because grace "here neither is (and remains) God's free and personal Word nor is (and remains) hearing faith." Barth cautions against calling Roman Catholic sacramental teaching "magic," which it is not; but, says Barth, such a view does understand the grace that lies at the heart of the church to be "a physical, not a historical, event."[148]

Barth goes on to contrast the Roman Catholic view of grace as fundamentally a sacramental event (and thus a physical rather than historical event), with the Reformers, who

> did not see themselves in a position to construe the grace of Jesus Christ in this way. They thought it should be understood, not as cause and effect, but as Word and faith. For this reason, they regarded the representative event at the centre of the Church's life as proclamation, as an act concerned with speaking and hearing, indicative of the fact that

what is at issue in the thing proclaimed too is not a material connexion but a personal encounter. In this light they had to regulate the mutual relations of preaching and sacrament in a very definite way.[149]

Proclamation "in the form of symbolic action" (sacrament) remained "essential to them," based as it is upon the proclamation of the promise "which has been laid once and for all," because it is the visible aspect of proclamation testifying to the surety of the divine promise. But, says Barth,

> [t]he former must exist for the sake of the latter, and therefore the sacrament for the sake of preaching alone, not *vice versa*. Hence not the sacrament alone nor preaching alone, nor yet, to speak meticulously, preaching and the sacrament in double track, but preaching with the sacrament, with the visible act that confirms human speech as God's act, is the constitutive element, the perspicuous centre of the Church's life.[150]

So, for Barth, the Word is primary and the sacrament secondary: Though they are to go together—"the Word is the audible sacrament and the sacrament is the visible Word"—yet the Word "stands alone, the sacrament cannot stand alone."[151] The sacrament is thus a means of grace, but only insofar as it stands as a mutual feature of proclamation along with preaching and, strictly speaking, stands subordinate to preaching. As such, a sacrament is that feature of proclamation that visibly attests to the surety of the one means of grace, Jesus Christ. This seems Zwinglian, which finds direct confirmation in Barth's view on baptism.

Late in life Barth became especially clear that baptism was not a means of grace as historically understood in the Reformed tradition. Baptism witnesses to Jesus Christ as our only means of grace; also, as our response to such a witness, baptism is the means by which we confess our transformation and pledge our life of obedience in faith. Barth's baptismal position thus, on his own admission, was more Baptist than Reformed, and was influenced strongly by the (much overlooked, then and now) exegetical study on baptism done by his son, Markus Barth.[152]

In similar fashion for Barth, though only briefly discussed, the Supper is the visible sign set apart by God to mark God's promise of grace. Commenting about the Supper, Barth cites Calvin that the tree of life in paradise, and the rainbow given to Noah, were merely a tree and a rainbow until God "engraved" his promise into them, whereupon they became signs of God's promise and therefore sacraments to Adam and to Noah, respectively.[153] On this reading, Barth's eucharistic theology is also Zwinglian, since his position exemplifies symbolic memorialism, embodying the view (as we saw above) that the sacrament both attests to Jesus Christ as our means of grace and pledges our obedience in faith.[154]

By contrast, the eucharistic theology of Donald Baillie seems, in its own reinterpretive way, to be Calvin-like.[155] In his typically artful, irenic, and clean style—such a contrast to that of Barth!—Baillie begins in a series of lectures by taking up "the sacramental universe," by which he means that not just under the dispensation to the people of Israel, nor only to those of "ethnic religions," but within nature itself, there are features that are sacramental. Since God is nature's creator, God "can make natural elements speak sacramentally to us; not in the sense of a 'natural theology' that can *prove* the purpose of God from a mere contemplation of nature, but in the sense that God by his Word can use, and therefore we by our faith can use, natural objects and some (like the rainbow) more naturally than others, as sacramental expressions of his mercy and faithfulness."[156] Baillie also approvingly cites Calvin's passage from the *Institutes* (4.14.18) about the tree of life and the rainbow, but he does so to broaden our thinking about sacraments. "Consider the lilies," Baillie reminds us, in a passage that not only shows the sacramental universe displayed in a Jesus saying, but which, by its repetition, actually can function at the moment to reveal the sacramental universe to the hearers themselves.

This moment that rises above the ordinary, above the tree or the rainbow or the flower, is what we should consider to be "spiritual," a word, argues Baillie, that in the New Testament means that which becomes "personal," that which rises above the "sub-personal" existence that merely dwells as a creature among creatures.[157] To be thus spiritual is to be personally with others in the world—a chair, for instance, is not "with" a table but rather is "alongside" a table—as God also is with us in the world. Thus divine "omnipresence does not mean that He occupies every part of space, but indicates rather a spiritual or we might say personal, relationship to the whole of His creation."[158] God is personally in the world by way of grace that brings forth faith in us, so that, in turn, our God-given faith becomes the medium by which we receive God, and we properly say that "sacraments *operate through* human faith."[159]

From this opening lecture on sacraments, grace, and faith, present in a sacramental universe wherein God personally dwells, Baillie turns to "The Sacraments and Sacred History" (Lecture II). He cautions against "treating the idea of a divine promise in too literal or mechanical a way," so that it functions as "a legal document, an I.O.U." Rather, the "promises of God are Yea and Amen in Christ Jesus," so that when it comes to dominical institution of the sacraments, the real point is that they come from "the *whole* episode of what God did in Christ."[160] Since that "episode" comes to us from the apostles in the Scriptures, "when the story is told, with the witness of the Church, the Holy Spirit does His work, takes of the things of Christ and gives them to us. Christ is present with us, not incarnate in the Church, but through the Holy Spirit working in the Church by Word and Sacrament." In this way only can we think of the church and its sacraments "as an extension of the incarnation," an extension that both travels back to its origins and forward to its consummation at the end time.[161]

Baillie devotes the next lecture to baptism (Lecture III); following that he turns to the "Real Presence" (Lecture IV). There Baillie begins with a section entitled "The Dramatic Symbolism of the Lord's Supper" (93–96). He notes that of course the sacraments are signs, although "[t]his is not to say that the sacraments are *merely* signs or symbols. They are more. But if there were not signs, they could not be more. It is through being signs, through their symbolism, that they come to be more."[162] Baillie then approvingly describes the way that some (Anglican and Benedictine) theologians consider the Supper as "*dramatic* symbolism" that "consists of a complex pattern of elements, words and actions, a pattern which has a symbolical meaning." He notes a Roman Catholic scholar who says that "the Mass, considered as a work of ritual art, is a pure masterpiece of tranquil beauty."[163] Baillie even quotes Barth as saying that "[t]he mass in its conception, content and construction is a religious masterpiece. It is the highwater mark in the development of the history of religion and admits no rival." But Baillie then gives Barth's next comment, that "[r]eligion with its masterpiece is one thing. Christian faith is another."[164] Baillie's point is that "every sacrament must use" dramatic symbolism, but "we have to ask about the sacrament of the Lord's Supper: what are the realities that it ought to symbolize if it is to be true to the Gospel of Christ? As a sacrament it uses 'sensible signs.' Signs of what? What are the things signified?"[165]

In the following section ("The Real Presence"), Baillie begins by noting "that even apart from the sacrament we are bound to distinguish several degrees or modes of the divine presence." Baillie returns first to what he discussed in "The Sacramental Universe," that God is omnipresent, which means that God is everywhere personally present with every entity, "a spiritual personal relationship which we have to symbolise by spatial metaphors." This personal "with-ness" that describes God's relationship to all creation has a particular "further stage" relevant to the human person whom God can address, and who can respond through faith, "so that God is specially present to the faith of the believer or, better still, to the faith of believers in worship." Baillie goes on to say that "faith is the channel by which God's most intimate presence comes to men [*sic*] in this earthly life."[166] Through the Supper, says Baillie, we are drawn "away from ourselves to that great divine reality which is even nearer and more truly real than the things we can see with our eyes and touch with our hands. The Lord's Supper is indeed the sacrament of the Real Presence."[167]

At the same time, says Baillie, we must realize that "[w]hile the Lord's Supper is indeed the sacrament of the Real Presence," such a presence "is not of the same mode as it was with His disciples in the days of His flesh, nor of the same mode as it will be when we come to see 'face to face.'"[168] It is in this sense that the Supper not only, says Baillie, concerns the divine presence now through the sacrament, but also looks back as "*a memorial feast*" and looks forward to the final consummation. In the sacrament, "we have the presence, the memory and the hope all in one."[169]

What Baillie has done, it seems to me, is attempt a Calvin-like eucharistic theology, in a new time and place, that takes seriously the issue that Barth raised about grace being the personal, God-given relationship of Word evoking faith, while also crediting the intimacy of immediate divine presence that comes with mystical union.[170] The gracious God who self-communicates as the "Yea and Amen in Jesus Christ" literally is with all entities always and everywhere ("omnipresence"), but especially with the human person through faith. Signs from the "sacramental universe" (bread and wine) are taken by Jesus and become part of "the *whole* episode of what God did in Christ." As "dramatic symbols" within the sacrament of the Supper, they bear us away from ourselves to the divine presence, self-revealed in Jesus Christ, who is "nearer and more truly real" than the things at hand, so that we receive the real presence.

6

RETROSPECT AND PROSPECT

While history never has the final word in Christian theology, it does have the first word, which is the point to returning to Scripture: however we most adequately construct our Christian worlds here and now, in the sight of God and thus according to the deepest conversation of our heart (2 Cor. 4:2),[1] we must theologically come to be in a way appropriate to the apostolic witness to Jesus, who was encountered as God's decisive revelation. There is no way from here to there except by way of history.[2] The first section of this chapter summarizes the historical theological material so far, in order to situate the Reformed tradition in the course of the eucharistic history that began with Jesus. The chapter then goes on to suggest briefly and constructively what the catholic and apostolic continuity of the Supper looks like when it begins with Jesus and, finally, what the "true presence" looks like when beginning with Jesus.

HISTORICAL SUMMARY:
FROM THE TABLE-SHARING OF JESUS

The sacrament of the Lord's Supper began with the table-sharing of Jesus, itself a variation of the fundamental meal-sharing tradition present in the Mediterranean basin at the time of Jesus. Like traditional Greco-Roman table-sharing, the table-sharing of Jesus aimed at building up the communal good and those within it. In a practice not unknown at the time, Jesus' table-sharing crossed boundaries: Jesus' table-sharing specifically practiced open commensality. Divides that stood between gender, class, and ethnic groups were transcended in what the community recalled as being a joyous event at which God's Wisdom (*Sophia*) was incarnate with the experience of God's reign: "'Behold, a glutton and a drunkard, a crony of tax collectors and sinners.' But *Sophia* is justified by her deeds" (Matt. 11:19, my trans.). The meal sharing of Jesus was, in other words, epiphanic of the divine presence. I will want to return here in a moment, once the historical outline is sketched out.

In oral cultures, over time and in community, traditional narratives were woven together with material presently at hand,[3] and Jesus' table-sharing became proclaimed through the Noble Death tradition. At Antioch Paul received this tradition and passed it to the church at Corinth, for whom in traditional fashion the supper part of the meal (*deipnon*) was followed by the edification (*symposium*). Sometimes the symposium was the Jesus Supper ritual (1 Cor. 11) and at other times a more ecstatic gathering with "tongues" and prophecy (1 Cor. 14). The Gospel writer Mark wove the Noble Death Supper tradition into a Passover story as he wrote amid his church's struggle within Second Temple Judaism, and the Passover "Last Supper" scene as we know it was created.[4]

By roughly 150 CE, the Lord's Supper had undergone two significant developments. In some contexts the elements themselves, bread and wine, were considered to be divine food, in some settings as early as the turn of the first century (John 6:51b–59; Ignatius). Second, what once had been a meal (table-sharing), and then became a ritual attached to a meal as the symposium (e.g., 1 Cor.), became completely separated as its own ritual and attached to a "word service" (Justin's *First Apology*). Ultimately this separate Supper rite became attached to baptism with some minimal prior instruction, so that the beginning of initiationism can be seen by roughly 150 CE (*First Apology*; redacted form of *The Didache*): properly instructed people are baptized and given the divine food of the Supper for the first time.

As the third- and fourth-century theologians reflected on their experience of God's immediate presence during the Supper, two principal traditions emerged. From North Africa, and finding fullest expression there in Augustine and later in Fulgentius of Ruspe, as well as in Gelasius I in Rome, a mystical (nonmetabolic) tradition prevailed. Engrafted into Christ through "initiation," believers during the Supper were taken by Christ deeper into his mystical body and thereby fed by his body and blood. From the Antioch area, and finding classic expression in John Chrysostom and Theodore of Mopsuestia, and from them Ambrose of Milan, a divine-food (metabolic) tradition prevailed. The elements themselves became transformed into the body and blood of Christ.

These two traditions were inherited by the Latin medieval West and were combined creatively, in various ways, during the early scholastic period. By the twelfth century a threefold scheme had developed—the bread and wine, the body and blood of Christ, and, ultimately, the sanctifying grace of God in Christ—that combined the eucharistic elements and both the metabolic and mystical (nonmetabolic) traditions. The Reformers of the sixteenth century inherited this long tradition. Luther at first emphasized the mystical true presence tradition, but eventually subsumed this into the metabolic tradition as one of its fruits, and then subsumed both under the Word of God.

The humanist reforming traditions, which turned back to the original writings of the patristic tradition, and then to the Scriptures, discovered

Augustine's eucharistic teaching of a mystical true presence. Engrafted into Christ himself, through faith and the Spirit, believers are fed yet again by his presence in the Supper. Erasmus found this tradition appealing but eventually assented to the authority of the late medieval church and its metabolic tradition. But the Reformed theologians of the first generation appealed strongly to the Augustinian tradition, even citing Augustine at length in precisely those tracts that careful modern scholarship has shown to be nonmetabolic in their description of Christ's real presence. Calvin and Bullinger continued this trajectory, both of them overcoming Zwingli's dualistic tendency by tying the sacramental event to the signs. Calvin's more instrumental view of the signs, and Bullinger's more outward testifying view of the signs, tightened the sign-reality connection that wobbled in Zwingli's theology, and both types of sign-theology were present in the Reformed confessions.

By way of summary, chapter 4 described the positions of the late medieval reformers—Roman Catholic and Protestant—to look like this:[5]

- Erasmus: medieval catholic eucharistic theology
- Luther: medieval catholic, evangelical eucharistic theology
- Zwingli, Bucer, Calvin, and Bullinger: patristic catholic, evangelical eucharistic theology

The Reformed confessions were univocal in their Reformed eucharistic theology, wherein believers, already engrafted into Christ, are nourished directly by the true body and blood of Christ as they are confirmed and deepened in their union with him. The confessions show developing articulation of how this mystical feeding connects to the signs themselves, with the later confessions typically displaying a position either Calvinist ("symbolic instrumentalism") or Bullinger-like ("symbolic parallelism").

We then saw that Schleiermacher keenly represented Reformed eucharistic theology. Those who already are mystically a part of Christ's body are fed directly by him through the Supper, which is a means of grace by which the Redeemer enters and transforms us yet more deeply, both personally and corporately. The Nevin-Hodge debate, which occurred in American Reformed theology in the nineteenth century, showed Nevin easily to have had the more adequate position historically, and to have braved a reinterpretation of the tradition. Yet Hodge did see something crucial about the personal quality to God's gracious presence. During the twentieth century, Barth represented Zwinglianism, with his view that the Word of God, working through the Spirit, actively evokes faith and the shaping of the Christian according to Christ himself. The Supper is an outward and visible sign that attests to the divine promise in Christ and to our responding pledge of obedience. Baillie represented a Calvin-like view of a sacramental world and the Supper as a God-given sign, from within a sacramental universe, which through faith (evoked by God) communicates to us the "real presence."

HISTORY, APOSTOLICITY, AND ENCOUNTERED BY GOD

The historical material concerning Jesus' table-sharing is somewhat supple and complex, and we would do well to pause and consider the tradition that was received from Jesus and how it functioned as revelatory.

What happened when someone was encountered by Jesus? Here the work of Willi Marxsen and the importance of form criticism must be accounted for.[6] Marxsen argues that when people were encountered by Jesus they had three possible reactions: Some were indifferent—they were left "cold"—because the encounter with him was not decisive one way or the other for who they were. After all, this was just the carpenter's son. For others, the encounter with Jesus was decisively negative. Jesus was Beelzebub; he was possessed. By contrast, for yet others, the encounter with Jesus was decisively positive; it was being encountered by the divine reality in such a way that the future opened in hope.[7] On Marxsen's careful analysis, and important for this study, several features about the encounter for this third group stand out.

First, we find this encounter embodied as pre-Synoptic material that is a witness ("kerygma") that calls people to response. Marxsen calls this earliest stratum of kerygma "the Jesus-kerygma," by which he distinguishes it from a later developing "Christ-kerygma" (as found, for example, in Paul's letters), or from the yet later "Jesus-Christ kerygma" that developed with the Gospel writers.[8] Most characteristic of this Jesus-kerygma is that people do not believe "*in*" Jesus; rather, "in the receipt and transmission of Jesus' words and deeds it is always made clear that people believe *him*," so that "Jesus' words and deeds are set forth as a saving event by people who have experienced salvation in this event."[9]

Second, the subject matter of the Jesus-kerygma is therefore "Jesus-as-proclaiming," in which Jesus' words are repeated, or "Jesus-as-acting," in which Jesus' deeds are repeated. We are dealing with Christology precisely and only "as soteriology" enacted.[10] "Saving well-being" came upon people so that,[11] in Marxsen's words, we can properly say that Jesus was an event ("Jesus von Nazareth—ein Ereignis").[12]

Third, the kerygmata of the Jesus-kerygma all function independently, yet each conveys fully the event of saving well-being. Marxsen reminds us that "*each* independent tradition contains the *whole*, even if from a different perspective in each case. In this way, each tradition both expresses and invites one into the experience of the whole."[13]

Finally, while it is well known that the kerygmata that form this earliest apostolic witness were proclamation and not mere reportage, the fact that these are *kerygma* means that "these independent traditions come from an *experience* that was repeated again and again and ever anew, and that they are for the sake of an *experience* that is to be repeated again and again and ever anew. But the experience is precisely the inbreaking of the rule of God."[14] Saving well-being lies neither in past events, nor in a yet-to-be-realized future, but in the present moment of witnessing and responding.

In his introductory essay that discusses Marxsen's significant contribution to both exegesis and constructive theology, Devenish carefully distinguishes Marxsen's category of "Jesus-kerygma" into several closely related types, one of which ("praxis-sacramental") can focus either on Jesus' words ("Jesus-as-proclaiming") or on Jesus' deeds ("Jesus-as-acting").[15] In either case, the earthly Jesus who "enacts an act of God" is made present again by reenacting ("repetition") his very words or deeds.[16] This was the point to reenacting the Supper by which Jesus enacted God's very act: *When followers of Jesus shared table as Jesus had shared table, God encountered people just as God had encountered them when Jesus shared table— saving well-being was experienced.*[17] As Willy Rordorf showed long ago, it was just this encounter at table that led the early church to designate its day of worship as "the Lord's day," which also means that the entire church year, from the Christmas cycle (Advent-Christmas-Epiphany) to the Easter cycle (Lent-Easter-Pentecost), ultimately derives not from a resurrection as such but from Jesus' table-sharing.[18]

In order to apply Marxsen's form-critical analysis to current practice, I want to make both formal and material comments about his results. Formally, the Jesus-kerygma (and in the case of the Supper, we are dealing with the "praxis-sacramental" type) stands as the "canon prior to the canon." This material is the norm ("canon") that stands *historically prior* to the collection of writings known as the canon, and it stands as the norm by which all Christian witnessing is assessed for its appropriateness to Jesus.[19] Marxsen observes that this earliest tradition that is the Jesus-kerygma, and that stands as normative for later traditions, is at one and the same time both Protestant and Roman Catholic, because simultaneously it is normative for both the later scriptural writings and the church tradition it originates. This formal observation is important, because when Protestant and Roman Catholic scholars discuss the Supper (Eucharist), they often discuss whether the apostolic norm ought to be the scriptural institution narrative(s) or the priestly tradition begun by Jesus that formed the church within which Scripture was produced.[20] Marxsen's observation means that the Jesus-kerygma that proclaims Jesus table-sharing ("praxis-sacramental") actually stands as apostolically normative for both

Protestant and Roman Catholic traditions about the Supper/Eucharist, so that the answer to the question of "scriptural warrant" or "priestly inception" is "Yes—the table-sharing of the Jesus-kerygma."

Materially the Jesus-kerygma comprises a dipolar event of witness-response whose ontic pole is the "kerygmatic-Jesus" ("Jesus-as-acting" or "Jesus-as-proclaiming") and whose noetic pole is, in Marxsen's language, the experience of saving well-being, which is to say, of the inbreaking of God's rule. Each pole deserves comment.

On the ontic pole, the key point is that "as the Jesus-kerygma sees him, the relevant Jesus is the related Jesus. In the technical terminology of classical dogmatics, the Jesus of the Jesus-kerygma *in se* is not (as in classical Christology) Jesus *a se* or *pro patri*, but rather Jesus *pro aliis*. If the subject matter of the Jesus-kerygma is itself a relation, then this is intrinsically (*in se*) relational."[21] So, for example, when it comes to translating Marxsen's phrase *die Sache Jesu geht weiter* ("the Jesus-business continues"),[22] Devenish says,

> I have chosen the phrase "the Jesus-business" in an effort to express that what is at issue is a simple, atomic "whole," the "event" of Jesus as a sign-act of enacted word or spoken deed. Thus, the basic point is not how the word *Sache* is translated, but rather that the phrase *die Sache Jesu* be rendered in such a way as to indicate that the datum or subject-matter to which it refers is an integral and noncomposite reality.[23]

The Jesus-kerygma therefore stands not as a rejection of the traditional christological doctrine of *vere homo–vere Deus* (true human being–true God) but rather as the apostolic benchmark by which such a later developing doctrine can be assessed. Marxsen explains that

> [i]n the phrase "the Jesus-business" the ancient christological confession of the *vere homo–vere deus* (true human being–true God) is as it were "joined together." This is not to be treated in isolation as a statement about the character of the person. Doing this leads to speculation about how to imagine divinity in the human being Jesus and how to imagine the humanity of him who, as the exalted one, sits on the throne of God. Through a human being (who was a human being, really human and nothing but human), there breaks in the rule of God that only God can bring. And as the one who brings God's rule, this human being is experienced really and entirely as God.[24]

This noetic pole, which we have seen Marxsen express elsewhere as the experience of saving well-being, or the experience of the inbreaking of God's rule, Marxsen here can equally express as someone's experience of Jesus, a human being who is "experienced really and entirely as God." The variations in expression, far from showing some imprecision in Marxsen's analysis, reflect that the Jesus-kerygma can be "explanatory"

and not just "sacramental" in character.[25] When the Jesus-kerygma functions to be explanatory, which can be sorted into two types ("praxis-
explanatory" and "person-explanatory"), theistic concepts or symbols
are *borrowed from their original context* and used to explain "the Jesus-
business" so as to kerygmatically proclaim him anew. So, for instance, as
examples of praxis-explanatory, "the rule of God has come near" (Mark
1:14–15) and the "finger of God" is upon someone (Luke 11:20) were
explanations about an "occurrence" initiated by God.[26] As examples of
person-explanatory, we find the numerous titles given to Jesus, such
as Messiah, Christ, Son of God, Son of David, bridegroom, and so on.[27]
What is true for all these explanatory forms of the Jesus-kerygma is that
the religious concepts or symbols already existed in their own right, and
they were then borrowed in order to explain for the sake of proclaiming.
Furthermore, what Marxsen said of the Jesus-kerygma overall is true of
its types as well—each of these explanatory efforts is entire and complete
in its own right. Each "contains the *whole*, even if from a different perspective." As Marxsen says about the explanatory titles given to Jesus,
"We may not add up these names of Jesus and say that, only once we
know the sum of the content of all the names can we state fully who Jesus
was. Rather, it was like this: since people who encountered Jesus had
experiences which they really only expected from God, each independent
title serves to make *the same* statement."[28]

Naturally, then, the noetic pole admits of as many confessional variations of the experiences of God as there might have been original contexts
and linguistic worlds of the people who had those experiences, which
themselves only occurred in and through such historically situated language.[29] So Marxsen's own varied descriptions of the noetic merely reflect
his borrowing from various kerygmata whose original contexts varied.

One final material comment remains. In the dipolar event whose witnessing ontic pole is the kerygmatic-Jesus and whose responding noetic
pole is the historically situated experience of that witness, what is being
handed on as decisive is *die Sache Jesu*, "the Jesus-business" wherein the
occurrence of God has come upon someone. This should be noted particularly for the Supper, because what is being handed on and (to use
Marxsen's language) "translated" in each Supper context is not Jesus'
table-sharing as such, but "the Jesus-business" that was embodied in the
table-sharing[30] and later was embodied as the symposium attached to the
deipnon (1 Cor.) and, historically even later, was embodied as a distinct rite
on Sunday morning. So, for example, the question is not whether the more
Hellenistic and philosophical Christianity of the fourth to fifth centuries
correctly translated Jesus' table-sharing by conceiving of divine food, but
whether the divine food tradition in its historically situated worldview
adequately embodied "the Jesus-business" in a way appropriate to how

Jesus' table-sharing adequately embodied "the Jesus-business" in the meal-sharing world of the first century of the common era.

THE TRUE PRESENCE AT SUPPER TODAY

As we have seen already, Marxsen understands that the foundational Christian datum, that which makes the church the church, so to speak, is the dipolar event whose ontic pole is the "kerygmatic-Jesus" ("Jesus-as-acting" or "Jesus-as-proclaiming") and whose noetic pole is, in Marxsen's language, the experience of saving well-being.[31] We also have seen that this means christologically that we are not interested in "Jesus 'in his person,' which is to say, Jesus as 'behind' or in one way or another inferred from word and deed."[32] Theological confessions such as Jesus internally being *vere homo–vere Deus* (true human being–true God) are themselves to be tested for appropriateness to the normative Jesus-kerygma, not the other way around.[33] Marxsen also makes the point that not only can an interest in the Jesus standing behind his words and deeds, whether speculation about his being or his consciousness or his cause, not be satisfied, since all we have is the "atomic," "non-composite" kerygmatic-Jesus, but that such interest also "corrupts faith completely; it is no longer faith at all. Kerygma theology undoubtedly saw this correctly."[34] As Marxsen so succinctly puts the matter, "Anyone who still wants historical security first when faced with the summons that has been issued to him refuses faith."[35]

Marxsen's exegetical insights are powerfully corroborated by the constructive efforts on Christology of Schubert Ogden, which help lead us forward in thinking about Jesus' true presence.[36] So, to begin again with Scripture, Marxsen's work reveals that one type of the Jesus-kerygma is the person-explanatory type:[37]

> People meet Jesus. They encounter his claim. They give themselves over to this claim. In so doing, they experience that they have to do with more than only human words; that they are confronted with God. They reflect on their experience and then, on the basis of the experience they have had with Jesus, they express *who* it is with whom they had this experience.[38]

Naturally, the titles that people conferred in order to explain the identity of Jesus came from within their own historically situated and language-constructed worlds. If people expected that God would encounter them as the Prophet, then Jesus was the Prophet; if as the Son of God, then Jesus was the Son of God; if as the Messiah, or High Priest, or Son of David, then Jesus was the Messiah, the High Priest, or the Son of David.

These various titles, as Marxsen noted above, cannot be summed together to get the "true Jesus." Rather, each title stands on its own to proclaim that God encounters someone when Jesus encounters him or her. As Marxsen says, "anyone who does risk surrendering to him and to his message will always use only the highest name one knows. And I *know* no higher name than when I say, 'Jesus is God'—because in Jesus and through Jesus I have to do with God."[39]

This dipolar event of the Jesus-kerygma, with its witnessing ontic pole as the kerygmatic-Jesus and its responding noetic pole as the experience of being encountered by God, finds its clearest constructive explanation in Ogden's long-standing and carefully developed argument that christological revelation is "re-presentational" rather than constitutive.[40] Rather than thinking that God constituted in Jesus a new way of being or relating to us that provided a saving relationship not otherwise present ("constitutive"), the encounter with Jesus re-presents (makes present again) the saving divine reality that could not fail to be present already, simply by virtue of God's original revelation in and to experience as such, a revelation that

> is not simply one event among others but, rather, the unique event which, being constitutive of human existence, always occurs insofar as we exist at all. It is the event in which God's ever-new self-presentation to the world in love not only takes place but is also received and somehow responded to understandingly as gift and demand.[41]

On Ogden's analysis, "the event of Jesus Christ" is not "*constitutive* of the possibility of salvation," but "is rather *representative* of this possibility, which is constituted solely and sufficiently by the primordial and everlasting love of God that is the sole primal source and the sole final end of all things."[42] Ogden goes on to illustrate this point:

> I trust that the distinction I have employed here between a constitutive and representative event is already familiar, in substance, if not also under these particular labels. But if an ordinary example of it is needed, I know of none better than that provided by the old story about the conversation between the three baseball umpires. The youngest and least experienced umpire allows, "I call 'em as I see 'em." Whereupon the second umpire says, "I call 'em as they are." But to all this, the oldest and shrewdest umpire responds with complete self-confidence, "They ain't nothin' till I call 'em!" By an event constitutive of the possibility of salvation I mean an event that is like the third umpire's calls, in that the possibility of salvation is nothing until the event occurs. On the contrary, what I mean by an event representative of the possibility of salvation is an event similar to the calls of the second umpire, in that it serves to declare a possibility of salvation that already is as it is—is already constituted as such—prior to the event's occurring to declare it.[43]

Thinking now about christological revelation as representational, if we return to Marxsen's comment that the kerygmata of the Jesus-kerygma "come from an *experience* that was repeated again and again and ever anew, and that they are for the sake of an *experience* that is to be repeated again and again and ever anew,"[44] we understand that the kerygma did and does function in the same way as the encounter with Jesus. They both declare as possible the salvation that already is at hand and, "as the objectification of God's original revelation," they are "the re-presentation of God's love itself as the ever-new gift and demand of my existence."[45]

On this view, to be encountered by the kerygma *is* to be encountered by the "true presence" of Jesus, which is why the Jesus-kerygma, as we have seen, does what Jesus does and proclaims what Jesus proclaims—it *is* "Jesus-as-acting" or it *is* "Jesus-as-proclaiming." This is a simple point that, it seems to me, cannot be made strongly enough: according to the normative apostolic witness of Jesus' table-sharing, to reenact the Supper by which Jesus enacted the act of God *is to have the true presence of Jesus* at the table, and the same is true today so long as we reenact the Supper appropriate to that Jesus-kerygma, which is its apostolic norm.

The Reformed Supper tradition, on my view, appropriately conforms to this normative scriptural witness, and I want to observe how that is so. First, the Reformed tradition has always viewed the celebration of the Supper as a form of the Word, which means that God has appointed it to convey to us the true presence of Christ. "This is the purpose of the gospel," wrote Calvin in his commentary on 1 Corinthians (1:9), "that Christ should become ours, and that we should be ingrafted into his body."[46] This Reformed perspective on the Word and the Supper embodies in its own context what we have seen in the Jesus-kerygma, where we are encountered by celebration of table-sharing, "Jesus-as-acting," and by word, "Jesus-as-proclaiming," both of which convey the true presence of the kerygmatic-Jesus, who is the only Jesus in whom we ultimately have interest.

Following on this point, both the Reformed tradition and the Jesus-kerygma understand that enacting the Supper according to the normative witness of Jesus is then to have Jesus' true presence at the table, encountering those gathered at table. In the chapters on Luther, Zwingli, and Calvin, this study traced how the Protestant Reformers of the late medieval period carried the debate about Jesus' true presence at the Supper into areas of classical Christology. In order to explain how the "true body and blood of Jesus" might be present, they debated not just confessions such as "the ascension" and "the session of Christ," but also concepts such as the *communicatio idiomatum* ("communication of properties") and their relationship to Jesus as *vere homo–vere Deus* (true human being–true God). This often entailed considerable exegetical discussion; but, as we have just seen, such discussions, while historically and proximately important, are ultimately to be assessed by the Jesus-kerygma, whose subject term (the kerygmatic-Jesus) neither exegetically nor constructively admits such discussions, as the work of Marxsen and Ogden has shown. Such christological discussions misconstrue the original subject term of christological reflection and thereby entertain christologies that could never, in principle, be shown to be either appropriately Christian or true.[47] Nevertheless, despite divergence in Christology from the Jesus-kerygma, the Reformed Supper traditions (like the Jesus-kerygma itself) have always maintained that the true presence of Jesus at the Supper is at table even today.

This leads directly to a third key point. We have learned from Marxsen that the normative apostolic Supper practice was itself a form of the Jesus-kerygma—the praxis sacramental type—so that *to reenact the Supper is to have Jesus truly be present*, enacting the act of God. Since the relevant subject term is "Jesus-as-acting," so that *vere homo–vere Deus* means (according to the normative Jesus-kerygma) that being encountered by the truly human Jesus was to be encountered by God's very presence, so also to be encountered by open table-sharing is to be encountered by God's very presence. Now, in parallel fashion, just as "the Jesus of the Jesus-kerygma *in se* is not (as in classical christology) Jesus *a se* or *pro patri*, but rather Jesus *pro aliis*,"[48] so also *the table-sharing with its elements* (bread and wine) *in se* is strictly "Jesus *pro aliis*." We neither have any more access to, nor interest in, the inner nature of the elements than we do to Jesus' inner nature, whether conceived in terms of matter (classical Christology) or in terms of psychology (revisionary Christology); nor is such an issue even relevant, since the true subject matter is "Jesus-as-acting," whereby God encounters us. The Reformed tradition rightly rejected from the start any speculation about the inner nature of the bread or wine as such, because the elements themselves are the divinely appointed instruments by which God self-communicates directly to us.[49]

One final objection needs to be met here, lest the charge of "mere memorialism" that was leveled against Zwingli—falsely, as this study has argued—be leveled falsely against the position that I have just sketched out. On the view here, beginning with the Jesus-kerygma and using Marxsen's exegetical terms from the Jesus-kerygma, the Supper reenacts the Jesus who enacts God's act. One could also use Ogden's constructive terms, saying that, just as with Jesus, the Supper *re-presents* the event of "God's ever-new self-presentation to the world in love."[50] Long ago, Ogden clarified that an aspect of the noetic pole of this self-presentation by God as love is that *strictly necessary feature* of life that Ogden calls "original confidence."[51] The source of our "ineradicable confidence in the final worth of our existence" thus lies in the objective character of God as self-revealing love, the divine original revelation that "is not simply one event among others but, rather, the unique event which, being constitutive of human existence, always occurs insofar as we exist at all."[52]

This is the divine presence, self-presenting in and to every moment, that constitutes our lives and that sustains us in our most intimate selves as surely and immediately as Jesus directly feeds our very souls with his very body and blood, to use the substance language of the Reformed Supper tradition. In both cases, this immediate and nourishing divine presence is mediated through the Supper, which is Jesus-present-to-us.[53] A key difference is that the view of the "mystical true presence" given here is not substantialist but rather—and here taking its cue from the discussion about grace that the last chapter raised—*personal* in how it views the direct nourishment of the Divine.

Barth articulated the Reformation view that the grace that lies at the center of the church is the divine personal relationship toward us that evokes our faithful obedience. Such grace is an historical event, not a physical event. Baillie gave an interpretation of the "real presence" that was personal, as indeed Nevin had attempted in his own way, with his "scientific" approach that tried to overcome the materialism in Calvin's "psychology." By understanding the mystical true presence to be realized when the Supper *re-presents* the event of "God's ever-new self-presentation to the world in love," the divine reality is here conceived as strictly personal. The divine activity of ineradicably valuing the world and all therein names the divine Other; it stands as the perfection of personal gracious activity, unrivaled because of its absolute universality and unrivaled because of its dependence upon nothing other than being the divine character as such. Further, and once more in careful attention to the normative scriptural witness, the historical encounter with the kerygmatic-Jesus ("Jesus-as-acting" and "Jesus-as-proclaiming") that decisively revealed this God was an encounter whose *agent* was personal and whose *agency* ("love," "forgiveness," and so on) was personal.[54]

Finally, the argument here seems to me to properly convert. The Supper can be adequately expressed as the mystical true presence that "*re-presents* the event of 'God's ever-new self-presentation to the world in love,'" just as Jesus re-presented the divine presence: The sacrament is the true presence that re-presents the divine presence. Put the other way around, Jesus who re-presented the divine presence can be said to be the true sacrament of God. With this christological assertion the argument now returns to, and completes, the excursus in chapter 1 that discussed the concept of "sacrament" historically and that ended with modern Roman Catholic and Protestant theology. Jesus stands as the *primal* sacrament, and the church as the *primary* sacrament.[55]

Now it might be objected that reading the Reformed Supper tradition in this way has introduced historical criticism (Marxsen), neoclassical metaphysics (Hartshorne), and existentialist theology (Bultmann and Ogden) into interpreting the meaning of the "true presence." For such an objection to hold merit, however, it would have to be shown that such interpretation is wrongly conceived, or wrongly carried out, or perhaps both. Just as surely as Schleiermacher and Barth each considered Reformed theology in their historical contexts, so as surely others can consider Reformed Supper theology in new contexts, as did Nevin and Baillie. Not to do so, and merely to repeat the words that were handed down to us without considering what they might mean in our setting, would be to commit the mistake that Calvin accused the ultra-Lutherans of making when, by merely repeating Luther's words a generation after him, they turned themselves into apes ("monkey see, monkey do"), rather than become true disciples of Luther.[56]

To put the matter more constructively, however briefly sketched this analysis of the "true presence" may be, such a reading of the Reformed doctrine of "true presence" as given here owes much to Augustine's mystical true presence—minus, of course, Augustine's substantialism and teaching on predestination. Simply by virtue of who God is, we already immediately and intimately experience the Divine, and the Supper that is the true presence of Christ deepens us and nourishes us in that reality. This position also owes much to the discussion of signs within sixteenth-century Reformed theology, and the Reformed insistence that Christ's "true presence" is not located in the elements, but is intimately connected to the elements in their God-given sign function.[57] Furthermore, Schleiermacher's teaching on original and decisive revelation, and his teaching on the mediator continuing as the church and nourishing us through the Supper, have influenced the position given here. So too the work of Nevin, who might be said to be the unintended forefather (*Urvater*) to this study, has confirmed the research, both in its historical aspect and in the charge to reinterpret for a new time and place. Barth's insistence on the kerygmatic quality to Scripture, and his insistence on the personal character to grace, has had its influence; as has the work of Baillie, which connects "real presence" with the "omnipresence" of God. In short, the analysis of the "true presence" given here simply is an interpretation of the tradition that is both deeply Augustinian and thoroughly Reformed by its appropriation of this Augustinianism via Calvin and various Reformed theologians who followed Calvin and interpreted the Reformed tradition.

NOTES

INTRODUCTION

1. The baptism book, and with it my cited *Church History* essay about Calvin and baptism, gives the dozens of critical studies concerning the relationship between Luther and Calvin. See John W. Riggs, *Baptism in the Reformed Tradition: An Historical and Practical Theology,* Columbia Series in Reformed Theology (Louisville, KY: Westminster John Knox Press, 2002); idem, "Emerging Ecclesiology in Calvin's Baptismal Thought, 1536–1543," *Church History* 64, 1 (1995): 29–43.

2. For the meaning of "humanist" in its historical context, see my comments, and the secondary scholarship cited, in John W. Riggs, *Postmodern Christianity* (Harrisburg, PA: Trinity Press, 2003), 56–57 and nn. 26–30.

3. Ezra Pound, "A Pact," in *Ezra Pound: New Selected Poems and Translations,* ed. Richard Sieburth (New York: New Directions Books, 2010), 39.

CHAPTER 1: FROM JESUS' TABLE-SHARING TO THE PROTESTANT REFORMATION

1. For entrance and bibliographic resources for this material, see the classic essay by Wilhelm Heitmüller, "Abendmahl: I. im Neuen Testament," in *Die Religion in Geschichte und Gegenwart* (Tübingen: J. C. B. Mohr, 1909), 1:19–51. In subsequent editions of *Die Religion in Geschichte und Gegenwart,* see the essays by Karl Ludwig Schmidt, "Abendmahl: I. im Neuen Testament," *RGG* (Tübingen: J. C. B. Mohr, 1927), 1:6–16; Eduard Schweizer, "Abendmahl: I. im NT," *RGG* (Tübingen: J. C. B. Mohr, 1957), 1:10–21; Ferdinand Hahn, "Abendmahl: I. Neues Testament," *RGG* (Tübingen: Mohr Siebeck, 1998), 1:10–15. Also see Gerhard Delling, "Abendmahl: II. Urchristliches Mahl—Verständnis," *Theologische Realenzyklopädie* (Berlin: Walter de Gruyter, 1977), 1:43–58. Among the many individual studies, in particular see Rudolf Bultmann, *The History of the Synoptic Tradition,* trans. John Marsh (New York: Harper & Row, 1963); Willi Marxsen, *Das Abendmahl als christologisches Problem* (Gütersloh: Gütersloher Verlagshaus Gerd Mohn, 1960) [Eng. trans. *The Lord's Supper as a Christological Problem,* trans. Lorenz Neiting (Philadelphia: Fortress Press, 1970)]; John Dominic Crossan, *The Historical Jesus* (San Francisco: HarperSanFrancisco, 1991); idem, *Jesus: A Revolutionary Biography* (San Francisco: HarperSanFrancisco, 1994); Robert Funk, ed., *The Acts of Jesus* (San Francisco: HarperSanFrancisco, 1998). In short, excellent historical scholarship that challenged Jesus's institution of Last Supper spanned the breadth of the twentieth century, beginning with Albert Eichhorn, *Das Abendmahl im Neuen Testament*

(Leipzig: J. C. B. Mohr, 1898), and most recently the ecumenical scholars working in the Jesus Seminar (*Acts of Jesus*, 139–42). For a summary of the state of scholarship, see Dennis E. Smith, "The Last Supper," in *The New Interpreter's Dictionary of the Bible* (Nashville: Abingdon Press, 2008), 3:582–85.

2. A critical summary of this approach, and bibliography, can be found in Paul F. Bradshaw, *The Search for the Origins of Christian Worship*, 2nd ed. (New York: Oxford University Press, 2002), 118–43. For an exemplary approach here, see Bradshaw, *Eucharistic Origins* (Oxford: Oxford University Press, 2004).

3. An excellent summary of this research and bibliography can be found in Hans-Josef Klauck, *Herrenmahl und Hellenistischer Kult* (Münster: Aschendorff, 1982), 1–30, who follows with his own scholarly appraisal.

4. Hans Lietzmann, *Mass and Lord's Supper*, trans. Dorothea H. G. Reeve (Leiden: E. J. Brill, 1953–55), 195–208.

5. Dom Gregory Dix, *The Shape of the Liturgy* (London: Dacre Press, 1978), 48–102.

6. Dennis E. Smith, *From Symposium to Eucharist* (Minneapolis: Fortress Press, 2003), 219–77. Also see his essay "Table Fellowship and the Historical Jesus," in *Religious Propaganda and Missionary Competition in the New Testament World: Essays Honoring Dieter Georgi*, ed. Lukas Bormann, Kelly del Tredici, and Angela Standhartinger (Leiden: E. J. Brill, 1994), 135–62.

7. Marxsen, *The Lord's Supper*. Also see Marxsen's essay, "The Meals of Jesus and the Lord's Supper of the Church," in *Jesus and the Church: The Beginnings of Christianity*, selected, translated, and introduced by Philip E. Devenish (Philadelphia: Trinity Press Int., 1992), 137–46.

8. Klauck, *Herrenmahl*, 11–13.

9. Note that this type of historical-critical approach more adequately interprets Marxsen's essays themselves. He was specifically interested in what Jesus' Supper, and its witness of faith, meant for the life of the subsequent church. For the best entry to Marxsen's work, see *Jesus and the Church*, xi–xxxv. In this volume of translated essays, also see "Toward the New Testament Grounding of Baptism" (147–71).

10. The best essay clarifying the task of historical, systematic, and practical theology, and their roles as aspects of a single Christian theology, remains Schubert M. Ogden, "What Is Theology?" in *On Theology* (San Francisco: Harper & Row, 1986), 1–21. See Ogden's further clarifications in *The Understanding of Christian Faith* (Eugene, OR: Cascade Books, 2010), 1–20, esp. 9–18.

11. On these issues, see chapter 6 of this book, "Retrospect and Prospect."

12. Bultmann, *Synoptic Tradition*, 265.

13. For entrance to this material, see Funk, *Acts of Jesus*, 139–42; Smith, "The Last Supper"; Andrew Brian McGowan, "'Is There a Liturgical Text in the Gospel?' The Institution Narratives and Their Early Interpretive Communities," *Journal of Biblical Literature* 118, no. 1 (1999): 73–87.

14. For discussion of the various proposals and secondary scholarship, see Klauck, *Herrenmahl*, 15–26; Joachim Jeremias, *The Eucharistic Words of Jesus*, 3rd ed., trans. Norman Perrin (New York: Charles Scribner's Sons, 1966), 26–31.

15. Jeremias, *Eucharistic Words*.

16. Eduard Schweizer, *The Lord's Supper according to the New Testament* (Philadelphia: Fortress Press, 1967). Despite continued confirmation of the editorial character of Mark's Passover scene, the Passover origin to the Lord's Supper continues

to find support. See, for example, Gillian Feeley-Harnik, *The Lord's Table: Eucharist and Passover in Early Christianity* (Philadelphia: University of Pennsylvania Press, 1981), 107–48. The argument against a Passover setting is simple and strong: the earliest Supper account, recited by Paul in 1 Cor. 11, shows no Passover context whatsoever; and when we find the scene first set in a Passover context (Mark), the inner material itself, as compared to Mark's framing, still shows no Passover material.

17. Marxsen, *Lord's Supper*.

18. The work of Lietzmann, it seems to me, can indeed be seen behind this argument, as Klauck suggests, *Herrenmahl*, 11–13. While this classification cannot be gainsaid, it does not, as I have argued above, do justice to Marxsen's historical-theological point.

19. Norman Perrin, *Rediscovering the Teaching of Jesus* (New York: Harper & Row, 1967), 102–8.

20. See Marcus J. Borg, *Conflict, Holiness and Politics in the Teaching of Jesus* (Harrisburg, PA: Trinity Press Int., 1998), 93–134; idem, *Jesus: A New Vision* (New York: Harper & Row, 1987), 101–2; Günther Bornkamm, *Jesus of Nazareth* (New York: Harper & Row, 1960), 80–81; James Breech, *The Silence of Jesus* (Philadelphia: Fortress Press, 1983), 22–64; Bruce Chilton, *The Temple of Jesus* (University Park: Pennsylvania State University, 1992), 137–54; idem, *A Feast of Meanings* (Leiden: E. J. Brill, 1994), 67–74; John Dominic Crossan, *The Historical Jesus* (San Francisco: HarperSanFrancisco, 1991), 260–64, 332–53; idem, *Jesus: A Revolutionary Biography* (San Francisco: HarperSanFrancisco, 1994), 48, 66–70, 76, 95–96, 103, 105–7, 110–11, 129–30, 177–78, 179–81; Elisabeth Schüssler Fiorenza, *In Memory of Her* (New York: Crossroad, 1983), 119–21, 126–30; Robert Funk and the Jesus Seminar, *The Acts of Jesus*, 31; Martin Hengel, *The Charismatic Leader and His Followers* (Philadelphia: Fortress Press, 1974), 67; Richard Horsley, *Jesus and the Spiral of Violence* (New York: Harper & Row, 1987), 178–80; Joachim Jeremias, *The Parables of Jesus*, 2nd rev. ed., trans. S. H. Hooke (New York: Charles Scribner's Sons, 1972), 128–32, 227; Hans-Josef Klauck, "Die Sakramente und der historische Jesus," in *Gemeinde-Amt-Sakrament: Neutestamentliche Perspektiven* (Würzburg: Echter, 1989), 273–85, esp. section II.4 ("Die Mahlgemeinschaft"), 281–82; Matthias Klinghardt, *Gemein-schaftsmahl und Mahlgemeinschaft: Soziologie und Liturgie frühchristlicher Mahlfeiern* (Tübingen: Francke Verlag, 1996); Jacob Neusner, "The Pharisees: Jesus' Com-petition," in *Judaism in the Beginning of Christianity* (Philadelphia: Fortress Press, 1984), 45–61; John W. Riggs, "From Gracious Table to Sacramental Elements: The Tradition-History of Didache 9 and 10," *The Second Century* 4 (1984): 83–102; idem, "The Sacred Food of Didache 9–10 and Second-Century Ecclesiologies," in *The Didache in Context*, ed. Clayton N. Jefford (Leiden: E. J. Brill, 1995), 256–62; E. P. Sanders, *Jesus and Judaism* (Philadelphia: Fortress Press, 1985), 174–211, 271–73; Smith, *From Symposium to Eucharist*; idem, "The Last Supper"; Morton Smith, *Jesus the Magician* (San Francisco: Harper & Row, 1978); Hal Taussig, *In the Begin-ning Was the Meal: Social Experimentation and Early Christian Identity* (Minneapolis: Augsburg Fortress Press, 2009); Geza Vermes, *Jesus the Jew* (London: Collins, 1973), 224. Although these scholars certainly interpret Jesus' table-sharing differently, the breadth and depth of their studies suggest a scholarly consensus about the importance of Jesus' table-sharing.

One could, of course, abandon the historical-critical task because of its complex-ity and alleged ambiguous results, and choose instead for the ecclesial narratives found in Scripture, thus reading the texts as "imaginative renderings of events and sayings, with meaning rather than chronicle as the purpose." For example, see the noted liturgical theologian David N. Power, *The Eucharistic Mystery* (New York: Crossroad, 1994), 23, 23–65; idem, "Eucharist," in *Systematic Theology II: Roman Catholic Perspectives*, ed. Francis Schüssler Fiorenza, John P. Galvin (Minneapolis: Fortress Press, 1991), 261–88; also see Raymond Moloney, *The Eucharist* (London: Geoffrey Chapman, 1995), 16–33.

On Power's view, the ecclesial setting and life of praxis gain authority over issues of dominical institution. Such an approach I can only regard as expedient at best and disingenuous at worst, a neglect of serious issues that not only separate Roman Catholic and Protestant traditions, but also pose a serious challenge to the very concept of *traditio*. Does each generation not have the obligation, in Paul's words, to pass on what it has received? If so, is there not a *norma normans sed non normata*—a norm that norms but itself is not normed, which must be the earliest apostolic testimony to Jesus, which can be found only through historical criticism? Note that two eminent Roman Catholic scholars of Christian origins, John Dominic Crossan and Hans-Josef Klauck, both look to Jesus' table-sharing as the so-called "dominical institution." Also note Moloney's all too simple transition from Jewish worship into liturgical forms used by the early church (*The Eucharist*, 3–61), a standard move made by prior generations of liturgical scholars who themselves were from so-called "liturgical traditions" and imagined that liturgies had to "evolve" or "develop" or "grow" from early forms. This perspective is questionable, given more recent scholarship on the diversity of late Judaism and early Christianity. For entrance to these discussions, see Bradshaw, *Search for Christian Origins*.

Interestingly, this appeal to later tradition, rather than the historical-critical task of some appeal to the historical Jesus, also appears among those who have a liturgical-text approach. See, for example, Andrew B. McGowan, "The Meals of Jesus and the Meals of the Church: Eucharistic Origins and Admission to Communion," in Maxwell E. Johnson and L. Edward Phillips, eds., *Studia Patristica Diversa: Essays in Honor of Paul E. Bradshaw* (Portland, OR: Pastoral Press, 2004), 101–15. McGowan's essay, it seems to me, not only fails to account for the now vast consensus about Jesus' meal-sharing, but, more importantly, fails to do justice to just the *Formgeschichte* issue that he himself raises (111ff.). For entrance to the importance of Marxsen's form-critical work, and why the encounter with Jesus is foundational for theology, producing the *norma normans sed non normata*, see the introductory essay by Philip E. Devenish, in Marxsen, *Jesus and the Church*, xi–xxxv. In the same volume, also see Marxsen's important essay, "Jesus of Nazareth: An Event" (55–75), to which I will later have recourse.

21. Crossan, *Jesus: A Revolutionary Biography*, 130.

22. In his study on banquets in the ancient world, *From Symposium to Eucharist* (122–23, 152), Smith argues strongly for the ecclesial character of the entire table-sharing material in the Gospels. Such material can tell us about the character of Jesus' ministry—that it was shared with unusual people and perhaps preferred the urban setting—but it tells us nothing about Jesus' historical practices themselves, including any supposed ministry of table-sharing (219–77). Smith's scholarship is so thorough that it seems to work against itself. Given the wealth of Gospel table-sharing materials, which come from a wide variety of oral and written sources, and which represent different locations across different eras, does

it make sense that all these Christian communities, independent of each other, turned to table-sharing to express the character of Jesus' ministry? Further, would early Christians really have made up a seemingly offensive saying about Jesus' table-sharing (Matt. 11:19 and Luke 7:34: "Behold a glutton and a drunk, a friend of tax collectors and sinners") that they might later have to explain away? Here the scholarly consensus makes more sense: Table-sharing was a crucial feature of Jesus' ministry and was appropriately remembered, in varying ways according to context, by later Christian communities.

23. See Smith, *Symposium*; Klinghardt, *Gemeinschaftsmahl und Mahlgemeinschaft*. The overall agreement between these two magisterial and independent works is remarkable, although they do parse the material a bit differently. For instance, where Smith names social features of the meals (boundaries, bonding, obligation, stratification, and equality) as they work toward producing community and fellowship, Klinghardt identifies values connected with the meals (community, equality and friendship, and grace-generosity-beauty that related to larger social and political values.

24. See the helpful chart provided in Smith, *Symposium*, 3.

25. Taussig, *In the Beginning*.

26. For more detailed argument with bibliography, see my essay "Sacred Food," 256–62. I want to thank the fellows of the Jesus Seminar, of the Westar Institute, for giving me the opportunity to present this material to the Jesus Seminar for discussion and voting (spring 2009). The New Testament scholars who comprise the fellows cast votes according to four categories: red (strongly agree), pink (agree), grey (disagree), black (strongly disagree).

The five theses presented for voting from my paper were (with vote results in parenthesis): (1) The historical origin of the Last Supper Gospel narratives lies in Jesus' table-sharing, not in a Passover setting (pink); (2) Jesus' table-sharing was itself a part of a wide-ranging meal tradition already culturally established (red); (3) The 1 Corinthians death motif of a last supper by Jesus (cited by Paul) comes from the Noble Death tradition, probably learned by Paul in Antioch (pink); (4) The shift from table-sharing to eucharistic divine food can be seen in the prayers of *Didache* 9 and 10, which lack the influence of the Noble Death tradition (pink); and, (5) The *Didache* shows a connection between the emergent emphasis on eucharistic divine food and fixed ecclesial offices so that Christian clergy controlled the means of life in a way analogous to patronage in the wider social context (pink).

Worth noting is that considerable discussion over (1) produced disagreement, not because this thesis was too radical for the Jesus Seminar, but because it was *too traditional*: It argues for *a table-sharing of Jesus that produced the experience of the Divine* and so was remembered and reenacted in new forms. (For more on this topic, see chapter 6 of this study, "Retrospect and Prospect," especially the subsection "History, Apostolicity, and Encountered by God.") Several scholars articulately objected to any notion of directly connecting the early church meal traditions with Jesus' table-sharing, arguing instead that the table-sharing narratives were composed for the symposia of early church meals.

27. E. Schüssler Fiorenza, *In Memory of Her*, 118–30.

28. Crossan, *Jesus: A Revolutionary Biography*, v. The entire book is a sophisticated development of just this simple theme. For more that Crossan has to say here, also see the references above (n. 1) and *The Birth of Christianity* (San Francisco: HarperSanFrancisco, 1998), 423–44.

29. For example, see Burton Mack, *A Myth of Innocence* (Philadelphia: Fortress Press, 1988), 102–13; David Seeley, *The Noble Death* (Sheffield: Sheffield Academic Press, 1990); Sam Williams, *Jesus' Death as a Saving Death* (Missoula, MT: Scholars Press, 1975). Seeley gives five characteristics of this Noble Death tradition: (1) obedience unto death for principles or divine calling; (2) overcoming physical trials and torture; (3) a military setting for a standoff with the hero in which loyalty comes to play; (4) a death that is vicarious for others through imitation; and (5) a death interpreted sacrificially by followers (13, 83, 87–99).

30. André Dupont-Sommer, *Le Quatrième Livre des Machabées*, Bibliothèque de l'École des Hautes Études 274 (Paris: Librairie Ancienne Honré Champion, 1939), 69–74; Moses Hadas, *The Third and Fourth Books of Maccabees* (New York: Harper & Bros., 1953), 109–13; Williams, *Jesus' Death*, 248–53. On 4 Maccabees and the Noble Death tradition, see Seeley, *Noble Death*, 92–99.

31. Mack, *Myth of Innocence*, 288–304.

32. See, e.g., Paul Achtemeier, "The Origin and Function of Pre-Markan Miracle Catenae," *Journal for Biblical Literature* 91 (1972): 198–221.

33. For an extended discussion of the meal tradition, see Smith, *Symposium*, 13–46. For a summary of scholarly attempts to reconstruct the Corinthian meal, see Klinghardt, *Gemeinschaftsmahl und Mahlgemeinschaft*, 276–86.

34. The construction offered here essentially parallels Klinghardt's (281–86) of *deipnon* (meal) followed by symposium (Lord's Supper), except that one ought to conceive of a single banquet whose symposium aspect is *the Jesus ritual* as Paul has received and handed down. This solution, it seems to me, simplifies the issues and avoids the problems that, according to Klinghardt, do arise with this structure. It also suggests a sensible historical phase between the earlier practice of the Lord's Supper as the meal itself and the later practice of the Lord's Supper as a ritual unto itself, detached from the meal and existing as part of a "Word service."

35. See Theissen's essays in *The Social Setting of Pauline Christianity: Essays on Corinth*, ed. and trans. John H. Schütz (Philadelphia: Fortress Press, 1982); see esp. "Social Integration and Sacramental Activity: An Analysis of 1 Cor. 11:17–34," 145–74, and "The Strong and the Weak in Corinth: A Sociological Analysis of a Theological Quarrel," 121–43. For a summary and evaluation of various positions taken here, see Klauck, *Herrenmahl*, 296–97.

36. Smith, *Symposium*, 173–217, esp. 191–200.

37. Paul's ethics show the same formal pattern of borrowing from context and interpreting with his christological framework. See the classic work by Victor P. Furnish, *Theology and Ethics in Paul* (Nashville: Abingdon Press, 1968).

38. Cf. Klinghardt, *Gemeinschaftsmahl und Mahlgemeinschaft*, who argues for the basic structure of *deipnon* followed by symposium (282–83). For a summary and bibliography of those who more traditionally viewed the Corinthian situation as a common meal followed by a sacred meal of the Lord's Supper, see Klinghardt, *Gemeinschaftsmahl und Mahlgemeinschaft*, 276–79. Here also see Marxsen, *Lord's Supper*, 99, and Klauck, *Herrenmahl*, 294–97.

39. For a short summary of the significant essays, see Klinghardt, *Gemeinschaftsmahl und Mahlgemeinschaft*, 333–36; also see Klauck, *Herrenmahl*, 346. Both Smith (*Symposium*, 200–214) and Klinghardt (*Gemeinschaftsmahl und Mahlgemeinschaft*, 333–36ff.) defend at some length the idea that 1 Cor. 11 and 14 represent the same event.

40. Klauck, *Herrenmahl*, 347–48; Smith, *Symposium*, 200.

41. Morton Smith, "Pauline Worship as Seen by Pagans," *Harvard Theological Review* 73 (1980): 241–49. For an excellent though older summary of the material in 1 Cor. 14, see Ferdinand Hahn, *The Worship of the Early Church*, trans. and intro. John Reumann (Philadelphia: Fortress Press, 1973), 68–76. On the issue of a single gathering, see Hahn's firm denial of such an event (72). For a more recent analysis, working with the meal-sharing traditions, and arguing for symposium nature of 1 Cor. 14, see Klinghardt, *Gemeinschaftsmahl und Mahlgemeinschaft*, 347–63.

42. This is the older, standard view of the relationship between the Corinthian meal and the Last Supper meal. For summary and bibliography on this view, see Klinghardt, *Gemeinschaftsmahl und Mahlgemeinschaft*, 333–35. Note also that Crossan has an overly simple categorization here (*Birth of Christianity*, 435–36).

43. This agrees with Crossan's basic point that Paul proclaims to the Corinthians that the meal and the bread-and-cup ritual form a single event called the Lord's Supper (*Birth of Christianity*, 435–38). The inherent unity comes, as Smith so thoroughly showed, from the basic meal pattern itself of *deipnon* followed by *symposion*. Cf. Klinghardt, *Gemeinschaftsmahl und Mahlgemeinschaft*, 282–83.

44. Marxsen, *Lord's Supper*, 99.

45. For a helpful summary of and distinction between the Jesus-kergyma (followers of Jesus), Christ-kerygma (before Paul, as well as in Paul and after Paul), and the Jesus Christ-kerygma (typified in the Synoptic Gospels), see Willi Marxsen, "Christology in the NT," *Interpreter's Dictionary of the Bible*, suppl. vol. (Nashville: Abingdon Press, 1976), 146–56.

46. Take, for example, two excellent works, both standards in their own way: James F. White, *Introduction to Christian Worship*, 3rd ed. rev. and expanded (Nashville: Abingdon Press, 2000), and Paul F. Bradshaw, *The Search for the Origins of Christian Worship*, 2nd ed. (New York: Oxford University Press, 2002).

47. See Justin Martyr, *First Apology*, chaps. 66–67. Justin's very significant text on Sunday service and the Eucharist can be found in Greek, with Latin translation, in Anton Hänggi and Irmgard Pahl, *Prex Eucharistica* (Fribourg: Éditions Universitaires Fribourg Suisse, 1968), 68–72 [Eng. trans., Cyril C. Richardson, *Early Christian Fathers* (Philadelphia: Westminster Press, 1953), 285–88].

48. For the initial work here, see Riggs, "From Gracious Table to Sacramental Elements." Also see Crossan, *Historical Jesus*, 360–65; idem, *Birth of Christianity*, 435–39; Aaron Milavec, "The Pastoral Genius of the Didache: An Analytical Translation and Commentary," in *Christianity*, ed. Jacob Neusner, Ernest S. Frerichs, Amy-Jill Levine, 89–125 (Atlanta: Scholars Press, 1989), 97.

49. Here see Peter Borgen's standard study, *Bread from Heaven* (Leiden: E. J. Brill, 1965).

50. Bultmann's assessment remains fundamentally intact. See Rudolf Bultmann, *The Gospel of John*, trans. G. R. Beasley-Murray (Philadelphia: Westminster Press, 1971), 234–37.

51. J. Louis Martyn, *History and Theology in the Fourth Gospel* (Nashville: Abingdon Press, 1979).

52. See the apt comments by Smith, *Symposium*, 274–75.

53. Marxsen, *Lord's Supper*, 11–113; idem, *Jesus and the Church*, 137–46.

54. See esp. Marxsen, *Jesus and the Church*, 144–46.

55. See, e.g., Martin Hengel, *Judaism and Hellenism*, trans. John Bowden (Philadelphia: Fortress Press, 1981); idem, *The "Hellenization" of Judaea in the First Century after Christ* (Philadelphia: Trinity Press, 1989).

56. Williams, *Jesus' Death*; Seeley, *Noble Death*.

57. Riggs, "Sacred Food and Second-Century Ecclesiologies."

58. *Smyrnaeans* 7.1.

59. *Ephesians* 20.2. Also see the comments by William Schoedel who, though interpreting Ignatius's comments on eucharistic realism more broadly, admits that such realism is still present in Ignatius's thought (William R. Schoedel, *Ignatius of Antioch* [Philadelphia: Fortress Press, 1985], 97–99, cf. 184–87, 240–42).

60. Justin's very significant text on Sunday service and the Eucharist can be found in Greek, with Latin translation, in Anton Hänggi and Irmgard Pahl, *Prex Eucharistica* (Fribourg: Éditions Universitaires Fribourg Suisse, 1968), 68–72 [Eng. trans. Cyril C. Richardson, *Early Christian Fathers* (Philadelphia: Westminster Press, 1953), 285–88].

61. *First Apology* 66.2.

62. Scholars often designate the early medieval period as beginning in 476 CE, when Odoacer, the king of several German tribes, conquered Ravenna and deposed the last of the Roman emperors, Romulus Augustulus. Since the Visigoths had overrun Roman territory a century earlier, when the Huns pushed them westward from their home north of the Black Sea, some take the late fourth century to mark the start of the medieval period. Others take the papacy of Gregory the Great (590–604), which was contemporaneous with the death of Venantius Fortunatus (d. ca. 600), the last of the great Latin poets, to mark the beginning of the medieval period. The high Middle Ages can be dated from the split of the Latin Western and Greek Eastern churches (1054) through the move of the papacy to Avignon, France (1309). The end of the late Middle Ages might be dated to 1550, after the onset of the Protestant Reformation and during the Council of Trent.

63. See Ramsay MacMullen, *Christianizing the Roman Empire (A.D. 100–400)* (New Haven, CT: Yale University Press, 1984), 32–33, 135–36n26; Robert M. Grant, *Early Christianity and Society* (San Francisco: Harper & Row, Publishers, 1977), 1–12. For further studies on the Christian population in the Roman Empire, see the bibliography in Grant (193–94) and the more recent studies to be found in MacMullen (*Christianizing*, 135–36n26).

64. E. Glenn Hinson, *The Evangelization of the Roman Empire* (Macon, GA: Mercer University Press, 1981), 161–92, 211–31.

65. For a very general introduction to patristic eucharistic theology, given from a particular point of view, see R. J. Halliburton, "The Patristic Theology of the Eucharist," in *The Study of Liturgy*, rev. ed., ed. Cheslyn Jones, Geoffrey Wainwright, Edward Yarnold, SJ, and Paul Bradshaw (New York: Oxford University Press, 1992), 245–51. For a more thorough essay and excellent bibliography, see the slightly older studies by Georg Kretschmar, "Abendmahl: III/1. Altkirche," in *Theologische Realenzyklopädie* (Berlin: Walter de Gruyter, 1977), 1:59–89; and Erwin Iserloh, "Abendmahl: III/2. Mittelalter," *Theologische Realenzyklopädie* (Berlin: Walter de Gruyter, 1977), 1:89–107. Among older books in English, see Darwell Stone, *A History of the Doctrine of the Eucharist* (London: Longmans, Green, 1909); Charles Gore, *The Body of Christ* (London: John Murray, 1901). The most comprehensive treatment in English is Edward J. Kilmartin, SJ, *The Eucharist in the West: History and Theology*, ed. Robert J. Daly, SJ (Collegeville, MN: The Liturgical Press, 1998). Among Kilmartin's other works that are helpful here, see *Christian Liturgy: Theology and Practice*, part I, *Systematic Theology of Liturgy* (Kansas City: Sheed & Ward, 1988); idem, "The Catholic Tradition of Eucharistic Theology:

Towards the Third Millennium," *Theological Studies* 55 (1994): 405–57; idem, "A Modern Approach to the Word of God and Sacraments of Christ: Perspectives and Principles," in *The Sacraments: God's Love and Mercy Actualized*, ed. Francis A. Eigo, OSA (Villanova, PA: The Villanova University Press, 1979), 59–109. Also see the important and thorough studies, with extensive bibliographies, by Johannes Betz, SJ, *Die Eucharistie in der Zeit der griechischen Väter*, 2 vols. (Freiburg: Herder, 1961, 1964); idem, *Eucharistie: In der Schrift und Patristik* (Freiburg: Herder, 1979). For this section and the next, I am thoroughly indebted to the lectures, seminars, and writings of my teacher, Edward J. Kilmartin, SJ.

66. On the redactional process in *Didache* 9 and 10, see Riggs, "From Gracious Table to Sacramental Elements"; idem, "The Sacred Food of Didache 9–10."

67. J. N. D. Kelly, *Early Christian Doctrines*, 2nd ed. (New York: Harper & Bros., 1960), 211, 211–16.

68. Stone, *Doctrine of the Holy Eucharist*, 22–42.

69. Stone, *Doctrine of the Holy Eucharist*, 23, 29, 33.

70. Stone, *Doctrine of the Holy Eucharist*, 29–37; Kilmartin, *Eucharist in the West*, 8–10; Betz, *Eucharistie: In der Schrift und Patristik*, 143–44.

71. Later scholarship has shown that the Tertullian language of image and prototype represents a different approach than Stone's third category and, as such, ought not be assimilated into the third category (*pace* Stone, *Doctrine of the Holy Eucharist*, 33).

72. Josef Rupert Geiselmann, *Die Eucharistielehre der Vorscholastik*, Forschungen zur christlichen Literatur- und Dogmengeschichte XV (Paderborn: F. Schönigh, 1926). Also see Pierre Batiffol, *L'Eucharistie, la présence réelle et la transsubstantiation*, 2nd ed. (Paris: Librairie Victor Lecoffre, 1905), 347–48, on these two distinct strands. This edition is difficult to find and in later editions the discussion of the two strands—Augustinian and Ambrosian—has been removed. See Batiffol's comments on Ambrose, *L'Eucharistie, la présence réelle et la transsubstantiation*, 5th ed. (Paris: Librairie Victor Lecoffre, 1913), 335–70; Friedrich Loofs, "Abendmahl II," *Realencyklopädie für protestantische Theologie und Kirche*, 3rd ed. (Leipzig: J. C. Hinrich, 1896), 1:60–64; Reinhold Seeberg, *Text-Book of the History of Doctrines*, trans. Charles E. Hay (Grand Rapids: Baker Book House, 1983), 323–34; F. Vernet, "Eucharistie du IXe a la fin du XIe siécle,"in *Dictionnaire de théologie catholique* (Paris, 1913), 5:1222.

73. Geiselmann, *Die Eucharistielehre der Vorscholastik*, 3–55.

74. Geiselmann, *Die Eucharistielehre der Vorscholastik*, 58–143.

75. Geiselmann, *Die Eucharistielehre der Vorscholastik*, 144–406.

76. See, for example, Kilmartin, *Eucharist in the West*, 3–78; Loofs, "Abendmahl II," 1:60–64; Allan J. Macdonald, *Berengar and the Reform of Sacramental Doctrine* (Merrick, NY: Richwood Publishing Co., 1930; repr. 1977), 227–62; Allan J. Macdonald, ed., *The Evangelical Doctrine of Holy Communion* (London: SPCK, 1936), 40–117, esp. 69–84; James F. McCue, "The Doctrine of Transubstantiation from Berengar through Trent: The Point at Issue," *Harvard Theological Review* 61 (1968): 385–430; Ralph W. Quere, *Melanchthon's Christum Cognoscere: Christ's Efficacious Presence in the Eucharistic Theology of Melanchthon* (Nieuwkoop: B. De Graaf, 1977), 11–31; Herman Sasse, *This Is My Body* (Minneapolis, MN: Augsburg Publishing House, 1959), 24–31, 178n117; cf. Henri de Lubac, *Corpus Mysticum: l'eucharistie et l'Église au Moyen âge*, 2nd ed. (Paris: Aubier, 1949), 139–61; also see Moloney, *The Eucharist*, 102–14. Note the helpful comments by Gary Macy, who cautions against

reading the varied Western eucharistic traditions according to later and partisan "Reformation" categories of real presence or symbolism; see Gary Macy, *The Theologies of the Eucharist in the Early Scholastic Period* (Oxford: Clarendon Press, 1984), 1–17; idem, *The Banquet's Wisdom* (New York: Paulist Press, 1992), 5–14. Macy's excellent study of early scholastic thought carries the Ambrosian/Augustinian distinction a bit farther, and he shows the diverse creativity of the early scholastic thinkers. Macy divides early scholastic thought into a metabolic or somatic approach ("Paschasian," 44–72), and two varieties of symbolic approaches ("Mystical," 73–105, and "Ecclesiastical," 106–32) in which the Eucharist as sign enlivens the individual or the community, comprised of believers, by the saving presence of Christ. Macy notes these as tendencies with overlaps that highlight the diversity of the early scholastic period.

77. Kilmartin, *Eucharist in the West*, xxiii. This section and the next are indebted to Kilmartin's analysis in *Eucharist in the West*, 3–168; idem, "The Catholic Tradition"; idem, "A Modern Approach." Also see the similar comments by Sasse, *This Is My Body*, 24–31.

78. Kilmartin, *Eucharist in the West*, xxiii.

79. For summaries and citations, see Stone, *Doctrine of the Holy Eucharist*, 42–54, 109–32. Steven J. Patterson gives an illuminating and important contribution on *why* early Christians interpreted Jesus' death as sacrifice, and *why* it remained important in a Greco-Roman social world welded together by sacrifice. See *Beyond the Passion: Rethinking the Death and Life of Jesus* (Minneapolis: Fortress Press, 2004), 69–101.

80. See the excursus at the end of this chapter for a discussion of the history of "sacrament" as such.

81. Leo the Great, "Sermon 74.2," in *St. Leo the Great: Sermons*. Trans. Jane Patricia Freeland and Agnes Josephine Conway, The Fathers of the Church, vol. 93 (Washington DC: Catholic University Press, 1996), 326. *Quod itaque Redemptoris nostri conspicuum fuit, in sacramenta transivit.* For a full discussion of the relation between *sacramentum* and *mysterium* in the Latin tradition, see Y. Congar, "Le 'mysterion' appliqué aux sacrements, traduit par 'sacramentum' dans l'église ancienne," in *Un peuple messianique* (Paris: Cerf, 1974), 47–55. See also Louis Bouyer, *The Christian Mystery* (Edinburgh: T. & T. Clark, 1989), esp. 5–18 and 31–171, for a treatment of "mystery" in the liturgy. My thanks to Dennis McManus for this reference to Leo and secondary scholarship.

82. Betz, *Eucharistie: In der Schrift und Patristik*, 101. For Chrysostom, see Betz, *Eucharistie: In der Schrift und Patristik*, 101–4; August Naegle, *Die Eucharistielehre des heiligen Johannes Chrysostomus, des Doctor Eucharistiae* (Strassburg: Herder, 1900), esp. 65–114.

83. *On the Priesthood*, 6, 4. Text in *Sources chrétiennes*, ed. H. de Lubac and Jean Daniélou (Paris: Éditions du Cerf, 1946), 272; hereafter cited as *SC*, followed by volume number.

84. *Instructions to the Catechumens*, 2.2. *SC* 366.

85. *Homilies on 2 Corinthians*, 30.2. Text in *Patrologiae Cursus Completus*, Series Graeca, ed. J. P. Migne (Paris, 1857–91); hereafter cited as *PG*, followed by volume number and page number.

86. *Homilies on 1 Corinthians*, 24.4; *PG* 61.203.

87. Edward J. Kilmartin, "The Eucharistic Gift: Augustine of Hippo's Tractate XXVII on Jn. 6:60–72," in *Preaching in the Patristic Age: Studies in Honor of Walter J. Burghardt, S.J.*, ed. David G. Hunter (New York: Paulist, 1989), 173–74.

88. The "sharpest thinker of the antiochene school"; Betz, *Eucharistie: In der Schrift und Patristik*, 105–8.

89. "Jesus did not say, 'This is a symbol (σύμβολον) of my body (σώματος) and a symbol of my blood,' but, 'This is (έστι) my body and my blood,' teaching us not to look at the nature (φύσις) of what is set before us, but that through the accomplished thanksgiving this becomes the body (σάρκα) and blood," in *On the Gospel of Matthew* 26:26; *PG* 66.713B.

90. On Theodore and anamnesis, see Betz, *Eucharistie: In der Schrift und Patristik*, 105–6. For summary comments on anamnesis in the Greek East, followed by analysis of the Greek theologians, see Betz, *Eucharistie: In der Schrift und Patristik*, 86–87 and 88–141.

91. See Kilmartin, *Eucharist in the West*, 35–40; Betz, *Eucharistie: In der Schrift und Patristik*, 112–24.

92. Betz, *Eucharistie: In der Schrift und Patristik*, 118–19.

93. Kilmartin, *Eucharist in the West*, 37–40; Betz, *Eucharistie: In der Schrift und Patristik*, 120–24.

94. Kilmartin, *Eucharist in the West*, 11–23.

95. Kilmartin, *Eucharist in the West*, 14–23, esp. 15, 21; Betz, *Eucharistie: In der Schrift und Patristik*, 147–48.

96. Exactly what Ambrose meant here has raised some controversy. For entrance to the discussion, see Kilmartin, *Eucharist in the West*, 15–16. For a summary of the arguments that have been given, see Raymond Johanny, *L'Eucharistie, centre de l'histoire du salut, chez Ambroise de Milan* (Paris: Beauchesne et ses fils, 1968), 104–24; also see Josef Schmitz, *Gottesdienst im altchristlichen Mailand: Eine liturgiewissenschaftliche Untersuchung über Initiation and Messfeier während des Jahres der Zeit des Bischofs Ambrosius* (Cologne: Peter Hanstein, 1975), 408–10.

97. *Nam sacramentum istud, quod accipis, Christi sermone conficitur. Quod si tantum valuit sermo Heliae, ut ignem de caelo deposceret: non valebit Christi sermo, ut species mutet elementorum? De totius mundi operibus legisti: Quia ipse dixit et facta sunt, ipse mandavit et creata sunt* [Psalm 148:5]. *Sermo ergo Christi, qui potuit ex nihilo facere quod non erat, non potest ea, quae sunt, in id mutare, quod non erant?* (Ambrose, *De mysteriis* 9.52. in *Corpus Scriptorum Ecclesiasticorum Latinorum* [Vindolsonae: C. Geroldi Filium Bibliopolam Academiae; F. Tempsky; Holdes-Pichles Tempsky, 1866–], 73:112.34–44; hereafter cited as *CSEL*, followed by the volume number, page number, and line number).

98. *De apologia prophetae David* 1.12.58; *CSEL* 32/2.339.18–340.5.

99. On Cyprian, see Kilmartin, *Eucharist in the West*, 10–11; cf. Betz, *Eucharistie: In der Schrift und Patristik*, 144–45.

100. E.g., *Explanatio psalmi* 38.25; *CSEL* 64.203.19–25; *De sacramentis* 4.6.27; *CSEL* 73.57.4–12. For more, see Kilmartin, *Eucharist in the West*, 18–19.

101. See Kilmartin, *Eucharist in the West*, xxiii, 3–6, 23–61; idem, "Eucharistic Gift"; Betz, *Eucharistie: In der Schrift und Patristik*, 150–54. Also see Gustave Martelet, *Résurrection, eucharistie, et genèse de l'homme; chemins théologiques d'un renouveau chrétien* (Paris: Desclée, 1972), 131–37 [Eng. trans. *The Risen Christ and the Eucharistic World*, trans. René Hague (New York: Seabury Press, 1976)]. Among the many studies of Augustine's eucharistic teaching, see Karl Adam, *Eucharistielehre des hl. Augustin* (Paderborn: F. Schöningh, 1908); idem, "Zur Eucharistielehre des hl. Augustinus," *Theologie Quartalschrift* 112 (1931); Marie-François Berrouard, "L'être sacramentel de l'eucharistie selon saint Augustin: Commentaire de Jean VI. 60–63 dans le *Tractatus* XXVII, 1–6

et 11–12 *in Iohannis Evangelium*," *Nouvelle Revue Theologique* 99, no. 5 (1977): 703–21 [49 (1977): 702–31]; Gerard Bonner, "Augustine's Understanding of the Church as a Eucharistic Community," in *Saint Augustine the Bishop: A Book of Essays*, ed. Fannie LeMoine, Christopher Kleinhenz (New York: Garland Publisher, 1994), 39–63; idem, "The Doctrine of Sacrifice: Augustine and the Latin Patristic Tradition," in *Sacrifice and Redemption: Durham Essays in Theology* (Cambridge: Cambridge University Press, 1991), 101–17; Th. Camelot, "Réalisme et symbolisme dans la doctrine eucharistique de s. Augustin," *Revue des sciences philosophiques et théologiques* 31 (1947): 394–410; H. M. Féret, "Sacramentum Res dans la langue théologique de S. Augustin," *Revue des sciences philosophiques et théologiques* 29 (1940): 218–40; Wilhelm Gessel, *Eucharistische Gemeinschaft bei Augustinus* (Würzburg: Augustinus-Verlag, 1966); Kilmartin, "Eucharistic Gift"; idem, *Eucharist in the West*, 23–30; Gaston Lecordier, *La Doctrine de l'Eucharistie chez saint Augustin* (Paris: Lecoffre, 1930); Joseph Lécuyer, "La sacrifice selon saint Augustin," in *Augustinus Magister* [Congrès international augustinien 1954] (Paris: Études augustiniennes, 1954–55), 905–14; Cornelius Mayer, "Die Feier der Eucharistie als Selbstdarstellung der Kirche nach der Lehre des hl. Augustinus," in *Der hl. Augustinus als Seelsorger, Augustinus-Colloquium 20–24 Mai, 1991* (St. Ottilien: EOS-Verlag, 1992), 94–102; Eugène Portalié, *A Guide to the Thought of Saint Augustine*, trans. Ralph J. Bastian (Chicago: H. Regnery Co., 1960); L. J. Van der Lof, "Eucharistie et présence réelle selon saint Augustin," *Revue des Études Augustiniennes* 10, no. 4 (1964): 295–304.

102. Batiffol, *L'Eucharistie*, 422.

103. For an introductory summary of this material, see Pamela Jackson, "Eucharist," in *Augustine through the Ages: An Encyclopedia*, Allan D. Fitzgerald, OSA, gen. ed. (Grand Rapids: Eerdmans, 1999), 330–34. For a classic summary of Augustine's realism, see Lecordier, *La Doctrine*, 26–39.

104. So, for example, Van der Lof argues that while Augustine may show some passages about "real presence," such as being "carried in his hands," these passages must be nuanced and are not "like Ambrose on their miraculous conversion into the body and blood of Christ" ("Eucharistie et présence réelle," 298–300). Likewise, Kilmartin makes clear that Augustine separates himself from the Chrysostom (and Ambrose) metabolic tradition ("Eucharistic Gifts," esp. 173–74). Note that in Lecordier's section on Augustine's realism, the words of Van der Lof ring true: Lecordier does not adduce passages where Augustine unambiguously is metabolic, on the order of Ambrose.

105. Bonner, "Augustine's Understanding of the Church," 48–49.

106. Camelot, "Réalisme et symbolism," 410; also see Féret, "Sacramentum Res," who argues that Augustine develops his idea of *sacramentum* and *res* from scriptural method in which the sign (e.g., a word) points to its reality, which is present (223–34). Thus the reality signified is not separated from the rite, but confers the mystery that is Christ; "Les yeux perçoivent le rite, l'intelligence et la foi la grace" (242–43). The connection between exegesis and rite exists because Augustine employs the concept of sign for (1) certain rituals of the Old Testament and New Testament; (2) a method of exegesis; and (3) "mysteries of the faith," such as the incarnation (222–23).

107. Jackson, "Eucharist."

108. Bonner, "Church as Eucharistic Community"; idem, "Doctrine of Sacrifice"; Gessel, *Eucharistische Gemeinschaft*, esp. 165–212; Lecuyer, "Le sacrifice"; Mayer, "Selbstdarstellung der Kirche."

109. Van der Lof names three tensions: (1) between real presence and bread and cup as images or signs; (2) between real presence and the Pauline idea of "soma" as person of Christ and "the church that lives in him and was born of his work"; and (3) between real presence and the union with the ascended, glorified Christ in heaven ("Eucharistie et présence réelle," 298–300).

110. Kilmartin, *Eucharist in the West*, 25.

111. Kilmartin gives a fascinating example of how medieval theologians, assuming the alternatives of symbolic or realistic, read Augustine as merely symbolic but paraphrased him in a way that made him a realist (*Eucharist in the West*, 27–28).

112. Henri de Lubac, *Corpus Mysticum*, 150. For this perspective I am indebted to Martelet, *Résurrection, eucharistie, et genèse de l'homme*, 131–37. Note, in passing, how Luther the Augustinian monk took exactly the turn—divine immensity of the physical body—that Martelet notes Augustine could not take.

113. *De civitate Dei* 10.6; *CSEL* 47.278–79.

114. *De civitate Dei* 10.20; *CSEL* 47.294.6–9.

115. *De civitate Dei* 10.6; *CSEL* 47.278–79. *Hoc est sacrificium christianorum: multi unum corpus in Christo. Quod etiam sacramento altaris fidelibus noto frequentat ecclesia, ubi et demonstratur, quod in ea re, quam offert, ipsa offeratur* (*CSEL* 47.279.52–55).

116. *Eucharist in the West*, 24.

117. See Kilmartin, "The Eucharistic Gift," 174–77.

118. Kilmartin, *Eucharist in the West*, 25, who notes Augustine's *Sermo* 272; *Patrologiae Cursus Completus*, Series Latina, ed. J. P. Migne (Paris, 1844–); hereafter cited as *PL*, followed by volume number and page numbers; *PL* 38:1246–48 and *Sermo* 227, 40; *SC* 116.234–42.

119. See Kilmartin, "The Eucharistic Gift: Augustine of Hippo's Tractate XXVII on Jn. 6:60–72." Kilmartin summarizes Augustine by saying that, "[i]n short, Augustine teaches that the Church is the true body of Christ (*verum corpus Christi*) while the eucharistic elements are the sacrament of the body of Christ (*sacramentum corporis Christi*). Hence the sacrament of the body of Christ is received in the true body of Christ. And the sacrament of the body of Christ is the sacrifice of the true body of Christ" (*Eucharist in the West*, 28).

120. On Gelasius, see the extended discussion and notes by Kilmartin, *Eucharist in the West*, 31–58. Note Kilmartin's comment that "Gelasius's theology of the sacraments of the Eucharist reflects the actual situation of the official Roman theology of the Eucharist at the end of the fifth century" (31).

121. See Betz, *Eucharistie: In der Schrift und Patristik*, 145.

122. Kilmartin, *Eucharist in the West*, 59.

123. Kilmartin, *Eucharist in the West*, 79.

124. For an extended discussion and critical notes with bibliography, see Kilmartin, *Eucharist in the West*, 79–82.

125. *De corpore et sanguine Domini* can be found in Corpus Christianorum Continuatio Mediaevalis 16 (Turnholti: Typographi Brepols, 1969); hereafter cited as *CCCM*, followed by volume number and page number; also see *PL* 120.1267–1350. Partial English translation can be found in *Early Medieval Theology*, trans. and ed. George E. McCracken, Library of Christian Classics IX (Philadelphia: The Westminster Press), 94–108. Translation of the full text can be found in German; see Melchior Hausherr, *Der heilige Paschasius Radbertus: eine Stimme über die Eucharistie vor tausend Jahren* (Mainz, 1862).

126. Critical Latin text, with French translation, for Ratramnus's *De corpore et sanguine Domini* can be found in J. N. Bakhuizen van den Brink, ed., *De corpore et sanguine Domini: texte originale et notice bibliographique* (Amsterdam: North Holland, 1974) [Eng. trans. in McCracken, *Early Medieval Theology*, 118–147].

127. For a general introduction to the controversy and subsequent scholarship, see John F. Fahey, *The Eucharistic Teaching of Ratramn of Corbie* (Mundelein, IL: Saint Mary of the Lake Seminary, 1951), 1–36. The following discussion follows Kilmartin, *Eucharist in the West*, 82–89, and Gustave Martelet, *Résurrection, eucharistie, et genèse de l'homme*, 138–44. But compare Geiselmann, who argued that Paschasius blended the older somatic, Antiochene tradition with the Augustinian tradition, producing the first catholic synthesis, while Ratramnus chose for the merely figurative view and turned the Augustinian "a-metabolic" position into an "anti-metabolic view" (*Eucharistielehre*,195–217).

128. "Epistula ad Fudegardum," *CCCM* 16.146. In 856 Paschasius wrote this letter to Frudegard, monk of Saint-Riquier, responding to Ratramnus; *CCCM* 16.190–95; also in *PL* 120.1351–66.

129. *Vera utique caro Christi quae crucifixa est et sepulta; CCCM* 16.30.81–82.

130. *percipiamus in pane quod pependit in cruce; CCCM* 16.151.185

131. Hrabanus Maurus, *Poenitentiale* 33; *PL* 110.493A.

132. Fahey, *Eucharistic Teaching*, 130–62; Martelet, *Résurrection, eucharistie, et genèse de l'homme*, 138–44.

133. Fahey, *Eucharistic Teaching*, 56–81, 82–91.

134. Here I follow Kilmartin, *Eucharist in the West*, 6–7. Commenting on Eph.1:7, Jerome argued: "Truly the blood of Christ and flesh are to be understood two-fold: either that which is spiritual and divine, about which he himself said, 'My flesh is truly food,' (Jn. 6:55), and 'Unless you eat my flesh and drink my blood,' (Jn. 6:53); or, the flesh and blood that was crucified, which was poured out by the soldier's lance" (*Commentarium in epistolam ad Ephesios 1; PL* 26.451A).

135. Kilmartin, *Eucharist in the West*, 67–76, 62–67.

136. Fahey, *Eucharistic Teaching*, 92.

137. Fahey, *Eucharistic Teaching*, 82–118; also see Martelet, *Résurrection, eucharistie, et genèse de l'homme*, 138–39.

138. Fahey, *Eucharistic Teaching*, 130–62.

139. Macy, *Eucharistic Theologies*, 73–132.

140. Kilmartin, *Eucharist in the West*, 62–67, 97–153; Power, *Eucharistic Mystery*, 163–207; Macy, *Banquet's Wisdom*, 92–95.

141. The critical modern edition of Berengar's works can be found in W. B. Beekenkamp, *De avondmaalsleer van Berengarius van Tours* (vol. 1) and *De Sacra Coena adversus Lanfrancum* (vol. 2) (The Hague: M. Nijhoff, 1941). The standard secondary work in English has been Macdonald, *Berengar*. For general background, see Gary Macy, *The Theologies of the Eucharist in the Early Scholastic Period* (Oxford: The Clarendon Press; New York: Oxford University Press, 1984), 18–43. For a general introduction and bibliography to Berengar, see O. Kapitani, "Berengar v. Tours," in *Lexikon des Mittelalters* (Munich, Zurich: Artemis-Verlag, 1977–99), 1:1937–39; Geoffrey Wainwright, *Encyclopedia of Religion* (New York: Macmillan, 1987), 2:112–13. For an overview of the theological writings of the early scholastics, see Artur Michael Landgraf, "Berengar of Tours," in *Einführung in die Geschichte der Theologischen Literatur der Frühscholastik* (Regensburg: Gregorius-Verlag, 1948) 2:112–13.

142. See Fahey, *Eucharistic Teaching*, 16–21; Kilmartin, *Eucharist in the West*, 97–102; Macdonald, *Berengar*, 227–330; Macdonald, *Evangelical Doctrine*, 85–117; Macy, *Theologies of the Eucharist*, 35–43; Martelet, *Résurrection, eucharistie, et genèse de l'homme*, 144–49.

143. *non solum sacramentum, sed etiam verum corpus et sanguinem Domini nostri Iesu Christi esse, et sensualiter, non solum sacramento, sed in veritate, manibus sacerdotum tractari et frangi et fidelium dentibus atteri* (Heinrich Denzinger and Adolf Schönmetzer, *Enchiridion symbolorum: definitionum et declarationum de rebus fidei et morum* [Barcinone: Herder, 1976], 690); hereafter referred to as *DS*, followed by document number).

144. Kilmartin, *Eucharist in the West*, 6–7, 65–66, 76, 78, 102, 107, 124.

145. Kilmartin, *Eucharist in the West*, 117–18.

146. Groundbreaking work was done by Ludwig Hödl, "Sacramentum et Res—Zeichen und Bezeichnetes: Eine begriffsgeschichtliche Arbeit zum frühscholastischen Eucharistietraktat," *Scholastik* 38 (1963): 161–82. Also see Kilmartin, "A Modern Approach," 60–62; idem, *Eucharist in the West*, 62–63, 119–20; Moloney, *The Eucharist*, 125–26; Macy, *Banquet's Wisdom*, 85–92.

147. Kilmartin, *Eucharist in the West*, 119–21; idem, *The Sacraments*, 60.

148. Kilmartin, *Eucharist in the West*, 62–65, 119–26. Compare the negative view of this early scholastic focus on the somatic presence in de Lubac, *Corpus Mysticum*, 252–67, 274–77.

149. Kilmartin, *Eucharist in the West*, 65–66; see discussion, 65–76.

150. Kilmartin, *Eucharist in the West*, 64, 143–53, esp. 144, 145–46; Hans Jorissen, *Die Entfaltung der Transsubstantiationslehre bis zum Beginn der Hochscholastik* (Münster: Aschendorff, 1965), 24–44; McCue, "The Doctrine of Transubstantiation"; Cummings, "Medieval Eucharistic Theology," 76–78; Gary Macy, "The Doctrine of Transubstantiation in the Middle Ages," *Journal of Ecclesiastical History* 45 (1994): 11–41, reprinted in *Treasures from the Storeroom* (Collegeville, MN: The Liturgical Press, 1999), 81–120; idem, *Banquet's Wisdom*, 102–14. A basic scholastic issue with transubstantiation was that neither "substance" (itself comprised of matter and form) nor "accident" existed separately, apart from a concrete reality; so the problem arose how the accidents of the elements could exist apart from their proper substances. Consubstantiation reasonably avoided this problem by positing that substances and accidents properly remained as features of their own reality; both bread and wine, and Jesus' body and blood, remain. However, for the scholastics several problems arose with consubstantiation. If the bread remained, could this not be construed as idolatry, since the elements were honored as the divine presence? Also, the sign function of the species (*sacramentum tantum*—bread and wine) would no longer properly point to the body and blood of Christ, but rather also to the substance of the bread and wine. Finally, the grammar of Jesus' "words of institution" supposedly ruled out a reference to "bread" still being substantially present (McCue, "Transubstantiation," 395–402).

151. For accessible overviews of this complex material, and entrance to technical studies, see Owen Cummings, "Medieval Eucharistic Theology," *Emmanuel* (March 1993): 73–79; Macy, *Banquet's Wisdom*, 102–34; Jaroslav Pelikan, *The Growth of Medieval Theology (600–1300)*, vol. 3 of *The Christian Tradition: A History of the Development of Doctrine* (Chicago: The University of Chicago Press, 1978), 184–204; Power, *Eucharistic Mystery*, 161–207; idem, "Eucharist"; Kilmartin, *Eucharist in the West*, 128–43, 153.

152. For the standard studies, see Peter Browe, *Die Verehrung der Eucharistie im Mittelalter* (1933; repr., Rome: Herder, 1967); and Edouard Dumoutet, *Le désir de voir l'hostie et les origines de la dévotion au sainct-sacrement* (Paris: Duchesne, 1926); Josef Jungmann, *The Mass of the Roman Rite*, trans. Francis A. Brunner, rev. Charles K. Riepe (New York: Benziger Bros., 1961), 1:107ff., 119–22. For an excellent and wider-ranging study of medieval eucharistic piety, see Nathan Mitchell, *Cult and Controversy: The Worship of the Eucharist outside Mass* (New York: Pueblo Publishing Co.), esp. 86–119, 163–86.

153. Browe, *Die Verehrung*, 59–68; Dumoutet, *Le désir de voir*, 18–28, 67–69; Jungmann, *Mass of the Roman Rite*, 1:119–22; Miri Rubin, *Corpus Christi: The Eucharist in Late Medieval Culture* (Cambridge and New York: Cambridge University Press, 1991), 108–29.

154. Peter Browe, "Die Elevation in der Messe," *Jahrbuch für Liturgiewissenschaft* 9 (1929): 20–66; Edouard Dumoutet, *Le Christ selon la chair et la vie liturgique au moyen-âge* (Paris: Beauchesne, 1932), 149–51.

155. For an overall introduction, see Steven Ozment, *The Age of Reform* (New Haven, CT: Yale University Press, 1980), 204–22. For penitential practices among the pious, see, for example, *The Ancrene Riwle*, trans. M. B. Salu (Notre Dame, IN: Notre Dame University Press, 1956); *Francis and Clare: The Complete Works*, trans. Regis J. Armstrong and Ignatius C. Brady (New York: Paulist Press, 1982). For a summary of this visual, late medieval piety, see Power, *Eucharistic Mystery*, 184–95.

156. Browe, *Die Verehrung*, 59–61; Dumoutet, *Le désir de voir*, 18–25.

157. *DS*, 812.

158. For entrance to the vast literature on Thomas Aquinas, see Otto Pesch, "Thomas von Aquino/Thomismus/Neuthomismus," in *Theologische Realenzyklopädie* (New York and Berlin: Walter de Gruyter, 2002), 33:433–74. For a summary of Aquinas's eucharistic teaching, with bibliographic references, see Power, *Eucharistic Mystery*, 208–40 (also see 269–90). Also see Kilmartin, *Eucharist in the West*, 247–66; Iserloh, "Abendmahl: III/2. Mittelalter," 1:95–97; E. Mangenot, "Eucharistie du XIIᵉ a la fin du XVᵉ siécle," *Dictionnaire de théologie catholique* (Paris, 1913), 5:1304–20, passim. For excellent shorter studies, more accessible to those not trained in scholastic theology, see Owen Cumings, "Medieval Eucharistic Theology," *Emmanuel* (March 1993): 73–79; Macy, *Banquet's Wisdom*, 104–9; Herbert McCabe, "Eucharistic Change," *Priests and People* 8, no. 6 (1994): 217–21; Moloney, *The Eucharist*, 39–150; Power, "Eucharist," 277–80. For an informative Catholic perspective on the sacraments in general, and thus the place of Thomas within this development, see Regis A. Duffy, "Sacraments in General," in *Systematic Theology: Roman Catholic Perspectives*, vol. 2, ed. Francis Schüssler Fiorenza and John P. Galvin (Minneapolis: Fortress Press, 1991), 183–210.

159. See Power, *Eucharistic Mystery*, 163–240, esp. 236–40.

160. Text given in Moloney, *The Eucharist*, 139. For the state of research on this passage and the authorship by Aquinas, see Pierre-Marie Gy, "L'Office du Corpus Christi et S. Thomas d'Aquin: état d'une recherche," *Revue des sciences philosophies et théologiques* 64 (1980): 491–507.

161. *Summa Theologiae* III, q. 73, arts. 1–6.

162. *Summa Theologiae* III, q. 76, arts. 1–2. For the following, see Power, *Eucharistic Mystery*, 219–26.

163. Power, *Eucharistic Mystery*, 221. *Summa Theologiae* III, q. 75, art. 1. ad 1m and ad 4m.

164. " . . . *Et ideo, proprie loquendo, corpus Christi, secundum modum essendi quem habet in hoc sacramento, neque sensu neque imaginatione perceptibile est: sed solo intellectu, qui dicitur oculos spiritualis"* (*Summa theologiae* 3a.76.7; trans. from Thomas Aquinas, *Summa Theologiae*, trans. Blackfriars [New York: McGraw Hill, 1964], 58:117).

165. On these issues, see the excellent essays by Gary Macy, "The Theological Fate of Berengar's Oath of 1059: Interpreting a Blunder Becomes Tradition," and "Berengar's Legacy as Heresiarch," in *Treasures from the Storeroom*, 20–35, 59–80.

166. How this precisely happened was debated. For instance, Thomas, following his teacher Albert the Great, held that the transformed substance, Christ's body and blood, remained with the accidents, but would not benefit the recipient whatsoever. The premise was simple: accidents and substances cannot be attached and detached as though random links of a chain. Bonaventure, following his master Alexander of Hales, argued instead that an unworthy recipient never received the sign itself (*sacramentum*) and so neither the substance. For a full discussion of positions taken during the thirteenth and fourteenth centuries, see Macy, *Treasures from the Storeroom*, 36–58.

The classical test case was the question of what a mouse might receive if it ate the eucharistic elements. For the standard treatment, which sets the issue amid technical medieval speculation, see Artur M. Landgraf, "Die in der Frühscholastik klassische Frage *Quid sumit mus*," in *Dogmensgeschichte der Frühscholastik* III/2 (Regensburg: Putset, 1955), 207–22. For a helpful summary of the issues, and a pastoral perspective on why such questions were raised, see Gary Macy, "Quid Mus Sumit as a Pastoral Question," *Researches de Théologie ancienne et médiévale* 58 (1991): 157–66. Also see Macy, *Treasures from the Storeroom*, 36–58.

167. For the following, see Macy, *Treasures from the Storeroom*, 36–58.

168. *Sacramentum et non sacramentaliter*: See, for example, Scotus's Oxford lectures (*Opus Oxoniensis*) in *Opera Omnia* 17 (Paris: Vives, 1894), 75; or his commentary on Lombard's *Sentences*, found in *Reportatio Parisiensia*, in *Omnia Opera* 24 (Paris: Vives, 1894), 27–28.

169. The seminal work on medieval diversity was by Pierre Allix, *Historia transsubstantiationis papalis* (London: Thomas Roycroft, 1675). Three important modern studies have confirmed and extended the argument for medieval eucharistic diversity on the issue of eucharistic change: Jorissen, *Entfaltung*; McCue, "Doctrine of Transubstantiation"; and Macy, *Treasures from the Storeroom*, 81–120.

170. McCue, "Doctrine of Transubstantiation." Also see Macy, *Treasures from the Storeroom* (81–120), who confirms and expands McCue's scholarship.

171. Jorissen, *Entfaltung*, 57–58; Macy, *Treasures from the Storeroom*, 84–91, 104.

172. Jorissen, *Entfaltung*, 55; Macy, *Treasures from the Storeroom*, 84–85.

173. Macy, *Treasures from the Storeroom*, 89–90. As Macy notes (90, 111n42) Luther expressly mentioned d'Ailly. Also see McCue, "Doctrine of Transubstantiation," 414–15.

174. Jorissen, *Entfaltung*, 56–57nn170–71; Macy, *Treasures from the Storeroom*, 107n15.

175. Indeed, the two great contributions of Gary Macy, in the studies already cited, are (1) the varied and creative ways that medieval theologians worked with the traditions that they inherited and (2) the specific pastoral questions that so often grounded what may appear to be merely speculative discussions about the Eucharist.

176. This was especially true when some, such as Berengar and the Cathars, took the issues to a reductio ad absurdum: For instance, if Christ's body were really consumed, how big would the heavenly Jesus have to be to account for all the consecrations and consumptions during the history of the church? Or, is Christ digested and then defecated? See Macy, *Treasures from the Storehouse*, 59–80, esp. 63–70.

177. The following excursus was originally written as background material for the Reformed-Roman Catholic dialogue group as it worked toward a common agreement on baptism. It appears in the final document, "Baptism Document: Seventh Round Reformed-Catholic Dialogue," within subsection 3, and I reproduce the text that I wrote there with some minor alterations. I want to thank my Roman Catholic colleagues, especially Joyce Zimmerman and Dennis McManus, as well as my Reformed colleagues, for their reading of this material and their helpful changes and additions.

178. See, for example, Günther Bornkamm, *Mysterion*, in Gerhard Kittel, ed., *Theological Dictionary of the New Testament*, trans. and ed. Geoffrey W. Bromiley (Grand Rapids: Eerdmans, 1967), 4:803ff.

179. To the idea of sacrament, Tertullian also added the faithful human response to God's redeeming work that comes to us through the *sacramentum*. For a general introduction to this material and a helpful bibliography, see Thomas M. Finn, "Sacraments," in *Encyclopedia of Early Christianity*, ed. Everett Ferguson (New York and London: Garland Publishing, Inc., 1990), 811–15. For *sacramentum*, see the discussion by Josef Finkenzeller, *Die Lehre von den Sakramenten im allgemeinen: Von der Schrift bis zur Scholastik* (Freiburg: Herder, 1980), 4–37, esp. 10–13, 25–30; also see J. de Ghellinck, SJ, *Pour l'histoire du mot "Sacramentum"* (Louvain: Spicelegium sacrum Lovaniense, 1924), esp. 12–18, 144–52. For a classic, late-nineteenth-century Protestant view on sacrament, see Ferdinand Kattenbusch, "Sakrament," in *Realencyklopädie für Theologie und Kirche*, 3rd ed. (Leipzig: Hinrichs, 1896–1913), 17:349–81. Kattenbusch denies a proper theological and etymological connection between *mysterion* and *sacramentum*, but agrees that Tertullian first made the connection, probably based on North African Latin translations of the New Testament (349–51). Also see Kevin W. Irwin, "Sacrament," in Joseph A. Komonchak, Mary Collins, and Dermot A. Lane, eds., *The New Dictionary of Theology* (Collegeville, MN: The Liturgical Press/A Michael Glazier Book, 1989, 1991), 910–22.

180. See Finkenzeller, *Lehre*, 22–23; cf. John Chrysostom, *Catechesis* 3, 13–19; Clement of Alexandria, *Paedagogus*; *PG* 8, 299; and Ambrose of Milan, *In Luc.*2, 85–89; *PL* 15, 1666–68.

181. For a summary of Augustine on sacrament as a sacred sign, see Finkenzeller, *Lehre*, 39–43. For a wider treatment, see Kilmartin, *Eucharist in the West*, 3–61.

182. *De civitate Dei* 10.6; *CSEL* 47.278–9. *Hoc est sacrificium christianorum: multi unum corpus in Christo. Quod etiam sacramento altaris fidelibus noto frequentat ecclesia, ubi et demonstratur, quod in ea re, quam offert, ipsa offeratur* (*CSEL* 47.279.52–55).

183. For Aquinas, see the references given above in note 158. For this summary of Aquinas's eucharistic teaching, and for bibliographic references, see Power, *Eucharistic Mystery*, 163–240, esp. 208–40 (also see 269–90).

184. Cf. Larger Catechism, QQ. 64–66; Scots Confession XVI; Second Helvetic Confession XVII.

185. E.g., Scots Confession XXI; Heidelberg Catechism Q. 68; Second Helvetic Confession XIX; Belgic Confession, art. 34; Westminster Confession XXVII.

186. Second Helvetic Confession XIX.

187. Second Helvetic Confession XXVII.

188. *Commentaries on the Last Four Books of Moses,* trans. Charles William Bingham (Grand Rapids: Eerdmans, 1950); *The Epistles of Paul the Apostle to the Romans and to the Thessalonians,* trans. Ross Mackenzie [Calvin's New Testament Commentaries, ed. David W. Torrance and Thomas F. Torrance, vol. 8] (Grand Rapids: Wm. B. Eerdmans, 1974–75); *The First Epistle of Paul the Apostle to the Corinthians,* trans. John W. Fraser [Calvin's New Testament Commentaries, ed. David W. Torrance and Thomas F. Torrance, vol. 9] (Grand Rapids: Wm. B. Eerdmans, 1974–75).

189. *Inst.* 1.5.9; *Christianae Religionis Institutio 1536,* in *Ioannis Calvini opera selecta,* ed. Peter Barth, Wilhelm Niesel, and Dora Scheuner, 5 vols. (Munich: Chr. Kaiser, 1926–52); hereafter cited as OS, with volume and page number; OS 3.53.18–23.

190. *Inst.* 1.5.1; OS 3.45.2–8.

191. Geneva Catechism Q. 25; OS 1.77.25–7.

192. *Inst.* 2.2.15; OS 3.258.11–14.

193. *Inst.* 2.2.15; OS 3.258.18–28.

194. *Inst.* 2.3.3–4; OS 3.274.20–276.38.

195. "The chief part of uprightness lacks where there is no zeal to glorify God" (*Inst.* 2.3.4; OS 3.29–30).

196. Canons of Dort III/IV, art. 4; cf. Belgic Confession, art. 14.

197. *Inst.* 4.14.18; OS 5.276.1–277.2.

198. *Inst.* 4.14.18; OS 5.276.35–277.2.

199. *Inst.* 4.14.19–26; OS 5.277.2–5.285.10.

200. Westminster Confession XXIII.

201. E.g., Scots Confession XXI; Heidelberg Catechism Q. 68; Second Helvetic Confession XIX; Belgic Confession, art. 34; Westminster Confession XXVII.

202. E.g., Tetrapolitan Confession, XVII–XVIII; First Basel Confession, VI; Second Basel Confession (First Helvetic Confession), 20 and 22 (Supper); Scots Confession XXI; Second Helvetic Confession XIX; French Confession, XXXIV–XXXVI; Belgic Confession, art. 33.

203. Second Helvetic Confession XIX.

204. Westminster Confession XXVII.

205. Westminster Confession XXVIII.1.

206. Westminster Confession, XXIX.7.

207. E.g., Scots Confession XXII; Second Helvetic Confession XVIII, XIX; Large Catechism, Q. 169.

208. Scots Confession XXII.

209. Second Helvetic Confession XIX.

210. OS 2.134.21–24.

211. Second Helvetic Confession XIX.

212. Westminster Confession XXVII.7.

213. Second Helvetic Confession XIX.

214. "ut unum prorsus atque idem sit" (*Inst.* 2.10.2; OS 3.404.1–3)

215. *Inst.* 2.10.2: OS 3.404.20–2.

216. *Inst.* 4.14.23; OS 5.280.25–28.

217. Scots Confession XXI.

218. Second Helvetic Confession XIX.

219. Otto Semmelroth, *The Preaching Word: On Theology of Proclamation,* trans. John Jay Hughes (New York: Herder & Herder, 1965); Eduard Schillebeeckx, *Christ*

the Sacrament of Encounter with God (New York: Sheed & Ward, 1963); and, among the many essays by Karl Rahner, see esp. "The Theology of Symbol," in *Theological Investigations* (Baltimore: Helicon, 1966), 4:221–52.

220. For an introduction to these thinkers from a Catholic perspective, see Regis A. Duffy, "Sacraments in General," in *Systematic Theology II*, ed. Francis Schüssler Fiorenza and John P. Galvin (Minneapolis: Fortress Press, 1991), 201–5; for a Protestant introduction, see Gerhard Ebeling, *The Word of God and Tradition*, trans. S. H. Hooke (Philadelphia: Fortress Press, 1968), 206–24.

221. See Semmelroth, *The Preached Word*, 27–71; Schillebeeckx, *Christ the Encounter*, 13–45. For the citation given, see Schillebeeckx, *Christ the Encounter*, 18. Note, however, that in this entire section of Schillebeeckx's work (1.2.1), entitled "Encounter with the earthly Christ as sacrament of the encounter with God" (13–17), as well as in the larger section of which this is a part ("Christ as the Primordial Sacrament," 13–39), Schillebeeckx assumes the inner embodiment of God's grace to us and our loving response back. The same holds for the section cited from Semmelroth's work. Strictly speaking, this assumption is not needed for the concept of Jesus as "encounter."

222. Schillebeeckx, *Christ the Encounter*, 40.

223. Rahner, *Theological Investigations*, 4:241. Note that here, as with Schillebeeckx, Christ and the church possess inwardly, and do not "merely designate," the grace of God (241). Again, the assumed inner nature of Christ, and the church, is not, strictly speaking, needed for the concept of encounter with God through church as primary sacrament.

224. Schillebeeckx, *Christ the Encounter*, 44.

225. See Schubert M. Ogden, *Faith and Freedom: Toward a Theology of Liberation*, rev. and enlarged ed. (Nashville: Abingdon Press, 1989), 81–102; idem, *Is There Only One True Religion or Are There Many?* (Dallas: SMU Press, 1992), 96–98; idem, *Doing Theology Today* (Valley Forge, PA: Trinity Press, 1996), 182–84.

226. For a fuller explanation of how Ogden's idea relates to Reformed eucharistic theology, see chapter 6 of this study.

227. For fuller explanation of this point, with references to Ogden's many works, see chapter 6 of this study.

228. Ogden, *Faith and Freedom*, 91–92.

CHAPTER 2: THE FIRST GENERATION: MARTIN LUTHER

1. Note, for example, that by the end of chapter 4 the Reformed tradition alone is sorted out into symbolic instrumentalism, symbolic parallelism, and symbolic anamnesis, all of which follow the Augustinian trajectory of real presence, as well as symbolic memorialism, which fills the category of "merely" symbolic or memorialist.

2. Many thanks to Ron Feenstra of Calvin Theological Seminary for first making this clear to me.

3. See chapter 1, n. 72.

4. Here I want to thank Philip Devenish, erstwhile professor at the Divinity School, the University of Chicago, and my Reformed colleagues on the Reformed-Roman Catholic dialogue group, for helping me think about this issue.

5. For an excellent entrée to these issues, see Dennis Tamburello, *Union with Christ: John Calvin and the Mysticism of St. Bernard* (Louisville, KY: Westminster John Knox Press, 1994), 3–12.

6. Ernst Troeltsch wrote that "[i]n the widest sense of the word, mysticism is simply the insistence upon a direct inward and present religious experience." See *The Social Teaching of the Christian Churches*, trans. Olive Wyon (New York: Macmillan, 1931), 2:730.

7. The historical-theological work of Bernard McGinn commands first attention. Among his many works, see his multivolume *The Presence of God: A History of Western Christian Mysticism* (New York: Crossroad, 1991–).

8. *Theologia mystica est cognitio experimentalis habita de Deo per amoris unitivi complexum.* See Jean Gerson, *Selections from "A Deo exivit," "Contra curiositatem studentium" and "De mystica theologia speculativa,"* ed. Steven E. Ozment (Leiden: E. J. Brill, 1969), 64–65. For the mystical theology of Gerson, see Steven E. Ozment, *Homo Spiritualis* (Leiden: E. J. Brill, 1969), 47–83, esp. 78–79, whose translation I here follow. Also see Tamburello, *Union with Christ*, 11–12.

9. See, e.g., the categories given by Ozment, *Age of Reform*, 73–134 (esp. 115–34), and note that Tamburello makes the connection from this type of mysticism, as exemplified by Bernard, to that of Calvin.

10. See nn. 50, 52 below.

11. See n. 53 below.

12. See, e.g., chapter 3, n. 15.

13. Note Tamburello's extraordinary list of references in Calvin, where he speaks about union with Christ (*Union with Christ*, 111–13). Also see B. A. Gerrish, *Grace and Gratitude* (Minneapolis: Fortress Press, 1993); and, Tamburello, *Union with Christ*, which shows the particular importance of this theme for Calvin's sacramental theology. See also the excellent but overlooked essay by Charles Partee, "Calvin's Central Dogma Again," *Sixteenth Century Journal* 18, no. 2 (1987): 191–99; and see Dawn DeVries, *Jesus Christ in the Preaching of Calvin and Schleiermacher* (Louisville, KY: Westminster John Knox Press, 1996), 95–96.

14. Joseph N. Tylenda, "Calvin on Christ's True Presence in the Lord's Supper," *American Ecclesiastical Review* 155 (1966): 321–33.

15. Calvin, *Commentary on 1 Cor 11.24*; *Ioannis Calvini opera quae supersunt Omnia*, ed. Wilhelm Baum, Edward Cunitz, and Edward Reuss, 59 vols., vols. 29–87 of *Corpus Reformatorum* (Brunswick: C. A. Schwetschke and Son [M. Bruhn], 1863–1900), 49.487; hereafter cited as C.O., with volume and page number.

16. *Und zwar S. Augustin halten sie fur ihr eigen*, W.A. 23.209.30; L.W. 37.104; see n. 19.

17. Martin Brecht's three-volume study has become the standard for Luther biography: *Martin Luther: His Road to Reformation, 1483–1521*, trans. James L. Schaaf (Philadelphia: Fortress Press, 1985); *Martin Luther: Shaping and Defining the Reformation, 1521–1532*, trans. James L. Schaaf (Minneapolis: Fortress Press, 1990); *Martin Luther: The Preservation of the Church, 1532–1546*, trans. James L. Schaaf (Minneapolis: Fortress Press, 1993). Shorter, one-volume biographies abound, among which Heiko Oberman's *Luther: Man between God and the Devil* (New Haven, CT: Yale University Press, 1989) remains the best, although it requires a basic background in the late medieval period. For a less demanding entrance to Luther, see James Kittleson, *Luther: The Story of the Man and His Career* (Minneapolis: Augsburg Publishing House, 1986). Of course, Roland Bainton, *Here I Stand!* (New

York: Abingdon-Cokesbury Press, 1950) remains a classic. Bernard Lohse, *Martin Luther: An Introduction to His Life and Work*, trans. Robert C. Schultz (Philadelphia: Fortress Press, 1986) enters the reader into Luther and the scholarly discussions that surround his life. Also see Mark U. Edwards Jr., "Luther's Biography," in *Reformation Europe: A Guide to Research II*, ed. William S. Maltby (St. Louis: Center for Reformation Research, 1992), 5–20.

18. For entrance to the discussion of young Martin's mental health, see Steve Ozment, *The Age of Reform* (New Haven, CT: Yale University Press, 1980), 223–31. Also see Randall C. Zachman, *The Assurance of Faith: Conscience in the Theology of Martin Luther and John Calvin* (Minneapolis: Fortress Press, 1993).

19. *D. Martin Luthers Werke: Kritische Gesamtausgabe* (Weimar: Hermann Böhlaus, 1888), 30,3:386.30–387.2; hereafter cited as W.A., with volume and page number [Eng. trans. in *Luther's Works*, ed. Jaroslav Pelikan and Helmut T. Lehmann, 55 vol. (St. Louis: Concordia Publishing House; Philadelphia: Fortress Press, 1955–), 34:103; hereafter cited as L.W., with volume and page number].

20. For entrance to the material, see Edwards, "Luther's Biography,"10–12. In particular, note the two collections by Berhard Lohse, ed., *Der Durchbruch der reformatorischen Erkenntnis bei Luther* (Darmstadt: Wissenschaftliche Buchgesellschaft, 1968), and *Der Durchbruch der reformatorischen Erkenntnis bei Luther: Neuere Untersuchungen* (Stuttgart: F. Steiner Verlag Wiesbaden, 1988).

21. On this perspective, and concerning the sacraments, see the summary comments by James McCue, "Luther and the Change in the Understanding of Sacrament," *Lutherjahrbuch 1985* (Göttingen: Vandenhoeck & Ruprecht, 1985), 282–83.

22. Carter Lindberg, *The European Reformations* (Oxford: Blackwell, 1996), 102; Ozment, *The Age of Reform*, 22–42, 231–39.

23. The place of Protestantism in late medieval Europe is an exceedingly complex topic that ranges far beyond this study. For an overview of scholarly views on the Protestant Reformation, see Steve Ozment, *Protestants: The Birth of a Revolution* (New York: Doubleday, 1992), 218–19. Also see Ozment, *The Reformation in the Cities* (New Haven, CT: Yale University Press, 1975), for a summary of views placing the Reformation in a late medieval context of ecclesial failures in piety and institution (2–14). In his work on the late medieval period and the Protestant Reformation, Ozment continued to develop the work begun by his teacher Heiko Oberman. Because this Oberman trajectory proves important for understanding Reformation sacramental issues, especially regarding Luther's thought, some introduction seems helpful.

In his work *The Harvest of Medieval Theology* (Cambridge, MA: Harvard University Press, 1963), Oberman began a rehabilitation of the fifteenth century by arguing that the century prior to the Protestant Reformation was a creative period of great harvest, not barrenness. In *Forerunners of the Reformation* (New York: Holt, Rinehart & Winston, 1966), Oberman argued that we ought to leave behind the old model of intellectual decline. The fourteenth and fifteenth centuries had diverse reforming trends that eventually, in hindsight, coalesced into both the Protestant Reformation and the so-called Counter Reformation, better conceived as the Catholic Reformation.

During his years after his move from Harvard University to the University of Tübingen, where he was the director of the Institute for Late Medieval and Reformation Studies, Oberman began to focus on the social history of the intellectual ideas with which he had so carefully worked, a task that he continued and extended at the University of Arizona, where he directed the Division for Late Medieval and Reformation Studies. His *Masters of the Reformation* (Cambridge: Cambridge University Press, 1981), which is the English title of a book published four years earlier at Tübingen, worked toward the social context from which new ideas developed, and the social contexts and processes in which such new ideas took root and made for changing lives. This book, conceived as a companion book to *The Harvest of Medieval Theology*, pointed forward to a book about Luther that would deal with "a man besieged by and responsive to the conditions and convictions of his day and age" (x). The Luther book would turn out to be *Luther: Man between God and the Devil*, first published in Berlin in 1982. In later works, such as *The Impact of the Reformation* (Grand Rapids: Eerdmans, 1994), Oberman worked at "total history," tracing the pattern of social conditions—reforming programs—and impact.

Through all this work, Oberman and his many students successfully challenged the so-called "decline theory" of the late medieval period, which had been argued by Etienne Gilson and can be summarized like this: Thomas Aquinas produced a great synthesis that combined nature and grace, reason and revelation, and state and church; but this theological vision of a unified reality gradually gave way to speculative works that reduced theology to subtleties and incessant logic. This speculative theology was an important contributor to the Western split into religious and secular cultures: the one looking to revelation and religion for what was true, the other looking to reason, philosophy, and science for what was true. For Gilson's major work, see *History of Christian Thought in the Middle Ages* (New York: Random House, 1955). Gilson summarizes the main themes in his Richards Lectures at the University of Virginia, in *Reason and Revelation* (New York: Charles Scribner's Sons, 1938).

The implications of the decline theory for the Protestant Reformation are clear. Protestantism was born a defective child from a defective era—the impoverished late medieval period. In Reformation studies the "decline theory" has been best argued by the Catholic scholar Joseph Lortz and his students. See, for example, Joseph Lortz, *Die Reformation in Deutschland*, vols. 1–2 (Freiburg, 1939–1940) [Eng. trans. *The Reformation in Germany* (New York: Herder & Herder, 1968)] and *Wie kam es zur Reformation?* (Einsiedeln: Johannes Verlag, 1955) [Eng. trans. *How the Reformation Came*, trans. Otto M. Knab (New York: Herder & Herder, 1964)]. Among Lortz's many notable students is Erwin Iserloh, whose study on the Eucharist in William of Ockham shows precisely the decline theory and situates Luther, who learned the *via moderna* at Erfurt, in that context; see *Gnade und Eucharistie in der philosophischen Theologie des Wilhelm von Ockham: Ihre Bedeutung für die Ursachen der Reformation* (Wiesbaden: F. Steiner, 1956).

24. Among studies over the last fifty years, as well as earlier studies that remain foundational, see Paul Althaus, *Die Theologie Martin Luthers* (Gütersloh: Gerd Mohn, 1962), 318–38 [Eng. trans. *The Theology of Martin Luther*, trans. Robert C. Schulz (Philadelphia: Fortress Press, 1966), 375–403]; Ernst Bizer, *Studien zur Geschichte des Abendmahlsstreits im 16. Jahrhundert* (Darmstadt: Wissenschaftliche Buchgesellschaft, 1962); Heinrich Bornkamm, *Luther's World of Thought*, trans. M. H. Bertram (St. Louis: Concordia Publishing House, 1958), 93–114; Mark Chapman, "Sacrament and Sacrifice in the Theology of the Mass according to Martin Luther," *One in Christ* 28 (1992): 248–66; Robert C. Croken, *Luther's First Front: The Eucharist as Sacrifice* (Ottawa: University of Ottawa Press, 1990); Jürgen

Diestelmann, *Über die lutherische Messe: Gemeindevorträge und Abhandlungen* (Gross Oesingen: Verlag der Lutherischen Buchhandlung Heinrich Harms, 1998), 1–23; Hermann Dietzfelbinger, "Luthers Abendmahlslehre im Zusammenhang seiner Gedankenwelt," *Theologische Beiträge* 14 (1983): 110–21; Werner Ellert, "Luther in Marburg," *Zeitwende* 5 (1929): 315–24; Paul C. Empie and James I. McCord, eds., *Marburg Revisited* (Minneapolis: Augsburg, 1966); J. A. Faulkner, "Luther and the Lord's Supper in the Critical Years, 1517–1522," *Lutheran Quarterly* 45 (April 1915): 202–16; idem, "Luther and the Real Presence," *The American Journal of Theology* 21 (1917): 225–39; Robert Fischer, "Luther's Stake in the Lord's Supper Controversy," *Dialog* 2 (1963): 50–59; B. A. Gerrish, "Eucharist," in *The Oxford Encyclopedia of the Reformation*, ed. Hans J. Hillerbrand (Oxford: Oxford University Press, 1996), 71–81; idem, "Discerning the Body: Sign and Reality in Luther's Controversy with the Swiss," *Journal of Religion* 68, no. 3 (1988): 377–95; Helmut Gollwitzer, *Coena Domini* (Munich: Chr. Kaiser, 1988); Hans Grass, *Die Abendmahlslehre bei Luther und Calvin; Eine Kritische Untersuchung* (Gütersloh: C. Bertelsmann, 1954); Friedrich Graebke, *Die Konstruktion der Abendmahlslehre Luthers in ihrer Entwicklung dargestellt: Eine dogmengeschichtliche Studie* (Leipzig: A. Deichert, 1908); Lowell C. Green, "Philosophical Presuppositions in the Lutheran-Reformed Debate on John 6," *Concordia Theological Quarterly* 56 (1992): 17–37; Basil Hall, "Hoc est corpus meum: The Centrality of the Real Presence for Luther," in *Luther: Theologian for Catholics and Protestants*, ed. George Yule (Edinburgh: T. & T. Clark, 1985), 112–44; Susi Hausamann, "Die Marburger Artikel—eine echte Konkordie?" *Zeitschrift für Kirchengeschichte* 87 (1966): 288–321; idem, "Realpräsenz in Luthers Abendmahlslehre," in *Studien zur Geschichte und Theologie der Reformation: Festschrift für Ernst Bizer*, ed. Luise Abramowski and J. F. Gerhard Goeters (Neukirchen-Vluyn: Neukirchener Verlag, 1969), 157–73; Hartmut Hilgenfeld, *Mittelalterlich-traditionelle Elemente in Luthers Abendmahlsschriften* (Zurich: Zürich Theologischer Verlag, 1971); Paul Hinlicky, "Christ's Bodily Presence in the Holy Supper—Real or Symbolic?" *Lutheran Forum* 33 (1999): 24–28; Albert Houssiau, "La Cène du Christ selon Luther," in *Luther aujourd'hui* (Louvain-la-Neuve: Publications de la Faculté de Théologie, 1983), 221–54; Eero Huovinen, "Opus Operatum: ist Luthers Verständnis von der Effektivität des Sakraments richtig verstanden?" in *Luther und Theosis* (Helsinki: Luther-Agricola-Gesellschaft; Erlangen: Luther-Akademie Ratzeburg, 1990), 187–214; Erwin Iserloh, *Gnade und Eucharistie*; Erwin Iserloh and Vilmos Vatja, "The Sacraments: Baptism and Lord's Supper," in *Confessing One Faith*, ed. George W. Forell and James F. McCue (Minneapolis: Augsburg Publishing House, 1982), 202–33, esp. 208–11; Hermann Keller, "Das Abendmahl als Gemeinschaftsmahl," *Reformierte Kirchenzeitung* 110 (1969): 76; Reinhold Koch, *Erbe und Auftrag: Das Abendmahlsgespräch in der Theologie des 20. Jahrhunderts* (Munich: Chr. Kaiser, 1957); Ernst Kinder, "'Realpräsenz' und 'Repräsentation', Feststellungen zu Luthers Abendmahlslehre," *Theologische Literaturzeitung* 84 (1959): 881–94; Gottfried Krodel, "The Lord's Supper in the Theology of the Young Luther," *The Lutheran Quarterly* 13 (1961): 19–33; Dennis Alan Laskey, *In Faith and Fervent Love: The Concept of Communio in Luther's Understanding of the Lord's Supper* (ThD thesis, Lutheran School of Theology at Chicago, 1983); Lothar Lies, "Realpräsenz bei Luther und den Lutheranern Heute," *Zeitschrift für Katholische Theologie* 119 (1997): 181–219; Joseph Lortz, "Sakramentales Denken beim jungen Luther," *Lutherjahrbuch 1969* (Göttingen: Vandenhoeck & Ruprecht, 1969), 9–40; Frido Mann, *Das Abendmahl beim jungen Luther* (Munich: M. Hueber, 1971); Peter

Meinhold, "Abendmahl und Opfer nach Luther," in *Abendmahl und Opfer*, ed. Peter Meinhold and Erwin Iserloh (Stuttgart: Schwabenverlag, 1960), 35–73; Norman Nagel, "The Presence of Christ's Body and Blood in the Sacrament of the Altar according to Luther," *Concordia Theological Monthly* 39 (1968): 227–38; Thomas Osborne, "Faith, Philosophy, and the Nominalist Background to Luther's Defense of the Real Presence," *Journal of the History of Ideas* 63 (2002): 63–82; Albrecht Peters, *Realpräsenz, Luthers Zeugnis von Christi Gegenwart im Abendmahl* (Berlin: Luther Verlagshaus, 1960); Ferdinand Pratzner, *Messe und Kreuzesopfer. Die Krise der sakramentalen Idee bei Luther und in der mittelalterlichen Scholastik* (Vienna: Herder, 1970); Ralph W. Quere, "Changes and Constants: Structure in Luther's Understanding of the Real Presence in the 1520s," *The Sixteenth Century Journal* 16, no. 1 (1985): 48–53; Regin Prenter, "A Lutheran Doctrine of Eucharistic Sacrifice?" *Studia Theologica* 19 (1965): 189–99; Herman Sasse, "Die Bedeutung der Realpräsenz," *Lutherischer Rundblick* 9 (1961): 70–87; idem, *This Is My Body: Luther's Contention for the Real Presence in the Sacrament of the Altar* (Minneapolis: Augsburg Publishing House, 1959); Rolf Schäfer, "Zum Problem der Gegenwart Christi im Abendmahl," *Zeitschrift für Theologie und Kirche* 84 (1987): 195–214; David Scaer, "In Response to Bengt Hägglund: Did Luther and Melanchthon Agree on the Real Presence?" *Concordia Theological Quarterly* 44 (1980): 141–47; Paul Schempp, "Das Abendmahl bei Luther," in *Paul Schempp: Gesammelte Aufsätze* (Munich: Chr. Kaiser, 1960), 88–106; Wolfgang Schwab, *Entwicklung und Gestalt der Sakramententheologie bei Martin Luther* (Frankfurt: P. Lang, 1977); Ernst Sommerlath, "Das Abendmahl bei Luther," in *Vom Sakrament des Altars*, ed. Herman Sasse (Leipzig: Dörffling & Francke, 1941), 95–132; idem, "Luthers Lehre von der Realpräsenz in Abendmahl im Zusammenhang mit seiner Gottesanschauung nach den Abendmahlsschriften von 1527–1528," in *Das Erbe Martin Luthers, Festschrift für Ludwig Ihmels*, ed. R. Jelke (Leipzig: Dörffling & Francke, 1928), 320–28; idem, *Der Sinn das Abendmahls nach Luthers Gedanken über das Abendmahl, 1527/29* (Leipzig: Dörffling & Francke, 1930); David Steinmetz, "Scripture and the Lord's Supper in Luther's Theology," *Interpretation* 37 (1983): 253–65; John R. Stephenson, "The Holy Eucharist: At the Center or Periphery of the Church's Life in Luther's Thinking?" in *A Lively Legacy: Essays in Honor of Robert Preuss*, ed. Kurt E. Marquat, John R. Stephenson, and Bjarne W. Teigen (Fort Wayne, IN: Concordia Theological Seminary, 1985), 154–63; idem, "Martin Luther and the Eucharist," *Scottish Journal of Theology* 36 (1983): 447–61; idem, *The Lord's Supper* (St. Louis: Luther Academy, 2003); idem, "Sanctification and the Lord's Supper," in *The Pieper Lectures: Sanctification, New Life in Christ*, ed. John A. Maxfield, 44–54 (St. Louis, MO: Concordia Historical Institute and the Luther Academy, 2003); Ursula Stock, *Die Bedeutung der Sakramente in Luthers Sermonen von 1519* (Leiden: E. J. Brill, 1982); Theobald Süss, "La présence réelle du Christ dans l'eucharist d'après les recherches protestantes actuelles," *Revue des sciences philosophiques et théologiques* 53 (1969): 433–57; Theodore Tappert, "Meaning and Practice of the Lord's Supper in the Reformation," in *Meaning and Practice of the Lord's Supper*, ed. Helmut Lehmann (Philadelphia: Muhlenberg, 1961), 85–109; J. Heywood Thomas, "Logic and Metaphysics in Luther's Eucharistic Theology," *Renaissance and Modern Studies* 23 (1979): 147–59; Mitchell Tori, "Luther and Cajetan on the Sacrifice of the Mass," *Logia* 9, no. 4 (2000): 29–36; Jared Wicks, "'Fides Sacramenti–Fides Specialis': Luther's Development in 1518," in *Luther's Reform: Studies on Conversion and the Church* (Mainz: Verlag P. von Zabern, 1992) , 117–47; Carl Wilsøff, *The Gift of Communion: Luther's*

Controversy with Rome on Eucharistic Sacrifice, trans. Joseph M. Shaw (Minneapolis: Augsburg, 1964).

25. Graebke, *Die Konstruktion.*

26. Faulkner, "Luther and the Lord's Supper"; idem, "Luther and the Real Presence." Long ago Hans Grass argued that up until 1526 Luther had an essentially standard eucharistic theology (*Die Abendmahlslehre,* 7–37) with a systematic development occurring thereafter (37–124).

27. Althaus, *Die Theologie,* 318–25 [Eng. trans. *Theology of Martin Luther,* 375–82].

28. Hausamann, "Realpräsenz."

29. Quere, "Changes and Constants."

30. See, e.g., Peters's study, *Realpräsenz,* which Hausamann criticizes for just such an approach ("Realpräsenz," 157–58n3).

31. See, for example, Krodel, "The Lord's Supper"; Schempp, "Das Abendmahl"; Sommerlath, *Der Sinn des Abendmahls*; Stephenson, "The Holy Eucharist."

32. *Sermon von dem Sakrament des Leibes und Blutes Christi wider die Schwarmgeister*; W.A. 19.482.15–483.19; L.W. 36.335 (*The Sacrament of the Body and Blood of Christ—Against the Fanatics,* hereafter *Sacrament of the Body and Blood.*)

33. W.A. 6.104–34; L.W. 42.117–66.

34. W.A. 2.714–23; L.W. 35.3–22.

35. W.A. 2.727–37; L.W. 24.23–43.

36. *Ein Sermon von dem hochwürdigen Sakrament des heiligen wahren Leichnams Christi und von den Brüderschaften,* W.A. 2.742–58; L.W. 34.45–73 (*The Blessed Sacrament of the Holy and True Body of Christ, and the Brotherhoods,* hereafter *The Blessed Sacrament.*)

37. See Luther's opening dedication to the Duchess Margaret, W.A. 2.713.

38. W.A. 2.742.15–16; L.W. 35.49.

39. W.A. 2.743.11–17; L.W. 35.51.

40. W.A. 2.744.8–11; L.W. 35.52.

41. W.A. 2.748.6–15; L.W. 35.58.

42. W.A. 2.743.27–744.7: L.W. 35.51–52.

43. W.A. 2.745.1–19; L.W. 35.53–54.

44. See, e.g., J. A. Faulkner, "Luther and the Lord's Supper," 205–6; Althaus, *Die Theologie Martin Luthers,* 275–78 [*Theology of Martin Luther,* 318–22]; Hausamann, "Realpräsenz," 160–62; Quere, "Changes and Constants."

45. Hausamann, "Realpräsenz," 161–62.

46. W.A. 2.749.36–750.3; L.W. 35.60–61.

47. So, e.g., Althaus, *Die Theologie,* 319–20 [*Theology of Martin Luther,* 377–78]; cf. Hausamann, "Realpräsenz," 160–64; Quere, "Changes and Constants."

48. See chap. 1, 13–21. Luther's (true Augustinian) strengthening of *signum-res,* so that the (nonmetabolic) real presence inheres in the sign seems to me the insight brought by Stephenson, "The Holy Eucharist," 154–57.

49. W.A. 2.748.27–35; L.W. 35.59. Also see Luther's bridal mysticism, n. 91 below.

50. Among Roman Catholic scholars, see Wilhelm Wagner, "Die Kirche als corpus Christi mysticum beim jungen Luther," *Zeitschrift für katholische Theologie* 61(1937): 29–99, esp. 91ff.; Houssiau, "La Cène du Christ," 227; cf. Mann, *Das Abendmahl,* 83–96, esp. 87–89. Among Protestant scholars, see Yngve Brilioth, *Eucharistic Faith and Practice: Evangelical and Catholic,* trans. A. G. Herbert (London: SPCK, 1953), 95–98, who explicitly mentions Luther's bridal metaphor ("Here the

imputed righteousness is not based on any forensic act, but on a deep inward fellowship, such as the *De libertate christiana* describes in the language of bridal mysticism," 96); Krodel, "The Lord's Supper," 28–30.

More generally, Protestant scholars have tended to emphasize Luther's view of *communio* as primarily forensic, even in the young Luther. For example, see Paul Althaus, *Communio Sanctorum* (Munich: Chr. Kaiser Verlag, 1929), 75–79; idem, *Die Theologie Martin Luthers*, 254–84, 318–21 [*Theology of Martin Luther*, 294–322, 375–79]; Jaroslav Pelikan, *Luther the Expositor* (St. Louis: Concordia Publishing House, 1959), 191–204. Even where the *communio* is connected to Christ's "real presence," the ethical life stems from the gift of real presence as such; see, e.g., Grass, *Die Abendmahlslehre*, 9–25; Werner Elert, *Eucharist and Church Fellowship in the First Four Centuries*, trans. N. E. Nagel (St. Louis: Concordia Publishing House, 1966), 36–40.

For an overall view of *communio* in Luther's theology and legacy, see Dennis Alan Laskey, "In Faith and Fervent Love: The Concept of *Communio* in Luther's Understanding of the Lord's Supper" (ThD diss., Lutheran School of Theology at Chicago, 1983).

51. See the excursus in chap. 1 above.

52. Krodel, "The Lord's Supper," 28–30. See Krodel's extended references to Luther's lectures on the Psalms in nn. 53–64.

53. Tuomo Mannermaa, *Christ Present in Faith: Luther's View of Justification*, ed. Kirsi Stjerna (Minneapolis: Fortress Press, 2005). For further introduction to the Finnish school, see Tuomo Mannermaa, "Theosis als Thema der finnischen Lutherforschung," in *Luther und Theosis* (Helsinki and Erlangen, 1990), 11–26; Stjerna, "Introduction," in *Christ Present in Faith*, 1–9. For a select bibliography on the Finnish school, see *Christ Present in Faith*, 121–33. For a summary of Mannermaa's position, see his essay "Why Is Luther So Fascinating?" in *Union with Christ: The New Finnish Interpretation of Luther*, ed. Carl E. Braaten and Robert W. Jenson (Grand Rapids: Eerdmans, 1998), 1–20; also see his essay, "Justification and *Theosis* in Lutheran–Orthodox Perspective," in *Union with Christ*, 25–41. Also see Simo Peura, "Christ as Favor and Gift: The Challenge of Luther's Understanding of Justification," in *Union with Christ*, 42–69 (esp. 53–56); idem, "What God Gives Man Receives: Luther on Salvation," in *Union with Christ*, 76–95 (esp. 91–94); Sammeli Juntunen, "Luther and Metaphysics: What Is the Structure of Being according to Luther?" in *Union with Christ*, 129–60.

Interestingly the Finnish scholarship often cites Luther's 1513–15 lectures on the Psalms (see n. 52 above). Note the comments by Dennis Bielfeldt, "Response to Sammeli Juntunen, 'Luther and Metaphysics,'" in *Union with Christ*, 161–66. Also see n. 73 below, where Luther calls the human heart the "true golden monstrance"; and see n. 91 below on Luther's bridal mysticism.

54. *De captivate Babylonica ecclesiae praeludium*, W.A. 6:497–573; L.W. 36:3–126.

55. W.A. 6.511.37–38; L.W. 36.35.

56. See Luther's "second captivity of the sacrament," in W.A. 6.508.1–512.6; L.W. 36.28–35. Pierre d'Ailly (1350–1420) had convinced Luther that it made more sense to hold that the real bread remained, not just the accidents. Luther also finds that Aristotelian logic as such was misconstrued by scholastics in positing transubstantiation, an argument that finds strong support in a recent study; see Thomas, "Logic and Metaphysics."

57. *Eyn Sermon von dem newen Testament. das ist von der heyligen Messe*, W.A. 6.3533–78; L.W. 35.75–111.

58. Note, for example, Graebke's comment (*Die Konstruktion*, 29) that this represented not merely a development, but a completely new (*eine völlig neue*) theology that was a total break from the old (*nach einem totalen Bruch*).

59. Althaus, *Die Theologie*, 320–21 [*Theology of Martin Luther*, 378–79].

60. *Babylonian Captivity*, W.A. 6.513.34ff.; L.W. 36.38–39.

61. *Treatise on the New Testament*, W.A. 6.358.35–359.12 (esp. 359.4–6); L W. 35.85–88.

62. W.A. 6.359.6–12; L.W. 35.86.

63. *Treatise on the New Testament*, W.A. 6.363.4–11; 373.32–374.9; 374.30–32; L.W. 35.91, 106, 107.

64. This discussion stepped forward in twentieth-century theology as scholars rethought the ontological categories that had been applied to biblical concepts that were personal. Within Lutheranism, note the comments on Luther by Friedrich Gogarten, *Verhängnis und Hoffnung der Neuzeit* (Stuttgart: Friedrich Vorwerk Verlag, 1953), 159–63: "This metaphysical thought is overcome in Luther's theology; *at least in principle*" (159, emphasis mine) [Eng. trans. *Despair and Hope for our Time*, trans. Thomas Wieser (Philadelphia, Boston: Pilgrim Press, 1970), 122–24]. For a traditionalist Lutheran criticism of this personal-ethical perspective as it concerns the Supper, see, e.g., John R. Stephenson, *The Lord's Supper*, 49–52, 73–74 (on Althaus).

65. Arthur Cushman McGiffert, *Christianity as History and Faith* (New York: Charles Scribner's Sons, 1934), 224–25.

66. "Where there is a divine promise, there every one must stand on their own; their own personal faith is demanded, all will account for themselves, and bear their own load, as it is said in the last chapter of Mark, 'He who believes and is baptized will be saved; but he who does not believe will be condemned.' Thus from the mass each one is able to benefit personally only by their own faith" (W.A. 6:497–573; 521.20–25; L.W. 36.49).

67. *omnia sacramenta ad fidem alendam sunt instituta* (W.A. 6.529.36; L.W. 36.61).

68. See Wicks, "'*Fides Sacramenti–Fides Specialis.*'"

69. For Luther and the sacrifice of the Mass, see Croken, *Luther's First Front*; Ulrich Kühn, "Abendmahl und Opfer" in Alexander Völker, ed., *Eucharistie. Beiträge zur Theologie der "Erneuerten Agende"* (Berlin, 1993), 61–75; Meinhold, "Abendmahl und Opfer"; Pratzner, *Messe und Kreuzesopfer*; Tori, "Luther and Cajetan"; Vatja, "Das Abendmahl. Gegenwart Christi—Feier der Gemeinschaft-Eucharistiches Opfer" in Erwin Iserloh, ed., *Confessio Augustana und Confutatio: der Augsburger Reichstag 1530 und die Einheit der Kirche: internationales Symposion der Gesellschaft zur Herausgabe des Corpus Catholicorum in Augsburg vom 3.-7. September 1979* (Münster, 1980), 545–77; Wilsøff, *The Gift of Communion*.

70. For a brief introduction to these developments, see W.A. 11.417–22; L.W. 36.271–74. For Luther and the Bohemians, see Brecht, *Martin Luther: Shaping and Defining*, 72–77.

71. *Vom Anbeten des Sarkraments des heiligen Leichnams Christi*, W.A. 11.431–56; L.W. 36.269–305.

72. W.A. 11.433.23–27; L.W. 36.278.

73. W.A. 11.433.15–18; L.W. 36.278. A monstrance is a vessel that holds the consecrated host for eucharistic adoration. A typical medieval monstrance had a crystal cylinder or window in a golden stand through which the consecrated host could be observed. Also see n. 53 above, on the Finnish interpretation of Luther.

74. W.A. 11.433.18–22.; L.W. 36.278. Also see W.A. 11.432.19–31; L.W. 36.277.

75. W.A. 15.394.12–20; L.W. 40.68.

76. For a detailed study of Cornelius Hoen, see Bart Jan Spruyt, *Cornelius Henrici Hoen (Hoenius) and His Epistle on the Eucharist (1525)* (Leiden: Brill, 2006). A critical edition of the Latin text can be found on pp. 226–35 and the 1526 German translation can be found on pp. 237–51. An English translation of Hoen's epistle is given by Heiko Oberman in *Forerunners of the Reformation: The Shape of Late Medieval Thought* (New York: Holt, Rinehart, & Winston, 1966), 268–78. For the presentation of Hoen's ideas to Luther, see Spruyt, *Hoen*, 199–202. Also see Oberman, *Forerunners*, 253; A. Hyma, "Hoen's Letter on the Eucharist and Its Influence upon Carlstadt, Bucer, and Zwingli," *The Princeton Theological Review* 24 (1926): 124–31.

77. See Spruyt, *Hoen*, 85–99.

78. W.A. 11.431.5–441.17; L.W. 36.279–87.

79. W.A. 11.438.15–17; L.W. 36.283.

80. W.A. 11.438.20–23; L.W. 36.284.

81. W.A. 11.440.34–441.8; L.W. 36.286–87 (emphasis mine). Cf. Simo Peura, "What God Gives Man Receives," 91–94.

82. *Wider die himmlischen Propheten, von den Bildern und Sakrament*, W.A. 18.62–214; L.W. 40.73–243.

83. For a descriptive summary and further references, see Brecht, *Martin Luther: Shaping and Defining*, 157–72.

84. *Ein Brief an die Christen zu Straßurg wider den Schwärmergeist*, W.A. 15.391–97; L.W. 40.65–77.

85. W.A. 18.146.15–182.10; L.W. 40.156–92.

86. W.A. 18.147.23–27; L.W. 40.157.

87. W.A. 18.203.27–204.21; L.W. 40.215–16.

88. *zum Sacrament odder Euangelio, da finde ich das wort, das mir solche erworbene vergebunge am creuz, austeilet, schenckt, darbeut und gibt* (W.A. 18.204.2–4; L.W. 40.214).

89. W.A. 18.204.21; L.W. 40.214.

90. W.A. 18.204.22–28; L.W. 40.214–15.

91. Works righteousness was a key complaint against the mystical traditions. For a good entrance to this material, including references, see Ozment, *Age of Reform*, 239–44. Note Luther's own use of the mystical marriage between Christ and the soul, where faith "unites the soul with Christ as a bride is united with her bridegroom. By this mystery, as the Apostle teaches, Christ and the soul become one flesh [Eph. 5:31–32]. And if they are one flesh and there is between them a true marriage—indeed the most perfect of all marriages, since human marriages are but poor examples of this one true marriage—it follows that everything they have they hold in common, the good as well as the evil" (W.A. 7.42–29; L.W. 31.351).

92. See Brecht, *Shaping and Defining*, 167, 300–303.

93. *Sermon von dem Sakrament des Leibes und Blutes Christi wider die Schwarmgeister*, W.A. 19.509.29–511.28; L.W. 36.352–53.

94. W.A. 19:118–25.

95. W.A. 19.474–81; L.W. 36.331–33.

96. W.A. 19.485.31 (Latin copy): "Accipe vitrum, bibe, das ist wittenbergisch bier."

97. W.A. 19.489.9–16; L.W. 36.340.

98. W.A. 19.489.23; L.W. 36.340.

99. W.A. 19.492.19–22; L.W. 36.342.

100. W.A. 19.493.7–8; L.W. 343.

101. W.A. 19.506.17–19; L.W. 36.349.

102. W.A. 19.507.31–33; L.W. 36.350.

103. Quere, "Changes and Constants," 66.

104. W.A. 19.509.29–511.28; L.W. 36.352–53.

105. For a list, see L.W. 37:8–11.

106. Brecht, *Shaping and Defining*, 311.

107. *Daß diese Worte Christi "Das ist mein Leib" noch fest stehen wider die Schwarm-geister*, W.A. 23.64–283; *That These Words of Christ, "This is my Body," Still Stand Firm Against the Fanatics*, L.W. 37.3–150.

108. *Vom Abendmahl Christi. Bekenntnis*, W. A. 26.261–509, here 401.23–402.3; *Confession concerning Christ's Supper*, L.W. 151–372, here 37.269.

109. For a brief description concerning Bucer's translation, see Brecht, *Shaping and Defining*, 304–5. At Marburg in 1529, Luther addressed Bucer with the words, "Tu es nequam" ("You are a naughty boy [a mischief-maker]") (Sasse, *This Is My Body*, 217n42).

110. W.A. 23.110.28–167.17; L.W. 37.46–78. The Weimar edition gives both Luther's manuscript and the printed edition. Unless otherwise noted, references will hereon be made simply to the printed edition.

111. W.A. 23.133.19–22; L.W. 37.57.

112. W.A. 23.145.13–19; L.W. 37.64.

113. W.A. 23.151.25–28; L.W. 37.69.

114. W.A. 23.151.13–15; L.W. 37.68 (emphasis mine). Also see Peters, *Realpräsenz*, 86–88.

115. Luther's relationship to the late medieval nominalism has been a much discussed topic. For general entrance to the material, see n. 7 above. For the issue of Luther's teaching on ubiquity and its relationship to nominalism, see Fischer, "Luther's Stake"; Hilgenfeld, *Mittelalterlich-traditionelle Elemente*; Iserloh, *Gnade und Eucharistie*; Nagel, "The Presence of Christ's Body"; Osborne, "Faith, Philosophy, and the Nominalist Background"; Peters, *Realpräsenz*; Reinhold Seeberg, *Text-Book of the History of Doctrines*, trans. Charles B. Hay (Grand Rapids: Baker Book House, 1983), 2.325–27; Sasse, *This Is My Body*; Schäfer, "Zum Problem."

116. W.A. 26.327.20–23; L.W. 36.215.

117. Something is circumscriptively in a place "if the space and the object occupying it exactly correspond and fit into the same measurements, such as wine or water in a cask. . . . In this mode, space and object correspond exactly" (W.A. 26.327.23–32; L.W. 27.215).

118. Something is definitively present "if the object or body is not tangibly in one place and is not measured according to the space of the location where it is but it can occupy either more room or less room" (W.A. 26.327.33–328.20; L.W. 37.215). Luther cites angels or devils as examples.

119. "a thing occupies a place repletively (that is, supernaturally) if it is simultaneously present in all places wholly and fully, and fills all places, yet without being measured or comprised by any place, in terms of the space which it occupies" (W.A. 26.329.27–30; L.W. 37.216). Only God has repletive presence.

120. For the former, see nn. 98–101 above; for examples of the latter, see W.A. 23.133.23–28; L.W. 37.57; W.A. 23.137.8–139.3; L.W. 37.59–60; W.A. 26.332.12–340.2; L.W. 37.218–28; W.A. 26.412.26–430.21; L.W. 37.275–86.

121. See, e.g., Fischer, "Luther's Stake"; Nagel, "The Presence of Christ's Body"; Osborne, "Faith, Philosophy, and the Nominalist Background"; Sasse, *This Is My Body*; Schäfer, "Zum Problem."

122. See, e.g., B. A. Gerrish, *Grace and Reason: A Study in the Theology of Martin Luther* (Oxford: Clarendon Press, 1962).

123. "Qui sine periculo volet in Aristotele Philosophari, necesse est ut ante bene stultificetur in Christo" (*Heidelberg Disputation*, W.A. 1.353–74, here 1.355.2–3; L.W. 31.35–70, here 35.41).

124. W.A. 23.167.18, 205.32; L.W. 37.78, 101.

125. W.A. 23.167.17–209.27; L.W. 37.78–104.

126. W.A. 23.209.27–241.23: L.W. 37.105–24.

127. *Und zwar S. Augustin halten sie fur ihr eigen* (W.A. 23.209.30: L.W. 37.104).

128. See above, chap. 1, pp. 14–15, nn. 102–11. E.g., see Van der Lof, "Eucharistie et présence réelle," *Revue des Études Augustiniennes* 10, no. 4 (1964): 298–300. See Luther's commentary, e.g., on Ps. 98:9.

129. *Amica exegesis, id est: expositio eucharistiae negocii ad Martinum Lutherum*, in *Huldreich Zwinglis sämtliche Werke*, ed. Emil Egli, Georg Finsler, et al., vols. 88–101 of *Corpus Reformatorum*, vol. I (Berlin: C. A. Schwetschke und Sohn, 1905); vols. II–V, VII–XII (Leipzig: M. Heinsius Nachfolger, 1908–28); vols. VI/1, VI/2, XIII–XIV (Zurich: Verlag Berichthaus, 1944–82), V.562–758; hereafter cited as Z.W., followed by volume, page, and line number [Eng. trans. in *Huldrych Zwingli Writings, Volume Two*, trans. Henry Preble, rev. and ed. H. Wayne Pipkin (Allison Park, PA: Pickwick Publications, 1984), 233–385].

130. See Brecht, *Shaping and Defining*, 314–17; L.W. 37.153–55.

131. W.A. 26.262.19–25; L.W. 37.163.

132. At the Marburg Colloquy (1529) Luther complained about theological errors from the Swiss (e.g., Trinity, person of Christ, original sin, baptism, justification, office, purgatory), and he demanded that agreement on these issues be found prior to discussing the Supper. The Swiss objected to Luther's high-handedly expanding the agenda. See Walther Köhler, *Das Marburger Religionsgespräch 1529* (Leipzig: M. Heinsius Nachfolger Eger & Sievers, 1929), 7–9 [Sasse, *This Is My Body*, 229–31]. The issues raised by Luther were already part of the seventeen Schwabach Articles, which were written prior to Marburg as a theological basis of the Wittenbergers, and which became the basis for the Marburg document as a whole. See Brecht, *Shaping and Defining*, 327, 332–34.

133. "For our people—this I know—I have made this text clear enough and laid down this rule: In Scripture we should let the words, as they read, be valid according to their own meaning and give no other interpretation except when a public article of faith compels otherwise. This rule is in my book" (W.A. 26.403.26–29; L.W. 37.270). "This then is our foundation: Where Holy Scripture is the ground of faith, we must not deviate from the words as they read, nor from the order in which they stand, except that an express article of faith compels us to another interpretation or ordering" (W.A. 18.147.23–26; L.W. 40.157).

134. W.A. 26.263.6–379.16; L.W. 37.163–252.

135. W.A. 26.282.10–285.37; L.W. 27.180–85.

136. Gottfried Locher, *Zwingli's Thought: New Perspectives* (Leiden: E. J. Brill, 1981), 173–78, comments that this "lent a 'Nestorian' coloring to the relationship of the two natures" (174).

137. W.A. 26.317.19–332.11; L.W. 37.206–14.

138. W.A. 26.379.16–432.37; L.W. 252–88.

139. Taking the opportunity to criticize both Oecolampadius and the much-disliked Zwingli, Luther wrote, "I did not know that Oecolampadius was so wicked-poor a logician or dialectician that he also would take substance for quality, and syllogize from accident to substance. For Zwingli this is no surprise; one of these self-made doctors who usually turn out this way" (W.A. 26.404.17–20; L.W. 37.271).

140. W.A. 26.428.28–33; L.W. 37.285.

141. W.A. 26.445.19–446.31; L.W. 37.303–5.

142. The polite but pointed reply by Oecolampadius, reflecting both his temperament and humanist training, was, "Where does it stand written that we should go through the scriptures with eyes shut tightly, Doctor?" (Köhler, *Marburger Religionsgespräch*, 13).

143. W.A. 26.476.30–34; L.W. 37.335.

144. W.A. 26.479.10; L.W. 37.338.

145. W.A. 26.478.38–479.6; L.W. 37.338.

146. W.A. 26.479.10–14; L.W. 37.339.

147. W.A. 26.490.19–498.27; L.W. 37.353–60.

148. W.A. 26.493.4–6; L.W. 37.356.

149. Brecht comments (*Shaping and Defining*, 167), speaking about the "enthusiast" conflicts that arose with Karlstadt, that it is "clear how burdensome and fateful for the later sacramentarian controversy it was that that conflict blended into the earlier confrontations with Karlstadt." To trace this blend of enthusiast and sacramentarian debate from 1525 to 1529, see Brecht, *Shaping and Defining*, 293–339.

150. W.A. 23.203.26–29; L.W. 37.100.

151. W.A. 23.205.20–25; L.W. 37.101.

152. Here I part ways with Quere, "Constants and Changes," whose principal point is that Luther left behind the two-storied, sign-reality, dualistic hermeneutic of Augustine for a truly monistic eucharistic theology. Quere, on my view, has mistaken the Augustinianism of the Latin, medieval West for Augustine's own views. When the Augustinian Ratramnus of Corbie opened his famous eucharistic treatise with the question, "Does what occurs in the eucharist happen *in mysterio* or *in veritate*?" he asked a question that (presumably) Augustine would not really have understood.

CHAPTER 3: THE FIRST GENERATION: HULDRYCH ZWINGLI AND MARTIN BUCER

1. Martin Luther, *Small Catechism*, VI.2: The "Sacrament of the Altar . . . is the true body and blood of our Lord Jesus Christ, under the bread and wine, given to us Christians to eat and to drink" (Theodore G. Tappert, *The Book of Concord: The Confessions of the Evangelical Lutheran Church* [Philadelphia: Fortress Press, 2000]).

2. The standard Zwingli biography is the four-volume work by Oskar Farner, who was the longtime pastor of the Grossmünster, and lecturer and professor at the University of Zurich. The final volume was completed and edited by Rudolf Pfister: see *Huldrych Zwingli*, 4 vols. (Zurich: Zwingli-Verlag, 1946–60). In English,

the fullest biography of Zwingli remains G. R. Potter, *Zwingli* (Cambridge: Cambridge University Press, 1976). Less extensive than the biography of Potter is that by Ulrich Gäbler, *Huldrych Zwingli: His Life and Work*, trans. Ruth L. C. Gritsch (Philadelphia: Fortress Press, 1986). Also see the shorter biography by Farner, *Zwingli the Reformer: His Life and Work*, trans. D. G. Sear (Hamden, CT: Archon Books, 1968). The essays by Gottfried Locher are important contributions to understanding various aspects of Zwingli's theology; see Locher, *Zwingli's Thought: New Perspectives* (Leiden: E. J. Brill, 1981). A good summary of Zwingli's theology, and of secondary scholarship, can be found in W. P. Stephens, *The Theology of Huldrych Zwingli* (Oxford: Clarendon Press, 1986).

3. See Stephens, *Huldrych Zwingli*, 5–50. On Zwingli's humanism, scholarship on Zwingli's theological formation was highly influenced by the work of Walter Köhler, who (especially early on) emphasized the influence of humanism upon Zwingli; more recent scholarship has seen the influence of humanism mitigated by Zwingli's fuller embrace of a christocentric and scriptural approach when he began his Zurich ministry. See the historiographic essay by Locher in *Zwingli's Thought*, 42–71. Also see Stephens, *Huldrych Zwingli*, 9–28.

Scholarship suggests that humanism signifies not material agreement on philosophical concepts of humankind and world, but rather the formal shift to original languages, texts, and conceptual tools such as rhetoric and grammar. See, for example, Donald Weinstein, "In Whose Image and Likeness? Interpretations of Renaissance Humanism," *Journal of the History of Ideas* 33 (1972): 165–76. Most of the Protestant Reformers of the sixteenth century were influenced by humanism. Ozment's apt comment remains true: "While the reformers set the humanist curriculum in place of the scholastic, doctrine was always the rider and the humanities the horse. The humanities became for the Protestant theologians what Aristotelian philosophy had been for late medieval theologians—the favored handmaiden of theology; the rhetorical arts served the more basic task of communicating true doctrine" (Steven Ozment, *The Age of Reform* [New Haven, CT: Yale University Press, 1980], 315; also see 290–317 for a suggestive overview of "Humanism and the Reformation"). For a still-helpful entrance to the material, see James D. Tracy, "Humanism and the Reformation," in *Reformation Europe: A Guide to Research*, ed. Steven Ozment (St. Louis: Center for Reformation Research, 1982), 33–57.

4. Zwingli's Reformation development happened gradually, as intellectual insights became personally appropriated through a variety of events—nearly dying from the plague, reflections on his personal life, the courage and religious stance of Luther, continued reading in the letters of Paul, the Gospel of John, and Augustine. In Zurich, Zwingli also began preaching a *lectio continua*, progressing in sermons through one book of the Bible at a time, rather than preaching from the snippets of Scripture that was the current lectionary system. See Stephens, *Huldrych Zwingli*, 21–34.

5. *Trahe, domine, pectus nostrum tui luminis gratia, ut digne, hoc est: ea fide, qua oportet, ad hoc sacrosanctum filii tui convivium addecamus, cuius ipse et hospes est et epulum; De canone missae epichiresis* (Z.W. II.607.22–25; *Attack on the Canon of the Mass*) [Eng. trans. in R. C. D. Jasper and G. J. Cuming, eds., *Prayers of the Eucharist* (New York: Pueblo Publishing Co., 1980), 186].

6. *Über Huldrych Zwingli haben Sie gelernt, daß er 'nur' ein Gedächtnismahl feiere, in welchem Brot und Wein Leib und Blut 'nur' symbolisieren* (Gottfried W. Locher, *Streit unter Gästen* [Zurich: Theologischer Verlag, 1972], 12) ("You have learned

about Huldrych Zwingli that he celebrates 'merely' a memorial meal in which bread and wine 'merely' symbolize body and blood").

7. On Zwingli's eucharistic theology, particularly the issue of Christ's presence, see Alexander Barclay, *The Protestant Doctrine of the Lord's Supper* (Glasgow: Jackson, Wylie, 1927); August Baur, *Zwinglis Theologie: ihr Werden und ihr System* (Halle: M. Niemeyer, 1885–89), 2 vols.; Karl Bauer, "Die Abendmahlslehre Zwinglis bis zum Beginn der Auseinandersetzung mit Luther," *Theologische Blätter* 5 (1926): 217–26; idem, "Symbolik und Realpräsenz in der Abendmahlsanschauung Zwinglis bis 1525. Eine Erwiderung," *Zeitschrift für Kirchengeschichte* 46 (1927): 97–105; J. Bichon, "La doctrine de la Sante-Cène chez Luther, Zwingli, et Calvin," *Foi et Vie* 43, no. 4 (1946): 404–9; Fritz Blanke, "Antwort auf Wilhelm Niesel: Zwinglis 'spätere Sakramentsanschauung,'" *Theologische Blätter* 11 (1931): 18; idem, "Zum Verständnis der Abendmahlslehre Zwinglis," *Pastoraltheologie. Monatsschrift zur Vertiefung des gesamten pfarramtlichen Wirkens* 27 (1931): 314–20; idem, "Zwinglis Sakramentsanschauung," *Theologische Blätter* 10 (1931): 283–90; Stefan Niklaus Bosshard, *Zwingli-Erasmus-Cajetan: Die Eucharistie als Zeichen der Einheit* (Wiesbaden: Steiner, 1978); Martin Brecht, "Hat Zwingli seinen Brief an Matthäus Alber über das Abendmahl abgesandt?" *Archiv* 58, no. 1 (1967): 100–102; Jaques Courvoisier, "Reflexions à propos de la doctrine eucharistique de Zwingli et de Calvin," in *Festgabe Leonhard von Muralt*, ed. Martin Haas and Rene Hauswirth (Zurich: Verlag Berichthaus, 1970), 258–64; idem, "Vom Abendmahl bei Zwingli," *Zwingliana* 11, no. 7 (1962): 415–26; idem, *Zwingli. A Reformed Theologian* (Richmond, VA: John Knox Press, 1963); B. A. Gerrish, "Lord's Supper in the Reformed Confessions," *Theology Today* 23 (July 1966): 224–43; idem, "Sign and Reality: The Lord's Supper in the Reformed Confessions," in *The Old Protestantism and the New* (Chicago: The University of Chicago Press, 1982), 118–30; idem, "Discerning the Body: Sign and Reality in Luther's Controversy with the Swiss," *The Journal of Religion* 68, no. 3 (1988): 377–95; idem, *Grace and Gratitude*; R. J. Goesser, "Word and Sacrament: A Study of Luther's Views as Developed in the Controversy with Zwingli and Karlstadt" (PhD diss., Yale University, 1960); Helmut Gollwitzer, "Zur Auslegung von Joh. 6 bei Luther und Zwingli," in *In Memoriam Ernst Lohmeyer*, ed. W. Schmauch (Stuttgart: Evangelisches Verlagswerk, 1951), 143–68; Richard Heman, *Mysterium Sanctum Magnum. Um die Auslegung des Abendmahls. Zwingli? Calvin? Luther? Rom?* (Lucerne: Verlag Räber, 1937); Gottfried Hoffmann, "Sententiae Patrum—Das patristische Argument in der Abendmahlskontroverse zwischen Oekolampad, Zwingli, Luther, und Melanchthon" (Diss., Heidelberg, 1971); Hyma, "Hoen's Letter"; Jasper and Cuming, *Prayers of the Eucharist*, 181–88; Markus Jenny, *Die Einheit des Abendmahlsgottesdienstes bei den elsässischen und schweizerischen Reformatoren*, Studien zur Dogmengeschichte und systematischen Theologie XXIII (Zurich: Zwingli Verlag, 1968); Walther Köhler, "Zu Zwinglis ältester Abendmahlsauffassung," *Zeitschrift für Kirchengeschichte* 45 (1926/1927): 399–408; idem, "Zum Abendmahlsstreite zwischen Luther und Zwingli," in *Lutherstudien. Zur 4 Jahrhundertfeier der Reformation* [Veröffentlicht von den Mitarbeitern der Weimarer Lutherausgabe] (Weimar: Böhlau, 1917), 114–39; idem, "Zum Gedächtnis der ersten evangelischen Abendmahlsfeier in Zürich," *Neue Züricher Zeitung*, 1925, no. 531; idem, "Zur Abendmahlskontroverse in der Reformationszeit insbesondere zur Entwicklung der Abendmahlslehre Zwinglis," *Zeitschrift für Kirchengeschichte* 47 (1928): 47–56; idem, "Zur Geschichte der privaten Abendmahlsfeier," *Zwingliana* 3, no. 2 (1913): 58–64; idem, *Zwingli und Luther. Ihr*

Streit über das Abendmahl nach seinen politischen und religiösen Beziehungen, 2 vols., Quellen und Forschungen zur Reformationsgeschichte VI–VII, vol. 1: Leipzig, 1924; vol. 2: Gütersloh, 1953; Hans Krönler, *Der Kult der Eucharistie in Sprache und Volkstum der deutschen Schweiz*, Schriften der Schweizer, Gesellschaft für Volkskunde XXXIII (Diss., Frieburg Basel, 1949); Gottfried W. Locher, "Die theologische und politische Bedeutung des Abendmahlsstreites im Licht von Zwinglis Briefen," *Zwingliana* 13, no. 5 (1971): 281–304; idem, *Im Geist und in der Wahrheit: die reformatorische Wendung im Gottesdienst zu Zürich* (Neukirchen: K. Moers, 1957); idem, *Zwingli's Thought*, 59–62, 220–28, 314–20, 328–29; idem, *Streit unter Gästen*; William D. Maxwell, *An Outline of Christian Worship: Its Developments and Forms* (London: Oxford University Press, 1949); H. Miéville, *La sainte cène d'après Ulrich Zwingli* (Lausanne : Georges Bridel, 1871); Wilhelm H. Neuser, "Zwinglis Abendmahlsbrief an Thomas Wyttenbach (1523)," in *Wegen en gestalten in het gereformeerd protestantisme* (Amsterdam: Ton Bolland, 1976), 35–46; Wilhelm Niesel, "Zwinglis 'spätere' Sakramentsanschauung," *Theologische Blätter* 11 (1932): 12–17; Cyril Richardson, *Zwingli and Cranmer on the Eucharist* (Evanston, IL: Seabury Western Theological Seminary, 1949); H. Rückert, "Das Eindringen der Tropuslehre in die schweizerische Auffassung vom Abendmahl," *Archiv für Reformationsgeschichte* 37 (1940): 199–221; Sasse, *This Is My Body*; D. G. Schrenk, "Zwinglis Hauptmotiv in der Abendmahlslehre und das Neue Testament," *Zwingliana* 5, no. 4 (1930): 176–85; H. von Schubert, "Das Marburger Gespräch als Anfang der Abendmahlskonkordie," *Zeitschrift für Kirchengeschichte* 30 (1909): 60–78; Julius Schweizer, *Reformierte Abendmahlsgestaltung in der Schau Zwinglis* (Basel: F. Reinhardt, 1954); C. A. Scott, "Zwingli's Doctrine of the Lord's Supper," *Expositor* 3 (1901): 161–71; Reinhold Seeberg, *Text-Book of the History of Doctrines*, trans. Charles B. Hay (Grand Rapids: Baker Book House, 1983); Rudolf Staehelin, *Huldreich Zwingli, sein Leben und Wirken* (Basel: B. Schwabe, 1895–97), 2 vols.; Joachim Staedtke, "Voraussetzungen der Schweizer Abendmahlslehre," *Theologische Zeitschrift* 16 (January / February 1960): 19–32; Stephens, *Huldrych Zwingli*, 218–59; Johann Stumpf, *Beschreibung des Abendmahlsstreites*, ed. Fritz Büsser (Zurich: Verlag Berichthaus, 1960); Bard Thompson, ed., *Liturgies of the Western Church* (New York: The World Publishing Co., 1961), 147–56; Leo Weisz, "Johannes Stumpfs Geschichte des Abendmahlsstreites," *Zwingliana* 5, no. 4 (1930): 193–221.

8. Baur, *Zwinglis Theologie*, 2.268–612, esp. 268–92; Staehelin, *Huldreich Zwingli*, 2.213–330, esp. 213–38; Seeberg, *Text-Book of the History of Doctrines*, 2.318–22 (§73.1–2). For an introduction to the research up to his era, see Köhler, *Zwingli und Luther*, 1:1–15. But also Bauer ("Symbolik und Realpräsenz," 97–99; also "Die Abendmahlslehre," 219, 221), who criticizes Köhler for not giving adequate attention to the nineteenth-century state of the question and its authors (e.g., Schenkel, Zeller, Sigwart, Dieckhoff), who, according to Bauer, already raised the issues that divided himself and Köhler.

9. Miéville, *La sainte cène*; Köhler, *Zwingli und Luther*, 1:16–117. Köhler himself thought this was the second point that his study made overall; its principal task was to place the Reformation history of eucharistic dogma into its sociopolitical matrix, since they mutually condition each other ("Zu Zwinglis ältester Abendmahlsauffassung," 400–402).

10. For the letter to Matthew Alber, see *Huldreich Zwinglis sämtliche Werke*, ed. Emil Egli, Georg Finsler, et al., vols. 88–101 of *Corpus Reformatorum*, vol. I (Berlin: C. A. Schwetschke und Sohn, 1905); vols. II–V, VII–XII (Leipzig: M. Heinsius

Nachfolger, 1908-28); vols. VI/1, VI/2, XIII-XIV (Zurich: Verlag Berichthaus, 1944-82), V.562-758; hereafter cited as Z.W., followed by volume, page, and line number; Z.W. III.335-54 [Eng. trans. in *Huldrych Zwingli Writings*, vol. 2, trans. H. Wayne Pipkin (Allison Park, PA: Pickwick Publications, 1984), 127-54].

11. For Zwingli's *Sixty-seven Articles*, see H. A. Niemeyer, ed., *Collectio confessionum in ecclesiis reformatis publicatarum* (Leipzig: Klinkhardt, 1840), who gives Zwingli's original Swiss text and a Latin translation [Eng. trans. in Arthur C. Cochrane, ed., *Reformed Confessions of the Sixteenth Century* (Philadelphia: The Westminster Press, 1966), 36-44]. For Zwingli's exposition of these articles, see *Ußlegen und gründ der schlußreden oder articklen durch Huldrychen Zwingli, Zürich uff den 29. Tag jenners im 1523, jar ußgangen*, Z.W. II.14-457 [Eng. trans. *An Exposition and Basis of the Conclusions or Articles published by Huldrych Zwingli, Zurich, 29 January 1523*, trans. E. J. Furcha, in *Huldrych Zwingli Writings*, vol. 1, *The Defense of the Reformed Faith* (Allison Park, PA: Pickwick Publications, 1984), 7-373].

12. Bauer, "Die Abendmahlslehre Zwinglis."

13. Köhler, "Zu Zwinglis ältester Abendmahlsauffassung."

14. Bauer, "Symbolik und Realpräsenz."

15. Köhler ("Zur Abendmahlskontroverse") lays out five views on the Supper (46-48): (1) late medieval curial view (transubstantiation); (2) "consubstantiation" of Luther (ubiquity); (3) mystical-spiritual view of Erasmus (also see Köhler's *Zwingli und Luther*, 1:49-61); (4) the memorialist view of Karlstadt and Hoen; (5) and the "trust-presence" ("die Lehre von der Fiduzialpräsenz") of Bucer and Calvin. What resulted, argues Köhler (49-56), is a lineage that goes Erasmus-Bucer-Zwingli-Calvin, not Zwingli-Bucer-Calvin (so, Bauer): Zwingli indeed moved from (1) to (5), but did so by first moving to an Erasmian position (3), influenced then by the memorialist position (4), but moved by Bucer to (5).

Bauer rejects a direct lineage from Erasmus to Zwingli, because he finds Zwingli to be community-oriented in a way that Köhler's "spiritual-mystical" description of Erasmus and Zwingli does not capture. Bauer summarizes his position by saying that on the issue of real presence Zwingli is not the successor (*Nachfolger*) of Erasmus, but the predecessor (*Vorgänger*) of Bucer and Calvin ("Symbolik and Realpräsenz," 102-5).

16. *Von symbolischer Auffasung findet sich nichts. Merkwürdig, daß man den Brief so gründlich mißverstehen konnte!* (Köhler, *Zwingli und Luther*, 1:28). Neuser tries to show the peculiarities of Zwingli's view on presence, as it moves toward memorialism ("Zwinglis Abendmahlsbrief," esp. 42-46.)

17. Miéville, *La sainte cène*; Barclay, *The Protestant Doctrine*, 41-106; Stephens, *Huldrych Zwingli*, 218-59; Fritz Blanke, "Antwort auf Wilhelm Niesel"; idem, "Zwinglis Sakramentsanschauung," *Theologische Blätter* 10 (1931): 283-90; Wilhelm Niesel, "Zwinglis 'spätere' Sakramentsanschauung."

18. See Courvoisier, "Reflexions"; idem, "Vom Abendmahl bei Zwingli"; idem, *Zwingli. A Reformed Theologian*; Schweizer, *Reformierte Abendmahlsgestaltung*; Locher, *Zwingli's Thought*, 59-62, 220-28, 314-20, cf. 328-29.

19. Gerrish, "Lord's Supper; idem, "Sign and Reality"; idem, "Discerning the Body"; idem, *Grace and Gratitude*; Jenny, *Die Einheit*, "Zwinglis Abendmahlsgottesdienst" (37-70), esp. 48-62.

20. Barclay, *The Protestant Doctrine*, 41-106.

21. Stephens, *Huldrych Zwingli*, 218-59.

22. Richardson, *Zwingli and Cranmer*, 3. Cf. "The elements are *reminders* of a past redemption, not *vehicles* of a present grace" (19). While recognizing subtleties in Zwingli, his approach to Zwingli takes that of real substance or mere memorial.

23. *So sy vesenklich gloubend, Christum ire sünd bezalt haben am crütz, und in sölchem glouben essend und trinckend sin fleisch und blůt, und erkennend inen das zů einer sichrung gegeben sin, ja inen werdend ire sünd verzigen, als were Christus erst am crütz gestorben. So krefftig und zů allen zyten gegenwürtig is Christus; denn er ist ein ewiger got. So is ouch sin lyden ewigklich fruchtbar, als Pauls redt Heb 9.: Wie vil me würt das blůt Christi, der sich selbs durch den ewigen geist unbefleckt hat got übergehen oder uffgeopret, unser conscientzen reinigen etc.* (Z.W. II.127.23–128.2; *Exposition*, 103).

24. "One should note that for the humanist, Platonized student of Augustine, *memoria*, 'remembrance,' does not mean a retrospective looking back but a re-presentation, an effective presence of the suffering of the Lord" (*"Dazu ist zu bemerken, daß für den humanistischen platonisierenden Augustinschüler 'memoria,' 'Erinnerung,' nicht Rückschau heißt, sondern Vergegenwärtigung, gültige Gegenwart des Leidens des Herrn"* [Locher, *Streit unter Gästen*, 10–11]).

For other places in the *Exposition* where Zwingli discusses *memoria* (*anamnesis*), see Z.W. II.137.19–24 (*Exposition*, 110)—a memorial by which we are united with God through Christ's sufferings and break forth in thanksgiving; Z.W. II.138.1–16 (*Exposition*, 111)—eating and drinking the body and blood is a memorial of what was done once; Z.W. II.144.17–26 (*Exposition*, 116)—once again, Zwingli says that what he means (subjectively) by memorial Luther mean objectively by "testament"; Z.W. II.150.19–25 (*Exposition*, 120)—eating the body and blood of Christ is a memorial (*widergedächtnus*) of Christ's suffering and is what Luther meant by "testament."

25. For those wanting a basic introduction to Plato, F. M. Cornford, *Before and after Socrates* (Cambridge: Cambridge University Press, 1932) remains as fine a book as likely will be written.

26. For an introduction to this epistemological material and its effect on the medieval period, and thus the Protestant Reformation, see Ozment's *Age of Reform*, 42–63.

27. Locher, *Zwingli's Thought: New Perspectives* (Leiden: E. J. Brill, 1981), 223.

28. Here Zwingli stands ironically close to the Roman Catholic teaching on eucharistic sacrifice, in which the sacrifice on the cross remains uniquely unrepeatable but is effectively re-presented in the Mass. For an exemplary explanation of the Roman Catholic position, learned in ecumenical dialogue and relevant to Reformed theology, see *Heidelberg Catechism Q. and A. 80 and the Roman Catholic Eucharist*, prepared by the Christian Reformed Church.

29. *Hie söllend aber die einvaltigen lernen, das man hie nit strytet, ob der fronlychnam und blůt Christi geeessen und truncken werde (**dann daran zwyflet dheinem Christen**), sunder ob es ein opffer sye oder nun ein widergedächtnus* (emphasis mine; Z.W. II.128.8–11; *Exposition*, 104).

30. See the discussion between Bauer and Köhler, nn. 12–15 above.

31. *hab ich das essen und trincken des fronluchnams unnd blůtes Christi genent ein widergedächtnus des lydens Christ* (Z.W. II.150.17–18; *Exposition*, 120).

32. *Zwingli an Thomas Wyttenbach*, Z.W. VIII.84–89.

33. Z.W. VIII.85.26–34.

34. *quicquid hic agitur, divina virtuti fieri, modum autem nobis penitus ignotum, quo deus illabatur animae* (Z.W. VIII.86.30–31)

35. *non essent amplius anxii, qui fieret, ut eum ederent, qui in dextera dei sedet?* (Z.W. VIII.86.37–87.1)

36. *Porro quod de custodia sentis, vehementer placet, nempe non custodiri, nisi in humani animo* (Z.W. VIII.87.1–3).

37. *ignem non esse in silice, nisi, dum excutitur, iam habundanter profluere; sic sub panis specie Christum non teneri, nisi, dum fide illic quaeritur ac petitur, iam edi, sed mirabilis modo, quem fidelis non anxie scrutatur* (Z.W. VIII.88.7–10).

38. *De canone missae epichiresis,* Z.W. II.556–608. An English translation of the eucharistic prayers can be found in Jasper and Cuming, *Prayers of the Eucharist,* 181–86. "For I have been compelled to complete everything there is within four days; the printer was pushing hard, preparing for the Frankfurt fair" (Z.W. II.557.25–27).

39. *quoniam Christus corpus suum et sanguine appellavit* (Z.W. II.568.25). *Nam eucharistie nomen aliud quam hunc cibum et potum liberale bonumque de donum et gratia mes praedicat* (Z.W. II.569.2–5).

40. *ut nobis corpus et sanguis fiat dilectissimi filii tui domini nostri Iesu Christi.*

41. *Hoc tamen impie dictum non est, si oramus, ut panis corpus et sanguis fiat dilectissimi filii dei; modo fieri hic non pro transsubstantiari theologorum nostrorum verbo accipias, sed ita sentias, ut panis et vinum cum fide edentibus fiat corpus et sanguis Iesu Christi, quocumque tandem modo id fiat* (Z.W. II.588.22–26).

42. *Ipsum enim panis, qui dat vitam mundo; frustra enim carnem filii tui et sanguine edemus et bibemus, nisi per fidem verbi tui hoc ante omnia firmiter credamus, quod idem filius tuus dominus noster Iesus Christus pro nobis cruci adfixus prevaricationem totius mundi expiarit. Nam ipse dixit carnem nihil prodesse, spiritum esse, qui vivificet* (Z.W. II.606.22–27).

43. See *Zwingli und Luther,* 1:49–58; "Zur Abendmahls Kontroverse."

44. Bauer, "Symbolik and Realpräsenz," 101–3.

45. "Reflexions," 258–61; *Zwingli,* 74–77, 100nn34, 35, also see general comments on 8.

46. Schweizer, *Abendmahlsgestaltung,* 84–106; *Aktion oder Brauch des Nachtmahls,* Z.W. II.13–24.

47. Hoffmann summarizes four ways that Zwingli learned from the patristic writers: (1) the words used by these writers to describe the Supper show the significance of Christ's body and blood but not a bodily presence ("eine leibliche Gegenwart"); (2) the patristic writers otherwise reject bodily presence; (3) faith as eating the body of Christ is their central point; and (4) at the Supper Christians gather to remember the Easter events and to live out communal love ("Sententiae Patrum," 139). Here, and especially with his discussion of Oecolampadius and Köhler's view on Oecolampadius (103–6), Hoffmann is hobbled by the binary categories of realistic/symbolic.

48. John B. Payne, *Erasmus: His Theology of the Sacraments* (n.p.: M. E. Brachter, 1970), 126–54.

49. Z.W. XII/I.138.38–151.37.

50. Zwingli repeats Augustine's well-known rhymed phrase *O Sacramentum pietatis! O signam unitatis! O vinculum charitatis!* ("O sacrament of piety! O sign of unity! O bond of love!") (Z.W. XII/I.144.33–35). Several times Zwingli writes in the margin "believe and you have eaten" (*crede et manducasti*) (Z.W. XII/I.144.21, 22). And he strikes out a line in Augustine's text that refers back to a physical eating and immortality, and he anticipates Augustine's next comment that the

bread and wine are to be understood as the spiritual union in the body of Christ, the church, when he writes that "the evangelist speaks in that chapter [John 6] only of spiritual eating, whereas Augustine here speaks of a bodily eating" (*Evangelista in illo capite loquitur tantum de manducatione spirituali, Augustinus vero hic loquitur de manducatione corporali* (Z.W. XII/I.144.39–145.1; see *Patrologiae Cursus Completus, Series Latina*, ed. J. P. Migne (Paris, 1844–91); hereafter cited as *PL*, followed by volume number and page numbers; *PL* 35.144.1–8).

51. See above, chap. 1, pp. 13–16.

52. *Ad Matthaeum Alberum, Rutlingensium ecclesiasten, de coena dominica Huldrychi Zuinglii epistola* (Z.W. III.335–54) [Eng. trans. *Letter to Matthew Alber concerning the Lord's Supper*, trans. Henry Preble, in *Huldrych Zwingli Writings*, vol. 2, rev. and ed. H. Wayne Pipkin (Allison Park, PA: Pickwick Publications, 1984), 127–45]. Whether the letter was sent to Alber, or remained an open letter, has had discussion. See Martin Brecht, "Hat Zwingli seinen Brief an Matthäus Alber über das Abendmahl abgesandt?" *Archiv für Reformationsgeschichte* 58 (1967): 100–2; Gottfried Locher, *Die Zwinglische Reformation im Rahmen der europäischen Kirchengeschichte* (Göttingen: Vandenhoeck & Ruprecht, 1979), 297n127.

53. Z.W. III.335.14–336.17; *Letter to Matthew Alber*, 131; cf. Z.W. III.344.8–9; *Letter to Matthew Alber*, 138.

54. Z.W. III.336.19–342.10; *Sic igitur docebis, charissime Matthaee, ante omnia, quid hic Christus per "edere," nempe, "credere" intelligat* ("Therefore you shall teach above all, dear Matthew, that here by 'eat' Christ certainly understands 'believe'") (Z.W. III.341.28–9; *Letter to Matthew Alber*, 136).

55. Z.W. III.344.9–345.21; *Letter to Matthew Alber*, 138–39.

56. Z.W. III.346.3–352.3; *Letter to Matthew Alber*, 139–43; *Atque huius rei ad memoriam, quod pro nobis esset atrociter necatus, ritum nobis volens relinquere* (Z.W. III.351.13–15; *Letter to Matthew Alber*, 143).

57. *Neque enim unquam puto fuisse, qui crederet, se Christum corporaliter et essentialiter in hoc sacramento edere. . . . Te cum aut non credidisti aut mentem, ne hic reclamaret, avocasti, aut vehementer anxius fuisti, quonam pacto veritas libere tandem prodiret* (Z.W. III.350.6–8, 11–13; *Letter to Matthew Alber*, 142).

58. *de corporali et essentiali corpore Christi in hoc sacramento* (Z.W. III.341.9–10; *Letter to Matthew Alber*, 136); *de essentiali corpore Christi loquuntur* (Z.W. III.341.14–15; *Letter to Matthew Alber*, 136); *Christum corporaliter et essentialiter in hoc sacramento edere* (Z.W. III.350.7–8; *Letter to Matthew Alber*, 142).

59. The direction of Zwingli's thought may be rooted in classical Greek mistrust of the senses, but it finally points to an important issue: Is all our perception sensationist, or do we not also immediately perceive in other ways as well, especially for Zwingli, through faith? For a basic introduction to modern thinkers who have gone beyond sensationist perception, and what this means for theology in a postmodern world, see my *Postmodern Christianity* (Harrisburg, PA: Trinity Press Int., 2003), 64–68 (and esp. notes), and 111–36.

"I believe," says Zwingli, "that in the Holy Supper of the eucharist (that is, the thanksgiving) the true body of Christ is present to the eye of faith" (*Octavo credo, quod in sacra eucharistiae [hoc est: gratiarum actionis] coena verum Christi corpus adsit fidei contemplatione*) (*Fidei ratio*, Z.W.VI/II.806.6–7).

From about the same time, see Zwingli's (1525) *De vera et falsa religione commentarius*, Z.W. III.590–912, 3.777.20–23; *On True and False Religion*, in *The Latin Works of Huldreich Zwingli*, ed. Samuel Macauley Jackson (Philadelphia: The Heidelberg

Press, 1929), 43–343, 202: "This comes, therefore, because you have in fact looked on me before, and look on me even now, with bodily eyes. But I do not speak of this kind of sight or approach, but of the light of faith" (*Hoc inde provenit, quod me quidem carnis oculis vidistis, dudum et etiamnum videtis. Sed ego de hoc visu vel accessu non loquor, sed de fidei luce*). Also see Z.W. III.786.12–14; *On True and False Religion*, 213: "Faith exists in our hearts through the Spirit of God, which we perceive. For it is not an obscure reality that there is a change of disposition, but we do not perceive it by the senses" (*Fides constat per spiritum dei in cordibus, quam sentimus. Non enim obscura res est, mentis esse immutationem, sed sensibus non percipimus*). Cf. Z.W. III.785.3–8; 786.33–34; 792.25–27; 798.15–16; *On True and False Religion*, 211, 213, 220–21, 227.

And, written just after the *Commentary on True and False Religion*, see Zwingli's clear remarks in *Subsidium sive coronis de eucharistia* (Z.W. IV.58–504; 4.490.22–28 [*Subsidiary Essay on the Eucharist*, in *Zwingli Writings*, vol. 2, 194–231, 215]). See n. 243 below and accompanying text for original and translation. Note the comments by Courvoisier, *Zwingli*, 69–70.

60. *Si carnem eius edamus, id est: pro nobis mortuam credamus; et sanguine eius bibamus, id est: quod sanguis eius pro nobis effuses sit, firmiter credamus: iam Christus sit in nobis et nos in ipso. Sed est ne Christus in quoquam corporaliter? Minime!* (Z.W. III.339.29–33; *Letter to Matthew Alber*, 134).

61. Z.W. III.773.26–775.19; *On True and False Religion*, 198–99; *Noluimus cibum dare, qum impestivum esset* (Z.W. III.774.16–17; *On True and False Religion*, 198).

62. *Est ergo cibus, quem quaerere iubet, fidere filio. Fides igitur cibus est, de quo tam graviter per totum hoc caput disserit* (Z.W. III.776.29–31; *On True and False Religion*, 201).

63. Z.W. III.795.9–799.21; *On True and False Religion*, 224–28.

64. *mortis Christi commemoratio est* (Z.W. III.799.4; *On True and False Religion*, 228).

65. *de corporea carne* (Z.W. III.782.25–26; *On True and False Religion*, 209); *de essentiali Christi corpore, aut corporea carne* (Z.W. III.782.35–36; *On True and False Religion*, 209); *verum, hoc est: corporeum et essentiale* (Z.W. III.784.2; *On True and False Religion*, 210); *realiter, corporaliter, aut essentialiter* (Z.W. III.785.34–35; *On True and False Religion*, 212); *essentiale corpus aut corpoream ac sensibilem carnem Christi* (Z.W. III.786.5–6; *On True and False Religion*, 212); *corpoream carnem* (Z.W. III.786.10; *On True and False Religion*, 213); *de corporali sensibilique Christi carne* (Z.W. III.790.22–23; *On True and False Religion*, 218); *de corporea carne aut sensibili corpore* (Z.W. III.792.10–11; *On True and False Religion*, 220); *corpoream Christi carnem* (Z.W. III.181.28; *On True and False Religion*, 251).

66. Z.W. III.783.16–784.4; *On True and False Religion*, 210.

67. Z.W. III.786.33–34; 792.25–27; 798.15–16; *On True and False Religion*, 213, 220–21, 227.

68. Z.W. III.785.6–8; *On True and False Religion*, 211.

69. *Vera religio, vel pietas, haec est, quae uni solique deo haeret* (Z.W. III.669.171–18; *On True and False Religion*, 92); *Falsa religio sive pietas est, ubi alio fiditur quam deo* (Z.W. III.674.21–22; *On True and False Religion*, 97).

70. Z.W. III.774.24–775.3; *On True and False Religion*, 198–99.

71. *Prodierunt hac nostra tempestate, qui dicerent symbolicum sensum in ista voce "hoc" deprehendi oportere, quorum ego fidem commendo, si modo ficta non est. Deus enim intuetur cor, nos ex facie iudicamus miseri. Commendo ergo magnopere illorum fidem, non*

qua nimis imprudenter haec verba tractare audent, sed qua viderunt considere nequire, ut hic corpoream carnem intellegamus. Veruntamen cuius Carybdis metus eos ad hanc Scyllam offendere coëgerit, nunc non dicam; nihil enim ad hanc rem (Z.W. III.792.35–793.6; *On True and False Religion*, 221).

72. Z.W. III.789.4–5; *On True and False Religion*, 216. Cf. Z.W. III.788.17–18; *On True and False Religion*, 215: *huius spiritualis-corporalis (sic enim inviti loqui cogimur) manducationis* ("this spiritual-bodily eating [for just so am I unwillingly forced to speak]").

73. Z.W. III.776.22–23; *On True and False Religion*, 201.

74. Z.W. III.780.20–37, 35; *On True and False Religion*, 206.

75. Z.W. III.786.12–13 (*On True and False Religion*, 213). Again, for Zwingli not all perception is sensationist, since this real perception comes through the "eye of faith." See note 59 above.

76. *Spiritus, inquam, dei miserum hominis spiritum dignatur ad se trahere, sibi iungere, alligare ac prorsus in se transformare* (Z.W. III.782.7–9, 10; *On True and False Religion*, 208). Also see Z.W. III.782.16–22; *On True and False Religion*, 208, where Zwingli contrasts this "spiritual" food, which is perceived by faith, with the "bodily flesh" and "essential body" that is perceived by the outer senses.

77. *qui ergo a patre intus docente discit, in eo nimirum deus est; ac simul, qui in Christo manet, in eo manet et Christus* (Z.W. III.781.12–13; *On True and False Religion*, 207).

78. Z.W. III.810.4–31; 814.35–815.28; *On True and False Religion*, 241–42, 246–47.

79. *Exposuit autem modum attributionis et doni sui, quomodo daret carnem suam manducare, dicens: "Quit manducat carnem meam et bibit sanguinem meum, in me manet et ego in illo" [Joh. 6.57]. Signum, quia manducavit et bibit, aliquis scilicet, hoc est, si manet et manetur, si habitat et inhabitatur, si haeret, et non deseratur. Hoc ergo nos docuit et admonuit mysticis verbis, ut simus non reliquentes unitatem eius* (Z.W. III.810.8–12; *On True and False Religion*, 241). The text given in Z.W. matches almost exactly the Augustinian text provided in *PL* 35.1616.9–14.

80. Schweizer, *Reformierte Abendmahlsgestaltung*, 103–6; Fritz Schmidt-Clausing, *Zwingli* (Berlin: Walter de Gruyter & Co., 1965), 102–12, esp. 105–8.

81. Markus Jenny, *Zwinglis Stellung zur Musik im Gottesdienst* (Zurich: Zwingli Verlag, 1966). Also see Oskar Farner, "Eine neuentdeckte Äusserung Zwinglis über den Gemeindegesang," in *Jahrbuch für Liturgik und Hymnologie* (1957).

82. Fritz Schmidt-Clausing, *Zwingli als Liturgiker. Eine liturgiegeschichtliche Untersuchung* (Göttingen: Vandenhoeck & Ruprecht, 1952), 63 (accurate for Zwingli but perhaps not for Luther).

83. *Action oder bruch des nachtmals*, Z.W. IV.13–24; *Action or Use of the Lord's Supper*, in *Liturgies of the Western Church*, ed. and trans. Bard Thompson (Cleveland and New York: Collins World, 1961), 14–156.

84. Zwingli's "Preface," *Und so die predig beschicht, wirt man ungeheblet brot und wyn ze vordrest im gefletz uff einem tisch haben* ("And as the sermon is happening, one shall have unleavened bread and wine on the table in the nave"); Z.W. IV.16.1–2 (see 15n10 and 16nn1–3); *Liturgies*, 150). Schweizer argued that the Table was set during the Word service (*Reformierte Abendmahlsgestaltung*, 94). Thompson follows this reading and likewise understands the word *predig* to refer to the entire Word service as such (*Liturgies*, 150, 156n5). Jenny thinks that from the beginning of the service the table was prepared, so that "during the whole church service the community is as a visitor at the Lord's table." He goes on to discuss the developing practice of setting the table after the sermon (*Die Einheit*, 56–58).

85. Z.W. IV.16.5–9; *Liturgies*, 150.

86. *O herr, allmechtiger gott, der uns durch dinen geyst in eynigkeit des gloubens zů einem dinem lyb gemacht hast, welchen lychnam du geheissen hast dir lob und danck sage numb die gůthät und frye gab, das du din eingebornen sun, unseren herren, Jesum Christum, für unser sünd in den tod ggeben hast, verlych uns, das wir dasselbig so getrüwlich tůgend, das wir mit kenier glychßnery oder valsch die unbetrognenn warheyt erzürnind. Verlych uns ouch, das wir so unschuldiklich läbind, als dinem lychnam, dinem gsind und kinderen zymme, damit ouch die unglöubigen dinem namen un eer lernind erkennen. Herr, behůt uns, das dyn nam und eer umb unsers läbens willen nienan geschmächt werde. Herr, mer uns all wäg den glouben, das ist: das vertruwenn in dich, du, der da läbst unnd rychßnest, gott in ewigkeyt! Amen!* (Z.W. IV.22.9–21; *Liturgies*, 154).

87. On the "transubstantiation" of the community, see Schweizer, *Reformierte Abendmahlsgestaltung*, 103–6. Agreeing with Schweizer, see Courvoisier, *Reformed Theologian*, 75–76; idem, "Reflexions," 259–60; Locher, *Zwingli's Thought*, 23, 60–61; idem, *Im Geist und in der Wahrheit* (Neukirchen: Kreis Moers, 1957), 24. Although Jenny says that Schweizer has perhaps "overemphasized" this reality, he takes it to be true at a fundamental level (*Die Einheit*, 62). But in disagreement, see Gerrish, "Discerning the Body," 387–89.

88. *Amica exegesis*, Z.W. V.348–758, 587.14–18; *Friendly Exegesis* in *Huldrych Zwingli Writings*, vol. 2, rev. and ed. H. Wayne Pipkin (Allison Park, PA: Pickwick Publications, 1984), 233–385, 254.

89. *Es ist ouch kein sacrament nie gewesen, das do gegenwürtig machte, daß es bedütet. . . . Also bringt das nachtmal Christi oder das brot und wyn darinn nit den lychnam oder tod Christi zůgegen; sunder die, so den tod Christi, der einist erlidten ist, erkennend ir läbend sin, bringend den in iren danckbaren hertzen ins nachtmal und nemend da mit iren mitgliederen das zeichen, das Christus ingesetzt hat, das es von denen sölle genommen werden unnd bezügen, die sinen tod verjehend; Über D. Martin Luthers Buch, Bekenntnis genannt, zwei Antworten von Johannes Oekolampad und Huldrych Zwingli* (Z.W. VI/II.1–248, 202.21–203.9; see 203nn3–6).

90. Gerrish, "Discerning the Body."

91. See the interesting discussion between Niesel and Blanke, who agree on this feature of Zwingli's late development, although both take Zwingli to be essentially "memorialist." Above, n. 7.

92. *Quo fit, ut omnia nostra impetus iustius adpelles quam libros* (Z.W. IV.462.31–32; *Subsidiary Essay*, 194).

93. Z.W. IV.82.32–484.9; *Subsidiary Essay*, 209–10. For a discussion of the issues with Am Grüt, the dream, and its subsequent discussion and reaction in the Prophezei (Zurich's process of public scripture study, inaugurated by Zwingli), see Köhler, *Luther und Zwingli*, 1:98–111.

94. *Est et aliud, quo rudiores peccant, videlicet ista vox "sensus". Hanc putant aut pro organis, aut pro carnis sensi capi, cum dicitum: hoc abhorret a sensu. . . . Cum sensus hic accipiatur pro "mente" ac "sententia", non carnis et sanguinis, sed quae spiritu dei discitur, et habetur in cordibus nostris* (Z.W. IV.490.22–28; *Subsidiary Essay*, 215).

95. Z.W. IV.491.23, 492.9; *Subsidiary Essay*, 216, 217.

96. *Diximus dudum, fidem rem esse, non scientiam, opinionem aut imaginationem. Sentit ergo homo intus in corde fidem* (Z.W. III.760.10–11; *On True and False Religion*, 182).

97. See above, nn. 65–77, and accompanying text on pp. 63–65.

98. See above, n. 94, and text on p. 46.

99. *Ein klare underrichtung vom nachtmal Christi* (Z.W. IV.789–862; *On the Lord's Supper*, trans. G. W. Bromiley, in *Zwingli and Bullinger* [Philadelphia: The Westminster Press, 1953], 185–238).

100. Z.W. IV.818.29–819.7; *On the Lord's Supper*, 206; Z.W. IV.822.13–17; *On the Lord's Supper*, 209; Z.W. IV.827.4–841.8; *On the Lord's Supper*, 212–22. For entrance to Zwingli's Christology, see Gottfried Locher, *Die Theologie Huldrych Zwinglis im Lichte seiner Christologie* (Zurich: Zwingli-Verlag, 1952), esp. 99–133; idem, *Zwingli's Thought*, 172–78.

101. *Zwingli's Thought*, 174.

102. One can commonly say that God suffered on our behalf because the one "who suffered according to his human nature is God as well as human (*daß der, der in menschlichen natur leid, glich als wol got was, als mensch*); but strictly speaking that would not be so, since the Godhead can not suffer (*nit das die gotheit lyden mög*)" (Z.W. IV.828.27–34; *On the Lord's Supper*, 213). Zwingli's Christology thus has a "'Nestorian' colouring" but all in the service of soteriology: As Zwingli saw the issue, a human redeemer had to assume a truly human nature in which there was no confusion with the Divine. For Zwingli "the divine nature is active whereas the human nature (as a creature) is passive, and the divine nature enters into the human, but is not absorbed by it. For Luther, the deity and manhood of Christ coincide, virtually to the point of identity" (Locher, *Zwingli's Thought*, 173–75, 173; also see *Die Theologie*, 127–33).

103. Z.W. IV.829.5–833.7; *On the Lord's Supper*, 213–16.

104. Z.W. V.565.13, also see n. 4; *Friendly Exegesis*, 240.

105. *Früntlich verglimpfung und ableynung über die predig des treffenlichen Martini Luthers wider die schwermer* (Z.W. V.771–94).

106. *Das dise wort: "Das ist min lychnam" . . . Huldrych Zwinglis christenlich antwurt* (Z.W. V.805–977).

107. Z.W. V.603.5–604.7; 617.15–621.7; 729.20–748.11; *Friendly Exegesis*, 265–66, 274–77, 350–64; Z.W. V.853.24–921.22; Z.W. VI/II.31.1–46.17. Cf. Z.W. V.795.9–799.21; *On True and False Religion*, 224–28; Z.W. IV.842.3–847.4; *On the Lord's Supper*, 223–27.

108. Z.W. V.626.14–627.2, 626.28ff.; *Friendly Exegesis*, 282–83.

109. Although Zwingli suggested that official minutes be taken for the colloquy, his suggestion was rejected. Some private notes were made and some reports written shortly after the colloquy. From these various sources, scholars have for almost three hundred years tried to sequence the conversations at Marburg. Sasse gives a summary of reconstructions (*This Is My Body*, 220–23) and then gives a reconstruction in English (223–68). Perhaps the most notable reconstruction was by Köhler (*Das Marburger Religionsgespräch 1529* [Leipzig: M. Heinsius Nachfolger Eger & Sievers, 1929]), who rendered the conversations into direct speech. (Sasse reports that using Köhler's dialogue students reenacted the colloquy on its fourhundredth anniversary [*This Is My Body*, 223n66].) The Weimar Edition (*D. Martin Luthers Werke: Kritische Gesamtausgabe* [Weimar: Hermann Böhlaus, 1888]; hereafter cited as W.A., with volume and page number; Eng. trans. in *Luther's Works*, ed. Jaroslav Pelikan and Helmut T. Lehmann, 55 vol. [St. Louis: Concordia Publishing House; Philadelphia: Fortress Press, 1955–], 34:103; hereafter cited as L.W., with volume and page number) (W.A. 30/3.92–159; L.W. 38.15–89) discusses the witnesses (30/3.99–101) and then gives some of the sources (Hedio, Anonymous, and Collins) grouped together in sections by dialogue in something of a synopsis (30/3.110–42), with other sources following one after the other (Osiander [144–51],

Brenz [152–56], the Rhapsodie [156–58], and Utinger [158–59]), and ending with the articles themselves (30/3.160–71).

110. Köhler, *Das Marburger Religionsgespräch*, 102–7; Sasse, *This Is My Body*, 256–58. Note Zwingli's precise charge that Luther begs the question (Köhler, *Das Marburger Religionsgespräch*, 115–16; Sasse, *This Is My Body*, 261); and also note that in the prelimnary conversations, Zwingli makes the same charge against Melanchthon (Sasse, *This Is My Body*, 227).

111. *Spiritus, inquam, dei miserum hominis spiritum dignatur ad se trahere, sibi iungere, alligare ac prorsus in se transformare* (Z.W. III.782.7–9; *On True and False Religion*, 208). On John 6:63, also see Z.W. VI/II.182.25–191.21 (also, note Zwingli's reference to Augustine's tractate 26 on the Gospel of John, Z.W. VI/II.191.20).

112. *Spiritum esse oportet, qui mentem vivificet, quique ad eam penetret, corpore pasci abhorret* (Z.W. V.622.13–15; *Friendly Exegesis*, 278)

113. In this chapter, see n. 59 above; also see n. 65 above for the outer correlation to the inner eye of faith. Also compare nn. 94, 137, and 140 above.

114. *Sed solummodo negamus corporis carnalis ad animam adhibitionem quicquam ad iustificationem facere, cum, quod corpore carneo vesci anima nequit, tum, quod Christus ipse spiritum esse oportere, quod iustificet carnem autem nihil poenitus prodesse, luculentissime disseruit* (Z.W. V.626.4–9; *Friendly Exegesis*, 282).

115. *. . . et quod stultissima erat, now plane beatos existimabamus, si quid talium solummodo aspexissemus. Promittebamus nobis ipsis abolita esse peccata, propiciam fortunam ac mundum totum* (Z.W. III.774.32–775.3; *On True and False Religion*, 199).

116. For the emphasis on the visual in the late medieval period, see chap. 1, nn. 123–27 and text. For Zwingli's comment to Luther about laity longing for the old ways, and Luther unfortunately abetting that desire, see Z.W. V.614.1–25; *Friendly Exegesis*, 314.

117. *Luter schmeckt aber nach dem knoblouch und böllen in Egypten* (Z.W. VI/II.70.6–7).

118. *Num duae sunt ad iusticiam viae? Altera credendi, altera corporaliter edendi? Quo ruimus?* (Z.W. V.706.9–11; *Friendly Exegesis*, 340).

119. Z.W. V.576.1–3, 591.4–25, 624.29–625.11, 670.17–671.8, 706.5–11, 707.3–708.13; *Friendly Exegesis*, 247, 258, 280–81, 313, 339–40, 340–41; Z.W. V.783.1–10. Also see his earlier comments, Z.W. III.780.38–782.22, 784.21–788.38; *On True and False Religion*, 206–8, 210–16.

120. *Secundo vero loco "praesens" accipitur naturaliter sive essentialiter, sic, ut corpus Christi fide fiat praesens. At quomodo, in spiritu aut mente, an etiam se ipso sive natura? Si spiritualis est ista corporis praesentia: puta, quod in mente fidimus Christo pro nobis mortuo, iam nihil dissidii inter nos manebit. Nos enim sic praesentiam istam adserimus, ut unam sciamus ad hanc rem sufficere, super qua digladiamur* (Z.W. V.587.14–18; *Friendly Exegesis*, 254). On translating *mens* by the word "heart," for Zwingli this often seems appropriate, because, as we have seen, faith primarily meant "trust," rather than cognitive belief (e.g., see the prayer in this chapter [p. 66, n. 86]). See Zwingli's argument to Luther in which he says that the "mind" (*mens/mentem*) finds its "keep (citadel) and palace" (*arx ac regia*) in the heart, which is not the physical heart but amounts to "nothing other than the soul" (*quod nihil est aliud quam animam*) (Z.W. V.673.7–13; *Friendly Exegesis*, 315).

121. See above, n. 65.

122. Z.W. V.679.6–701.18; *Friendly Exegesis*, 319–36 ("On the Alloiosis of the Two Natures of Christ"); Z.W. V.922.1–959.12 ("On the Two Natures of Christ and

their Exchange"); Z.W. VI/II.126–159.15 ("On the Exchange or Alloiosis"); Z.W. V/II.159.16–181.6 ("That Christ's Body Would Be Circumscribed and Finite"); *qui naturas in Christo confundant, non iam per alloeosim naturarumque et idiomatum commutationem, sed vere de humana praedicare volentes, quod divinae modo est, et de divina, quod humanae tantum* (Z.W. V.564.11–14; *Friendly Exegesis*, 564).

123. Locher, *Zwingli's Thought*, 173–78; idem, *Die Theologie*, 128–33, also see 135–55.

124. Z.W. V.354.6–7.

125. *Nunc autem, quum Christus propter verbum suum (hoc Neoterici ordinatam vocant potentiam) ailibi esse corpore non possit, quam ubi definivit, impossibile est, eum in pane edi. Ad dexteram est; isthic sessurum se dixit, usque dum arbiter omnium futures redeat. "In uno loco esse oportet,"* quod ad humanam adtinet (Z.W. V.671.15–20; *Friendly Exegesis*, 314). Also see Z.W. V.695.2–696.8; *Friendly Exegesis*, 331–32; Z.W. IV.822.13–17; *On the Lord's Supper*, 209; Z.W. IV.827.4–841.8 9; *On the Lord's Supper*, 212–22.

126. Köhler, *Das Marburger Religionsgespräch*, 93; Sasse, *This Is My Body*, 252–53.

127. Locher, *Zwingli's Theology*, 173–74.

128. Susi Hausamann, "Die Marburger Artikel—eine echte Konkordie?" *Zeitschrift für Kirchengeschichte* 87 (1966): 288–321, argues that Marburg produced "eine Scheinkonkordie" in which both sides found their voice, but left real differences unresolved, so that later conflicts were inevitable. The same material can be viewed more positively, as Stephens shows, by noting the balancing of emphasis between the positions of Luther and Zwingli (*Theology of Huldrych Zwingli*, 249–50). Compromise ecclesial documents, in which both sides see themselves represented but that do not attempt a single perspective, go back at least as far as Chalcedon.

129. *The Tetrapolitan Confession* (1530). Latin text in H. A. Niemeyer, ed., *Collectio confessionum in ecclesiis reformatis publicatarum* (Leipzig: Klinkhardt, 1840) [Eng. trans. in Arthur C. Cochrane, ed., *Reformed Confessions of the Sixteenth Century* (Philadelphia: The Westminster Press, 1966), 54–88].

130. *Si tu et tui interim "Apologeticos" parassetis ad caesarem et principes, in quibus quam piissime, citra cuiusquam, quantum fieri potest, suggillationem fidei vestre rationem redderetis, ita tamen, ut no nederentur, nisi consultum nobis, qui hic agimus, visum fuisset, non credo omnino operam et impensam perdituros vos* (Jacob Sturm an Zwingli, Z.W. X.604.3–7).

131. *Fidei ratio*; Z.W. VI/II.790–817 (*An Account of the Faith* in *The Latin Works of Huldreich Zwingli II*, gen. ed. Samuel Macauley Jackson, ed. William John Hinke [Philadelphia: The Heidelberg Press, 1922], 35–61). Also see the recent critical edition by Wilhelm H. Neuser in *Reformierte Bekenntnisschriften* 1/1, ed. Heiner Faulenbach and Eberhard Busch, in conjunction with Emidio Campi et al. (Neukirchen-Vluyn: Neukirchener, 2002), 412–46. Note that the 1530 Froschauer edition can be downloaded in PDF format from the *Zentralbibliothek Zürich* at http://www.e-rara.ch/zuz/content/titleinfo/298459.

132. *Christi corpus per essentialiam et realiter, hoc est: corpus ipsum naturale, in caena aut adsit aut ore dentibusque nostris manducatur* (Z.W. VI/II.806.12–14); *verum Christi corpus adsit fidei contemplatione* (Z.W. VI/II.806.7); *An Account of the Faith*, 49.

133. *Repulsio Articulorum Zwinglii*; *Refutation of Zwingli by Eck*, in *The Latin Works of Huldreich Zwingli II*, 62–104.

134. *Illustrissimis Germaniae principibus in comitiis Augustanis congregatis*, Z.W. VI/III.249–91; *Letter to the Princes of Germany*, in *The Latin Works of Huldreich Zwingli II*, 105–27.

135. *Cum vero panis et vinum, quae ipsis domini verbis consecratea sunt, simul fratribus distribuuntur, an nam totus Christ velut sensibiliter (ut etiam, si verba requirantur, plus dicam, quam vulgo solet) sensibus etiam offertur?* (Z.W. VI/III.260.3–7; *Letter to the Princes of Germany*, 110–11).

136. Z.W. VI/III.260.7–261.3; *Letter to the Princes of Germany*, 111.

137. *Et nos nunquam negavimus corpus Christi sacramentaliter ac in mysterio esse in coena, tum propter fidei contemplationem, tum propter symboli, ut diximus, totam actionem. . . . Cum igitur omnis ista praesentia nihil sit sine fidei contemplatione, iam fidei est ista esse aut fieri praesentia, non sacramentorum* (Z.W. VI/III.264.23–365.6; *Letter to the Princes of Germany*, 112–13).

138. Z.W. VI/III.265.21–277.15; *Letter to the Princes of Germany*, 113–21; *non istud spirituale, quod nos edimus* (Z.W. VI/III.274.6; *Letter to the Princes of Germany*, 119). On Zwingli's affirmation that the elements are converted into Christ's sacramental body, though not his natural body, see Z.W. VI/III.271.13–272.3; *Letter to the Princes of Germany*, 117–18.

139. Z.W. VI/III.280.22–24, see n. 4; *Letter to the Princes of Germany*, 123. For the whole section on the ring, see Z.W. VI/III.278.19–282.7; *Letter to the Princes of Germany*, 122–24.

140. *Sic, inquam, nos coenam domini splendidam Christi praesentia habemus. At in his omnibus an non sacramentaliter et fidei contemplatione corpus Christi praesens esse, ut semper diximus, summa totius rei est?* (Z.W. VI/III.281.3–6; *Letter to the Princes of Germany*, 123; emphasis added).

141. Z.W. VI/III.272.12–13; *Letter to the Princes of Germany*, 118. Zwingli made this same point to Luther when he said that the Supper does not make present to believers the death or body of Christ; see n. 89 above.

142. See above, nn. 73–77.

143. Locher would seem right on target when he calls this presence of Christ a "re-presentation" (*Vergegenwärtigung*). See n. 24 above; cf. n. 27.

144. Edward J. Kilmartin, SJ, *The Eucharist in the West: History and Theology*, ed. Robert J. Daly, SJ (Collegeville, MN: The Liturgical Press, 1998), 25.

145. For example, see above, nn. 59, 65.

146. *Zwingli an Capito und Bucer* (Z.W. XI.339–43). *Ad summam nostrae confessionis venio: non est ut hoc quisquam a nobis exigat, an credamus Christum esse in coena; nam nisi adsit, abhorrebimus a coena. Non de Christo dissidium est; etiam quum Luterus dicit eum esse ubique, nobiscum enim sentit. De hoc autem est certamen, Christi naturale istud ac substantia corpus natura substantiaque praesens hic loci in coena et porrigatur et edatur. De qua re dudum habetis sententiam nostram, in uno loco esse oportere hoc modo. Sed ista nunc mittimus. Christi corpus scimus adesse in coena; verum non naturaliter aut corporaliter, sed sacramentaliter adesse credimus nudae, religiosae ac sanctae menti, hoc est: fidei contemplatione* (Z.W. XI.340.7–16).

147. Z.W. XI.339.4–9.

148. *Hoc me solicitum tenet, quod et monui, quum Augustae esses, quod ad diuturnam contumaciam istorum hominum cessistis loco et iam verbis illorum loquimini, quae si solum symbolicos intelligitis. . . . Qualia sunt, ut in Germanice scripta confessione vestra extat: corpus suum verum vere dedit Chrsitus in coena, et etiam num dat, in cibum animae. Nam Christus non praebuit corpus suum in cibum animae, sed corporis sui prebiti iam dudum, quum in terra nasceretur, praebendique quum crastino cruci adfigeretur, in cibum animae symbolum dedit* (Z.W. IX.340.24–28).

149. For Bucer's biography, see Martin Greschat, *Martin Bucer: Ein Reformator und seine Zeit* (Munich: Verlag C. H. Beck, 1990), now in an English translation, which includes additional material added by Greschat that covers scholarship since the German edition (Greschat, *Martin Bucer: A Reformer and His Times*, trans. Stephen E. Buckwalter [Louisville, KY, and London: Westminster John Knox Press, 2004]). Also see the older work by Hasting Eells, *Martin Bucer* (New Haven, CT: Yale University Press, 1931). See Brian G. Armstrong, "Calvin and Calvinism," in *Reformation Europe: A Guide to Research II*, ed. William S. Maltby (St. Louis: Center for Reformation Research, 1992), 92–93. For a short introduction to Bucer, see Martin Greschat, "Das Profil Martin Bucers," in *Martin Bucer and Sixteenth-Century Europe*, 2 vols. (Leiden: E. J. Brill, 1993), ed. Christian Krieger and Marc Lienhard, 9–16. For Bucer in Strasbourg, see Miriam Usher Chrisman, *Strasbourg and the Reform: A Study in the Process of Change* (New Haven, CT: Yale University Press, 1967). Also see the far-reaching essays in Krieger and Lienhard, eds., *Martin Bucer*, especially those concerning Bucer's relationship with other Reformers, 1:343–470.

Secondary literature on Bucer can be found in *Bucer-Bibliographie/Bibliographie Bucer 1975–1998*, ed. Thomas Wilhelmi, Bernd Paul, Michael Mermann, and Danièle Fischer, preface by Matthieu Arnold and Gottfried Seebass (Strasbourg: Association des Publications de la Faculté de Théologie Protestante, 1999). The director of the Bucer-Forschungsstelle in Heidelberg, Gottfried Seebass, reviewed Bucer research since 1991 in "Bucer—Forschung seit dem Jubiläumsjahr 1991," *Theologische Rundschau* 62 (1997): 271–300.

150. For the standard older work, see Constantin Hopf, *Martin Bucer and the English Reformation* (Oxford: Basil Blackwell, 1946). But for recent studies, see N. Scott Amos, "The Alsatian among the Athenians: Martin Bucer, Mid-Tudor Cambridge and the Edwardian Reformation," *Reformation and Renaissance Review* 4, no. 1 (2002): 94–124; idem, "'It Is Fallow Ground Here': Martin Bucer as Critic of the English Reformation," *Westminster Theological Journal* 61 (1999): 41–52; idem, "Martin Bucer and the Revision of the 1549 Book of Common Prayer: Reform of Ceremonies and the Didactic Use of Ritual," *Reformation and Renaissance Review* (1999): 107–26; Diarmaid MacCulloch, *Thomas Cranmer* (New Haven, CT: Yale University Press, 1996); Jochen Remy, "Die 'Kölner Reformation' und ihre Bedeutung für die englische Kirchengeschichte. Anmerkung zu einer Verhältnisbestimmung zwischen dem 'Einfältigen Bedenken' und dem 'Book of Common Prayer,'" *Veröffentlichungen des Kölnischen Geschichtsvereins* 67 (1993): 119–40.

151. The view of Köhler (*Zwingli und Luther*; "Zur Abendmahls Kontroverse") that Bucer played the pragmatic and irenic mediator between Zwingli and Luther, keeping Zwingli from ultimately becoming a mere memorialist, was challenged by the work of Thomas Kaufmann. See Kaufmann, *Die Abendmahlstheologie der Straßburger Reformatoren bis 1529* (Tübingen: J. C. B. Mohr, 1992); also see a summary essay of his argument, "Streittheologie und Friedensdiplomatie. Die Rolle Martin Bucers im frühen Abendmahlstreit," in Krieger and Lienhard, eds., *Martin Bucer*, 239–56. Kaufmann argues that while ecumenically conciliatory to the Lutherans in public, Bucer and the Strasbourg theologians were privately working against Luther. For example, a 1524 letter-writing effort disingenuously spread Karlstadtian ideas against Luther while not being clear to Luther about the differences between him and Bucer (Kaufmann, *Die Abendmahlstheologie*, 217–37); and Strasbourg pursued concord with Wittenberg, while Bucer emended Bugenhagen's

Psalm commentary in order to bend Bugenhagen's views toward his own and wrote pastors in South Germany urging them to reject Luther's eucharistic views (Kaufmann, *Die Abendmahlstheologie*, 303–32).

Rather than irenic, Bucer appears to Kaufmann to be so complexly and personally involved in the eucharistic controversies that he bordered on being just plain duplicitous (e.g., "Streittheologie und Friedensdiplomatie," 250–51). Even Bucer biographers such as Eells find Bucer "a peculiar and puzzling personality" (Eells, *Martin Bucer*, 87); and Greschat finds Bucer a "complex personality"—a subtheme of his book—and perhaps not at his best in the early disputes with Luther (Greschat, *Martin Bucer: Ein Reformator*, 86–89; Greschat, *Martin Bucer: A Reformer*, 74–77). Note Greschat's measured comments on Kaufmann's work (Greschat, *Martin Bucer: A Reformer*, 259–60), including the rejection of Kaufmann's suggestion that anyone (even from the "Stupperischschule"—see Kaufmann, "Streittheologie und Friedensdiplomatie," 239n1)—ever took Bucer to be purely and simply irenic.

152. For instance, see Eells, *Martin Bucer*, 415–22; W. P. Stephens, *The Holy Spirit in the Theology of Martin Bucer* (Cambridge: Cambridge University Press, 1970), 5–10; Chrisman, *Strasbourg and the Reform*, 85–88; but also see Reinhold Friedrich, "Martin Bucer: Ökumene im 16. Jahrhundert," in Krieger and Lienhard, eds., *Martin Bucer and Sixteenth-Century Europe*, 257–68, who notes Bucer's scriptural boundary for ecumenism; and see Hamman, "La démarche théologique de Bucer," in Krieger and Lienhard, eds., *Martin Bucer and Sixteenth-Century Europe*, 71–81, who note the work of the Spirit in Bucer's ecumenical and pragmatic efforts. See also Seebass, "Bucer—Forschung seit dem Jubiläumsjahr 1991"; and Greschat, *Martin Bucer: A Reformer*, 255–71.

153. For a detailed analysis of Bucer's eucharistic teachings, see Ian Hazlett, "The Development of Martin Bucer's Thinking on the Sacrament of the Lord's Supper in Its Historical and Theological Context" (Thesis, Westfälische Wilhelms-Universität zu Münster, 1975). Hazlett provides a helpful chronological summary of Bucer's writings that related to the Supper (9–15). Also see Irena Backus, "Bucer's Commentary on the Gospel of John," in *Martin Bucer: Reforming Church and Community*, ed. D. F. Wright (Cambridge: Cambridge University Press, 1994), 61–71; Eells, *Martin Bucer*, 70–98; idem, "The Genesis of Martin Bucer's Doctrine of the Supper," *Princeton Theological Review* 24 (1926): 225–51; Greschat, *Martin Bucer: Ein Reformator*, 83–91, 102–14, 142–52 [*Martin Bucer: A Reformer*, 70–79, 91–103, 132–42]; Ian Hazlett, "Eucharistic communion: Impulses and directions in Martin Bucer's thought," in *Martin Bucer: Reforming Church and Community*, ed. D. F. Wright (Cambridge: Cambridge University Press, 1994), 72–82; Hyma, "Hoen's Letter"; Kaufmann, *Die Abendmahlstheologie*; Köhler, *Zwingli und Luther*; Wilhelm Neuser, "Martin Bucer als Mittler im Abendmahlsstreit (1530/31)," in *Kaum zu glauben. Von der Häresie und dem Umgang mit ihr*, ed. Athina Lexutt and Vicco von Bülow (Rheinbach-Merzbach: CMZ-Verlag, 1998), 140–61; Stephens, *The Holy Spirit*, 238–59; Robert Stupperich, "Strassburgs Stellung im Beginn des Sakramentsstreits," *Archiv für Reformationsgeschichte* 38 (1941): 249–72; Nicholas Thompson, *Eucharistic Sacrifice and Patristic Tradition in the Theology of Martin Bucer, 1534–1546* (Leiden and Boston: Brill, 2005).

154. Stephens, *Martin Bucer*, 239; Eells, "The Genesis," 251.

155. *Bucers Lehre der Real-Präsenz und der Abendmahlsgabe lässt sich leider nicht in einigen Worten auf eine griffige Kurzformen bringen. Dies ist teilweise in Bucers außerordentlich vorsichtiger Denkart begründet. Dazu kommt, dass seine Aussagen in den*

verschiedenen Zeiten, bezogen auf die jeweiligen Adressaten, unterschiedlich sind, ohne dass er das Wesentliche in seiner Auffassung preisgibt (Hazlett, "The Development," 413.) Also see Eells, who makes much the same comment (*Martin Bucer*, 87).

156. Hazlett, "The Development," 43–56, Eells, *Martin Bucer*, 70–73; idem, "The Genesis," 225–26; Stephens, *Martin Bucer*, 240; Friedhelm Krüger, *Bucer und Erasmus* (Wiesbaden: F. Steiner Verlag, 1970), 183–224.

157. See Krüger, *Bucer und Erasmus*, 186–96. See Köhler, *Zwingli und Luther*, 69–71, for Zwingli's reaction to Luther here.

158. "Letter to Germanus," in *Correspondance de Martin Bucer*, vol. 2, ed. Jean Roth (Leiden: E. J. Brill, 1989), 50–54; hereafter referred to as BCor, followed by volume, page, and line. See BCor 2.51.12–28.

159. *Ain Sermon auf Euangeli Johannis*; W.A. 12.580–84. For the publication of this sermon in Strasbourg, see Hazlett, "The Development," 60–61. Also see Greschat, *Martin Bucer: Ein Reformator*, 84–85 [*Martin Bucer: A Reformer*, 71–72]; Stupperich, "Straßburgs Stellung," 254.

160. *Das essen und trincken ist nichts anders dann glauben* (W.A. 12.582.10–11). Cf. W.A. 12.582.31–36.

161. Eells, *Martin Bucer*, 71–72; idem, "The Genesis," 226–28; Hyma, "Hoen's Letter"; Hazlett, "The Development," 90–95; Stupperich, "Straßburgs Stellung," 254–55.

162. Hazlett, "The Development," 70–85; Greschat, *Martin Bucer: Ein Reformator*, 84 [*Martin Bucer: A Reformer*, 71–72]; Eells, *Martin Bucer*, 71–73; idem, "The Genesis," 226–28; Hyma, "Hoen's Letter"; Krüger, *Bucer und Erasmus*, 194–207; Stupperich, "Straßburgs Stellung," 252–55.

163. *Martin Bucers Deutsche Schriften*, Bd. 1 (Gütersloh: Gütersloher Verlagshaus Gerd Mohn; Paris: Presses universitaires de France, 1960), 194–278; hereafter referred to as BDS, followed volume, page, and line. For Bucer's description of the miracles attributed to St. Aurelien's grave, such as her making insane and biting off the fingers of grave robbers; and for reforms made according to the Word of God, such as the removal of the coffin, in which bones "very large and dissimilar" (*ser groß und ungleich*) were found—bones that could not have come from a girl— see BDS 1.273.9–274.5.

164. Numbering them in order (no numbering was given by Bucer): (1) Reforms to the Lord's Supper (BDS 1.205.19–208.39); (2) The Name of the Lord's Supper (BDS 209.1–210.26); (3) Lord's Supper as a Memorial of Lord's Death, in No Way a Sacrifice (BDS 210.27–218.6); (4) Abolishing the Elevation (BDS 218.7–230.23); (6) Priestly Prayers and Gestures Abolished and Changed; the Table (Called the Altar) Shifted (BDS 236.15–242.9); (7) Lord's Supper on Sundays and in Congregation (BDS 242.10–246.2); (8) How the Lord's Supper Is Now Celebrated (BDS 246.3–254.20).

165. *Weyter, so man dis brot und den kelch auffgehaben hat, haben es die leüt angebettet als iren gott und Christum, da leiplich zůgegen, mit etlichen seltzamen gebettlin, die haben dann vil krefftiger müssen sein, dann zů andern zeiten, so doch die rechte heilsame gegenwertigkeit gottes und Christ durch den waren glauben is unsichtbarlicher weyß* (BDS 1.228.3–7; see 1.228.12–20). Also see BDS 1.227.5–25; 1.249.22–5; 1.252.1–2; 1.253.21–25. See BDS 1.48.9–13 for this same contrast made with John 4:23–24 ("worship the Father in Spirit and truth"); and see Bucer citing John 4:23–24 as contrary to all the many offensive and hypocritical priestly gestures that are "such magical trickery" (*solich gauckelwerck*) (BDS 1.237.21–238.8, 238.5).

166. BDS 1.228.12–20.

167. "Letter to Germanus," in *Correspondance de Martin Bucer*, ed. Jean Roth (Leiden: E. J. Brill, 1989), 2.50–54. Bucer wrote that he never had really been convinced of a bodily presence of Christ (*prasentiam carnalem Christi in pane eucharistia*), but held on because of Luther's own authority, only to come to the idea of "a spiritual eating of Christ," because of Luther's own teaching on John 6; see BCor 2.51.12–28.

168. For example, the title to section 2 reads "[t]hat the Supper of the Lord should be held as a memorial of the death of our Lord and in no way be taken to be a sacrifice" (*Das das Nachtmal des herrn zů gedachtnuß des tods unsers herren und keinswegs für ein auffopfferung sol gehalten werden*) (BDS 1.210.27–28). On the Supper as a memorial known inwardly but not seen outwardly, as in the elevation, see, e.g., BDS 1.227.5–25.

169. BDS 1.247.38–252.30.

170. *das wir uns gern wolten befleissen, die leüt vom fleisch, von leiplichen elementen auff den geist und geistliche übungen zů furen* (BDS 1.248.9–11).

171. BDS 1.248.33–249.21.

172. *das wort macht mir die ausserlichen ding frey und heist mich sye gebrauchen zů besserung der nechsten, und darumb, weiwohl ich frey bin von jederman, hab ich doch mich selb jederman zum knecht gemacht, auff das ich ir vil geinne. Den juden bin ich worden asl ein jud, den schwachen ein schwacher und jederman allerley, das ich doch etlich geinne and selig machte*, 1 Cor. 9 (BDS 1.223.15–20).

173. So Stupperich (BDS 2.433) in his introduction to the letter, which can be found in BDS 2.434–60.

174. For the controversy with Brenz, see Hazlett, "The Development," 115–17, 128–33; Eells, *Martin Bucer*, 75–76. On Bucer's concept that the Word at the table offers the true body of Christ, which is inwardly received through the Spirit and faith, see Johannes Brenz, *Anecdota Brentiana: ungedruckte Briefe und Bedenken*, ed. Theodor Pressel (Tübingen: J. J. Heckenhauer, 1868), "Der Prediger von Strassburg an die Herrn von Gemmingen (December 1, 1525)," 9–10; e.g.,"the bread was a sign of the body of Christ, with which the body of Christ was handed over to the faithful—however through the Word—and so the mouth eats only the bread, but the spirit eats the body of Christ through faith" (*das brot sey ein zeychen des leips Cristi, mit dem den glaubigen der leip Cristi, werd ubergeben, Aber durchs wort, und also esse der mundt nur das brodt, der geyst aber den leip Cristi durch den glauben*).

175. Hazlett, "The Development," 187–97, 214–22, 225–26.

176. *Enarrationum in evangelia Matthaei, Marci et Lucae libri duo* (1527). The second volume, which contains exegesis on Matt. 26:26, survives in only one known extant copy, but can be found in August Lang, *Der Evangelienkommentar Martin Butzers und die Grundzüge seiner Theologie*, in N. Bonwetsch and R. Seeberg, eds., Studien zur Geschichte der Theologie und der Kirche, Bd II (Leipzig: Dieterich'sche Verlags-Buchhandlung Theodore Weicher, 1900) .

177. *Sicut tunc vobis trado panem edendum, ore corporis, ita dono vobis corpus meum edendum animo, nam dabitur iam pro vita vestra in mortem, symbolum hoc corporis mei est, ut sicut panem a me acceptum, ore comedititis et in ventrem traiicitis, ut inde vita vestra sustentetur, et ad opera valeat, ita animo credatis corpus meum pro vobis tradi, ut hinc fiducia in deum alatur, et corroboretur, qui indubie filios et haeredes vos agnoscet, pro quibus ego corpus meum, in mortem tradidero* (Lang, *Der Evangelienkommentar*, 435).

178. *Martini Buceri Opera Latina,* vol. 2: *Enarratio in Evangelion Iohannis (1528, 1530, 1536),* ed. Irena Backus (Leiden: E. J. Brill, 1988); hereafter referred to as BOL2, followed by page number. On Bucer's continued double manducation, see Hazlett, "The Development," 214–26. For the ecclesial dimension of union in Christ and (nonmetabolic but real) nourishment by his body, see Backus, "Bucer's Commentary," 62–63, 66–67, 70.

179. *"Qui edit carnem meam et bibit sanguine meum, in me manet" [Io. 6, 57]. Totum siquidem rapi in Christum et transmutari oportet eum qui sola fide agnoverit et perpenderit quam immense nos dilectione complexus sit, dum nostri causa mori sustinuit. In hoc vicissim agit et vivit Christus, omnia in eo suo Spiritu perficiens idque est "Christum manere in illo" [Io 6, 57]*; BOL2, 272.

180. Hazlett, "The Development," 227–414; Greschat, *Martin Bucer: Ein Reformator,* 104–15 [*Martin Bucer: A Reformer,* 93–104]; Eells, *Martin Bucer,* 93–118; idem, "Genesis," 246–57.

181. *Der leib unnd das blut Christi selbs warhafftig, zugegen seye, nit schlecht* effective, *kräfftiglich, würklich, gaistlich, sondern* vere, substantialiter, essentialiter, *wesentlich unnd warhafftig, unnd werde gegeben unnd empfangen mit brott und wein. Dann mann müesse underscheiden* sacramentum et rem sacramenti, *nemblich dasz der lieb unnd das blut Christ (allsz* res sacramenti*) gegeben unnd empfangen werde, mit dem brott unnd wein im abendtmahl* ("Éclaircissement de Bucer devant ses collègues sur la Concorde de Wittenberg," in *Martin Bucer: Études sur la Correspondance,* vol. 1, ed. J. V. Pollet [Paris: Presses Universitaires de France, 1958], 166.14–21).

182. Hazlett, "The Development," 392. For Bucer's reply to Ceneau, see *Martini Buceri Opera Latina Volume V: Defensio adversus axioma catholicum id est criminationem R. P. Roberti Episcopi Abrincensis (1534),* ed. William Ian P. Hazlett (Leiden: Brill, 2000); hereafter referred to as BOL5, followed by page number. Bucer wrote his *Defensio* as a reply to a work by Robert Ceneau, bishop of Avraches and theologian at the University of Paris, who attacked Bucer's position on the Supper as given in his commentary on the Gospels. The give-and-take between Ceneau and Bucer occurred amid a complex political scene that included a possible rapprochement between Roman Catholic and Reformation thinkers, a possibility rejected by the theologians at Paris unless the Protestants first recanted and returned home to the Roman church. For historical background, see BOL5, ix–xxxvii.

183. See above, n. 65.

184. See above, n. 65.

185. In his reply to Ceneau, Bucer once again appealed to both Thomas and patristic writers, and in the passage cited here Bucer has taken up views of Hilary with which he agrees, and he says that "by the Son remaining physically in us, and by our bodily and inseparable union in him, the mystery of a true and natural union may be proclaimed" (*per manentem in nobis carnaliter Filium, et in eo nobis corporaliter et inseparabiliter unitis, mysterium verae ac naturalis unitatis sit praedicandum*); BOL5, 99.

186. *Martin Bucer Deutsche Schriften V: Straßburg und Münster im Kampf um den rechten Glauben 1532–1534,* ed. Robert Stupperich (Gütersloh: Gütersloher Verlagshaus Gerd Mohn, 1978), herafter referred to as BDS5, followed by page number: *unser heyland, Gott und Herr, der die liebe selb ist, in uns lebet, so seind wir auch mit allen unseren mitgliedern im warer göttlicher liebe vereiniget, ein leibe, ein brot, die do eins brots gemeinschafft, 1 Cor. 10 [16]. . . . darum seind alle wort und sacrament des Herren*

daruff erstlich gericht, das uns, in denen die gemeinschafft unsers Herren Jesu, das er uns nit allein by dem vatter vertrette, sonder auch in uns lebe . . . (BDS5, 250–51).

187. For the following, see Hazlett, "The Development," 392–96. Bucer used the opportunity of the *Defensio* to lay groundwork for concord with the Lutherans; see Hazlett, "The Development," 384–88.

188. *nam et ipse nullam aliam Domini manducationem agnoscit, quam verum, quam ea, quae semper salvifica est, quantum quidem Domini manducatio est, et si eadem interdum ex accedente indignitate sim iudicium aliquod accersat* (BOL5, 116).

189. Where Luther understood the Bread from Heaven discourse to be about faith, and to stand subordinate to the institution narratives; and where Zwingli found an exegetical point about the uselessness of sense-related perception as compared to the real perception that is faith's and that brings union with Christ through the Spirit; Bucer saw John 6 as itself a truly eucharistic passage, a discourse about the Supper itself. See Hazlett, "The Development," 136–37; idem, "Eucharistic communion," esp. 81–82.

190. Hazlett, "The Development," 32.

CHAPTER 4: THE SECOND GENERATION: JOHN CALVIN AND HEINRICH BULLINGER

1. Theodore Beza (1519–1605) wrote his first Calvin biography in the preface to Calvin's *Commentary on the Book of Joshua* (1564) (see C.O. 21.21–50). For a helpful and fascinating study of the genre of *Lives* and early Calvin biographies—pro and con—see Irena Backus, "Calvin. Saint, Hero or the Worst of All Possible Christians?" in *Calvinus sacrarum literarum interpres*, ed. Herman J. Selderhuis (Göttingen: Vandenhoeck & Ruprecht, 2008), 223–43. Emil Doumergue, *Jean Calvin. Les Hommes et les choses de son temps*, 7 vols. (Lausanne: Georges Bridel, 1899–1924), remains a wealth of information and context. Williston Walker, *John Calvin: The Organizer of Reformed Protestantism, 1509–1564* (New York: G. P. Putnam's Sons, 1906), remains a classic that needs to be read alongside the far more recent T. H. L. Parker, *John Calvin: A Biography* (Philadelphia: The Westminster Press, 1975). Also see Ronald S. Wallace, *Geneva and the Reformation: A Study of Calvin as Social Reformer, Churchman, Pastor, and Theologian* (Grand Rapids: Baker Book House, 1988), and Randall Zachman's summary of Calvin the teacher, standing at the confluence of humanism and the gospel, *John Calvin as Teacher, Pastor, and Theologian* (Grand Rapids: Baker Academic, 2006). Important also is William Bouwsma, *John Calvin: A Sixteenth-Century Portrait* (New York: Oxford University Press, 1988), which places Calvin the person amid the culture that shaped him and which gives an iconic rendering of the sixteenth century. For entrance to the scholarly debate over Bouwsma's book, see John Hesselink, "Reactions to Bouwsma's 'Portrait' of John Calvin," in *Calvinus Sacrae Scripturae Professor*, ed. Wilhelm Neuser (Grand Rapids: Eerdmans, 1994), 209–13. For overall bibliographic essays, see David C. Steinmetz, "The Theology of Calvin and Calvinism," in Steven Ozment, ed., *Reformation Europe: A Guide to Research* (St. Louis: Center for Reformation Research, 1982), 211–32; and, Brian G. Armstrong, "Calvin and Calvinism," in William S. Maltby, *Reformation Europe: A Guide to Research II* (St. Louis: Center for Reformation Research, 1992), 75–103. Also see the fall issue of the *Calvin Theological Journal* from 1971 onward for exhaustive bibliographies of Calvin

studies that year, organized according to topics. This work extends the older Calvin bibliography found in Wilhelm Niesel, *Calvin-Bibliographie, 1901–1959* (Munich: C. Kaiser, 1961).

2. Parker, *Calvin*, 4–8.

3. Alexandre Ganoczy, *The Young Calvin*, trans. David Foxgrover and Wade Provo (Philadelphia: The Westminster Press, 1987), 173, 57–63, 168–78 [Ganoczy, *Le Jeune Calvin, Genèse et évolution de sa vocation réformatrice* (Wiesbaden: Franz Steiner Verlag, 1966)]; Heiko Oberman, "*Initia Calvini*: the Matrix of Calvin's Reformation," in Neuser, ed., *Calvinus*, 117–27; Alistair E. McGrath, "John Calvin and Late Medieval Thought," *Archiv für Reformationsgeschichte* 77 (1986): 58–78 (note the cautious, general summary, 77–78); Thomas F. Torrance, *The Hermeneutics of John Calvin* (Edinburgh: Scottish Academic Press, 1988), 3–57 ("The Parisian Background") and 73–95 ("Late Mediaeval Thought and Piety"); Richard C. Gamble, "Current Trends in Calvin Research, 1982–1990," in Neuser, ed., *Calvinus*, 96–108.

4. Parker, *Calvin*, 13–33; also see Parker's discussion of chronology in appendix 1, 156–61.

5. Parker, *Calvin*, 24–28.

6. *Christianae Religionis Institutio 1536*, in *Ioannis Calvini opera selecta*, ed. Peter Barth, Wilhelm Niesel, and Dora Scheuner, 5 vols. (Munich: Chr. Kaiser, 1926–52), 1:11–280; hereafter cited as OS, with volume and page number. In 1975 Ford Lewis Battles produced a translation of the 1536 *Institutes*, along with annotations and four appendices, which was revised and republished in 1986 to recognize the 450th anniversary of the 1536 *Institutes*. See John Calvin, *Institutes of the Christian Religion, 1536 Edition*, trans. and annot. Ford Lewis Battles, rev. ed. (Grand Rapids: Eerdmans, 1986); hereafter referred to as *1536 Edition*, followed by page number.

7. See William G. Naphy, *Calvin and the Consolidation of the Genevan Reformation* (Louisville, KY: Westminster John Knox Press, 2003).

8. Raymond Abba, "Calvin's Doctrine of the Lord's Supper," *The Reformed Theological Review* 9, no. 2 (Winter 1950): 1–12; Yoshimitsu Akagi, "A Fundamental Problem of Calvin's Doctrine of the Eucharist," *Shingaku* 59 (1997): 11–26; Willem Balke, "Calvijns avondmaalsleer," in *Omgang met de reformatoren* (Kampen: Uitgeverij de Groot Goudriaan, 1992), 145–57; idem, "Calvijns avondmaalspraktijk," in *Omgang met de reformatoren* (Kampen: Uitgeverij de Groot Goudriaan, 1992), 175–81; idem, "Calvijns avondmaalsstrijd," in *Omgang met de reformatoren* (Kampen: Uitgeverij de Groot Goudriaan, 1992), 158–74; Hans-Martin Barth, "'. . . sehen, wie freundlich der Herr ist?' Das Verhältnis von Wort, Bild und Sakrament im Protestantismus," *Kerygma und Dogma* 39 (July 1993): 247–63; Peter Barth, "Calvins Stellung im Abendmahlsstreit," *Die christliche Welt* 43 (1929): 922–29; Ford Lewis Battles, "God Was Accommodating Himself to Human Capacity," *Interpretation* 31 (1977): 19–38; Joachim Beckmann, *Vom Sakrament bei Calvin: Die Sakramentslehre Calvins in ihren Beziehungen zu Augustin* (Tübingen: J. C. B. Mohr, 1926); G. C. Berkouwer, *The Sacraments*, trans. Hugo Bekker (Grand Rapids: Eerdmans, 1969); J. Todd Billings, *Calvin, Participation, and the Gift: the Activity of Believers in Union with Christ* (Oxford, New York: Oxford University Press, 2007); Ernst Bizer, *Studien zur Geschichte des Abendmahlsstreits im 16. Jahrhundert* (Darmstadt: Wissenschaftliche Buchgesellschaft, 1962); Jean Cadier, *La doctrine Calviniste de la Sainte Cène* (Montpellier: Institut protestant de théologie, 1951); Henry Chavannes, "La presence réelle chez saint Thomas et chez Calvin," *Verbum Caro* 13, no. 50 (1959): 151–70; Jaques Courvoisier, "Reflexions à propos de la doctrine eucharistique de

Zwingli et de Calvin," in *Festgabe Leonhard von Muralt*, ed. Martin Haas and Rene Hauswirth (Zurich: Verlag Berichthaus, 1970); William R. Crockett, "Calvin," in *Eucharist: Symbol of Transformation* (New York: Pueblo Publishing Co., 1989), 148–63; Richard Cross, "Catholic, Calvinist, and Lutheran Doctrines of Eucharistic Presence: A Brief Note toward a Rapprochement," *International Journal of Systematic Theology* 4, no. 3 (2002): 301–18; W. F. Dankbaar, *De Sacramentsleer van Calvijn* (Amsterdam: H. I. Paris, 1941); Thomas J. Davis, *The Clearest Promises of God: The Development of Calvin's Eucharistic Teaching* (New York: AMS Press, 1995); idem, *This Is My Body: The Presence of Christ in Reformation Thought* (Grand Rapids: Baker Academic, 2008); August Ebrard, *Das Dogma vom heiligen Abendmahl und seine Geschichte*, 2 vols. (Frankfurt am Main: Heinrich Zimmer, 1845–46), 2:402–33; Mary Potter Engel, *John Calvin's Perspectival Anthropology* (Atlanta: Scholars Press, 1988); Douglas Farrow, "In Support of a Reformed View of Ascension and Eucharist," in *Reformed Theology: Identity and Ecumenicity*, ed. Michael Welker and Wallace M. Alston Jr. (Grand Rapids: Eerdmans, 2003), 351–71; idem, "Between the Rock and a Hard Place: In Support of (something like) a Reformed View of the Eucharist," *International Journal of Systematic Theology* 3, no. 2 (2001): 167–86; Joseph Fitzer, "The Augustinian Roots of Calvin's Eucharistic Teaching," *Augustinian Studies* 7 (1976): 69–98; H. Jackson Forstman, *Word and Spirit: Calvin's Doctrine of Biblical Authority* (Palo Alto, CA: Stanford University Press, 1962); R. William Franklin, "Eucharistic Humanism Lost and Regained," in *The Case for Christian Humanism*, ed. William Franklin and Joseph Shaw (Grand Rapids: Eerdmans, 1991), 116–39; Ulrich Gäbler, "Das Zustandekommen des Consensus Tigurinus im Jahre 1549," *Theologische Literaturzeitung* 104, no. 5 (1979): 321–32; Richard C. Gamble, "Sacramental Continuity among Reformed Refugees: Peter Martyr Vermigli and John Calvin," in *Peter Martyr Vermigli and the European Reformations*, ed. Frank A. James III (Leiden: Brill, 2004), 97–112; idem, "Calvin's Controversies," in *The Cambridge Companion to John Calvin*, ed. Donald K. McKim (Cambridge: Cambridge University Press, 2004), 188–203; Alexandre Ganoczy, "L'action sacramentaire de Dieu par le Christ selon Calvin," in *Sacrements de Jésus-Christ*, ed. Joseph Doré (Paris: Desclée, 1983), 109–29; idem, *Calvin: Theologien de l'Eglise et du Ministère* (Paris: Éditions du Cerf, 1964); idem, "Calvin als paulinischer Theologe," in *Calvinus Theologus: Die Referate des Europäischen Kongresses für Calvinforschung vom 16. bis 19. September 1974 in Amsterdam*, ed. W. H. Neusner (Neukirchen-Vluyn: Neukirchener Verlag, 1976); idem, *The Young Calvin*, trans. David Foxgrover and Wade Provo (Philadelphia: Westminster Press, 1987); Timothy George, "John Calvin and the Agreement of Zurich (1549)," in *John Calvin and the Church: A Prism of Reform*, ed. Timothy George (Louisville, KY: Westminster John Knox Press, 1990), 42–58; Brian A. Gerrish, "Calvin's Eucharistic Piety," *Reformed Liturgy and Music* 31, no. 2 (1997): 93–100; idem, "The Flesh of the Son of Man: John W. Nevin on the Church and the Eucharist," in *Tradition in the Modern World: Reformed Theology in the Nineteenth Century* (Chicago: University of Chicago Press, 1978), 49–70; idem, "Gospel and Eucharist: John Calvin on the Lord's Supper," in *The Old Protestantism and the New: Essays on the Reformation Heritage* (Chicago: University of Chicago Press, 1982), 106–17; idem, "The Pathfinder," in *The Old Protestantism and the New*, 27–48; idem, "Sign and Reality: The Lord's Supper in the Reformed Confessions," in *The Old Protestantism and the New: Essays on the Reformation Heritage* (Chicago: University of Chicago Press, 1982), 118–30; idem, *Grace and Gratitude: The Eucharistic Theology of John Calvin* (Minneapolis: Fortress

Press, 1993); Ronald N. Gleason, "Calvin and Bavinck on the Lord's Supper," *Westminster Theological Journal* 45, no. 2 (Fall 1983): 273–303; Hans Grass, *Die Abendmahlslehre bei Luther und Calvin: Eine kritische Untersuchung* (Gütersloh: C. Bertelsmann, 1954); Eleanor B. Hanna, "Biblical Interpretation and Sacramental Practice: John Calvin's Interpretation of John 6:51–58," *Worship* 73, no. 3 (1999): 211–30; Gerrit Pieter Hartvelt, *Verum Corpus: Een Studie over een Centraal Hoofdstuk uit de Avondmaalsleer van Calvijn* (Delft: W. D. Meinema, 1960); Alasdair I. C. Herron, "'If Luther Will Accept Us with Our Confession . . .': The Eucharistic Controversy in Calvin's Correspondence up to 1546," *Hervormde Teologiese Studies* 62, no. 3 (2006): 867–84; idem, *Table and Tradition: Toward an Ecumenical Understanding of the Eucharist* (Philadelphia: Westminster Press, 1983); I. John Hesselink, "The Role of the Holy Spirit in Calvin's Doctrine of the Sacraments," in *Essentialia et Hodierna: oblate P. C. Potgieter*, ed. D. François Tolmie (Bloemfontein: University of the Free State, 2002), 66–88; Charles Hodge, "The Mystical Presence: A Vindication of the Reformed or Calvinistic Doctrine of the Holy Eucharist, by Rev. John W. Nevin, D.D.," *Princeton Review* 20 (April 1848): 227, 275–77, 278; idem, in *Systematic Theology*, 3 vols. (Grand Rapids: Eerdmans, 1989), 3:626–50; George Hunsinger, "The Bread That We Break: Toward a Chalcedonian Resolution of the Eucharistic Controversies," *The Princeton Seminary Bulletin* 24, no. 2 (2003): 241–58; Wim Janse, "Calvin, a Lasco und Beza: Eine gemeinsame Abendmahlserklärung (May 1556)?" in *Calvinus Praeceptor Ecclesiae*, ed. Herman J. Selderhuis (Geneva: Droz, 2004), 209–32; idem, "Calvin's Eucharistic Theology: Three Dogma-Historical Observations," in *Calvinus sacrarum literarum interpres*, ed. Herman J. Selderhuis (Göttingen: Vandenhoeck & Ruprecht, 2008), 37–69; Heinrich Janssen, "Die Abendmahlslehre Johannes Calvin," *Una Sancta* 15, no. 2 (1960): 125–38; Paul H. Jones, "Reformation Concepts: John Calvin," in *Christ's Eucharistic Presence: A History of the Doctrine*, ed. Paul H. Jones (New York: Peter Lang, 1994), 134–67; Christopher B. Kaiser, "Climbing Jacob's Ladder: John Calvin and the Early Church on Our Eucharistic Ascent to Heaven," *Scottish Journal of Theology* 56, no. 3 (2003): 247–67; idem, "John Calvin Climbing Jacob's Ladder" *Perspectives* 13, no. 4 (1998): 10–12; Nathan R. Kerr, "Corpus Verum: On the Ecclesial Recovery of Real Presence in John Calvin's Doctrine of the Eucharist," in *Radical Orthodoxy and the Reformed Tradition*, ed. James K. A. Smith and James H. Olthuis (Grand Rapids: Baker Academic, 2005), 229–42; Bertold Klappert, "Das Abendmahl als Verheißungs-und Bekenntniszeichen: Calvins Abendmahlslehre und die Interpretation Wilhelm Niesels," in *Wilhelm Niesel—Theologe und Kirchen-politiker*, ed. Martin Breidert and Hans-Georg Ulrichs (Wuppertal: Foedus, 2003), 111–52; Charles P. Krauth, "Calvin on the Lord's Supper," in *The Conservative Reformation and Its Theology* (Philadelphia: Lippincott, 1871), 493–502; Bernhard Lang, "The West-Side Story (2) Calvin's Theory of Christ's Spiritual Presence," in *Sacred Games: A History of Christian Worship* (New Haven, CT: Yale University Press, 1997), 322–27 (472, notes); Mark J. Larson, "Moving beyond Zwingli: The Calvinist Doctrine of the Lord's Supper," *The Outlook* 54, no. 4 (2004): 11–13; Auguste Lecerf, "The Liturgy of the Holy Supper at Geneva in 1542," *Reformed Liturgy* 3, no. 2 (1966–67): 17–24; Cees Leijenhorst, "Place, Space and Matter in Calvinist Physics," *The Monist* 84, no. 4 (2001): 520–41; Immanuel Leuschner, "Bullinger und Calvin einigen sich in der Abendmahlsfrage," in *Heinrich Bullinger, Vater der reformierten Kirche*, ed. Fritz Blanke and Immanuel Leuschner (Zurich: Theologischer Verlag, 1990), 216–24; Donald MacLeod, "Calvin into Hyppolytus?" in *To Glorify God: Essays on*

Modern Reformed Liturgy, ed. Bryan Spinks and Iain Torrance (Grand Rapids: Eerdmans, 1999), 255–67; Pierre Marcel, "La communication du Christ avec les siens: a parole et la cène," *La Revue Réformée* 37 (1986): 1–64; Matthew W. Mason, "A Spiritual Banquet: John Calvin on the Lord's Supper," *Churchman* 117, no. 4 (2003): 329–46; Keith A. Mathison, *Given for You: Reclaiming Calvin's Doctrine of the Lord's Supper* (Phillipsburg: Presbyterian and Reformed, 2002); Kilian McDonnell, "Calvin's Eucharistic Doctrine," *Reformed Liturgics* 5, no. 2 (Fall 1968): 13–21; idem, *John Calvin, the Church, and the Eucharist* (Princeton, NJ: Princeton University Press, 1967); Donald K. McKim, "Sacramental Controversy: What Is the Lord's Supper?" in *Theological Turning Points: Major Issues in Christian Thought* (Atlanta: John Knox Press, 1988), 134–50, 197–99; Joseph C. McLelland, "Lutheran-Reformed Debate on the Eucharist and Christology," in Paul C. Empie and James I. McCord, eds., *Marburg Revisited* (Minneapolis: Augsburg, 1966), 39–54; Boniface Meyer, "Calvin's Eucharistic Doctrine: 1536–39," *Journal of Ecumenical Studies* 4, no. 1 (1967): 47–65; idem, "Sacramental Theology in the Institutes of John Calvin," *American Benedictine Review* 15 (1964): 360–80; Martha L. Moore-Keish, "Calvin, Sacraments, and Ecclesiology," in *Call to Worship: Liturgy, Music, Preaching and the Arts*, ed. Theodore A. Gill Jr. (Louisville, KY: Geneva Press, 2002), 25–41; Henry Mottu, "Nos convictions réformées au sujet de la saints cène," *Les Cahiers Protestants* (October 1987): 5–11; Brian Nicholson, "Calvin's Doctrine of the Spiritual Presence of Christ in the Lord's Supper," *Antithesis* 2, no. 2 (1991): 35–38; Wilhelm Niesel, *Calvins Lehre vom Abendmahl im Lichte seiner letzen Antwort an Westphal*, 2nd ed. (Munich: Chr. Kaiser Verlag, 1935); idem, *The Theology of Calvin*, trans. Harold Knight (Philadelphia: Westminster Press, 1956); Hughes Oliphant Old, "Biblical Wisdom Theology and Calvin's Understanding of the Lord's Supper," in *Calvin Studies VI*, ed. John H. Leith (Davidson, NC, 1992), 77–86; Maurice Eugene Osterhaven, "Eating and Drinking Christ: The Lord's Supper as an Act of Worship in the Theology and Practice of John Calvin," *Reformed Review* 37 (1983–84): 83–93; idem, "The Sacraments," in *The Faith of the Church: A Reformed Perspective on Its Historical Development* (Grand Rapids: Eerdmans, 1982), 125–54; Charles Partee, "Calvin's Central Dogma Again," *The Sixteenth Century Journal* 18 (1987): 191–99; Gordon E. Pruett, "A Protestant Doctrine of the Eucharistic Presence," *Calvin Theological Journal* 10, no. 2 (November 1975): 142–74; Jill Raitt, *The Eucharistic Theology of Theodore Beza. Development of the Reformed Doctrine* (Chambersburg, PA: American Academy of Religion, 1972); W. Stanford Reid, "The Lord's Supper and Church Unity in the Thought of John Calvin," *Theological Forum* 12 (July 1985): 2–6; Joachim Rogge, *Virtus und Res: Um die Abendmahlswirklichkeit bei Calvin* (Stuttgart: Calwer Verlag, 1965); Paul Rorem, "Calvin and Bullinger on the Lord's Supper, part 1, The Impasse," *Lutheran Quarterly* 2, no. 2 (1988): 155–84; idem, "Calvin and Bullinger on the Lord's Supper, part 2, The Agreement," *Lutheran Quarterly* 2, no. 3 (1988): 357–89; idem, *Calvin and Bullinger on the Lord's Supper* (Nottingham: Grove Books Ltd., 1989); idem, "The Consensus Tigurinus (1549): Did Calvin Compromise?" in *Calvinus sacrae scripturae professor: Calvin as Confessor of Holy Scripture*, ed. Wilhelm H. Neuser (Grand Rapids: Eerdmans, 1994), 72–90; Peter Rodolphe, "Calvin et le liturgie d'après l'Institution," *Ètudes théologiques et religieuses* 60, no. 3 (1985): 385–401; Herman Sasse, "Calvin's Attempt to Solve the Problem of the Sacrament," in *This Is My Body*, 320–30; Laurence C. Sibley Jr., "The Church as Eucharistic Community: Observations on John Calvin's Early Eucharistic Theology (1536–1545)," *Worship* 81, no. 3 (2007): 249–67; Luchesius Smits, *Saint*

Augustin dans l'oeuvre de Jean Calvin (Assen: Van Gorcum, 1956); Willem van't Spijker, "Bucer's Influence on Calvin: Church and Community," in *Martin Bucer: Reforming Church and Community*, ed. David Frederick Wright (New York: Cambridge University Press, 1994), 32–44; David C. Steinmetz, "The Theology of Calvin and Calvinism," in *Reformation Europe*, 211–32; Laurence Hull Stookey, "Calvin: Virtualism," in *Eucharist: Christ's Feast with the Church* (Nashville: Abingdon Press, 1993), 55–62; Henri Strohl, "Bucer et Calvin," *Bulletin de Histoire du Protestantisme francaise* 87 (1938): 354–56; Jane E. Strohl, "God's Self-Revelation in the Sacrament of the Altar," in *By Faith Alone*, ed. Joseph A. Burgess and Marc Kolden (Grand Rapids: Eerdmans, 2004), 97–109; Dennis Tamburello, *Union with Christ: John Calvin and the Mysticism of St. Bernard* (Louisville, KY: Westminster John Knox Press, 1994); Michael J. Taylor, "Calvin," in *The Protestant Liturgical Renewal: A Catholic Viewpoint* (Westminster, MD: Newman Press, 1963), 82–92; Max Thurian, "The Real Presence," in *The Eucharistic Memorial*, trans. J. G. Davies (Richmond: John Knox Press, 1961), 108–24; Melvin Tinker, "Language, Symbols, and Sacraments: Was Calvin's View of the Lord's Supper Right?" *Churchman* 112, no. 2 (1998): 131–49; Joseph N. Tylenda, "The Calvin-Westphal Exchange: The Genesis of Calvin's Treatises against Westphal," *Calvin Theological Journal* 9, no. 2 (November 1974): 182–209; idem, "Calvin and Westphal: Two Eucharistic Theologies in Conflict," in *Calvin's Books: Festschrift Dedicated to Peter De Klerk on the Occasion of His Seventieth Birthday*, ed. Wilhelm H. Neuser, Herman J. Selderhuis, and Wilhem van't Spijker (Heerenveen: J. J. Groen, 1997), 99–122; idem, "Calvin and Christ's Presence in the Supper—True or Real," *Scottish Journal of Theology* 27 (1974): 65–75; idem, "Calvin on Christ's True Presence in the Lord's Supper," *The American Ecclesiastical Review* 155 (November 1966): 321–33; idem, "The Ecumenical Intentions of Calvin's Early Eucharistic Teaching," in *Reformatio Perennis*, ed. Brian A. Gerrish (Pittsburgh: Pickwick Press, 1981), 27–47; idem, "A Eucharistic Sacrifice in Calvin's Theology?" *Theological Studies* 37 (1976): 456–66; G. S. M. Walker, "The Lord's Supper in the Theology and Practice of Calvin," in *Calvin: A Collection of Essays*, ed. G. E. Duffield (Grand Rapids: Eerdmans, 1966), 131–48; Ronald S. Wallace, *Calvin's Doctrine of the Word and Sacrament* (Edinburgh: Oliver & Boyd, 1953); François Wendel, *Calvin: The Origins and Development of His Religious Thought*, trans. Philip Mairet (London: William Collins & Sons Co., 1963); Timothy Wengert, "'We Will Feast Together in Heaven Forever': The Epistolary Friendship of John Calvin and Philip Melanchthon," in *Melanchthon in Europe: His Work and Influence beyond Wittenberg*, ed. Karin Maag (Grand Rapids: Baker, 1999), 19–44; E. David Willis, "Calvin's Use of Substantia," in *Calvinus Ecclesiae Genevensis Custos*, ed. Wilhelm H. Neuser (Frankfurt: Peter Lang, 1984), 289–301; idem, "A Reformed Doctrine of the Eucharist and Ministry and Its Implications for Roman Catholic Dialogues," *Journal of Ecumenical Studies* 21, no. 2 (Spring 1984): 295–309; Jennifer Lynn Woodruff, "John Calvin, the Wesleys, and John Williamson Nevin on the Lord's Supper," *Methodist History* 41, no. 4 (2003): 159–78.

9. Ebrard, *Das Dogma*, 411–18.

10. *Confessio Fidei de Eucharistia*; OS 1:435–36 [Eng. trans. in *Calvin: Theological Treatises*, The Library of Christian Classics XXII, ed. J. K. S. Reid (Philadelphia: The Westminster Press, 1954), 168–69].

11. *eine reale Erneuerung und Föderung jener continuirlichen Lebenseinheit*; Ebrard, *Das Dogma*, 429–31.

12. Ebrard, *Das Dogma*, 433.

13. John Williamson Nevin, *The Mystical Presence: A Vindication of the Reformed or Calvinistic Doctrine of the Holy Eucharist* (Philadelphia: J. B. Lippincott, 1846). For more on Nevin and his debate with Charles Hodge, see the next chapter. For entrance to the ecclesial feature of Nevin's essay, within nineteenth-century context and an eye to its enduring qualities, see B. A. Gerrish, "John W. Nevin on the Church and the Eucharist," in *Tradition and the Modern World: Reformed Theology in the Nineteenth Century* (Chicago: University of Chicago Press, 1978), 49–70.

14. This essay originally appeared in the *Mercersburg Review* and, along with *The Mystical Presence*, can be found in John W. Nevin, *The Mystical Presence and Other Writings on the Eucharist*, ed. Bard Thompson and George H. Bricker (Philadelphia, Boston: United Church Press, 1966).

15. Commenting on Nichols's remark that "[a]s an historical monograph, it [*Mystical Presence*] remained without a rival in English until the twentieth century" (James Hastings Nichols, ed., *The Mercersburg Theology* [New York: Oxford University Press, 1966], 246), Gerrish says, "One wonders, indeed, what there is to rival it in English even today" (Gerrish, "John W. Nevin on the Church and the Eucharist," 66).

16. Davis, *The Clearest Promises*; Wim Janse, "Calvin's Eucharistic Theology: Three Dogma-Historical Observations," in *Calvinus sacrarum literarum interpres*, ed. Herman J. Selderhuis (Göttingen: Vandenhoeck & Ruprecht, 2008).

17. See chap. 1, n. 72.

18. Beckmann, *Vom Sakrament*, 161: "In den beiden für das Wesen des Abendmahls konstitutiven Grundgedanken fanden wir völlige Identität."

19. In his study "The Augustinian Roots," Fitzer takes up and develops the work of Luchesius Smits (*Saint Augustin dans l'oeuvre de Jean Calvin, I: Etude de Critique Litteraire* [Assen: Van Gorcum, 1956]) and concludes that "the eucharistic teaching of Calvin's 1559 *Institutes* does seem to be a faithful mirror of Augustine's eucharistic teaching" (96).

20. Note, for example, the summary comment, "The nature of the Supper *communio cum Christo* is for Calvin like Augustine community with Christ in the Spirit; and it is the community as the body of Christ, which celebrates its membership community as the body of Christ, and therein allows itself to be fed from the head, through the Holy Spirit, with the power of eternal life. The body of Christ, we can also say, can be filled through the reception of the Supper with a new spiritual life from the personality of Christ, in order to be the true body of Christ, the spirit-filled community, which is one with Christ and therefore truly with one another and wants to become so more and more" (Beckmann, *Vom Sakrament bei Calvin*, 161).

21. See the comments by Wilhelm Niesel in *Calvins Lehre vom Abendmahl*, 2nd ed. (Munich: Chr. Kaiser Verlag, 1935), 2–3.

22. Niesel, *Calvins Lehre*, 2–3 (comments on Rome), 33–53 (communication of Christ's body and blood and the blessings therein), 56–90 (the limitations of the Lutheran position), and 90–98 (the work of the Spirit and the salvific, real presence of Christ in the community). On Niesel's view, Calvin had found himself in a controversy with fellow Protestants that he found distasteful (*zuwider*) and, in developing his teaching on the Supper, had made rapprochement as far as possible with the Lutherans by subscribing to the Augustana (according to the intent of its author, Melanchthon) and as far as possible with the Swiss by subscribing to the Consensus Tigurinus, insofar as they had moved from an early Zwinglian position (5;54–55n1).

23. *Calvins Lehre vom Abendmahl im Lichte seiner letzen Antwort an Westphal*; Niesel, *Calvins Lehre*, 11.

24. Alexander Barclay, *The Protestant Doctrine of the Lord's Supper* (Glasgow: Jackson, Wylie, 1927).

25. E.g., cf. Barclay, *The Protestant Doctrine*, 121, 130, 132, with Ebrard, *Das Dogma*, 417–18, 427, 430.

26. Barclay, *The Protestant Doctrine*, 165–79; also see 115 and cf. Ebrard, *Das Dogma*, 141. On Calvin and the Consensus Tigurinus, see the careful comments by Davis (*The Clearest Promises*, 29–68), and his comments on Barclay (34).

27. For the development of the modern liturgical renewal movement, see John W. Riggs, *Baptism in the Reformed Tradition* (Louisville, KY: Westminster John Knox Press, 2002), 2–8.

28. G. P. Hartvelt, *Verum Corpus: Een Studie over een Centraal Hoofdstuk uit de Avondmaalsleer van Calvijn* (Delft: W. D. Meinema, 1960), 113–14; see section 3 ("Communio cum corpore et sanguine Christi"), 85–113.

29. Hartvelt, *Verum Corpus*, 96–97.

30. Hartvelt, *Verum Corpus*, 78. Hartvelt cites Calvin's 1536 discussion on baptism and the following example of Cornelius (cited by Hartvelt from the *Corpus Reformatorum* [1:115]; see OS 1.133; Battles, *1536 Edition*, 99). Hartvelt's interpretation of this passage, as well as that of Davis, who follows Hartvelt, will be taken up later.

31. Kilian McDonnell, *John Calvin, the Church and the Eucharist* (Princeton, NJ: Princeton University Press, 1967). Among numerous notable scholars whom McDonnell thanks, he gives special thanks to Hans Küng (vii).

32. Despite the "role his polemic writings played," writes McDonnell, "Calvin is more concerned to build a biblical theology and a eucharistic doctrine in which mystical union with Christ through faith, and fellowship with Christ through faith, is normative" (108).

33. "With the fact of real presence, Calvin had no difficulty. . . . Rather than denying the real presence, as he has been accused of doing, he presupposes it. None of the Reformers defended it more forcibly than Calvin" (McDonnell, *John Calvin*, 223–24).

34. McDonnell, *John Calvin*, 179–80. For several years now, it has been my privilege to serve on a bilateral ecumenical discussion group of Reformed and Roman Catholic theologians from across the United States. The question of what distinctive gift is offered in the Supper, according to Calvin, has arisen frequently. To be fair, the same question has arisen from notable Protestant Calvin scholars as well; e.g., see Wendel, *Calvin*, 352–54; and Werner Krusche, *Das Wirken des Heiligen Geistes nach Calvin* (Göttingen: Vandenhoeck & Ruprecht, 1957), 272.

35. Thomas Davis (*The Clearest Promises*, 214) has put this precisely when he says, "It is at this point that Nevin was right in his instincts: there is a eucharistic gift in Calvin. It is *Christ* and the *knowledge* of his presence. The gift, in a sense, cannot be a special presence, for Calvin has set up this theology so that the definition of being a Christian is to be in union with Jesus Christ. In that sense, McDonnell and others have asked Calvin a question foreign to his outlook."

36. See chap. 1, pp. 13–16, nn. 101–16.

37. E.g., McDonnell, *John Calvin*, 40–43.

38. McDonnell, *John Calvin*, 3.

39. Jean Calvin, *Institution de la religion Chrestienne*, édition critique avec introduction, notes et variantes, ed. Jean-Daniel Benoit, 5 vols. (Paris: J. Vrin, 1957–63);
hereafter referred to as Benoit, *Institution*, followed by volume and page number.
As one of several examples, in the 1560 French *Institutes* (*Inst.* 4.14.9) Calvin says,
concerning the gift that opens the eyes and ears of our faith, that "the Holy Spirit
has that very office, in our hearts, of a special grace outside the course of nature"
(*mais le sainct Esprit a ce mesme office en nos âmes d'une grâce speciale outre le course de
nature* [Benoit, *Institution* 4.298]). The 1559 Latin *Institutio* had had a christological
reference there: "Christ by a special grace outside the measure of nature does the
same thing in our hearts" (*Christus autem praeter naturae modum speciali gratia idem
in animis nostris agit* [OS 5.267.4–5]).

40. Davis, *Clearest Promises*.

41. Davis, *Clearest Promises*, 15–68.

42. For Davis's own summary, see *Clearest Promises*, 7–8.

43. See Riggs, *Baptism*, 39–70; idem, "Emerging Ecclesiology in Calvin's Baptismal Thought," *Church History* 64, no. 1 (1995): 29–43.

44. So Wim Janse, "Calvin's Eucharistic Theology," 38n7.

45. Janse, "Calvin's Eucharistic Theology," 37, 39.

46. Hartvelt, *Verum Corpus*, 78; Davis, *Clearest Promises*, 86, 94nn58–59; Janse,
"Calvin's Eucharistic Theology," 38–39.

47. *Non quia sacramento tales gratiae illigatae inclusaeque sit, quo nobis conferantur,
sed duntaxat, qui hac tessera voluntatem suam nobis Dominus testificatur, nempe: se haec
omnia nobis velle largiri* (OS 1.133; *1536 Edition*, 99).

48. "De Baptismo," OS 1.127–36; *1536 Edition*, 94–102.

49. "Baptism has been given to us by God, *first* to serve our faith toward him,
and *then* to serve our confession toward others" (*Baptismus nobis a Deo datus est,
primum ut fidei nostrae apud se, deinde ut confessioni apud homines serviret*; OS 1.127;
1536 Edition, 94). For the fullest treatment of Calvin's teaching on baptism, see
Riggs, *Baptism*, 39–70.

50. OS 1.122; *1536 Edition*, 90–91.

51. *Summa theologiae*; trans. from Thomas Aquinas, *Summa Theologiae*, trans.
Blackfriars (New York: McGraw Hill, 1964), I.ii.q. 82, a.3.

52. The Decree on Original Sin given at the Council of Trent asserts that infants
are born with original sin that deprives them of eternal life and that such original
sin is actually taken away so that they are "born again" and made new (Decree
on Original Sin, 4–5). The Decree on Justification makes clear what being "born
again" means by way of justification. God intervenes with the graces necessary
for coming to faith, as well as possessing the other theological virtues of hope and
charity, so that one "unites perfectly with Christ" and "faith is the beginning of
salvation" (Decree on Justification, chaps. 5–8). In Protestant terms, the baptized
child is actually made just and the condition of sanctification has begun. See Heinrich Denzinger, *The Sources of Catholic Dogma*, trans. Roy J. Deferrari (St. Louis:
Herder, 1957), 247–48, 250–52.

Euchologically the earlier Gelasian Sacramentary put this well in its famous
prayer consecrating the baptismal font for the Easter Vigil, which reads in part:
*open the font of baptism to renew the nations of the world over, that by the command of
your majesty it may acquire the grace of your Only-Begotten by the Holy Spirit; who,
by the secret mingling of his light, might make fertile the water prepared for human*

regeneration, that there may come forth from the immaculate womb of the divine font, in which sanctification was conceived, a divine offspring, reborn into a new creature; and that grace, the mother, may bring forth in one childhood all whom either age or sex distinguishes. L. C. Mohlberg, ed., *Liber Sacramentorum Romanae Aeclesiae Ordinis Anni Circuli*, Rerum Ecclesiasticarum Documenta, Series Major, vol. IV (Rome, 1960).

53. *Iam perspicuum est, quam falsum sit quod docuerunt nonnulli, nos per baptismum solvi et eximi ab originali peccato et ea corruptione quae ab Adam in universam posteritatem propagata est, atque in eandem iustitiam naturaeque puritatem restitui, quam obtinuisset Adam, si in ea, qua primum creatus fuerat, integritate stetisset* (OS 1.130).

54. *Caeterum, ex hoc sacramento nihil assequimur, nisi quantum fide accipimus; si fides desit, erit in testimonium accusationis nostrae coram Deo, quod promissioni monium accusationini nostrae coram Deo, quod promissioni illic datae incredulit fuerimus* (OS 1.133; emphasis in English is mine).

55. Riggs, *Baptism in the Reformed Tradition*, 41–52.

56. *offere nobis ac proponere Christum*; OS 1.123–4; *1536 Edition*, 91. Calvin's later, more typical verb, *exhibere*, speaks for a refinement of this early position, not a change from this position, in which Calvin maintains that God's instrumentally does what God says God will do, be present with the offer of grace in the sacrament. Note also that the reference to the Word does not indicate that the sacraments are merely moments of symbolic witness, but rather that the Word itself functions like a sacrament and actually presents Christ.

57. Riggs, *Baptism in the Reformed Tradition*, 53–60.

58. Riggs, *Baptism in the Reformed Tradition*, 66–69.

59. OS 1.137; *1536 Edition*, 102.

60. *quod sic Christum nobis, sic nos illi vicissim insertos esse agnoscimus, ut quidquid ipsius est, nostrum vocare, quidquid nostrum est, ipsius censere liceat* (OS 1.137; *1536 Edition*, 102).

61. OS 1.137–38; *1536 Edition*, 103.

62. OS 1.138; *1536 Edition*, 103–4 (*Sacramentum ergo non panem vitae Christum esse facit, sed quatenus in memoriam nobis revocat panem esse factum, quo assidue vescamur*).

63. Tylenda, "Ecumenical Intentions," 29.

64. Davis, *Clearest Promises*, 80.

65. For the following I am indebted to Tylenda, "Ecumenical Intentions," 28–32.

66. OS 1.139; *1536 Edition*, 104 (emphasis mine).

67. OS 1.139; *1536 Edition*, 104.

68. OS 1.140; *1536 Edition*, 104.

69. Following Ganoczy, *The Young Calvin* (153), Davis calls Calvin's position "ambiguous" (79). Ganoczy's discussion, however, hardly deals with precisely this issue, and citing him for support seems a bit tenuous.

70. Also see Davis, *Clearest Promises*, 82–83.

71. Davis, *Clearest Promises*, 83–84.

72. See, e.g., Ganoczy, *The Young Calvin*, 109–10.

73. *Theological Treatises*, 44. See Calvin's numerous citations to Augustine (40–42), including passages that were taken up in chap. 1 of this study.

74. *Theological Treatises*: working from Augustine's homily on John (41), and developing a more sustained biblical theology on this point (42–44).

75. *Theological Treatises*, 44.

76. OS 1.435; *Theological Treatises*, 168. On Calvin's eucharistic theology and this confession, see Heinrich Janssen, "Die Abendmahlslehre Johannes Calvin," *Una Sancta* 15, no. 2 (1960): 125–38.

77. OS 1.435; *Theological Treatises*, 168.

78. OS 1.435; *Theological Treatises*, 168.

79. OS 1.435; *Theological Treatises*, 168.

80. Davis, *Clearest Promises*, 101–5.

81. Concerning the Supper, the catechism says that the body of Christ once was given for us and still is ours and always will be ours (*le corps du Seigneur a une fois tellement este donne pour nous, quil est maintenant nostre et le sera aussy perpetuellement*; OS 1.412). Christ's immortal flesh (*sa chair immortelle*) thus vivifies our flesh (OS 1.413), and such communication happens "spiritually" (*spirituellement*), by which Calvin means through the work of the Spirit (OS 1.413).

82. See my extended references in *Baptism in the Reformed Tradition*, 42n29. Also see Willem van 't Spiker, *Calvin: A Brief Guide to His Life and Thought*, trans. Lyle D. Bierma (Louisville, KY: Westminster John Knox Press, 2009), 28–30; and Wulfert de Greef, *The Writings of Calvin: An Introductory Guide*, expanded ed., trans. Lyle D. Bierma (Louisville, KY, London: Westminster John Knox Press, 2009), 182–85. Ironically, we know of no French translation of this edition of the *Institutes*, even though it aimed to be a pedagogical and confessional work for French evangelicals.

83. For the 1539 *Institutes* Calvin wrote in his remarks to the reader that it was his "purpose in this labor to prepare and instruct candidates in sacred theology for the reading of the divine Word" (OS 3.6.18–20; *Inst.* "John Calvin to the Reader"). This change in the *Institutes* also allowed Calvin to move the long theological discussions that often had been part of Scripture commentaries out of the commentaries themselves. For summary comments, see de Greef, *The Writings of John Calvin*, 76, 186–87.

84. Davis, *Clearest Promises*, 107.

85. Doumergue, *Jean Calvin*, 2:434; Aimé Louis Herminjard, *Correspondance des Réformateurs dans les pays de langue française*, 9 vols. (Geneva: H. Georg, 1866–97), 5:231; Walker, *John Calvin*, 228.

86. As a whole Latin text, the 1539 *Institutes* can be found in John Calvin, *Institutes of the Christian Religion of John Calvin 1539: Text and Concordance*, 4 vols., ed. Richard F. Wevers (Grand Rapids: The H. Henry Meeter Center for Calvin Studies, 1988). Wevers worked from the first edition of the 1539 *Institutes*, as printed in Strasbourg by Wendelin Rihel, and he has given internal paragraph and line numbers to the chapters of the 1539 *Institutes*. I will cite the 1539 edition according to chapter, paragraph, and line, then followed by the actual page number in the Wevers edition. While all of the 1539 text can be found in the 1559 *Institutes* given in volume 5 of the *Opera Selecta*, the 1539 text itself has become rearranged in the later edition. The great virtue of Wevers's great labor is to provide Calvin's coherent, sequential 1539 argument.

87. *nos spiritus modo participes faciunt, praeteria carnis et sanguinis mentione. Quasi vero illa omnia de nihilo dicta forent: carnem eius vere esse cibum, sanguinem eius vere esse potum. Non habere vitam, nisi qui carnem illam manducaverit, et sanguinem biberit* (*1539 Institutes*, 12.10.2–6; p. 293).

88. Wevers, *1539 Institutes*, 12.10.17; p. 293.

89. Wevers, *1539 Institutes*, 12.11.1–3; p. 293 (*Christum ab initio, vivificum illud patris verbum fuisse, vitae fontem et originem, unde omnia, ut viverent, semper acceperunt*).

90. *ubi fons ille vitae habitare in carne nostra coepit, iam non procul nobis absconditus latet, sed coram se participandum **exhibit*** (Wevers, *1539 Institutes*, 12.11.14–16; p. 294; emphasis added to note use of *exhibere*.)

91. Wevers, *1539 Institutes*, 12.11.17–19; p. 294.

92. Wevers, *1539 Institutes*, 12.12.15–18; p. 294 (*Ita Christi caro instar fontis est divitis et inexhausti, quae vitam a divinitate in seipsam scaturientem ad nos transfundit. Iam quis non videt communionem carnis et sanguinis Christi, necessariam esse omnibus, qui ad coelestem vitam adspirant?*). For the liberty of translating *instar* with the word "icon," see the magisterial study by Randall C. Zachman, *Image and Word in the Theology of John Calvin* (Notre Dame, IN: University of Notre Dame Press, 2007).

93. Wevers, *1539 Institutes*, 12.12.22–23; p. 294.

94. Wevers, *1539 Institutes*, 12.13–18; pp. 294–98.

95. Wevers, *1539 Institutes*, 12.19–20; pp. 298–99.

96. Davis, *Clearest Promises*, 114.

97. See the opening description in chap. 2 about "mystical true presence" and the choice to take "mystical" to mean "experiential knowledge of God through the embrace of unitive love."

98. See the discussion above about Tylenda's analysis of the 1536 *Institutes* in "Ecumenical Intentions," 28–32.

99. Also see the discussion by Davis of Calvin's description of Christ's flesh as Calvin develops that in his Romans commentary; *Clearest Promises*, 113.

100. Davis, *Clearest Promises*, 117–20.

101. *Petit Traicté de la Saincte Cene de Nostre Seigneur Jesus Christ*, OS 1.503–30 [Eng. trans. in *Theological Treatises*, 142–66]. Also see the translation in *Selected Works of John Calvin: Tracts and Letters*, 6 vols., ed. Henry Beveridge and Jules Bonnet (Grand Rapids: Baker Book House, 1983), 2:163–98.

102. OS 1.504–5; *Theological Treatises*, 143.

103. OS 1.505; *Theological Treatises*, 144.

104. OS 1.506–7; *Theological Treatises*, 145.

105. For the following, see Zachman, *Image and Word*, 11–17, 436–37, passim.

106. "to have our life in Christ our souls should be fed on his body and blood" (*pour avoir nostre vie en Christ, noz ames soient repeues de son corps et son sang*) (OS 1.508; *Theological Treatises*, 147).

107. OS 1.507; *Theological Treatises*, 146; cf, *Calvin's Selected Works*, 2:169 (*que la matiere et substance des Sacramens c'est le Seigneur Iesus*).

108. OS 1.508; *Theological Treatises*, 147.

109. OS 1.508; *Theological Treatises*, 147.

110. OS 1.509; *Theological Treatises*, 147–48.

111. Calvin gives a wonderfully concise explanation of the historical issues between the Lutheran and Reformed theologians of the first generation in his final section of this treatise; OS 1.526–30; *Theological Treatises*, 163–66.

112. *C'est un mystere spirituel, lequel ne se peut voir à l'oeil, ne comprendre en l'entendement humain* (OS 1.509; *Theological Treatises*, 147).

113. OS 1.529–30; *Theological Treatises*, 166.

114. van 't Spijker, *Calvin*, 59–60; Tylenda, "Ecumenical Intention," 45–46n46. Calvin himself says, in a letter dated March 17, 1546, that the piece was written "ten years earlier," which would place its composition in Geneva, and one must take the dating to be a general comment that indicates his Strasbourg period (C.O. 12.316; *Calvin's Selected Works* 5.39–40).

115. Tylenda, "Ecumenical Intention," 37–41.

116. A reference in Herminjard, and repeated by Parker with a note to Herminjard, indicates that Luther is said to have praised Calvin's *Short Treatise* to a friend, at least for its learned and ecumenical tone. See Herminjard, *Correspondance* 9.374n8; Parker, *John Calvin*, 136–37.

117. Tylenda, "Ecumenical Intention," 36–37.

118. B. A. Gerrish, *The Old Protestàntism and the New* (Chicago: The University of Chicago Press, 1982), 39–45.

119. Davis, *Clearest Promises*, 145. For a full treatment of this material, see 145–200.

120. *Iohannis Calvini Commentarii in priorem Epistolam Pauli ad Corinthios*; C.O. 49:293–574 [Eng. trans. by John W. Fraser in Calvin's New Testament Commentaries, ed. David W. Torrance and Thomas F. Torrance (Edinburgh: Oliver & Boyd, 1960; repr. ed., Grand Rapids: Eerdmans, 1980)]; hereafter cited as *1 Corinthians*. For the following I am indebted to Davis, *Clearest Promises*, 155–63.

121. C.O. 49:489. See also Calvin's comments at 11:26 (C.O. 49:491; *1 Corinthians*, 250).

122. See, e.g., Calvin's comments on 2:12 (C.O. 49: 342; *1 Corinthians*, 59).

123. Davis, *Clearest Promises*, 162.

124. McDonnell, *John Calvin*, 179–80.

125. It does not seem out of place to recall here Bultmann's answer to the question of what distinctive new content is given in the divine revelation through Jesus. Bultmann says by analogy, "What 'more,' then, do I know when I am in an actual relationship of friendship? Nothing! at any rate, nothing more *about* friendship. What 'more' I do know is that I now know my friend and also know myself anew, in the sense that, in understanding my friend, my concrete life in its work and its joy, its struggle and its pain, is qualified in a new way" ("The Historicity of Man and Faith," in *Existence and Faith: Shorter Writings of Rudolf Bultmann*, trans. Schubert M. Ogden [New York: Meridian Books, 1960], 100).

126. See, e.g., Calvin's letter to John Marbach (August, 24, 1554), in which he says, "If Luther were alive—that illustrious servant of God, and faithful teacher of the church—he would not be so bitter nor implacable as not willingly to admit of this confession; that those things are really imparted to us in the sacraments, which are there symbolically represented; and that it is for that reason that in the holy Supper we are made partakers of the body and blood of Jesus Christ. For how often did he profess that he had no other motive for his contestation, unless that it should be clearly recognized, that the Lord does not mock us with empty signs, but that he fill us inwardly with what he represents to our eyes, and that so the effect is connected with the visible sign!" (C.O. 15:212–13; *Calvin's Selected Works*, 6:56).

127. The published title in 1551 was *Consensio Mutua in Re Sacramentaria Ministrorum Tigurinae Ecclesia et D. Ioannis Calvini Ministri Genevensis Ecclesiae*; OS 2:247–53; *Calvin's Selected Works*, 2:212–19. For article 24, see OS 2:252.25–253.4; *Calvin's Selected Works*, 2:219. For a helpful introduction to the Consensus, including secondary scholarship, see Davis, *Clearest Promises*, 29–68, who also has his own particular point of few: the document represents a pastoral and political compromise by Calvin, and "the Consensus Tigurinus is not Calvin's victory, not Calvin's document, not even a fairly balanced juxtaposition of theologies. The Consensus did, as Beza claimed, knit Geneva and Zurich in the closest of ties. Yet, these ties

were by and large political ties, not theological ones, at least where the Eucharist was concerned. Calvin's Defence makes clear that the Consensus, in order to be claimed as representative of his views, had to be radically interpreted" (Davis, *Clearest Promises*, 56).

128. *Defense of the Sane and Orthodox Doctrine of the Sacraments and of their Nature, Power, End, Use and Fruit (Defensio sanae et orthodoxae doctrinae de sacramentis eorumqum natura, vi, fine, usu et fructu)*, OS 2:246–87 (2:259–87 for the *Defense* as such). *Calvin's Selected Works*, 2:199–244, contains the original order of the material, where the *Opera Selecta* has the three parts place in relative chronological order (Consensus, letter, and exposition).

129. Davis, *Clearest Promises*, 29–68.

130. OS 2:248; *Calvin's Selected Works*, 2:213–14.

131. Davis, *Clearest Promises*, 41.

132. This chapter, pp. 92–93 and nn. 77–79.

133. See also article 9.

134. OS 2:272.12–16; here quoting Calvin, *Selected Works*, 2:226.

135. OS 2:283.19–24; here quoting Calvin, *Selected Works*, 2:239.

136. OS 272.29–280.34.

137. OS 2:252; *Calvin's Selected Works*, 2:219.

138. Above, p. 81.

139. Calvin's second and third responses were *Second Defense of the Pious and Orthodox Faith concerning the Sacraments, in Answer to the Calumnies of Joachim Westphal (Secunda defensio piae et orthodoxae de sacramentis fidei contra Ioachimi Westphali Calumnias)*, C.O. 9:41–120; *Selected Works* 2:252–345; and *Last Admonition of John Calvin to Joachim Westphal (Ultima Admonitio ad Ioachimum Westhphalum)*, C.O. 9:137–252; *Selected Works* 2:346–494.

140. *Efficaciter exhiberi in coena dixi Christi corpus, non naturaliter, secundum virtutem, non secundum substantiam. Quo posteriore membro, localis substantiae inclusio a me notata fuit* (C.O. 9:70–71); citing *Selected Works*, 2:278.

141. C.O. 9:77–78; Calvin, *Selected Works*, 2:287–88

142. *Christi substantiam in nos transfundi* (C.O. 9:80); citing Calvin, *Selected Works*, 2:290–291.

143. C.O. 9:148; *Selected Works*, 2:355. In this third reply, also see Calvin's appeal to Melanchthon in C.O. 9:230 (reply 45); Calvin, *Selected Works*, 2:477. Also see Calvin's letter to Schalling (1557); C.O. 16.430.

144. C.O. 9:141–49, 149 (*non magis a me Philippum quam a propriis visceribus in hac causa posse divelli*); citing Calvin, *Selected Works* 2:356.

145. C.O. 9:149–77; Calvin, *Selected Works*, 2:356–95.

146. C.O. 9:153–66 (mystical true presence), 166–77 (ascension); Calvin, *Selected Works* 2:361–79, 379–95.

147. C.O. 9:164; Calvin, *Selected Works*, 376.

148. C.O. 9:164–65; Calvin, *Selected Works* 2:377.

149. *Atque haec integra est sacrae coenae veritas, ut Christus nos inserendo in corpus suum, non modo participes faciat corporis et sanguinis sui, sed vitam, cuius in ipso residet plenitudo, in nos inspiret* (C.O. 9:165; Calvin, *Selected Works*, 377). See, also in this letter, his comments to Magdeburg that "[t]he whole question turns on this—Are we fed by the flesh and blood of Christ, when by them he infuses life into us; or is it necessary that the substance of his flesh (*substantiam carnis*) should be swallowed up by us in order to be meat, and that the blood should be substantially quaffed

(*substantialiter hauriri*) in order to be drink?" (C.O. 9:183; Calvin, *Selected Works* 2:402). As Calvin so often says in this reply to Westphal, and to the Lutherans, the difference between their positions is not whether we are fed by Christ's true body and blood; the "difference is only in the mode" (*tantum in modo dissension est*) (C.O. 9:182; Calvin, *Selected Works* 2:401).

150. This chapter, pp. 92–93, nn. 76–79.

151. *In Evangelium secundum Iohannem, Commentarius Iohannis Calvini* (Geneva, 1553); C.O. 47:1–458; *Commentaire sur l'Evangile selon Sainct Iean* (Geneva, 1553). See De Greef, *Writings of Calvin*, 82–83.

152. C.O. 25:145; emphasis to the English translation has been added: *Neque enim fides Christum intuetur duntaxat quasi procul remotum, sed eum amplectitur, ut noster fiat et in nobis habitet: facit ut coalescamus in eius corpus, communem habeamus cum ipso vitam, unum denique simus cum ipso* [Eng. trans. from Calvin's New Testament Commentaries 4:159].

153. C.O. 25:155; Calvin's New Testament Commentaries 4:170.

154. It seems worthwhile, in passing, to note that Melanchthon, like the Reformed scholars of his day, was a humanist, in what we now know to be the fullest sense of the word; "humanism" for that period; to be a method issue, not a material issue; to be a return to the sources via certain types of approach that included language study, rhetoric, a broad sense of historical consciousness, and so on. For a short summary of these issues, and parsing scholarly approaches to humanism, see my work *Postmodern Christianity* (Harrisburg, PA: Trinity Press Int., 2003), 56–57. My point is simply that we ought to be well beyond the mid-twentieth-century debate between neo-orthodoxy and liberal Protestantism that contrasted biblical theology with humanist Christianity. By their humanist approach, Reformed scholars, as well as Melanchthon, and of course Erasmus, returned to reading the patristic scholars and discovered in Augustine a most catholic view that bespoke the mystical true presence (nonmetabolic real presence).

155. The long-standing biography of Bullinger is that by Carl Pestalozzi, *Heinrich Bullinger: Leben und ausgewählte Schriften* (Elberfeld: R. L. Fridrechs, 1858). First replacing this work was the study by Fritz Blanke and Immanuel Leuschner, *Heinrich Bullinger: Vater der reformierten Kirche* (Zurich: Theologischer Verlag, 1990); but also see the recent two-volume study by Fritz Büsser, *Heinrich Bullinger (1504–1575): Leben, Werk und Wirkung* (Zurich: Theologischer Verlag, 2004). For the ongoing critical editing of Bullinger's enormous corpus of work (over 100 books and over 15,000 letters), see Fritz Büsser, *Henirich Bullinger Werke* (Zurich: Theologischer Verlag, 1972–). For Bullinger's theological development, see Fritz Blanke, *Der junge Bullinger* (Zurich: Zwingli Verlag, 1942), and Joachim Staedtke, *Die Theologie des jungen Bullinger* (Zurich: Zwingli Verlag, 1962). Also see the helpful discussion by Robert C. Walton, "Heinrich Bullinger 1504–1575," in *Shapers of Religious Traditions in Germany, Switzerland, and Poland 1560–1600*, ed. Jill Raitt (New Haven, CT: Yale University Press, 1982), 69–87.

156. For Bullinger's teaching on the Supper, see Hans Bächtold, "Heinrich Bullinger und Oberschwaben," *Zeitschrift für Bayerische Kirchengeschichte* 64 (1995): 1–19; J. Wayne Baker, "Covenant and Community in the Thought of Heinrich Bullinger," in *The Covenant Connection: From Federal Theology to Modern Federalism*, ed. Daniel J. Elazar and John Kincaid (Lanham, MD: Lexington Books, 2000), 15–29; Barclay, *The Protestant Doctrine of the Lord's Supper*; Hans G. vom Berg,

"Die Brüder vom Gemeinsamen Leben und die Stiftsschule von St. Martin zu Emmerich. Zur Frage des Einflusses der Devotio moderna auf den jungen Bullinger," in *Heinrich Bullinger 1504–1575: Gesammelte Aufsätze zum 400. Todestag,* vol. 1, ed. Ulrich Gäbler and Erland Herkenrath (Zurich: Theologischer Verlag, 1975), 1–12; idem, "Spätmittelalterliche Einflüsse auf Bullingers Theologie," in Gäbler and Herkenrath, *Gesammelte Aufsätze,* 43–53; Bizer, *Studien zur Geschichte;* Fritz Blanke, *Der Junge Bullinger, 1504–1531* (Zurich: Zwingli-Verlag, 1942), 29–30, 56–58; André Bouvier, *Henri Bullinger, Réformateur et Conseiller Oecuménique: Le Successeur de Zwingli* (Neuchâtel: Imprimerie Delachaux et Niestlé, 1940), 110–49, 471–76; Martin Brecht, "Luthers Beziehungen zu den Oberdeutschen und Schweizern von 1530–1531 bis 1546," in *Leben und Werk Martin Luthers von 1526 bis 1546,* ed. Hjalmar Junghans (Göttingen: Vandenhoeck & Ruprecht, 1983), 497–517; G. W. Bromiley, ed., *Zwingli and Bullinger,* The Library of Christian Classics, vol. 24 (Philadelphia: Westminster Press, 1953); Pierre Bühler, "Bullinger als Systematiker: Am Beispiel der Confessio Helvetica Posterior," *Zwingliana* 31 (2004): 215–36; Amy Nelson Burnett, "Basel and the Wittenberg Concord," *Archiv für Reformationsgeschichte* 96 (2005): 33–56; Edward Dowey, "Der Theologische Aufbau des Zweiten Helvetischen Bekenntnisses," in *Glauben und Bekennen: Vierhundert Jahre Confessio Helvetica Posterior Beiträge zu ihrer Geschichte und Theologie,* ed. Joachim Staedtke (Zurich: Zwingli-Verlag,1966), 205–34; idem, "Das Wort Gottes als Schrift und Predigt im Zweiten Helvetischen Bekenntnis," in Staedtke, *Glauben und Bekennen,* 235–50; Leanne van Dyk, "The Reformed View," in *The Lord's Supper: Five Views,* ed. Gordon T. Smith (Downers Grove, IL: IVP Academic, 2008), 67–82; Martin Friedrich, "Heinrich Bullinger und die Wittenberger Konkordie: Ein Ökumeniker im Streit um das Abendmahl," *Zwingliana* 24 (1997): 59–79; Ulrich Gäbler, "Das Zustandekommen des Consensus Tigurinus im Jahre 1549," *Theologische Literaturzeitung* 104 (1979): 321–32; Timothy George, "John Calvin and the Agreement of Zurich (1549)," in *John Calvin and the Church: A Prism of Reform* (Louisville, KY: Westminster John Knox Press, 1990), 42–58; Gerrish, "Sign and Reality," 118–30; Bruce Gordon and Emidio Campi, eds., *Architect of Reformation: An Introduction to Heinrich Bullinger, 1504–1575* (Grand Rapids: Baker Academic, 2004); Hans Grass, "Der Consensus Tigurinus," in *Die Abendmahlslehre bei Luther und Calvin* (Gütersloh: Bertelsmann, 1954), 193–24, also 275–78; Susi Hausamann, *Römerbriefauslegung zwischen Humanismus und Reformation: eine Studie zu Heinrich Bullingers Römerbriefvorlesung von 1525* (Zurich: Zwingli-Verlag, 1970), 186–91; Rainer Henrich, "Zu den Anfängen der Geschichtsschreibung über den Abendmahlsstreit bei Heinrich Bullinger und Johann Stumpf," *Zwingliana* 20 (1993): 11–51; Herbert Hug, "Heinrich Bullinger: Eine Ökumenische Gestalt," *KBRS* 96 (1940): 194–97; Wim Janse, "Calvin's Eucharistic Theology"; David Keep, ed., *Henry Bullinger: 1504–1575: British Anniversary Colloquium, 1975* (Woodbury, Exeter: D. J. Keep, 1976); Ernst Koch, *Die Theologie der Confessio Helvetica Posterior,* Beiträge zur Geschichte und Lehre der Reformierten Kirche, vol. 27 (Neukirchen: Neukirchener Verlag des Erziehungsvereins, 1968), 326–27; Walther Köhler, *Dogmengeschichte als Geschichte des christlichen Selbstbewusstseins: Das Zeitalter der Reformation* (Zurich: Max Neihans, 1951), 322; Gottfried Locher, "Die Lehre vom Heiligen Geist in der Confessio Helvetica Posterior," in Staedtke, ed., *Glauben und Bekennen,* 300–336; Joseph C. McLelland, "Meta-Zwingli or Anti-Zwingli? Bullinger and Calvin in Eucharistic Concord," in *Huldrych Zwingli, 1484–1531: A Legacy of Radical Reform. Papers from the 1984 International Zwingli Symposium,* ed. E. J. Furcha (Montréal: McGill University Faculty of Religious Studies, 1985), 179–95; idem, "Die Sakramentslehre der Confessio Helvetica Posterior," in Staedtke, ed., *Glauben und Bekennen*, 368–91; Peter Opitz, "Eine Theologie der Gemeinschaft im Zeitalter der Glaubensspaltung," *Zwingliana* 31 (2004): 199–214; Pestalozzi, *Bullinger*, 10–11, 202; Paul Rorem, "Calvin and Bullinger on the Lord's Supper, part 1, The Impasse," *Lutheran Quarterly* 2, no. 2 (1988): 155–84; idem, "Calvin and Bullinger on the Lord's Supper, part 2, The Agreement," *Lutheran Quarterly* 2, no. 3 (1988): 357–89; idem, *Calvin and Bullinger on the Lord's Supper* (Bramcote, Nottingham: Grove Books, 1989); idem, "The Consensus Tigurinus (1549): Did Calvin Compromise?" in *Calvinus Sacrae Scripturae Professor*, ed. Wilhelm H. Neuser (Grand Rapids: Eerdmans, 1994), 72–90; Kurt J. Rüetschi, "Bucer und Bullinger in ihren persönlichen Beziehungen," in *Martin Bucer and Sixteenth-Century Europe: Actes du Colloque de Strasbourg, 28–31 Août 1991*, vol. 1, ed. Christian Krieger and Marc Lienhard (Leiden: E. J. Brill, 1993), 429–39; Paul Sanders, "Heinrich Bullinger et le «Zwinglianisme Tardif» aux Lendemains du «Consensus Tigurinus»," *Zwingliana* 19 (1992): 307–23; Philip Schaff, "The Second Helvetic Confession. A.D. 1566," in *The Creeds of Christendom*, 4th ed., vol. 1 (New York: Harper & Bros., 1919), 390–95; Gottlob Schrenk, *Gottesreich und Bund im älteren Protestantismus* (Darmstadt: Wissenschaftliche Buchgesellschaft, 1967), 40–44; Gustav Von Schultheß-Rechberg, *Heinrich Bullinger: Der Nachfolger Zwinglis*, Schriften des Vereins für Reformationsgeschichte, vol. 82 (Halle: Verein für Reformationsgeschichte, 1904); Willem van't Spijker, "De Leer van de Doop bij Zwingli, Bullinger en Bucer," in *Rondom de Doopvont*, ed. Willem van't Spijker (Kampen, Netherlands: De Groot Goudriaan, 1983), 221–62; Joachim Staedtke, "Voraussetzungen der Schweizer Abendsmahlslehre," *Theologische Zeitschrift* 16 (1960): 19–32; idem, *Die Theologie des Jungen Bullinger*, Studien zur Dogmengeschichte und Systematische Theologie, vol. 16 (Zurich: Zwingli-Verlag, 1962), 20–27; idem, "Bullingers Theologie—eine Fortsetzung der Zwinglischen?" in *Bullinger-Tagung 1975*, ed. Ulrich Gäbler and Endre Zsindely (Zurich: Institut für Schweizerische Reformationsgeschichte, 1977), 87–98; Peter Stephens, "The Sacraments in the Confessions of 1536, 1549, and 1566: Bullinger's Understanding in the Light of Zwingli's," *Zwingliana* 33 (2006): 51–76; Otto Strasser, "Der Consensus Tigurinus," *Zwingliana* 9 (1949): 1–16; Tylenda, "The Calvin-Westphal Exchange"; Peter Walser, *Die Prädestination bei Heinrich Bullinger im Zusammenhang mit seiner Gotteslehre*, Studien zur Dogmengeschichte und Systematischen Theologie, vol. 11 (Zurich: Zwingli-Verlag, 1957), 244; Robert C. Walton, "Heinrich Bullinger," in *Shapers of Religious Traditions in Germany, Switzerland and Poland, 1560–1600*, ed. Jill Raitt (New Haven, CT: Yale University Press, 1981), 69–88; idem, "Let Zwingli be Zwingli," in *Prophet, Pastor, Protestant: The Work of Huldrych Zwingli after Five Hundred Years*, ed. E. J. Furcha and H. Wayne Pipkin (Allison Park, PA: Pickwick Publications, 1984), 171–90.

157. See Ernst Koch, *Die Theologie der Confessio Helvetica Posterior* (Neukirchen-Vluyn: Neukirchener Verlag des Erziehungsvereins, 1968), 387–408; idem, "Paulusexegese und Bundestheologie: Bullingers Auslegung von Gal 3:17–26," in Olivier Fatio and Pierre Fraenkel, eds., *Histoire de l'exégèse au XVIe siècle* (Geneva: Droz, 1979), 342–50; J. Wayne Baker, *Heinrich Bullinger and the Covenant: The Other Reformed Tradition* (Athens: Ohio University Press, 1980); Charles S. McCoy and J. Wayne Baker, *Fountainhead of Federalism: Heinrich Bullinger and the Covenant*

Tradition (Louisville, KY: Westminster/John Knox Press, 1991). Also see Koch's generally positive review of Baker's book in *Theologische Literaturzeitung* 109 (1984) and his suggestion that Baker has perhaps streamlined the issue and made Bullinger's views on covenant more consistent over time than they were (43–44). Not all scholars, however, have seen Bullinger as a covenant theologian, or as representing a covenant (and thus nonpredestinarian) Reformed position. See Edward A. Dowey Jr., who criticizes the work of both Baker and Koch, in "Heinrich Bullinger's Theology: Thematic, Comprehensive, Schematic," in *Calvin Studies V*, ed. John Leith (Richmond, VA: Union Theological Seminary in Virginia, 1991), 41–60. Also see Cornelis P. Venema, "Heinrich Bullinger's Correspondence on Calvin's Doctrine of Predestination, 1551–1553," *Sixteenth Century Journal* 17 (1986): 449. See, esp., Venema, *Heinrich Bullinger and the Doctrine of Predestination: Author of "the Other Reformed Tradition"?* (Grand Rapids : Baker Academic, 2002).

158. Rorem, *Calvin and Bullinger*, 13–14. This book is a reprint of the two essays that first appeared in *The Lutheran Quarterly* (see above, n. 8). On the many influences on the young Bullinger, see the introductory comments and the notes by Peter Opitz, "Bullinger's *Decades*: Instructions in Faith and Conduct," in *Architect of Reformation: An Introduction to Heinrich Bullinger, 1504–1575*, ed. Bruce Gordon and Emidio Campi (Grand Rapids: Baker Academic, 2004), 102–3.

159. So, e.g., in *De pane eucharistiae declamationes*, 19 March 1526, ed. Bernhard Schneider, in *Werke*, 3d Abt., *Theologische Schriften*, Bd. 2 (Zurich: Theologischer Verlag Zürich, 1991), 111–18; hereafter referred to as *Bullinger Theologische Schriften*, followed by volume number and page numbers, Bullinger says about the realistic language of John 6:51ff., "To sum, it teaches nothing else in this epilogue other than he was sent into this world to suffer for us. He who truly believes his flesh was sacrificed for the salvation of the human race shall be saved; he who does not believe will be condemned" (*In summa nihil docet aliud in hoc epilogo, nisi quod in hunc mundum missus sit, ut pateretur pro nobis. Id vero qui credat carnem suam pro salute humani generis caesam, salvus sit, qui non credit, quod is condamnabitur*).

160. *Das Abendmahl is nicht nur Danksagungs- und Erinnerungsfest, bei dem die Gemeinde im Glauben sich das Gnadenopfer Christi vergegenwärtigt, sondern sakramentaler Akt der Zueignung und Vergegenwärtigen . . . so, daß die gläubige, gedenkende Gemeinde der passive, emfangende Teil ist und der sich schenkende Christus das allein handelnde Subjekt* (vom Berg, "Spätmittelalterliche Einflüsse auf die Abendmahlslehre," 233). Also see Opitz, "Bullinger's *Decades*," 102–3 and nn.

161. As we saw in the first chapter, John 6 was the scriptural *locus classicus* for the Augustinian mystical true presence.

162. See *Wider das Götzenbrot*, 15 July 1525, ed. Hans-Georg vom Berg, in *Bullinger Theologische Schriften*, 2:46–65; *De institutione eucharistiae*, 10 December 1525, ed. Bernhard Schneider, in *Bullinger Theologische Schriften*, 2:86–107; *De pane eucharistiae declamationes*, 19 March 1526, ed. Bernhard Schneider, in *Bullinger Theologische Schriften*, 2:108–26.

163. *Bullinger Theologische Schriften* 2:52–53; 2:59 (*Eins nimbt mich wunder, wie sie doch das 6. cap. Joh. laßind außleggen, dieweil die wort auch steiff tönend von dem fleisch und von dem blut [Joh 6,v51ff]. Aber es ist nüt dann ein lötiger kib*).

164. *Bullinger Theologische Schriften*, 2:93, where he mentions Augustine's commentary on Ps. 73.

165. *Bullinger Theologische Schriften*, 2:95.

166. *Bullinger Theologische Schriften*, 2:98–9.
167. *Bullinger Theologische Schriften*, 2:103.
168. *Bullinger Theologische Schriften*, 2:111–18.
169. *Warhaffte Bekanntnuss der Dieneren der Kirchen zů Zürych* (Zurich: Froschauer, 1545); see the listing in Heinrich Bullinger, *Werke*, Erste Abteilung: *Bibliographie*, Band 1, ed. Joachim Staedtke (Zurich: Theologischer Verlag, 1972), no. 161. My text is taken directly from the 1545 original, a copy of which resides in the extensive and rich rare book collection of Eden Seminary, and references are to this edition. This particular 1545 Froschauer edition also reprints, at the end of the Zurich confession, a copy of Luther's 1544 Short Confession. For a detailed analysis of this document and, with regard to Bullinger's Supper theology, the relationship of the True Confession to the Zurich Agreement, see Rorem, *Calvin and Bullinger*, 18–20.
170. *Warhaffte Bekanntnuss*, 70 verso–71 recto.
171. For the critical text of Bullinger's *Decades*, see *Bullinger Theologische Schriften*, 3.1 (*Decades* 1–4,2) and 3.2 (*Decades* 4,3–5,10). For an introduction to Bullinger's *Decades*, see Peter Opitz, "Bullinger's *Decades*," 101–16. Also see Peter Opitz, *Heinrich Bullinger als Theologe. Eine Studie zu seinen "Decades"* (Zurich: Theologischer Verlag, 2004). For a brief history of the publication of the *Decades*, see Opitz, "Bullinger's *Decades*," 104n15. For Bullinger's sermon on the Supper (*Decades* 5, 9), see "De sancta domini coena," *Sermo IX* in *Bullinger Theologische Schriften*, 3.2:995–1041. An English translation can be found in *The Decades of Henry Bullinger*, 3 vols., trans. H. I. and ed. Thomas Harding (Cambridge: The University Press, 1852); also see the reprint edition with new introductions by George Ella and Joel R. Beeke, 2 vols. (Grand Rapids: Baker, 2004).
172. *Interim diserte profiteor me non omnem Christi praesentiam in ecclesia et in ipsa quoque actione coenae damnare aut oppugnare simpliciter. Oppugno enim significanter corporalem illam praesentiam Christi in pane, quam tuentur et obtrudunt ecclesiae dei papistae* (*Bullinger Theologische Schriften*, 3.2:1026.7–10; *The Decades of Henry Bullinger*, 452).
173. *Bullinger Theologische Schriften*, 3.2:1014.21–22, 25–26; *The Decades of Henry Bullinger*, 433.
174 *Caeterum haec promissio et communio Christi non nunc primum ad nos in coena aut per coenam defertur* (*Bullinger Theologische Schriften* 3.2:1014.35–6; *The Decades of Henry Bullinger*, 434).
175. *Bullinger Theologische Schriften*, 3.2:1014.36–1015.7; *The Decades of Henry Bullinger*, 434.
176. *ita in ipsa actione seu celebratione coenae reparatur nobis promissio, et nos communionem illam Christi, in qua sumus, renovamus et continuamus corpore et sanguine Christi spiritualiter vita et donis eius omnibus vere per fidem participantes. Atque hoc modo corpus domini edimus, et sanguinem eius bibimus* (*Bullinger Theologische Schriften*, 3.2:1015.8–12; *The Decades of Henry Bullinger*, 434).
177. *Bullinger Theologische Schriften*, 3.2:1028.19–1035.12; *The Decades of Henry Bullinger*, 456–67.
178. Rorem notes this numerous times; *Calvin and Bullinger*, see 20–55.
179. *Porro communionem illam spiritualem et promissionem vitae per Christum ipse dominus symbolis visibilibus, epulo, inquam, panis et vini verbo vel promissioni suae adiunctis visibiliter attestatur et obsignat se videlicet esse panem et potum vivificum, nos autem (symbolis, fide et obedientia susceptis) obsignari in nobis promissionem illam et communionem Christi sustinemus impresso vel traiecto in corpus nostrum corporis et*

sanguinis domini sigillo vel sacramento (*Bullinger Theologische Schriften*, 3.2:1015.12–18; *The Decades of Henry Bullinger*, 434–35).

180. *sacramentum et sigillum atque obsignatio sunt panis et poculum mysticum* (*Bullinger Theologische Schriften*, 3.2:1035.11–12; *The Decades of Henry Bullinger*, 467).

181. Opitz, "Bullinger's *Decades*," 102–3. On the 1548–49 discussions between Calvin and Bullinger, see Rorem, *Calvin and Bullinger*, 20–28; for further discussions between Calvin and Bullinger over signs, see 33–37, 42–45, 49–55.

182. See Rorem, *Calvin and Bullinger*, 30–37; C.O. 35:703 (*Deus solus agit; cessant igitur instrumenta*).

183. Rorem, *Calvin and Bullinger*, 35–36.

184. Rorem, *Calvin and Bullinger*, 36–37.

185. Note Rorem's well-put comment, "In the sixteenth century a military alliance often depended upon an explicit confessional agreement. In this case, Calvin knew that the Swiss Protestant cities would never form an effective military confederation without an open doctrinal consensus, which met its greatest barrier at precisely this point, the Lord's Supper" (*Calvin and Bullinger*, 27).

186. For the following, see Rorem, *Calvin and Bullinger*, 41–45.

187. Rorem, *Calvin and Bullinger*, 41.

188. See n. 176 above.

189. In a way, it seems to me, what was being discussed was the question that Kilian McDonnell raised centuries later when, conceding a true presence of Christ in the Supper according to Calvin's teaching, he asked about what the Supper gives that is not already present. See notes 31–35 in this chapter.

190. See Rorem, *Calvin and Bullinger*, 39–45.

191. Rorem, *Calvin and Bullinger*, 44.

192. Ulrich Gäbler, "Das Zustandekommen des Consensus Tigurinus," *Zwingliana* 9, no. 1 (1949): 323ff.; idem, "Consensus Tigurinus," in *Theologische Realenzyklopädie* (1981), 8:189.

193. Original text in Wilhelm Niesel, ed., *Bekenntnisschriften und Kirchenordnungen der nach Gottes Wort reformierten Kirchen*, 3rd ed. (Zollikon-Zurich: Evangelischer Verlag, 1940), 265:24–26 [trans. here from *The Constitution of the Presbyterian Church (U.S.A.)*, Part I, *Book of Confessions* (Louisville, KY: The Office of the General Assembly, Presbyterian Church (U.S.A.), 2004), 5.196].

194. See the comment by Ernst Koch in *Die Theologie der Confessio Helvetica Posterior* (Neukirchen-Vluyn: Neukrichener Verlag, 1968), 318. On precisely this point, theologically, see the seminal essay Gerrish, "Sign and Reality."

195. So, while Rorem rightly notes that Bullinger always stopped short of using Calvin's instrumental language, "[h]e does, however, seem to affirm a close temporal relationship. Did Bullinger use 'meanwhile' (*interim*) as a synonym for 'at the same time' (*simul*)? If so, the evolution of Bullinger's thought, and perhaps therefore the influence of Calvin and of the Consensus Tigurinus, consists in this, that here the parallelism of analogy is simultaneous. Bullinger had earlier objected to the term *simul* in Calvin's 1548 propositions, as he read it. Yet later, here in the Second Helvetic Confession, Bullinger not only tolerates but proposes a sort of simultaneity of sacramental sign and spiritual reality. If, however, *interim* does not imply simultaneity or as close a temporal relationship as *simul*, then Bullinger's position evolved very little through his entire life, through a close relationship to Zwingli's legacy and close negotiations with Calvin" (*Calvin and Bullinger*, 53–54).

196. Gerrish, "Sign and Reality."

CHAPTER 5: THE REFORMED TRAJECTORY

1. *Selected Works of John Calvin: Tracts and Letters*, 6 vols., ed. Henry Beveridge and Jules Bonnet (Grand Rapids: Baker Book House, 1983), 2:196.

2. The principal collection of Reformed confessions was always that by E. F. Karl Müller, ed., *Die Bekenntnisschriften der reformierten Kirche* (Leipzig: A. Deichert [Georg Böhme], 1903; repr. ed., Waltrop: Spenner, 1999). Two earlier critical collections should be mentioned: H. A. Niemeyer, ed., *Collectio confessionum in ecclesiis reformatis publicatarum* (Leipzig: Klinkhardt, 1840); and Philip Schaff, *Bibliotheca Symbolica Ecclesiae Universalis: The Creeds of Christendom, with a History and Critical Notes*, 3 vols., 4th ed. (New York: Harper & Bros., 1919). More recently there was the collection by Wilhelm Niesel, ed., *Bekenntnisschriften und Kirchenordnungen der nach Gottes Wort reformierten Kirchen*, 3rd ed. (Zollikon-Zurich: Evangelischer Verlag, 1940).

In recent years, new critical texts have appeared in *Reformierte Bekenntnisschriften*, 1/1, 1/2, 1/3, ed. Heiner Faulenbach and Eberhard Busch, in conjunction with Emidio Campi et al. (Neukirchen-Vluyn: Neukirchener, 2002, 2006, 2007); *Reformierte Bekenntnisschriften* 2/1, 2/2, ed. Andreas Mühling and Peter Opitz, in conjunction with Emidio Campi et al. (Neukirchen-Vluyn: Neukirchener, 2009); hereafter referred to as *Reformierte Bekenntnisschriften*, followed by volume, page, and line. These critical texts attempt to fill out, for the sake of scholars and the Reformed community, a complete collection of Reformed confessions: See, e.g., the chart in *Reformierte Bekenntnisschriften* 1/1:8–25 that compares previous editions of published confessions with the planned publication, of which sixty-four confessions have been published through 2/2.

For an introduction to the complex issues concerning the Reformed confessions, see B. A. Gerrish, "The Confessional Heritage of the Reformed Church," *McCormick Quarterly* 19 (1966): 120–34, including nn. 1–18 for further resources; idem, *The Faith of Christendom: A Source Book of Creeds and Confessions* (Cleveland and New York: The World Publishing Co., 1963), 17–46, 126–50, 354–60. Also see Arthur C. Cochrane, ed., *Reformed Confessions of the Sixteenth Century* (Philadelphia: The Westminster Press, 1966), 11–31; and Jan Rohls, *Reformed Confessions: Theology from Zurich to Barmen*, trans. John Hoffmeyer, intro. Jack L. Stotts (Louisville, KY: Westminster John Knox Press, 1998), xi–xxiii, 3–28.

3. For an overall summary, see John W. Riggs, *Baptism in the Reformed Tradition* (Louisville, KY: Westminster John Knox Press, 2002), 74–75.

4. See Gerrish, "The Confessional Heritage."

5. B. A. Gerrish, *The Old Protestantism and the New* (Chicago: The University of Chicago Press, 1982), 118–30.

6. Gerrish, *The Old Protestantism and the New*, 118–24. "There seem to be, then, three doctrines of the Eucharist in the Reformed confessions, which we may label 'symbolic memorialism,' 'symbolic parallelism,' and 'symbolic instrumentalism'" (128).

7. After each of these categories, I have picked the adjective that, where needed, I will use for each of these positions. I have left "Zwinglian" for the category to which it has usually been applied, the category of memorialism, and I have used "Zwingli-like" for the category of symbolic anamnesis, since this category is that which really is "like Zwingli." For Bullinger I have chosen "Bullinger-like," to avoid something else that would be even more ill-sounding.

8. *Reformierte Bekenntnisschriften* 1/2:34–35.

9. The First Helvetic Confession (*Confessio helvetica prior*) can be found in "Confessio Helvetica Prior von 1536," ed. Ernst Saxer, in *Reformierte Bekenntnisschriften* 1/2:44–56 (German), 57–68 (Latin) [Eng. trans. (of *German* text) in Cochrane, *Reformed Confessions*, 97–111]. Also see Müller, 101–9 (German); and for the Latin and German, also see Schaff, 3:211–31.

10. *Reformierte Bekenntnisschriften* 1/2:52.4–5, 64.7–8: *sed signis simul et rebus constant/sondern sy bstand in zeychenn und wesenlichen dingen.*

11. Note Saxer's comments in his introduction to this confession; *Reformierte Bekenntnisschriften* 1/2:35–36.

12. *Reformierte Bekenntnisschriften* 1/2:52.12–18, 64.13–17.

13. *Coenam vero mysticam, in qua dominus corpus et sanguinem suum, id est, seipsum suis vere ad hoc offerat, ut magis magisque in illis vivat et illi in ipso* (*Reformierte Bekenntnisschriften* 1/2:65.7–9).

14. *Non quod pani et vino corpus et sanguis domini vel naturaliter uniantur: vel hic localiter includantur, vel ulla huc carnali praesentia statuantur* (*Reformierte Bekenntnisschriften* 1/2:65.9–11).

15. *Reformierte Bekenntnisschriften* 1/2:65.24–66.3.

16. *Reformierte Bekenntnisschriften* 1/2:66.3–5.

17. *Reformierte Bekenntnisschriften* 1/2:35–36. Notice, for example, that article 22 in the Latin is entitled "Eucharistia" ("Eucharist"), while in Jud's German translation it is entitled, "Vom Nachtmal des herren oder von der Dancksagung" ("Concerning the Lord's Supper or Concerning the Thanksgiving"). So, also, where the Latin text begins by calling the Supper the "mystical Supper" (*coenam mysticam*), Jud's German text begins by calling the Supper the "Holy Supper" (*heylgen nachtmal*). I also noted earlier Jud's omission of the temporal and coordinating adverb *simul* (at the same time, together) that occurs in the Latin text when referring to the signs and the reality that they offer (see *Reformierte Bekenntnisschriften* 1/2:64.7, 52.4–5).

18. The Genevan Instruction and Confession of Faith (*Instruction et confession de foy*) can be found in "Genfer Bekenntnis 1536/7," ed. Anette Zillenbiller, in *Reformierte Bekenntnisschriften* 1/2:97–136. For the Confession of Faith (*Confession de la foy*), see Müller, 111–16; C.O. 9:693–700 [Eng. trans. in Cochrane, *Reformed Confessions*, 117–26].

19. *Reformierte Bekenntnisschriften* 1/2:131.25–26, 40–41. For the discussion of Calvin's development of, and change from, Augustine's definition of a sacrament, see Riggs, *Baptism*, 45–47.

20. *Reformierte Bekenntnisschriften* 1/2:132.35–39; 133.1–3.

21. *Reformierte Bekenntnisschriften* 1/2:133.9–14.

22. It is exactly following the sentence on the work of the Spirit that Calvin writes, "For although Christ, elevated to heaven, has left his dwelling place here on earth, where we all are pilgrims still, nevertheless no distance can dissolve his power to nourish his own with himself" (*Car combine que Christ, eslevé au ciel, a laissé l'habitation de la terre en laquelle nous sommes encores pellerins, toutesfois nulle distance ne peult dissouldre sa vertu, qu'il ne repaisse de soy mesmes les siens*) (*Reformierte Bekenntnisschriften* 1/2:132.39–41).

23. *La Cene nostre Seigneur est ung signe par lequel soubs le pain et le vin il nous represente la vraie communication spirituelle que nous avons en son corps et son sang* (C.O. 9.697).

24. For a critical edition of the French edition, see "Genfer Katechismus von 1542," ed. Ernst Saxer, in *Reformierte Bekenntnisschriften* 1/2:279–362; for the Latin edition, see "Catechismus Ecclesiae Genevensis," in *Christianae Religionis Institutio 1536*, in *Ioannis Calvini opera selecta*, ed. Peter Barth, Wilhelm Niesel, and Dora Scheuner, 5 vols. (Munich: Chr. Kaiser, 1926–52), 2:59–151 [Eng. trans. in *Calvin's Selected Works* 2:33–99].

25. *Reformierte Bekenntnisschriften* 1/2:349.13–17; *Christianae Religionis Institutio 1536*, in *Ioannis Calvini opera selecta*, ed. Peter Barth, Wilhelm Niesel, and Dora Scheuner, 5 vols. (Munich: Chr. Kaiser, 1926–52); hereafter cited as OS, with volume and page number; OS 2:130.17–20; *Calvin's Selected Works* 2:83–84.

26. *Reformierte Bekenntnisschriften* 1/2:349.30–32; OS 2:131.4–6; *Calvin's Selected Works* 2:84.

27. *Reformierte Bekenntnisschriften* 1/2:350.2–3; OS 2:131.9–11; *Calvin's Selected Works* 2:84.

28. *la communicaton de son corpse et son sang, noz ames sont nourries* (*Reformierte Bekenntnisschriften* 1/2:355.35–36).

29. *ut corporis et sanguinis sui communicatione educari in spem vitae aeternae animas nostras nos doceret* (OS 2:137.18–19).

30. *il faut que nous le possedions. Veu que ses beins ne sont pas nostres, sinon que premierement il se donne à nous* (*Reformierte Bekenntnisschriften* 1/2:356.17–18); *ipsum a nobis possediri necesse est. Neque enim bona nobis sua aliter communcat, nisi dum se nostrum facit* (OS 2:138.4–6).

31. *Reformierte Bekenntnisschriften* 1/2:356.30–31; OS 2:138.16–17; *Calvin's Selected Works* 2:90.

32. *Reformierte Bekenntnisschriften* 1/2:357.1–2; OS 2:138.23; *Calvin's Selected Works* 2:90.

33. OS 2:139.5. The (1545) Latin more fully accentuates the benefits, and reflects the Augustinian tradition, and thus advances the French (1542), in which the Supper "more fully confirms in us" (*plus amplement confermée en nous*) and "ratifies" (*ratifée*) this mystical union (*Reformierte Bekenntnisschriften* 1/2:357.8–9).

34. *Reformierte Bekenntnisschriften* 1/2:358.30; OS 2:140.14–15; *Calvin's Selected Works* 2:91.

35. A critical text of the Second Helvetic Confession can be found in "Confessio Helvetica posterior, 1566," ed. Emidio Campi, in *Reformierte Bekenntnisschriften* 2/2:243–345. English references to the Second Helvetic Confession will be made to *The Constitution of the Presbyterian Church (U.S.A.)*, Part I, *Book of Confessions* (Louisville, KY: The Office of the General Assembly, Presbyterian Church (U.S.A.), 2004); hereafter cited as *Book of Confessions (PCUSA)*, followed by the given internal paragraph numbers. For the Second Helvetic Confession and for any of the documents that currently serve in the confessional canon for a given church—as examples, the Heidelberg Catechism (PC(USA), CRC) or the Belgic Confession (CRC)—I will give the English directly from the ecclesial documents, rather than offering my own translation. This would not be the case, for example, with the French Confession, where the translation will be mine.

36. For this interesting discussion, I am indebted to Rorem, *Calvin and Bullinger*, 33–43, esp. 43. These sixteenth-century Reformers seem to have had a nuance between these words—*instrumentum* and *organum*—that is not entirely clear (or to Rorem either).

37. See Rorem's excellent and detailed analysis of the letters exchanged between Calvin and Bullinger, between June 1548 and January 1549 (*Calvin and Bullinger*, 29–37).

38. *Vide tamen quale sit tuum argumentum: Deus solus agit; cessant igitur instrumenta. Quid?* (C.O. 7:703; Ad VII).

39. For the history of the document, see *Reformierte Bekenntnisschriften* 2/2:256–61.

40. *Reformierte Bekenntnisschriften* 2/2:232.14–23, 324.5–11; *Book of Confessions (PCUSA)* 5.169, 5.172. Among Protestant scholars of the late medieval period and the Protestant Reformation, it was above all the late Dutch scholar Heiko Oberman who most overturned the Gilsonian decline theory of the late medieval period, which argued that Protestants were the bastard children of a bastardized decline of the great Thomistic synthesis. Instead, argued Oberman, the late medieval period that blossomed into the Protestant Reformation bridged the gap between the sacred and profane by conceiving of God as strictly personal and covenanting; a God not of overflow of Being into creation but a God who personally speaks, to which faith responds. For a basic introduction here, see Riggs, *Postmodern Christianity* (Harrisburg, PA: Trinity Press Int., 2003), 52–54, esp. 69n13. Also see Steven Ozment, *The Age of Reform* (New Haven, CT: Yale University Press, 1980), 1–21.

41. *Book of Confessions (PCUSA)* 5.172; *Reformierte Bekenntnisschriften* 2/2:234.10–11 (*Et verbum Dei habetur instar tabularum vel literarum, sacramenta vero instar sigillorum: quae literis Deus appendit solus*).

42. The still-classic study on oral cultures remains that by Albert Bates Lord, *The Singer of Tales*, ed. Stephen Mitchell and Gregory Nagy (Cambridge, MA: Harvard University Press, 2000). Here I have in mind the much-overlooked but important work by Walter Ong, whose analysis of oral culture, and its differences to chirographic culture, informs my comments. See especially Walter J. Ong, *The Presence of the Word: Some Prolegomena for Cultural and Religious History* (New Haven, CT: Yale University Press, 1967); also see *Interfaces of the Word: Studies in the Evolution of Consciousness and Culture* (Ithaca, NY: Cornell University Press, 1971); and *Orality and Literacy: The Technologizing of the Word* (London and New York: Routledge, 2002).

43. Note the view on sacraments given by Barth that this chapter takes up later.

44. *Book of Confessions (PCUSA)* 5.175; *Reformierte Bekenntnisschriften* 2/2:324.21–24 (*substantiam et materiam sacramentorum*).

45. *Book of Confessions (PCUSA)* 5.205; *Reformierte Bekenntnisschriften* 2/2:332.19–23.

46. *Book of Confessions (PCUSA)* 5.197; *Reformierte Bekenntnisschriften* 2/2:330.21–24 (*Neque enim credit vetustas pia, neque nos credimus, corpus Christi manducari ore corporis corporaliter, vel essentialiter*).

47. *Book of Confessions (PCUSA)* 5.205; *Reformierte Bekenntnisschriften* 2/2:23 (*Corpus Christi in coelis est, ad dexteram patris*).

48. *Book of Confessions (PCUSA)* 5.196; *Reformierte Bekenntnisschriften* 2/2:330.9–13.

49. *Book of Confessions (PCUSA)* 5.196–201; *Reformierte Bekenntnisschriften* 2/2:330.3–331.19. So, e.g., the eating is "certainly not in a corporeal way but in a spiritual way, by the Holy Spirit" (*non corporali modo, sed spirituali, per spiritum sanctum*) (*Book of Confessions (PCUSA)* 5.198; *Reformierte Bekenntnisschriften* 2/2:330.28–29).

50. *Book of Confessions (PCUSA)* 5.199–201; *Reformierte Bekenntnisschriften* 2/2:331.6–8, 12–14, 17–19. So, e.g., "In this matter we follow the teaching of the Savior himself, Christ the Lord, according to John, ch. 6" (*In qua se sequimur per omnia doctrinam ipsius Salvatoris Christi domini, apud Ioan in cap 6.*) (*Book of Confessions (PCUSA)* 5.201; *Reformierte Bekenntnisschriften* 2/2:331.17–19).

51. *Book of Confessions (PCUSA)* 5.196; *Reformierte Bekenntnisschriften* 2/2:330.3–10: Note that in the Latin, the words for "at the same time" and "inwardly" occur together at the beginning of the second part of the assertion: *intus interim opera Christi per spiritum sanctum, percipiunt etiam carnem et sanguinem domini.*

52. Gerrish, *The Old Protestantism and the New*, 24, 128; also see Rohls, *Reformed Confessions*, 226.

53. Also note the key confession already discussed in chap. 4; see n. 10 and accompanying analysis of the text.

54. See Gerrish, *Faith of Christendom*, 126–50, for an introduction to the French Confession (*Confessio gallicana*).

55. For a history of the French Confession and its sources, see Jacques Pannier, *Les origines de la confession de foi et de la discipline des église réformées de France* (Paris: F. Alcan, 1936). Esp. see Hannelore Jahr, *Studien zur Überlieferungsgeschichte der Confession de foi von 1559* (Neukirchen-Vluyn: Neukirchener Verlag des Erziehungsvereins, 1964). Jahr does careful textual work on the Confession (19–29), discusses the spread and influence of the French Confession (29–57), and has more recent bibliographic material (156–62). For a critical edition, see "Confessio Gallicana, 1559/1571, mit dem Bekenntnis der Waldenser, 1560," ed. Emidio Campi, in *Reformierte Bekenntnisschriften* 2/1:1–29 (French text, 17–29); the French text can also be found in Müller, 221–32; for the Latin text, see Niemeyer, 327–39 [Eng. trans. in Cochrane, *Reformed Confessions*, 144–58].

56. *Reformierte Bekenntnisschriften* 2/1:27.21–28.1: *Nous confessons que la Cène (qui est le second Sacrement) nous est tesmoignage de l'unité que nous avons avec Jésus Christ, d'autant qu'il n'est pas seulement une fois mort et ressucité pour nous, mais aussi nous repaist et nourrist vrayement de sa chair et son sang à ce que nous soyons un avec luy et que vie nous soit commune. Or combine qu'il soit au ciel iusques à ce qu'il vienne pout iuger tout le monde, toutesfois nous croyons que par la vertu secrete et incompréhensible de son Espirit il nourrist et vivifie de las substance de son corps et de son sang.*

57. *Dieu nous donne réallement et par effect ce qu'il y figure* (*Reformierte Bekenntnisschriften* 2/1:28.7).

58. *Reformierte Bekenntnisschriften* 2/1:28.9–12: *Et par ainsi tous ceux qui apportent à la table sacrée de Christ une pure foy comme un vaisseau reçoyvent vrayement ce que les signes y testifient. C'est que le corps et le sang de Iésus Christ ne servent pas moins de manger et boire à l'âme que le pain et le vin font au corps.*

59. For a critical text of the Belgic Confession, and a helpful introduction, see "Confessio Belgica von 1561," ed. Eberhard Busch, in *Reformierte Bekenntnisschriften* 2/1:319–69, which gives both the 1561 French text (2/1:324–43) and the 1618 Latin text (2/1:343–69). The Latin text can also be found in Müller, 233–49; and the French version can be found in Schaff (3:383–436), who used the official version from the Synod of Dort (1618–19), which differed from the original French confession in several areas. For an English overview of the Belgic Confession and literature, see Cochrane, *Reformed Confessions*, 185–88. Also see Michael A. Hakkenberg, "Belgic Confession," in *The Oxford Encyclopedia of the Reformation*, ed. Hans J. Hillerbrand (Oxford: Oxford University Press, 1996), 1:137–39. For the

English, I will cite from *Ecumenical Creeds and Reformed Confessions* (Grand Rapids: CRC Publications, 1988) and make reference only to the original 1561 French text in *Reformierte Bekenntnisschriften* 2/1.

60. *Reformierte Bekenntnisschriften* 2/1:339.17–20; *Ecumenical Creeds and Reformed Confessions*, 111.

61. *Reformierte Bekenntnisschriften* 2/1:339.21–2; *Ecumenical Creeds and Reformed Confessions*, 111.

62. *et entez en sa familie, qui est son Eglise* (*Reformierte Bekenntnisschriften* 2/1:340.38; *Ecumenical Creeds and Reformed Confessions*, 114). This beginning is reminiscent of the baptismal material that reflects the strength and faithfulness of the gathered church. As I said in the baptismal analysis, we should remember that "the Belgic Confession came from a threatened minority, was written to defend the Reformed faith as orthodox and nonseditious, and was given to Philip II in the hope of toleration" (Riggs, *Baptism*, 80).

63. *Reformierte Bekenntnisschriften* 2/1:341.5–8; *Ecumenical Creeds and Reformed Confessions*, 115.

64. *nourissant, fortifiant et consolant nostre poure ame desolee par le manger de sa chair, et l'enyurant par le bruuage de son sang* (*Reformierte Bekenntnisschriften* 2/1:339.17–20; *Ecumenical Creeds and Reformed Confessions*, 116).

65. See my comments in n. 62 above.

66. For a critical text of the Heidelberg Catechism, see "Heidelberger Katechismus von 1563," ed. Wilhelm H. Neuser, in *Reformierte Bekenntnisschriften* 2/2:167–212; also Müller, *Die Bekenntnisschriften*, 682–719. The catechism follows an earlier catechism of Zacharias Ursinus, who had studied at Wittenberg with Melanchthon. The threefold structure of law–gospel–new life comes from Melanchthon, although the last section reflects Calvin's so-called "third use of the law." The sacramental theology has been taken to be Calvinist (Müller, *Die Bekenntnisschriften*, iii; Schaff, *Bibliotheca*, 1:543); or of the "Zwinglian tradition" (Neuser, "Heidelberger Katechismus," 170), although not so for the general sacramental questions (65–68); but Gerrish has argued that the eucharistic doctrine "owes more to Zwingli and particularly to Bullinger than to Calvin" (*The Old Protestantism and the New*, 125–26). By meticulous textual study, Neuser has argued that the baptismal material is indebted primarily to Melanchthon, while synthesizing Luther, Melanchthon, and Calvin. See Wilhelm H. Neuser, *Die Tauflehre des Heidelberger Katechismus: Eine aktuelle Lösung des Problems der Kindertaufe* (Munich: Chr. Kaiser Verlag, 1967). For an introduction to the catechism, see Neuser, ed., "Heidelberger Katechismus," 167–72; in English, see Edward A. Dowey Jr., *A Commentary on the Confession of 1967 and an Introduction to The Book of Confessions* (Philadelphia: Westminster Press, 1968), 187–200; Rohls, *Reformed Confessions*, 20–21; Jack Rogers, *Presbyterian Creeds: A Guide to the Book of Confession* (Philadelphia: Westminster Press, 1985), 96–112; *The Heidelberg Catechism: 400th Anniversary Edition*, trans. Allen O. Miller and M. Eugene Osterhaven (New York: United Church Press, 1962), 5–8.

For this Supper material from the Heidelberg Catechism, I will cite from the English given in the 2012 officially approved Christian Reformed Church translation of the catechism; see *The Heidelberg Catechism* (Grand Rapids: Faith Alive Christian Resources, 2012). I will also give the references to the paragraphs in the *Book of Confessions (PCUSA)*. The two translations differ slightly from each other, and they differ slightly from the critical text given by Neuser, and I have chosen the CRC translation, because it seems to me slightly closer to the German, perhaps better arranged on the page, and it also retains the Scripture references in the text itself.

67. Gerrish, *The Old Protestantism and the New*, 125.

68. Gerrish, *The Old Protestantism and the New*, 125.

69. *Reformierte Bekenntnisschriften* 2/2:193.33–194.3; *Heidelberg Catechism*, 26; *Book of Confessions (PCUSA)* 4.075.

70. *Reformierte Bekenntnisschriften* 2/2:194.7–16; *Heidelberg Catechism*, 27; *Book of Confessions (PCUSA)* 4.076.

71. In 1998 the CRC synod asked for a study of Q. 80 and its answer, particularly the last three paragraphs, which end with calling the Roman Catholic Mass "a condemnable idolatry." After some remarkable scholarship and ecumenical dialogue with Roman Catholic theologians, the CRC decided to bracket these final three paragraphs. The official 2012 version of the catechism says, "In response to a mandate from Synod 1998, the Christian Reformed Church's Interchurch Relations Committee conducted a study of Q&A 80 and the Roman Catholic Mass. Based on this study, Synod 2004 declared that 'Q&A 80 can no longer be held in its current form as part of our confession.' Synod 2006 directed that Q&A 80 remain in the CRC's text of the Heidelberg Catechism but that the last three paragraphs be placed in brackets to indicate that they do not accurately reflect the official teaching and practice of today's Roman Catholic Church and are no longer confessionally binding on members of the CRC" (*The Heidelberg Catechism*, 29; cf. *Book of Confessions (PCUSA)* 4.080.)

72. Sometimes referred to as the six Johns, the committee was comprised of John Knox (ca. 1514–82), John Willock (d. 1585), John Spottiswoode (1510–85), John Douglas (ca. 1494–1574), John Winram (ca. 1492–1582), and John Row (ca. 1525–80); see *Reformierte Bekenntnisschriften* 2/1:2111–12.

For a critical text of the Scots Confession, see "Confessio Scotica 1560," ed. Ian Hazlett, in *Reformierte Bekenntnisschriften* 2/1:209–99; also see Niesel, 79–117, who gives the Scots text and the Latin text on opposing pages. For an introduction and comprehensive bibliography, see *Reformierte Bekenntnisschriften* 2/1:209–39. Also see Cochrane, *Reformed Confessions*, 159–62; Dowey, *Commentary*, 173–86; and Rogers, *Presbyterian Creeds*, 79–91. Also see Alex Cheyne, "The Scots Confession of 1560," *Theology Today* 17 (1960): 323–38; and William Ian Petrie Hazlett, "The Scots Confession 1560: Context, Complexion and Critique," *Archiv für Reformationsgeschichte* 78 (1987): 287–320.

73. Dowey, *Commentary*, 175.

74. *Book of Confessions (PCUSA)* 3.21; *Reformierte Bekenntnisschriften* 2/1:282.6–9 ("Christ Jesus is sa joinit with us that he becumis the verray nurischment and fude of our saulis").

75. *Book of Confessions (PCUSA)* 3.21; *Reformierte Bekenntnisschriften* 2/1:283:2–4.

76. *Book of Confessions (PCUSA)* 3.21; *Reformierte Bekenntnisschriften* 2/1:284.3–286.3.

77. *Book of Confessions (PCUSA)* 3.21; *Reformierte Bekenntnisschriften* 2/1:286.5–8.

78. For a critical text, see "The Articles of Religion of the Church of England (1563/1571) commonly called the 'Thirty-Nine Articles,'" ed. W. J. Torrance Kirby, in *Reformierte Bekenntnisschriften* 2/1:371–410, which gives both the Latin and English texts. Also see Müller, 522–25. For an introduction, see *Reformierte Bekenntnisschriften* 2/1:371–75; for an overview of catechisms in the Anglican tradition, see James Hartin, "Catechisms," in Stephen Sykes and John Booty, *The Study of Anglicanism* (London: SPCK, 1988), 154–63. Also see Francis Procter, *A New History*

of the Book of Common Prayer, rev. and rewritten by Walter Howard Frere (London: Macmillan & Co., Ltd., 1955), 597–602. The English text will be cited from *The Book of Common Prayer* (New York: Seabury Press, 1979), 867–76.

79. Gerrish, *The Old Protestantism and the New,* 126.

80. *Book of Common Prayer,* 873; *Reformierte Bekenntnisschriften* 2/1:400.22–23. The Latin says, *Corpus Christi datur, acciptur, et manducatur in Coena, tantum coelestis et spirituali ratione (Reformierte Bekenntnisschriften* 2/1:400.7–8).

81. Text in Müller, 522–25. The sacramental sections were added in 1604 by Bishop Overall, dean of St. Paul's Cathedral. In 1662 the catechism was printed in the *Book of Common Prayer* and placed between the rites for Baptism and Confirmation.

82. Müller, 524.20–23.

83. For a brief introduction to the Westminster Assembly, with notes and a select bibliography, see John H. Leith, *Assembly at Westminster: Reformed Theology in the Making* (Richmond, VA: John Knox Press, 1973).

84. For an introduction, see Dowey, *Commentary,* 214–50; Leith, *Assembly at Westminster,* 65–107; and Rogers, *Presbyterian Creeds,* 140–65. The text for the two catechisms can be found in Müller, 612–52, who gives the English version of the Shorter Catechism and the Latin version of the Larger Catechism. I will cite the English from the *Book of Confessions (PCUSA).* A critical text for the Confession can be found in Müller, 542–642, which gives both Latin and English.

85. Gerrish, *The Old Protestantism and the New,* 126.

86. *Book of Confessions (PCUSA)* 6.167.

87. *Book of Confessions (PCUSA)* 7.264.

88. *Book of Confessions (PCUSA)* 7.272.

89. *Book of Confessions (PCUSA)* 7.278.

90. *Book of Confessions (PCUSA)* 7.280; emphasis is mine.

91. Schleiermacher bibliography can be found in Terrence N. Tice, *Schleiermacher Bibliography: With Brief Introductions, Annotations, and Index* (Princeton, NJ: Princeton Theological Seminary, 1966); idem, *Schleiermacher Bibliography (1784–1984): Updating and Commentary* (Princeton, NJ: Princeton Theological Seminary, 1985); idem, "Schleiermacher Bibliography: Update 1987," *New Athenaeum/Neues Athenaeum* 1 (1989): 280–350; "Schleiermacher Bibliography: Update 1990," *New Athenaeum/ Neues Athenaeum* 2 (1991): 131–65; "Schleiermacher Bibliography: Update 1994," *New Athenaeum/Neues Athenaeum* 4 (1995): 139–94; idem, *Schleiermacher's Sermons: A Chronological Listing and Account* (Lewiston, NY: E. Mellen Press, 1997). For those not familiar with Schleiermacher, by far the best introduction to his theology is the work by B. A. Gerrish, *A Prince of the Church: Schleiermacher and the Beginnings of Modern Theology* (Philadelphia: Fortress Press, 1984). Also see the more recent work by Terrence N. Tice, *Schleiermacher* (Nashville: Abingdon Press, 2006); and Catherine C. Kelsey, *Thinking about Christ with Schleiermacher* (Louisville, KY: Westminster John Knox Press, 2003). Martin Redeker's *Schleiermacher: Life and Thought,* trans. John Wallhauser (Philadelphia: Fortress Press, 1973), remains a standard introduction to Schleiermacher's life and thought. Richard R. Niebuhr gives a more complete introduction to Schleiermacher's theology in his book *Schleiermacher on Christ and Religion* (New York: Charles Scribner's Sons, 1964).

92. See Redeker, *Schleiermacher,* 94–100, 151–208.

93. See Riggs, *Baptism,* 90–93.

94. Friedrich Schleiermacher, *The Christian Faith* (Philadelphia: Fortress Press, 1976); the critical German edition is *Der christliche Glaube nach den Grundsätzen der*

evangelischen Kirche im Zusammenhange dargestellt, 7th ed., ed. Martin Redeker (Berlin: Walter de Gruyter & Co, 1960). Here and following, the citation will be according to propositions and subsections, followed by the page number in the English edition, and in parentheses the volume and page number in Redeker's critical edition. Unless otherwise noted, I have used the English translation given here in the text, see *Christian Faith,* §106.1, 476 (2:147).

95. *Christian Faith,* §127.3, 589–90 (2:127–28).

96. *Christian Faith,* §137.1–2, 628–29 (2:328–30).

97. *Christian Faith,* §137.2, 629–31 (2:330–32).

98. "Denn wird die Taufe schlecht empfangen, wenn sie ohne Glauben empfangen wird; so ist sie auch nicht gut gegeben" (*Christian Faith,* §137.2, 630 [2:331]). Note the irony that Schleiermacher's position on Word, faith, and baptism stands very close to that of his later archcritic, Karl Barth; see Riggs, *Baptism,* 94–95.

99. *Christian Faith,* §107.1, 479 (2:151).

100. "Now of course it is by the very same act that the individual is regenerated and that he becomes a spontaneously active member of the Christian Church" (*Christian Faith,* §114.2, 531 [2:214]).

101. *Christian Faith,* §136.3, 622–23 (2:321–23).

102. *Christian Faith,* §138.2, 636 (2:338).

103. *Christian Faith,* §139.1, 638 (2:340–41).

104. *Christian Faith,* §139.1, 639 (2:341–42).

105. *Christian Faith,* §139.2, 640–41 (2:343); *die erlösende und gemeinschaftstiftende Liebe Christi nicht nur darstellt, sondern immer aufs neue kräftig regt* (2:343).

106. *Christian Faith,* §139.2, 640–41 (2:343).

107. *Christian Faith,* §140, 644 (2:347).

108. *Christian Faith,* §140.2, 646 (2:349).

109. *Der Hauptgrund also, warum wir, abgesehen davon, daß sie sich hermeneutisch nicht rechtfertigen läßt, die Theorie der katholischen Kirchen verwerfen* ("Hence the chief reason why [apart from its exegetical unsoundness] we reject the theory of the Catholic Church") (*Christian Faith,* §140.2, 646 [2:350]).

110. *Christian Faith,* §140.2, 646 (2:350).

111. *Christian Faith,* §140.3, 646–7 (2:350).

112. *Christian Faith,* §140.4, 648–651 (2:352–55).

113. *welche an allen diesen Klippen nich scheitere* (*Christian Faith,* §140.4, 650–51 [2:355]).

114. "The one benefit of this participation is stated as being the confirming of our fellowship with Christ; and this includes the confirming of Christians in their union with each other, for the latter rests so entirely on their union with Christ (*Vereinigung mit Christo*) that the union of an individual with Christ is unthinkable apart from his union with believers" (*Christian Faith,* §141.1, 651 [2:356]).

115. *Christian Faith,* §142.1, 655 (2:361).

116. *Christian Faith,* §142.1, 656 (2:361–62).

117. *Christian Faith,* §142.2, 656 (2:362).

118. *Christian Faith,* §142.2, 656 (2:362).

119. See John W. Nevin, *The Mystical Presence and Other Writings on the Eucharist,* ed. Bard Thompson and George H. Bricker, Lancaster Series on the Mercersburg Theology, vol. 4 (Boston and Philadelphia: United Church Press, 1966). This was the volume that over the years I have used to read Nevin's eucharistic writings. For this current chapter, however, I read from an excellent recent volume that not only is physically easy to read and attractive (and financially obtainable), but also

has a more complete and updated bibliography and has informational notes and translations of Nevin's Latin texts, which would help the general reader: see John Williamson Nevin, *The Mystical Presence and the Doctrine of the Reformed Church on the Lord's Supper*, ed. Linden J. DeBie, gen. ed. W. Bradford Littlejohn, The Mercersburg Theology Study Series, vol. 1 (Eugene, OR: Wipf & Stock, 2012). In the following notes, I will give the pagination from the DeBie and Littlejohn edition, followed in parentheses by the pages in the Thompson and Bricker edition, which still remains standard for many readers. For introduction to the material, see Thompson and Bricker, *Mystical Presence*, 7–14; De Bie and Littlejohn, *Mystical Presence*, xxiii–xlii; and B. A. Gerrish, *Tradition and the Modern World: Reformed Theology in the Nineteenth Century* (London, Chicago: The University of Chicago Press, 1978), 49–70.

120. De Bie and Littlejohn, eds., *Mystical Presence*, 174–211 (201–66); on John 6:51–58, see 205–11 (243–52).

121. De Bie and Littlejohn, eds., *Mystical Presence*, 245–51, esp. 250–51 (297–305, esp. 303–5).

122. Gerrish, *Tradition and the Modern World*, 66.

123. John W. Nevin, *My Own Life: The Early Years*, Papers of the Eastern Chapter, Historical Society of the Evangelical and Reformed Church, no. 1 (Lancaster, PA, 1964), 2.

124. Nevin, *My Own Life*, 8–10.

125. Nevin, *My Own Life*, 139.

126. Nevin, *My Own Life*, 143.

127. De Bie and Littlejohn, eds., *Mystical Presence*, 40–41 (27–28). The italicization of "felt" belongs to Nevin.

128. De Bie and Littlejohn, eds., *Mystical Presence*, 57–65, 258–92 (46–56, 315–59).

129. De Bie and Littlejohn, eds., *Mystical Presence*, 58 (47–48).

130. Charles Hodge, review of *The Mystical Presence: A Vindication of the Reformed or Calvinistic Doctrine of the Holy Eucharist*, by Rev. John W. Nevin, D.D., *Princeton Review* 20, no. 2 (1848): 227–78, 227.

131. Hodge, "Mystical Presence," 227–31.

132. Hodge, "Mystical Presence," 229.

133. Hodge, "Mystical Presence," 251.

134. Hodge, "Mystical Presence," 251.

135. De Bie and Littlejohn, eds., *Mystical Presence*, 227 (271).

136. De Bie and Littlejohn, eds., *Mystical Presence*, 241, 258–92, 292–314 (291–92, 315–59, 359–401).

137. Gerrish, *Tradition and the Modern World*, 61–63.

138. Hodge, "Mystical Presence," 271.

139. Gerrish, *Tradition and the Modern World*, 61–63.

140. Gerrish, *The Old Protestantism and the New*, 110–11; emphasis belongs to Gerrish.

141. A quick check with colleagues who teach preaching has revealed what I had suspected. Despite employing a great many heuristic tools to explain what preaching does—linguistic theory, phenomenology, political theory and language, and so on—no substantial monograph that anyone can think of addresses what I take to be the key Reformation insight: preaching communicates the divine reality itself.

142. Karl Barth, *Church Dogmatics: The Doctrine of the Word of God*, I/1, ed. G. W. Bromiley and T. F. Torrance (Edinburgh: T. & T. Clark, 1975). Hereafter cited as CD, followed by volume number, part number, and page number.

143. Karl Barth, *Church Dogmatics: The Doctrine of Reconciliation*, IV/4, ed. G. W. Bromiley and T. F. Torrance (Edinburgh: T. & T. Clark, 2009).

144. CD I/1, 11.

145. CD I/1, 47.

146. CD I/1, 67–68.

147. CD I/1, 68.

148. CD I/1 68.

149. CD I/1, 69–70.

150. CD I/1 70.

151. CD IV/1, 71: Barth here citing with approval the Lutheran Hermann Bezzel. Barth gives the reference for the quotation as Johannes Rupprecht, *Hermann Bezzel als Theologe* (Munich: C. Kaiser, 1925), 369.

152. Markus Barth, *Die Taufe—Ein Sakrament?* (Zollikon-Zurich: Evangelischer Verlag, 1951). For entrance to Karl Barth on baptism, and his changing views on baptism, see Riggs, *Baptism*, 94–95.

153. CD IV/1, 88; citing *Institutes* 4.14.18.

154. Here the comments by Donald K. McKim are concisely accurate; see *Theological Turning Points* (Atlanta: John Knox Press, 1988), 174.

155. Donald M. Baillie, *The Theology of the Sacraments and Other Papers* (New York: Charles Scribner's Sons, 1957). The chapters on the sacraments (37–124) were originally lectures given at the Presbyterian Theological Seminary, San Anselmo, California, during 1952 (9).

156. Baillie, *Theology of the Sacraments*, 42–47, 45–56.

157. Baillie, *Theology of the Sacraments*, 47–49.

158. Baillie, *Theology of the Sacraments*, 51.

159. Baillie, *Theology of the Sacraments*, 53.

160. Baillie, *Theology of the Sacraments*, 59.

161. Baillie, *Theology of the Sacraments*, 61–67.

162. Baillie, *Theology of the Sacraments*, 93.

163. Baillie, *Theology of the Sacraments*, 94–95.

164. Baillie, *Theology of the Sacraments*, 96.

165. Baillie, *Theology of the Sacraments*, 96.

166. Baillie, *Theology of the Sacraments*, 97–99.

167. Baillie, *Theology of the Sacraments*, 102.

168. Baillie, *Theology of the Sacraments*, 102–3.

169. Baillie, *Theology of the Sacraments*, 102–6.

170. At its best, this seems to have been Hodge's point to Nevin when he argued that central to the Reformed faith is the "sacrificial virtue" of the body broken for us, which secures our forgiveness and which we accept in faith. Nevin's reply was essentially twofold—one part historical, the other part constructive ("scientific"). Nevin was simply correct that, historically speaking, the Reformed tradition, and certainly Calvin and all the key confessions, asserted that believers were mystically engrafted into Christ and were deepened in that union through the Supper, which was indeed a nourishment by the true body and the true blood of Christ.

At the same time, Nevin realized that the basic concepts that Calvin used for mystical union were themselves historically situated, and so Nevin interpreted the Reformed witness of mystical union using concepts credible to a modern context (De Bie and Littlejohn, eds., *Mystical Presence*, 138–73 [15–200]). For Nevin, Calvin struggled at three key points, all because he had "a false psychology as applied either to the person of Christ or the person of his people" (138). By rethinking what we would call philosophical anthropology—the fundamental structure of self-hood in relationship to the structure of reality as such—Nevin tried to put Calvin's teaching on mystical union in the Supper on more solid ground, and he tried to do so with an approach that he thought was appropriate to the biblical witness (De Bie and Littlejohn, eds., *Mystical Presence*, 174–221 [201–66]).

CHAPTER 6: RETROSPECT AND PROSPECT

1. On this Scripture passage, see my theological commentary on Proper 4 of the Revised Common Lectionary, in *Feasting on the Word: Year B, Vol. 1*, ed. David L. Bartlett and Barbara Brown Taylor (Louisville, KY: Westminster John Knox Press, 2008), 422–27.

2. See the comments by Schubert Ogden in *The Understanding of Christian Faith* (Eugene, OR: Cascade Books, 2010), 9–13.

3. See Albert Bates Lord, *The Singer of Tales* (Cambridge, MA: Harvard University Press, 1981).

4. Again, see chap. 1 (pp. 4–9) and esp. nn. 26–61.

5. For these descriptions, and why they have been given, see the beginning of chap. 4.

6. Much of Marxsen's most important work now has been translated into English. For the best introduction to his insights, and why form criticism remains so important, see the introductory essay by Philip Devenish in *Jesus and the Church: The Beginnings of Christianity* (Philadelphia: Trinity Press Int., 1992), xi–xxxv. Also see Marxsen, *The Beginnings of Christology; together with The Lord's Supper as a Christological Problem*, trans. Paul J. Achtemeier and Lorenz Nieting, intro. John Reumann (Philadelphia : Fortress Press, 1979); idem, "Christology in the NT," in *The Interpreter's Dictionary of the Bible: Supplementary Volume* (Nashville: Abingdon Press, 1976); idem, "The Limits to the Possibility of Christological Assertions," in *Witness and Existence: Essays in Honor of Schubert M. Ogden*, ed. Philip E. Devenish and George L. Goodwin, trans. Philip E. Devenish, 43–54 (Chicago: University of Chicago Press, 1989); idem, *New Testament Foundations for Christian Ethics*, trans. O. C. Dean Jr. (Edinburgh : T. & T. Clark, 1993).

7. In particular see Marxsen, *Jesus and the Church*, xxix–xxx, 1–15 ("Jesus Has Many Names"), and 55–75 ("Jesus of Nazareth: An Event").

8. Marxsen, *Jesus and the Church*, 76–95 ("When Did Christian Faith Begin?"); idem, "Christology in the NT."

9. "Christology in the NT," 147.

10. "Christology in the NT," 147.

11. *Jesus and the Church*, 64–66.

12. *Jesus and the Church*, 55–75.

13. *Jesus and the Church*, 67.

14. *Jesus and the Church*, 65; the italics belong to Marxsen.

15. Marxsen, *Jesus and the Church*, xvi–xix.

16. Marxsen, *Jesus and the Church*, 60; idem, "Christology in the NT," 147.

17. Note that by borrowing from Marxsen's description of the normative Christian canon (the form-critical kerygmata), wherein continually "Jesus enacted the

act of God" (*Jesus and the Church*, 60), we end with a triune structure to this description of the Supper. The three "persons" have the same intrinsic character: "Father" (acting inwardly in and to each moment, accepting all through divine grace); "Son" (en-acting outwardly at table this radical acceptance of God); and "Spirit" (re-en-acting outwardly at table God's gracious acting that Jesus enacted).

"Father"	Inward	Act
"Son"	Outward	En-act
"Spirit"	Outward	Re-en-act

18. Rordorf convincingly argues that it was just such an epiphanic encounter at table, after Jesus' crucifixion, that first led to the proclamation of the "Lord's day," and *then later* to the dating of Jesus' resurrection as occurring on the "Lord's Day," which was to become "Sunday." Put another way, the point to Rordorf's study is simply that Sunday was chosen as the central worship day of the early church, not by linking it to *an historical event* ("resurrection"), but because of *the existential encounter* with Jesus at table-sharing after the crucifixion. On this view, the classic and successful interpretation of the development of the whole church year as beginning from Sunday (McArthur) can now be seen *to begin with Jesus' table-sharing* and not the resurrection of Jesus. See Willy Rordorf, *Sunday*, trans. A. A. K. Graham (Philadelphia: Westminster Press, 1968); A. Allan McArthur, *The Evolution of the Christian Year* (London: SCM Press, 1953). Also see John W. Riggs, "Eschatology of Table Sharing: On the Origins of Christian Worship," *Eden Journal* 1, no. 2 (May 1992): 45–60, which makes this argument in detail, taking up the influential works of Thomas Talley, *The Origins of the Liturgical Year* (Collegeville, MN: Liturgical Press, 1991), and August Strobel, *Ursprung und Geschichte des frühchristlichen Osterkalenders* (Berlin: Akademie-Verlag, 1977).

19. See Willi Marxsen, *Das Neue Testament als Buch der Kirche* (Gütersloh: Gütersloher Verlagshaus Gerd Mohn, 1966) [Eng. trans. *The New Testament as the Church's Book*, trans. James E. Mignard (Philadelphia: Fortress Press, 1966)]; Schubert M. Ogden, *On Theology* (San Francisco: Harper & Row, 1986), 45–68; idem, "Sources of Religious Authority in Liberal Protestantism," *Journal of the American Academy of Religion* 44 (1976): 403–16; idem, *Doing Theology Today*, 36–51, which somewhat develops the previous approach by distinguishing the norm of "fittingness."

20. As I mentioned earlier, it was my privilege to serve eight years on the Reformed-Roman Catholic dialogue group that took up the subjects of baptism and the Supper, producing significant ecumenical documents in the process.

21. See *Jesus and the Church*, xxv–xxviii.

22. For this phrase, see Marxsen, *Die Sache Jesu geht weiter* (Gütersloh: Gütersloher Verlagshaus Gerd Mohn, 1976). This book contains an essay, translated in the collection *Jesus and the Church* ("The Jesus-business: In Defense of a Concept," 16–35), whose opening sentence provided the title of the book "The Jesus-business continues!"

23. *Jesus and the Church*, xxviii.

24. *Jesus and the Church*, 34–35.

25. *Jesus and the Church*, xvi–xxiv.

26. *Jesus and the Church*, 60–61.

27. *Jesus and the Church* ("Jesus Has Many Names"), 1–15.

28. *Jesus and the Church*, 67, 8.

29. This is why "Jesus has many names" (*Jesus and the Church*, 1–15). In this regard, Marxsen's form-critical observations are strikingly postmodern. See Riggs, *Postmodern Christianity* (Harrisburg, PA: Trinity Press Int., 2003), 115.

30. See, e.g., *Jesus and the Church*, 144–46.

31. While in their own way all the essays of *Jesus and the Church* make this point, see particularly "Jesus of Nazareth: An Event" (55–75) and "When Did Christian Faith Begin?" (76–95).

32. *Jesus and the Church*, xxv, xxv–xviii.

33. As for being "normative," I repeat what was said above in the text: The Jesus-kerygma stands as the *norma normans sed non normata* (the norm that norms but is not normed) for what is appropriate to Jesus—its "Christianness," so to speak—which is not to say that it is the only theological norm, although it *is* the ultimate norm for whether something is "Christian" as such.

34. *Jesus and the Church*, 48–49. By "kerygma theology" Marxsen, of course, refers to the "dialectical theology" (48) typified by the work of Rudolf Bultmann and Karl Barth.

35. *Jesus and the Church*, 48.

36. For the beginning shape of the christological question and Ogden's answer, see his classic study on Bultmann, *Christ without Myth* (New York: Harper, 1961). Ogden lays out the christological point in detail in *The Point of Christology* (San Francisco: Harper & Row, 1982). Also see Ogden, "A Priori Christology and Experience," in *Doing Theology Today* (Valley Forge, PA: Trinity Press, 1996), 123–38, where Ogden shows that constitutive Christologies, whether classical or revisionary, "presuppose an a priori christology that stipulates a condition for making or implying the assertion truly that no experience could ever show to be fulfilled" (135).

37. See Marxsen's classic essay, "Jesus Has Many Names," in *Jesus and the Church*, 1–15.

38. *Jesus and the Church*, 9.

39. *Jesus and the Church*, 15.

40. For Ogden's foundational studies, see *Christ without Myth* and "The Reality of God," in *The Reality of God and Other Essays* (New York: Harper & Row, 1966), 1–70. For further explication of revelation as re-presentational, see *On Theology* (San Francisco: Harper & Row, 1986), 22–44; *Faith and Freedom*, rev. and enl. ed (Nashville: Abingdon Press, 1989); *Is There Only One True Religion or Are There Many?* (Dallas: Southern Methodist Press, 1992); "Is There Only One True Religion or Are There Many?" in *Doing Theology Today*, 169–84; and "A Priori Christology and Experience," in *Doing Theology Today*, 123–38.

41. Ogden, *On Theology*, 43.

42. Recall, again, Marxsen's phrase, "Jesus of Nazareth—an event" (*Jesus von Nazareth—ein Ereignis*). For this citation, see Ogden, "Is There Only One True Religion or Are There Many?" 182.

43. Ogden, "Is There Only One True Religion or Are There Many?" 182.

44. *Jesus and the Church*, 65.

45. Ogden, *On Theology*, 43. Note also that Bultmann correctly saw there to be direct continuity between the so-called "historical Jesus" and the kerygma as such. (Also note, in passing, that I have tried to avoid the mistaken alternatives

of "historical Jesus" and "kerygmatic Christ" by talking about the "kerygmatic-Jesus" that is the ontic pole of the kerygmatic encounter.) See also *Jesus and the Church*, xxv–xxviii, 36–54 ("Jesus–Bearer or Content of the Gospel?"). For a thorough critique of the so-called New Quest, and numerous references to Bultmann's understanding of continuity between Jesus and the kerygma, see Schubert M. Ogden and Van A. Harvey, "How New is the 'New Quest of the Historical Jesus'?" in *The Historical Jesus and the Kerygmatic Christ*, ed. Carl E. Braaten and Roy A. Harrisville (New York: Abingdon Press, 1964), 197–242.

46. *The First Epistle of Paul to the Corinthians*, trans. John W. Fraser (Calvin's New Testament Commentaries, vol. 9, ed. David W. Torrance and Thomas F. Torrance) (Grand Rapids: Eerdmans, 1979), 24.

47. Ogden, *Doing Theology Today*, 123–38.

48. *Jesus and the Church*, xxvi.

49. In the Reformed-Roman Catholic dialogue, during one session I commented to our Roman Catholic colleagues that, from a Reformed perspective, the Reformed teaching on the Supper has a structure of "Thou-I," while the Roman Catholic teaching has a structure of "Thou-It/It-I." To this comment, which I had expected to bring unhappy retort, my Roman Catholic colleagues said, "Yes, that's right, the elements are *so* important." At that point I realized how different were the pieties that underlay our teachings.

50. Ogden, *On Theology*, 43. These two sets of descriptions seem to me dynamically equivalent, one from the exegetical perspective of "Jesus-as-acting," the other from the constructive perspective of Jesus as representational revelation.

51. *The Reality of God*, 37–43; also compare 120–43. Note carefully that the phrase "strictly necessary" properly points to the realm of metaphysics, which concerns those features of reality that simply must apply and cannot fail to be assumed by anyone. As Ogden says of original confidence, "Always presupposed by even the most commonplace of moral decisions is the confidence that these decisions have an unconditional significance. No matter what the content of our choices may be whether for this course of action or for that, we can make them at all only because of our invincible faith that they somehow make a difference which no turn of events in the future has the power to annul" (*Reality of God*, 36, also see 41–43).

For the groundwork of this metaphysics in Ogden's work, and its connection to Christology, see *Christ without Myth*. Also see Ogden, *The Reality of God*, 90–98, and more recently, *Doing Theology Today*, 187–209. For entrance to the analysis by Charles Hartshorne, whose metaphysics has largely been appropriated by Ogden, see "Metaphysical Statements as Nonrestrictive and Existential," *Review of Metaphysics* (September 1958): 35–47; and, *The Logic of Perfection* (LaSalle, IL: Open Court, 1962), 280–97. As Hartshorne puts the matter in simple terms, "metaphysical truths may be described as such that no experience can contradict them, but also such that any experience must illustrate them." For example, says Hartshorne, "Take the sayings, 'Life has a meaning,' or 'There are real values,' or 'Some ways of thinking and acting are better than others.' In no case can these affirmations rightfully be denied, for if life itself is never worthwhile, then neither is the denial of life's worthwhileness ever worthwhile, since this denial itself is a piece of life, an act of a living being. And to say that no way of thinking is better than any other is to say that the way of thinking thus expressed is no better than the contradictory way, and such a manner of talking nullifies itself" (*The Logic of Perfection*, 285–87). Hartshorne goes on to say that "metaphysics gives us no fact, ordinary or superior, but it gives us the key to fact, on both levels, the clue or ideal by which factual experience is to be interpreted. It gives us a sense of what a German theologian has called the accompanying melody, *Begleitmelodie*, of all existence. The import of the word 'God' is no mere special meaning in our language, but the soul of significance in general, for it refers to the Life in and for which all things live" (*The Logic of Perfection*, 297).

Relative to the Supper, the question of metaphysics needs to be raised briefly, because Roman Catholic theologians in the Reformed–Roman Catholic Dialogue raised the issue—rightly so, on my view—that, whereas their (metaphysical) teaching on the "real presence" specifies how the "real presence" happens in reality itself, the Reformed teaching, which historically has lacked a metaphysics, falls short in its ability to explain meaningfully the "true presence" of Jesus and so lapses into mere confessionalism.

52. *The Reality of God*, 37; *On Theology*, 43.

53. Compare Ogden's comment that "[w]hereas original revelation, we may say, is *immediately* and *proximately* necessary to our authenticity, decisive revelation is only *mediately* and *remotely* necessary to it, being necessary in the first instance not to the constitution of our possibility, but to its full and adequate explication (cf. Wesley: 2:451–52, 456–57)" (*On Theology*, 41).

54. For a further discussion on this point, see Philip E. Devenish, "The Sovereignty of Jesus and the Sovereignty of God," *Theology Today* 53 (1996): 63–73; also see Riggs, *Postmodern Christianity*, 111–18.

55. See chapter 1, pp. 32–33, nn. 219–28.

56. "But when forsooth they do not possess a single one of Luther's virtues, by their lusty bawling they give themselves out for his genuine disciples. As if indeed to *ape*, and to *imitate*, any person, were not very different things" (Calvin to Martin Sideman, March 14, 1555, *Selected Works of John Calvin: Tracts and Letters*, 6 vols., ed. Henry Beveridge and Jules Bonnet (Grand Rapids: Baker Book House, 1983), 6:159–60; xxix–xxx CO 15:501–2).

57. On the convergence here between the Reformed tradition and a modern Roman Catholic eucharistic teaching, see Jill Raitt, "Roman Catholic New Wine in Reformed Old Bottles? The Conversion of the Elements in the Eucharistic Doctrines of Theodore Beza and Edward Schillebeeckx," *Journal of Ecumenical Studies* 8 (1971): 581–604.

BIBLIOGRAPHY

Abba, Raymond. "Calvin's Doctrine of the Lord's Supper." *Reformed Theological Review* 9, no. 2 (Winter 1950): 1–12.

Achtemeier, Paul. "The Origin and Function of Pre-Markan Miracle Catenae." *Journal for Biblical Literature* 91 (1972): 198–221.

Adam, Karl. *Eucharistielehre des hl. Augustin.* Paderborn: F. Schöningh, 1908.

———. "Zur Eucharistielehre des hl. Augustinus." *Theologie Quartalschrift* 112 (1931).

Allix, Pierre. *Historia transsubstantiationis papalis.* London: Thomas Roycroft, 1675.

Althaus, Paul. *Communio Sanctorum.* Munich: Chr. Kaiser Verlag, 1929.

———. *Die Theologie Martin Luthers.* Gütersloh: Gerd Mohn, 1962. Translated by Robert C. Schulz as *The Theology of Martin Luther* (Philadelphia: Fortress Press, 1966).

Amos, N. Scott. "The Alsatian among the Athenians: Martin Bucer, Mid-Tudor Cambridge and the Edwardian Reformation." *Reformation and Rennaisance Review* 4, no. 1 (2002): 94–124.

———. "'It Is Fallow Ground Here': Martin Bucer as Critic of the English Reformation." *Westminster Theological Journal* 61 (1999): 41–52.

———. "Martin Bucer and the Revision of the 1549 Book of Common Prayer: Reform of Ceremonies and the Didactic Use of Ritual." *Reformation and Renaissance Review* (1999): 107–26.

Aquinas, Thomas. *Summa Theologica.* Translated by Blackfriars. New York: McGraw-Hill, 1964.

Armstrong, Brian G. "Calvin and Calvinism." In *Reformation Europe: A Guide to Research II,* edited by William S. Maltby, 75–103. St. Louis: Center for Reformation Research, 1992.

Bächtold, Hans. "Heinrich Bullinger und Oberschwaben." *Zeitschrift für Bayerische Kirchengeschichte* 64 (1995): 1–19.

Backus, Irena. "Bucer's Commentary on the Gospel of John." In *Martin Bucer: Reforming Church and Community,* edited by D. F. Wright, 61–71. Cambridge: Cambridge University Press, 1994.

———. "Calvin. Saint, Hero or the Worst of All Possible Christians?" In *Calvinus sacrarum literarum interpres,* edited by Herman J. Selderhuis, 223–43. Göttingen: Vandenhoeck & Ruprecht, 2008.

Baillie, Donald M. *The Theology of the Sacraments and Other Papers.* New York: Charles Scribner's Sons, 1957.

Bainton, Roland. *Here I Stand!* New York: Abingdon-Cokesbury Press, 1950.

Baker, J. Wayne. "Covenant and Community in the Thought of Heinrich Bullinger." In *The Covenant Connection: From Federal Theology to Modern Federalism*, edited by Daniel J. Elazar and John Kincaid, 15–29. Lanham, MD: Lexington Books, 2000.

———. *Heinrich Bullinger and the Covenant: The Other Reformed Tradition.* Athens: Ohio University Press, 1980.

Bakhuizen van den Brink, J. N., ed. *De corpore et sanguine Domini: Texte originale et notice bibliographique.* Amsterdam: North Holland, 1974.

Balke, Willem. *Omgang met de reformatoren.* Kampen: Uitgeverij de Groot Goudriaan, 1992.

Barclay, Alexander. *The Protestant Doctrine of the Lord's Supper.* Glasgow: Jackson, Wylie, 1927.

Barth, Hans-Martin. "'. . . sehen, wie freundlich der Herr ist?' Das Verhältnis von Wort, Bild und Sakrament im Protestantismus." *Kerygma und Dogma* 39 (July 1993): 247–63.

Barth, Karl. *Church Dogmatics.* Vol. I/1, *The Doctrine of the Word of God.* Edited by G. W. Bromiley and T. F. Torrance. Edinburgh: T. & T. Clark, 1975.

———. *Church Dogmatics.* Vol. IV/4, *The Doctrine of Reconciliation.* Edited by G. W. Bromiley and T. F. Torrance. Edinburgh: T. & T. Clark, 2009.

Barth, Markus. *Die Taufe—Ein Sakrament?* Zollikon-Zurich: Evangelischer Verlag, 1951.

Barth, Peter. "Calvins Stellung im Abendmahlsstreit." *Die christliche Welt* 43 (1929): 922–29.

Batiffol, Pierre. *L'Eucharistie, la présence réelle et la transsubstantiation.* 2nd ed. Paris: Librairie Victor Lecoffre, 1905. 5th ed. Paris: Librairie Victor Lecoffre, 1913.

Battles, Ford Lewis. "God Was Accommodating Himself to Human Capacity." *Interpretation* 31 (1977): 19–38.

Bauer, Karl. "Die Abendmahlslehre Zwinglis bis zum Beginn der Auseinandersetzung mit Luther." *Theologische Blätter* 5 (1926): 217–26.

———. "Symbolik und Realpräsenz in der Abendmahlsanschauung Zwinglis bis 1525. Eine Erwiderung." *Zeitschrift für Kirchengeschichte* 46 (1927): 97–105.

Baur, August. *Zwinglis Theologie: Ihr Werden und ihr System.* 2 vols. Halle: M. Niemeyer, 1885–89.

Beckmann, Joachim. *Vom Sakrament bei Calvin: Die Sakramentslehre Calvins in ihren Beziehungen zu Augustin.* Tübingen: J. C. B. Mohr, 1926.

Beekenkamp, W. B. *De avondmaalsleer van Berengarius van Tours.* Kerkhistorische studien 1. The Hague: M. Nijhoff, 1941.

———. *De Sacra Coena adversus Lanfrancum.* Kerkhistorische studien 2. The Hague: M. Nijhoff, 1941.

Berg, Hans G. vom. "Die Brüder von Gemeinsamen Leben und die Stiftsschule von St. Martin zu Emmerich. Zur Frage des Einflusses der Devotio moderna auf den Jungen Bullinger." In *Heinrich Bullinger 1504–1575: Gesammelte Aufsätze zum 400. Todestag.* Vol. 1. Edited by Ulrich Gäbler and Erland Herkenrath. Zurich: Theologischer Verlag, 1975.

Berkouwer, G. C. *The Sacraments*. Translated by Hugo Bekker. Grand Rapids: Eerdmans, 1969.

Berrouard, Marie-François. "L'être sacramentel de l'eucharistie selon saint Augustin: Commentaire de Jean VI. 60–63 dans le Tractatus XXVII, 1–6 et 11–12 in Iohannis Evangelium." *Nouvelle Revue Theologique* 99, no. 5 (1977): 702–21.

Betz, Johannes, SJ. *Eucharistie: In der Schrift und Patristik*. Freiburg: Herder, 1979.

———. *Die Eucharistie in der Zeit der griechischen Väter*. 2 vols. Freiburg: Herder, 1961, 1964.

Bichon, J. "La doctrine de la Sante-Cène chez Luther, Zwingli, et Calvin." *Foi et Vie* 43, no. 4 (1946): 404–9.

Bielfeldt, Dennis. "Response to Sammeli Juntunen, 'Luther and Metaphysics.'" In *Union with Christ: The New Finnish Interpretation of Luther*, edited by Carl E. Braaten and Robert W. Jenson, 161–66. Grand Rapids: Eerdmans, 1998.

Billings, J. Todd. *Calvin, Participation, and the Gift: The Activity of Believers in Union with Christ*. Oxford and New York: Oxford University Press, 2007.

Bizer, Ernst. *Studien zur Geschichte des Abendmahlsstreits im 16. Jahrhundert*. Darmstadt: Wissenschaftliche Buchgesellschaft, 1962.

Blanke, Fritz. "Antwort auf Wilhelm Niesel: Zwinglis 'spätere Sakramentsanschauung.'" *Theologische Blätter* 11 (1931): 18.

———. *Der junge Bullinger*. Zurich: Zwingli Verlag, 1942.

———. "Zum Verständnis der Abendmahlslehre Zwinglis." *Pastoraltheologie. Monatsschrift zur Vertiefung des gesamten pfarramtlichen Wirkens* 27 (1931): 314–20.

———. "Zwinglis Sakramentsanschauung." *Theologische Blätter* 10 (1931): 283–90.

Blanke, Fritz, and Immanuel Leuschner. *Heinrich Bullinger: Vater der reformierten Kirche*. Zurich: Theologischer Verlag, 1990.

Bonner, Gerard. "Augustine's Understanding of the Church as a Eucharistic Community." In *Saint Augustine the Bishop: A Book of Essays*, edited by Fannie LeMoine and Christopher Kleinhenz, 39–63. New York: Garland, 1994.

———. "The Doctrine of Sacrifice: Augustine and the Latin Patristic Tradition." In *Sacrifice and Redemption: Durham Essays in Theology*, 101–17. Cambridge: Cambridge University Press, 1991.

The Book of Common Prayer. New York: Seabury Press, 1979.

Borg, Marcus J. *Conflict, Holiness and Politics in the Teaching of Jesus*. Harrisburg, PA: Trinity Press International, 1998.

———. *Jesus: A New Vision*. New York: Harper & Row, 1987.

Bornkamm, Günther. *Jesus of Nazareth*. New York: Harper & Row, 1960.

———. "Mysterion." In *Theological Dictionary of the New Testament*, edited by Gerhard Kittel, translated and edited by Geoffrey W. Bromiley, 4:803ff. Grand Rapids: Eerdmans, 1967.

Bornkamm, Heinrich. *Luther's World of Thought*. Translated by M. H. Bertram. St. Louis: Concordia Publishing House, 1958.

Bosshard, Stefan Niklaus. *Zwingli-Erasmus-Cajetan: Die Eucharistie als Zeichen der Einheit*. Wiesbaden: Steiner, 1978.

Bouvier, André. *Henri Bullinger, Réformateur et Conseiller Oecuménique: Le Successeur de Zwingli*. Neuchâtel: Imprimerie Delachaux et Niestlé, 1940.

Bouwsma, William. *John Calvin: A Sixteenth-Century Portrait*. New York: Oxford University Press, 1988.

Bouyer, Louis. *The Christian Mystery*. Edinburgh: T. & T. Clark, 1989.

Bradshaw, Paul F. *Eucharistic Origins*. Oxford: Oxford University Press, 2004.

———. *The Search for the Origins of Christian Worship*. 2nd ed. New York: Oxford University Press, 2002.

Brecht, Martin. "Hat Zwingli seinen Brief an Matthäus Alber über das Abendmahl abgesandt?" *Archiv* 58, no. 1 (1967): 100–102.

———. "Luthers Beziehungen zu den Oberdeutschen und Schweizern von 1530–1531 bis 1546." In *Leben und Werk Martin Luthers von 1526 bis 1546*, edited by Hjalmar Junghans, 497–517. Göttingen: Vandenhoeck & Ruprecht, 1983.

———. *Martin Luther: His Road to Reformation, 1483–1521*. Translated by James L. Schaaf. Philadelphia: Fortress Press, 1985.

———. *Martin Luther: Shaping and Defining the Reformation, 1521–1532*. Translated by James L. Schaaf. Minneapolis: Fortress Press, 1990.

———. *Martin Luther: The Preservation of the Church, 1532–1546*. Translated by James L. Schaaf. Minneapolis: Fortress Press, 1993.

Breech, James. *The Silence of Jesus*. Philadelphia: Fortress Press, 1983.

Brenz, Johannes. *Anecdota Brentiana: Ungedruckte Briefe und Bedenken*. Edited by Theodor Pressel. Tübingen: J. J. Heckenhauer, 1868.

Brilioth, Yngve. *Eucharistic Faith and Practice: Evangelical and Catholic*. Translated by A. G. Herbert. London: SPCK, 1953.

Bromiley, G. W., ed. *Zwingli and Bullinger*. Library of Christian Classics 24. Philadelphia: Westminster Press, 1953.

Browe, Peter. "Die Elevation in der Messe." *Jahrbuch für Liturgiewissenschaft* 9 (1929): 20–66.

———. *Die Verehrung der Eucharistie im Mittelalter*. 1933. Reprint, Rome: Herder, 1967.

Bucer, Martin. *Correspondance de Martin Bucer*. Edited by Jean Roth. Leiden: E. J. Brill, 1989.

———. *Enarrationum in evangelia Matthaei, Marci et Lucae libri duo*. Vol. 2. In August Lang, *Der Evangelienkommentar Martin Butzers und die Grundzüge seiner Theologie*. Studien zur Geschichte der Theologie und der Kirche, Bd II, edited by N. Bonwetsch and R. Seeberg. Leipzig: Dieterich'sche Verlags-Buchhandlung Theodore Weicher, 1900.

———. *Martin Bucers Deutsche Schriften*. Bd. 1. Gütersloh: Gütersloher Verlagshaus Gerd Mohn; Paris: Presses universitaires de France, 1960.

———. *Martini Buceri Opera Latina*. Vol. V, *Defensio adversus axioma catholicum id est criminationem R. P. Roberti Episcopi Abrincensis (1534)*. Edited by William Ian P. Hazlett. Leiden: Brill, 2000.

———. *Martini Buceri Opera Latina*. Vol. 2, *Enarratio in Evangelion Iohannis (1528, 1530, 1536)*. Edited by Irena Backus. Leiden: E. J. Brill, 1988.

Bühler, Pierre. "Bullinger als Systematiker: Am Beispiel der Confessio Helvetica Posterior." *Zwingliana* 31 (2004): 215–36.

Bullinger, Henry. *The Decades of Henry Bullinger*. Edited by Thomas Harding. 3 vols. Cambridge: University Press, 1852.

———. *Warhaffte Bekanntnuss der Dieneren der Kirchen zů Zürych*. Zurich: Froschauer, 1545.

———. *Werke*. 3d Abt. *Theologische Schriften*, Bd. 2. Edited by Bernhard Schneider. Zurich: Theologischer Verlag Zürich, 1991.

Bultmann, Rudolf. *Christ without Myth*. New York: Harper, 1961.

———. *Existence and Faith: Shorter Writings of Rudolf Bultmann*. Translated by Schubert M. Ogden. New York: Meridian Books, 1960.

———. *The Gospel of John*. Translated by G. R. Beasley-Murray. Philadelphia: Westminster Press, 1971.

———. *The History of the Synoptic Tradition*. Translated by John Marsh. New York: Harper & Row, 1963.

Burnett, Amy Nelson. "Basel and the Wittenberg Concord." *Archiv für Reformationsgeschichte* 96 (2005): 33–56.

Büsser, Fritz. *Heinrich Bullinger (1504–1575): Leben, Werk und Wirkung*. Zurich: Theologischer Verlag, 2004.

———. *Henirich Bullinger Werke*. Zurich: Theologischer Verlag, 1972–.

Cadier, Jean. *La doctrine Calviniste de la Sainte Cène*. Montpellier: Institut protestant de théologie, 1951.

Calvin, John. *Commentaries on the Last Four Books of Moses*. Translated by Charles William Bingham. Grand Rapids: Eerdmans, 1950.

———. *The Epistles of Paul the Apostle to the Romans and to the Thessalonians*. Translated by Ross Mackenzie. Calvin's New Testament Commentaries 8. Grand Rapids: Wm. B. Eerdmans, 1974–75.

———. *The First Epistle of Paul the Apostle to the Corinthians*. Translated by John W. Fraser. Calvin's New Testament Commentaries 9. Grand Rapids: Wm. B. Eerdmans, 1974–75.

———. *Institutes of the Christian Religion of John Calvin 1539: Text and Concordance*. Edited by Richard F. Wevers. 4 vols. Grand Rapids: H. Henry Meeter Center for Calvin Studies, 1988.

———. *Ioannis Calvini opera quae supersunt Omnia*. Edited by Wilhelm Baum, Edward Cunitz, and Edward Reuss. Volumes 29–87 of *Corpus Reformatorum*. Brunswick: C. A. Schwetschke and Son (M. Bruhn), 1863–1900.

———. *Ioannis Calvini opera selecta*. Edited by Peter Barth, Wilhelm Niesel, and Dora Scheuner. 5 vols. Munich: Chr. Kaiser, 1926–52.

———. *Selected Works of John Calvin: Tracts and Letters*. Edited by Henry Beveridge and Jules Bonnet. 6 vols. Grand Rapids: Baker Book House, 1983.

Camelot, Th. "Réalisme et symbolisme dans la doctrine eucharistique de s. Augustin." *Revue des sciences philosophiques et théologiques* 31 (1947): 394–410.

Chapman, Mark. "Sacrament and Sacrifice in the Theology of the Mass according to Martin Luther." *One in Christ* 28 (1992): 248–66.

Chavanes, Henry. "La presence réelle chez saint Thomas et chez Calvin." *Verbum Caro* 13, no. 50 (1959): 151–70.

Cheyne, Alex. "The Scots Confession of 1560." *Theology Today* 17 (1960): 323–38.

Chilton, Bruce. *A Feast of Meanings*. Leiden: E. J. Brill, 1994.

———. *The Temple of Jesus*. University Park: Pennsylvania State University, 1992.

Cochrane, Arthur C., ed. *Reformed Confessions of the Sixteenth Century*. Philadelphia: Westminster Press, 1966.

Congar, Y. "Le 'mysterion' appliqué aux sacrements, traduit par 'sacramentum' dans l'église ancienne." In *Un peuple messianique*, 47–55. Paris: Cerf, 1974.

Constitution of the Presbyterian Church (U.S.A.), Part I, *Book of Confessions*. Louisville, KY: Office of the General Assembly, Presbyterian Church (U.S.A.), 2004.

Cornford, F. M. *Before and after Socrates*. Cambridge: Cambridge University Press, 1932.

Corpus Scriptorum Ecclesiasticorum Latinorum. Vindolsonae: C. Geroldi Filium Bibliopolam Academiae; F. Tempsky; Holdes-Pichles Tempsky, 1866–.

Courvoisier, Jaques. "Reflexions à propos de la doctrine eucharistique de Zwingli et de Calvin." In *Festgabe Leonhard von Muralt*, edited by Martin Haas and Rene Hauswirth, 258–64. Zurich: Verlag Berichthaus, 1970.

———. "Vom Abendmahl bei Zwingli." *Zwingliana* 11, no. 7 (1962): 415–26.

———. *Zwingli: A Reformed Theologian*. Richmond, VA: John Knox Press, 1963.

Crisman, Miriam Usher. *Strasbourg and the Reform: A Study in the Process of Change*. New Haven, CT: Yale University Press, 1967.

Crockett, William R. "Calvin." In *Eucharist: Symbol of Transformation*, 148–63. New York: Pueblo Publishing, 1989.

Croken, Robert C. *Luther's First Front: The Eucharist as Sacrifice*. Ottawa: University of Ottawa Press, 1990.

Cross, Richard. "Catholic, Calvinist, and Lutheran Doctrines of Eucharistic Presence: A Brief Note toward a Rapprochement." *International Journal of Systematic Theology* 4, no. 3 (2002): 301–18.

Crossan, John Dominic. *The Birth of Christianity*. San Francisco: HarperSanFrancisco, 1998.

———. *The Historical Jesus*. San Francisco: HarperSanFrancisco, 1991.

———. *Jesus: A Revolutionary Biography*. San Francisco: HarperSanFrancisco, 1994.

Cumings, Owen. "Medieval Eucharistic Theology." *Emmanuel* (March 1993): 73–79.

Dankbaar, W. F. *De Sacramentsleer van Calvijn*. Amsterdam: H. I. Paris, 1941.

Davis, Thomas J. *The Clearest Promises of God: The Development of Calvin's Eucharistic Teaching*. New York: AMS Press, 1995.

———. *This Is My Body: The Presence of Christ in Reformation Thought*. Grand Rapids: Baker Academic, 2008.

Delling, Gerhard. "Abendmahl: II. Urchristliches Mahl—Verständnis." In *Theologisches Realenzyklopädie*, 1:43–58. Berlin: Walter de Gruyter, 1977.

Denzinger, Heinrich. *The Sources of Catholic Dogma*. Translated by Roy J. Deferrari. St. Louis: Herder, 1957.

————, and Adolf Schönmetzer. *Enchiridion symbolorum: Definitionum et declarationum de rebus fidei et morum*. Barcinone: Herder, 1976.

Devenish, Philip E. "Introduction." In *Jesus and the Church: The Beginnings of Christianity*, selected, translated, and introduced by Philip E. Devenish, xi–xxxv. Philadelphia: Trinity Press International, 1992.

————. "The Sovereignty of Jesus and the Sovereignty of God." *Theology Today* 53 (1996): 63–73.

DeVries, Dawn. *Jesus Christ in the Preaching of Calvin and Schleiermacher*. Louisville, KY: Westminster John Knox Press, 1996.

Diestelmann, Jürgen. *Über die lutherische Messe: Gemeindevorträge und Abhandlungen*. Gross Oesingen: Verlag der Lutherischen Buchhandlung Heinrich Harms, 1998.

Dietzfelbinger, Hermann. "Luthers Abendmahlslehre im Zusammenhang seiner Gedankenwelt." *Theologische Beiträge* 14 (1983): 110–21.

Dix, Dom Gregory. *The Shape of the Liturgy*. London: Dacre Press, 1978.

Doumergue, Emil. *Jean Calvin. Les Hommes et les choses de son temps*. 7 vols. Lausanne: Georges Bridel, 1899–1924.

Dowey, Edward A., Jr. *A Commentary on the Confession of 1967 and an Introduction to The Book of Confessions*. Philadelphia: Westminster Press, 1968.

————. "Heinrich Bullinger's Theology: Thematic, Comprehensive, Schematic." In *Calvin Studies V*, edited by John Leith, 41–60. Richmond, VA: Union Theological Seminary in Virginia, 1991.

————. "Der Theologische Aufbau des Zweiten Helvetischen Bekenntnisses." In *Glauben und Bekennen: Vierhundert Jahre Confessio Helvetica Posterior Beiträge zu ihrer Geschichte und Theologie*, edited by Joachim Staedtke, 205–34. Zurich: Zwingli-Verlag,1966.

Duffy, Regis A. "Sacraments in General." In *Systematic Theology: Roman Catholic Perspectives*, edited by Francis Schüssler Fiorenza and John P. Galvin, 2:183–210. Minneapolis: Fortress Press, 1991.

Dumoutet, Edouard. *Le Christ selon la chair et la vie liturgique au moyen-âge*. Paris: Beauchesne, 1932.

————. *Le désir de voir l'hostie et les origines de la dévotion au sainct-sacrement*. Paris: Duchesne, 1926.

Dupont-Sommer, André. *Le Quatrième Livre des Machabées*. Bibliothèque de l'École des Hautes Études 274. Paris: Librairie Ancienne Honré Champion, 1939.

Dyk, Leanne van. "The Reformed View." In *The Lord's Supper: Five Views*, edited by Gordon T. Smith, 67–82. Downers Grove, IL: IVP Academic, 2008.

Ebeling, Gerhard. *The Word of God and Tradition*. Translated by S. H. Hooke. Philadelphia: Fortress Press, 1968.

Ebrard, August. *Das Dogma vom heiligen Abendmahl und seine Geschichte*. 2 vols. Frankfurt am Main: Heinrich Zimmer, 1845–46.

Edwards, Mark U., Jr. "Luther's Biography." In *Reformation Europe: A Guide to Research II*, edited by William S. Maltby, 5–20. St. Louis: Center for Reformation Research, 1992.

Eells, Hasting. "The Genesis of Martin Bucer's Doctrine of the Supper." *Princeton Theological Review* 24 (1926): 225–51.

————. *Martin Bucer*. New Haven, CT: Yale University Press, 1931.

Eichhorn, Albert. *Das Abendmahl in Neuen Testament*. Leipzig: J. C. B. Mohr, 1898.

Elert, Werner. *Eucharist and Church Fellowship in the First Four Centuries*. Translated by N. E. Nagel. St. Louis: Concordia Publishing House, 1966.

Ella, George, and Joel R. Beeke. Introductions to *The Decades of Henry Bullinger*, edited by Thomas Harding. 2 vols. Grand Rapids: Baker, 2004.

Ellert, Werner. "Luther in Marburg." *Zeitwende* 5 (1929): 315–24.

Empie, Paul C., and James I. McCord, eds. *Marburg Revisited*. Minneapolis: Augsburg, 1966.

Engel, Mary Potter. *John Calvin's Perspectival Anthropology*. Atlanta: Scholars Press, 1988.

Farner, Oskar. "Eine neuentdeckte Ausserung Zwinglis über den Gemeindegesang." *Jahrbuch für Liturgik und Hymnologie* 3 (1957): 130.

————. *Zwingli the Reformer: His Life and Work*. Translated by D. G. Sear. Hamden, CT: Archon Books, 1968.

Farrow, Douglas. "Between the Rock and a Hard Place: In Support of (something like) a Reformed View of the Eucharist." *International Journal of Systematic Theology* 3, no. 2 (2001): 167–86.

————. "In Support of a Reformed View of Ascension and Eucharist." In *Reformed Theology: Identity and Ecumenicity*, edited by Michael Welker and Wallace M. Alston Jr., 351–71. Grand Rapids: Eerdmans, 2003.

Faulkner, J. A. "Luther and the Lord's Supper in the Critical Years, 1517–1522." *Lutheran Quarterly* 45 (April 1915): 202–16.

————. "Luther and the Real Presence." *American Journal of Theology* 21 (1917): 225–39.

Feeley-Harnik, Gillian. *The Lord's Table: Eucharist and Passover in Early Christianity*. Philadelphia: University of Pennsylvania Press, 1981.

Féret, H. M. "Sacramentum Res dans la langue théologique de S. Augustin." *Revue des sciences philosophiques et théologiques* 29 (1940): 218–40.

Finkenzeller, Josef. *Die Lehre von den Sakramenten in allgemeinen: Von der Schrift bis zur Scholastik*. Freiburg: Herder, 1980.

Finn, Thomas M. "Sacraments." In *Encyclopedia of Early Christianity*, edited by Everett Ferguson, 811–15. New York and London: Garland Publishing, 1990.

Fischer, Robert. "Luther's Stake in the Lord's Supper Controversy." *Dialog* 2 (1963): 50–59.

Fitzer, Joseph. "The Augustinian Roots of Calvin's Eucharistic Teaching." *Augustinian Studies* 7 (1976): 69–98.

Forstman, H. Jackson. *Word and Spirit: Calvin's Doctrine of Biblical Authority*. Palo Alto, CA: Stanford University Press, 1962.

Francis of Assisi and Clare of Assisi. *Francis and Clare: The Complete Works*. Translated by Regis J. Armstrong and Ignatius C. Brady. New York: Paulist Press, 1982.

Franklin, R. William. "Eucharistic Humanism Lost and Regained." In *The Case for Christian Humanism*, edited by William Franklin and Joseph Shaw, 116–39. Grand Rapids: Eerdmans, 1991.

Friedrich, Martin. "Heinrich Bullinger und die Wittenberger Konkordie: Ein Ökumeniker im Streit um das Abendmahl." *Zwingliana* 24 (1997): 59–79.

Funk, Robert, ed. *The Acts of Jesus*. San Francisco: HarperSanFrancisco, 1998.

Furnish, Victor P. *Theology and Ethics in Paul*. Nashville: Abingdon Press, 1968.

Gäbler, Ulrich. "Consensus Tigurinus." In *Theologische Realenzyklopädie*, 8:189. New York and Berlin: Walter de Gruyter, 1981.

———. *Huldrych Zwingli: His Life and Work*.Translated by Ruth L. C. Gritsch. Philadelphia: Fortress Press, 1986.

———."Das Zustandekommen des Consensus Tigurinus." *Zwingliana* 9, no. 1 (1949): 323ff.

———. "Das Zustandekommen des Consensus Tigurinus im Jahre 1549." *Theologische Literaturzeitung* 104, no. 5 (1979): 321–32.

Gahey, John F. *The Eucharistic Teaching of Ratramn of Corbie*. Mundelein, IL: Saint Mary of the Lake Seminary, 1951.

Gamble, Richard C. "Calvin's Controversies." In *The Cambridge Companion to John Calvin*, edited by Donald K. McKim, 188–203. Cambridge: Cambridge University Press, 2004.

———. "Sacramental Continuity among Reformed Refugees: Peter Martyr Vermigli and John Calvin." In *Peter Martyr Vermigli and the European Reformations*, edited by Frank A. James III, 97–112. Leiden: Brill, 2004.

Ganoczy, Alexandre. "L'action sacramentaire de Dieu par le Christ selon Calvin." In *Sacrements de Jésus-Christ*, edited by Joseph Doré, 109–29. Paris: Desclée, 1983.

———. "Calvin als paulinischer Theologe." In *Calvinus Theologus: Die Referate des Europäischen Kongresses für Calvinforschung vom 16. bis 19. September 1974 in Amsterdam*, edited by W. H. Neusner. Neukirchen-Vluyn: NeukirchenerVerlag, 1976.

———. *Calvin: Theologien de l'Eglise et du Ministère*. Paris: Éditions du Cerf, 1964.

———. *Le Jeune Calvin, Genèse et évolution de sa vocation réformatrice*. Wiesbaden: Franz Steiner Verlag, 1966.Translated by David Foxgrover and Wade Provo as *The Young Calvin* (Philadelphia: Westminster Press, 1987).

Geiselmann, Josef Rupert. *Die Eucharistielehre der Vorscholastik*. Forschungen zur christlichen Literatur- und Dogmengeschichte 15. Paderborn: F. Schönigh, 1926.

George, Timothy. "John Calvin and the Agreement of Zurich (1549)." In *John Calvin and the Church: A Prism of Reform*, edited by Timothy George, 42–58. Louisville, KY: Westminster John Knox Press, 1990.

Gerrish, Brian A. "Calvin's Eucharistic Piety." *Reformed Liturgy and Music* 31, no. 2 (1997): 93–100.

———. "The Confessional Heritage of the Reformed Church." *McCormick Quarterly* 19 (1966): 120–34.

———. "Discerning the Body: Sign and Reality in Luther's Controversy with the Swiss." *Journal of Religion* 68, no. 3 (1988): 377–95.

———. "Eucharist." In *The Oxford Encyclopedia of the Reformation*, edited by Hans J. Hillerbrand. Oxford: Oxford University Press, 1996.

———. *The Faith of Christendom: A Source Book of Creeds and Confessions.* Cleveland and New York: World Publishing Co., 1963.

———. *Grace and Gratitude: The Eucharistic Theology of John Calvin.* Minneapolis: Fortress Press, 1993.

———. *Grace and Reason: A Study in the Theology of Martin Luther.* Oxford: Clarendon Press, 1962.

———. "Lord's Supper in the Reformed Confessions." *Theology Today* 23 (July 1966): 224–43.

———. *The Old Protestantism and the New: Essays on the Reformation Heritage.* Chicago: University of Chicago Press, 1982.

———. *A Prince of the Church: Schleiermacher and the Beginnings of Modern Theology.* Philadelphia: Fortress Press, 1984.

———. *Tradition and the Modern World: Reformed Theology in the Nineteenth Century.* Chicago: University of Chicago Press, 1978.

Gerson, Jean. *Selections from "A Deo exivit," "Contra curiositatem studentium" and "De mystica theologia speculativa."* Edited by Steven E. Ozment. Leiden: E. J. Brill, 1969.

Gessel, Wilhelm. *Eucharistische Gemeinschaft bei Augustinus.* Würzburg: Augustinus-Verlag, 1966.

Ghellinck, J. de, SJ. *Pour l'histoire du mot "Sacramentum."* Louvain: Spicelegium sacrum Lovaniense, 1924.

Gilson, Etiene. *History of Christian Thought in the Middle Ages.* New York: Random House, 1955.

———. "Richards Lectures at the University of Virginia." In *Reason and Revelation.* New York: Charles Scribner's Sons, 1938.

Gleason, Ronald N. "Calvin and Bavinck on the Lord's Supper." *Westminster Theological Journal* 45, no. 2 (Fall 1983): 273–303.

Goesser, R. J. "Word and Sacrament: A Study of Luther's Views as Developed in the Controversy with Zwingli and Karlstadt." PhD diss., Yale University, 1960.

Gogarten, Friedrich. *Verhängnis und Hoffnung der Neuzeit.* Stuttgart: Friedrich Vorwerk Verlag, 1953. Translated by Thomas Wieser as *Despair and Hope for Our Time* (Philadelphia and Boston: Pilgrim Press, 1970).

Gollwitzer, Helmut. *Coena Domini.* Munich: Chr. Kaiser, 1988.

———. "Zur Auslegung von Joh. 6 bei Luther und Zwingli." In *In Memoriam Ernst Lohmeyer,* edited by W. Schmauch, 143–68. Stuttgart: Evangelisches Verlagswerk, 1951.

Gordon, Bruce, and Emidio Campi, eds. *Architect of Reformation: An Introduction to Heinrich Bullinger, 1504–1575.* Grand Rapids: Baker Academic, 2004.

Gore, Charles. *The Body of Christ.* London: John Murray, 1901.

Graebke, Friedrich. *Die Konstruktion der Abendmahlslehre Luthers in ihrer Entwicklung dargestellt: Eine dogmengeschichtliche Studie.* Leipzig: A. Deichert, 1908.

Grant, Robert M. *Early Christianity and Society.* San Francisco: Harper & Row, 1977.

Grass, Hans. *Die Abendmahlslehre bei Luther und Calvin: Eine kritische Untersuchung.* Gütersloh: C. Bertelsmann, 1954.

Greef, Wulfert de. *The Writings of Calvin: An Introductory Guide.* Expanded ed. Translated by Lyle D. Bierma. Louisville, KY: Westminster John Knox Press, 2009.

Green, Lowell C. "Philosophical Presuppositions in the Lutheran-Reformed Debate on John 6." *Concordia Theological Quarterly* 56 (1992): 17–37.

Greschat, Martin. *Martin Bucer: Ein Reformator und seine Zeit.* Munich: Verlag C. H. Beck, 1990. Translated by Stephen E. Buckwalter as *Martin Bucer: A Reformer and His Times.* Louisville, KY: Westminster John Knox Press, 2004.

———. "Das Profil Martin Bucers." In *Martin Bucer and Sixteenth-Century Europe,* edited by Christian Krieger and Marc Lienhard, 2:9–16. Leiden: E. J. Brill, 1993.

Gy, Pierre-Marie. "L'Office du Corpus Christi et S. Thomas d'Aquin: état d'une recherche." *Revue des sciences philosophies et théologiques* 64 (1980): 491–507.

Hadas, Moses. *The Third and Fourth Books of Maccabees.* New York: Harper & Bros., 1953.

Hahn, Ferdinand. "Abendmahl: I. Neues Testament." In *Die Religion in Geschichte und Gegenwart,* 1:10–15. Tübingen: Mohr Siebeck, 1998.

———. *The Worship of the Early Church.* Translated and introduction by John Reumann. Philadelphia: Fortress Press, 1973.

Hakkenberg, Michael A. "Belgic Confession." In *The Oxford Encyclopedia of the Reformation,* edited by Hans J. Hillerbrand. Oxford: Oxford University Press, 1996.

Hall, Basil. "Hoc est corpus meum: The Centrality of the Real Presence for Luther." In *Luther: Theologian for Catholics and Protestants,* edited by George Yule, 112–44. Edinburgh: T. & T. Clark, 1985.

Halliburton, R. J. "The Patristic Theology of the Eucharist." In *The Study of Liturgy,* rev. ed., edited by Cheslyn Jones, Geoffrey Wainwright, Edward Yarnold, SJ, and Paul Bradshaw, 245–51. New York: Oxford University Press, 1992.

Hanna, Eleanor B. "Biblical Interpretation and Sacramental Practice: John Calvin's Interpretation of John 6:51–58." *Worship* 73, no. 3 (1999): 211–30.

Hartshorne, Charles. *The Logic of Perfection.* LaSalle, IL: Open Court, 1962.

———. "Metaphysical Statements as Nonrestrictive and Existential." *Review of Metaphysics* (September 1958): 35–47.

Hartvelt, G. P. *Verum Corpus: Een Studie over een Centraal Hoofdstuk uit de Avondmaalsleer van Calvijn.* Delft: W. D. Meinema, 1960.

Hausamann, Susi. "Die Marburger Artikel—eine echte Konkordie?" *Zeitschrift für Kirchengeschichte* 87 (1966): 288–321.

———. "Realpräsenz in Luthers Abendmahlslehre." In *Studien zur Geschichte und Theologie der Reformation: Festschrift für Ernst Bizer,* edited by Luise Abramowski and J. F. Gerhard Goeters, 157–73. Neukirchen-Vluyn: Neukirchener Verlag, 1969.

———. *Römerbriefauslegung zwischen Humanismus und Reformation: Eine Studie zu Heinrich Bullingers Römerbriefvorlesung von 1525.* Zurich: Zwingli-Verlag, 1970.

Hausherr, Melchior. *Der heilige Paschasius Radbertus: Eine Stimme über die Eucharistie vor tausend Jahren.* Mainz, 1862.

Hazlett, Ian. "The Development of Martin Bucer's Thinking on the Sacrament of the Lord's Supper in Its Historical and Theological Context." Thesis, Westfälischen Wilhelms-Universität zu Münster, 1975.

———. "Eucharistic Communion: Impulses and Directions in Martin Bucer's Thought." In *Martin Bucer: Reforming Church and Community*, edited by D. F. Wright, 72–82. Cambridge: Cambridge University Press, 1994.

———. "The Scots Confession 1560: Context, Complexion and Critique." *Archiv für Reformationsgeschichte* 78 (1987): 287–320.

Heitmüller, Wilhelm. "Abendmahl: I. im Neuen Testament." In *Die Religion in Geschichte und Gegenwart*, 1:19–51. Tübingen: J. C. B. Mohr, 1909.

Heman, Richard. *Mysterium Sanctum Magnum. Um die Auslegung des Abendmahls. Zwingli? Calvin? Luther? Rom?* Lucerne: Verlag Räber, 1937.

Hengel, Martin. *The Charismatic Leader and His Followers.* Philadelphia: Fortress Press, 1974.

———. *The "Hellenization" of Judaea in the First Century after Christ.* Philadelphia: Trinity Press, 1989.

———. *Judaism and Hellenism.* Translated by John Bowden. Philadelphia: Fortress Press, 1981.

Henrich, Rainer. "Zu den Anfängen der Geschichtsschreibung über den Abendmahlsstreit bei Heinrich Bullinger und Johann Stumpf." *Zwingliana* 20 (1993): 11–51.

Herminjard, Aimé Louis. *Correspondance des Réformateurs dans les pays de langue française.* 9 vols. Geneva: H. Georg, 1866–97.

Herron, Alasdair I. C. "'If Luther Will Accept Us with Our Confession . . .': The Eucharistic Controversy in Calvin's Correspondence up to 1546." *Hervormde Teologiese Studies* 62, no. 3 (2006): 867–84.

———. *Table and Tradition: Toward an Ecumenical Understanding of the Eucharist.* Philadelphia: Westminster Press, 1983.

Hesselink, John I. "Reactions to Bouwsma's 'Portrait' of John Calvin." In *Calvinus Sacrae Scripturae Professor*, edited by Wilhelm Neuser, 209–13. Grand Rapids: Eerdmans, 1994.

———. "The Role of the Holy Spirit in Calvin's Doctrine of the Sacraments." In *Essentialia et Hodierna: Oblate P. C. Potgieter*, edited by D. François Tolmie, 66–88. Bloemfontein: University of the Free State, 2002.

Hilgenfeld, Hartmut. *Mittelalterlich-traditionelle Elemente in Luthers Abendmahlsschriften.* Zurich: Zürich Theologischer Verlag, 1971.

Hinlicky, Paul. "Christ's Bodily Presence in the Holy Supper—Real or Symbolic?" *Lutheran Forum* 33 (1999): 24–28.

Hinson, E. Glenn. *The Evangelization of the Roman Empire.* Macon, GA: Mercer University Press, 1981.

Hodge, Charles. "Doctrine of the Reformed Church on the Lord's Supper." In *Systematic Theology*, 3:626–50. Grand Rapids: Eerdmans, 1989.

———. "The Mystical Presence: A Vindication of the Reformed or Calvinistic Doctrine of the Holy Eucharist, by Rev. John W. Nevin, D.D." *Princeton Review* 20, no. 2 (1848): 227–78.

Hödl, Ludwig. "Sacramentum et Res—Zeichen und Bezeichnetes: Eine begriffsgeschichtliche Arbeit zum frühscholastischen Eucharistietraktat." *Scholastik* 38 (1963): 161–82.

Hoffmann, Gottfried. "Sententiae Patrum—Das patristische Argument in der Abendmahlskontroverse zwischen Oekolampad, Zwingli, Luther, und Melanchthon." Diss., Heidelberg, 1971.

Hopf, Constantin. *Martin Bucer and the English Reformation*. Oxford: Basil Blackwell, 1946.

Horsley, Richard. *Jesus and the Spiral of Violence*. New York: Harper & Row, 1987.

Houssiau, Albert. "La Cène du Christ selon Luther." In *Luther aujourd'hui*, 221–54. Louvain-la-Neuve: Publications de la Faculté de Théologie, 1983.

Hunsinger, George. "The Bread That We Break: Toward a Chalcedonian Resolution of the Eucharistic Controversies." *Princeton Seminary Bulletin* 24, no. 2 (2003): 241–58.

Huovinen, Eero. "Opus Operatum: Ist Luthers Verständnis von der Effektivität des Sakraments richtig verstanden?" In *Luther und Theosis*, 187–214. Helsinki: Luther-Agricola-Gesellschaft; Erlangen: Luther-Akademie Ratzeburg, 1990.

Hyma, A. "Hoen's Letter on the Eucharist and Its Influence upon Carlstadt, Bucer, and Zwingli." *Princeton Theological Review* 24 (1926): 124–31.

Irwin, Kevin W. "Sacrament." In *The New Dictionary of Theology*, edited by Joseph A. Komonchak, Mary Collins, and Dermot A. Lane, 910–22. Collegeville, MN: Liturgical Press/A Michael Glazier Book, 1989, 1991.

Iserloh, Erwin. "Abendmahl: III/2. Mittelalter." In *Theologisches Realenzyklopädie*, 1:89–107. Berlin: Walter de Gruyter, 1977.

———. *Gnade und Eucharistie in der philosophischen Theologie des Wilhelm von Ockham: Ihre Bedeutung für die Ursachen der Reformation*. Wiesbaden: F. Steiner, 1956.

Iserloh, Erwin, and Vilmos Vatja. "The Sacraments: Baptism and Lord's Supper." In *Confessing One Faith*, edited by George W. Forell and James F. McCue, 202–33. Minneapolis: Augsburg Publishing House, 1982.

Jackson, Pamela. "Eucharist." In *Augustine through the Ages: An Encyclopedia*, edited by Allan D. Fitzgerald, OSA, 330–34. Grand Rapids: Eerdmans, 1999.

Jahr, Hannelore. *Studien zur Überlieferungsgeschichte der Confession de foi von 1559*. Neukirchen-Vluyn: Neukirchener Verlag des Erziehungsvereins, 1964.

Janse, Wim. "Calvin, a Lasco und Beza: Eine gemeinsame Abendmahlserklärung (May 1556)?" *Calvinus Praeceptor Ecclesiae*, ed. Herman J. Selderhuis, 209–32. Geneva: Droz, 2004.

Janse, Wim. "Calvin's Eucharistic Theology." In *Henry Bullinger: 1504–1575: British Anniversary Colloquium, 1975*, edited by David Keep. Woodbury, Exeter: D. J. Keep, 1976.

———. "Calvin's Eucharistic Theology: Three Dogma-Historical Observations." In *Calvinus sacrarum literarum interpres*, edited by Herman J. Selderhuis, 37–69. Göttingen: Vandenhoeck & Ruprecht, 2008.

Janssen, Heinrich. "Die Abendmahlslehre Johannes Calvin." *Una Sancta* 15, no. 2 (1960): 125–38.

Jenny, Markus. *Die Einheit des Abendmahlsgottesdienstes bei den elsässischen und schweizerischen Reformatoren.* Studien zur Dogmengeschichte und systematischen Theologie 23. Zurich: Zwingli Verlag, 1968.

———. *Zwinglis Stellung zur Muzik im Gottesdienst.* Zurich: Zwingli Verlag, 1966.

Jeremias, Joachim. *The Eucharistic Words of Jesus.* 3rd ed. Translated by Norman Perrin. New York: Charles Scribner's Sons, 1966.

———. *The Parables of Jesus.* 2nd ed. Translated by S. H. Hooke. New York: Charles Scribner's Sons, 1972.

Johanny, Raymond. *L'Eucharistie, centre de l'histoire du salut, chez Ambroise de Milan.* Paris: Beauchesne et ses fils, 1968.

Jones, Paul H. "Reformation Concepts: John Calvin." In *Christ's Eucharistic Presence: A History of the Doctrine,* edited by Paul H. Jones, 134–67. New York: Peter Lang, 1994.

Jorissen, Hans. *Die Entfaltung der Transsubstantiationslehre bis zum Beginn der Hochscholastik.* Münster: Aschendorff, 1965.

Jungmann, Josef. *The Mass of the Roman Rite.* Translated by Francis A. Brunner, rev. Charles K. Riepe. New York: Benziger Bros., 1961.

Juntunen, Sammeli. "Luther and Metaphysics: What Is the Structure of Being according to Luther?" In *Union with Christ: The New Finnish Interpretation of Luther,* edited by Carl E. Braaten and Robert W. Jenson, 129–60. Grand Rapids: Eerdmans, 1998.

Justin Martyr. *First Apology.* In *Prex Eucharistica,* edited by Anton Hänggi and Irmgard Pahl, 68–72. Fribourg: Éditions Universitaires Fribourg Suisse, 1968. English translation by Cyril C. Richardson in *Early Christian Fathers,* 285–88 (Philadelphia: Westminster Press, 1953).

Kaiser, Christopher B. "Climbing Jacob's Ladder: John Calvin and the Early Church on Our Eucharistic Ascent to Heaven." *Scottish Journal of Theology* 56, no. 3 (2003): 247–67.

———. "John Calvin Climbing Jacob's Ladder." *Perspectives* 13, no. 4 (1998): 10–12.

Kapitani, O. "Berengar v. Tours." In *Lexikon des Mittelalters,* 1:1937–39. Munich and Zurich: Artemis-Verlag, 1977–99.

Kattenbusch, Ferdinand. "Sakrament." In *Real-Encyklopädie für Theologie und Kirche,* 3rd ed., 17:349–81. Leipzig: Hinrichs, 1896–1913.

Kaufmann, Thomas. *Das Abendmahlstheologie der Straßburger Reformatoren bis 1529.* Tübingen: J. C. B. Mohr, 1992.

Keller, Hermann. "Das Abendmahl als Gemeinschaftsmahl." *Reformierte Kirchenzeitung* 110 (1969): 76.

Kelly, J. N. D. *Early Christian Doctrines.* 2nd ed. New York: Harper & Bros., 1960.

Kelsey, Catherine C. *Thinking about Christ with Schleiermacher.* Louisville, KY: Westminster John Knox Press, 2003.

Kerr, Nathan R. "Corpus Verum: On the Ecclesial Recovery of Real Presence in John Calvin's Doctrine of the Eucharist." In *Radical Orthodoxy and the Reformed Tradition,* edited by James K. A. Smith and James H. Olthuis, 229–42. Grand Rapids: Baker Academic, 2005.

Kilmartin, Edward J., SJ. "The Catholic Tradition of Eucharistic Theology: Towards the Third Millennium." *Theological Studies* 55 (1994): 405–57.

———. *Christian Liturgy: Theology and Practice*. Part 1, *Systematic Theology of Liturgy*. Kansas City: Sheed & Ward, 1988.

———. *The Eucharist in the West: History and Theology*. Edited by Robert J. Daly, SJ. Collegeville, MN: Liturgical Press, 1998.

———. "The Eucharistic Gift: Augustine of Hippo's Tractate XXVII on Jn. 6:60–72." In *Preaching in the Patristic Age: Studies in Honor of Walter J. Burghardt, S.J.*, edited by David G. Hunter, 173–74. New York: Paulist, 1989.

———. "A Modern Approach to the Word of God and Sacraments of Christ: Perspectives and Principles." In *The Sacraments: God's Love and Mercy Actualized*, edited by Francis A. Eigo, OSA, 59–109. Villanova, PA: Villanova University Press, 1979.

Kinder, Ernst. "'Realpräsenz' und 'Repräsentation,' Feststellungen zu Luthers Abendmahlslehre." *Theologische Literaturzeitung* 84 (1959): 881–94.

Kittleson, James. *Luther: The Story of the Man and His Career*. Minneapolis: Augsburg Publishing House, 1986.

Klappert, Bertold. "Das Abendmahl als Verheißungs-und Bekenntniszeichen: Calvins Abendmahlslehre und die Interpretation Wilhelm Niesels." In *Wilhelm Niesel—Theologe und Kirchenpolitiker*, edited by Martin Breidert and Hans-Georg Ulrichs, 111–52. Wuppertal: Foedus, 2003.

Klauck, Hans-Josef. *Herrenmahl und Hellenistischer Kult*. Münster: Aschendorff, 1982.

———. "Die Sakramente und der historische Jesus." In *Gemeinde-Amt-Sakrament: Neutestamentliche Perspektiven*, 273–85. Würzburg: Echter, 1989.

Klinghardt, Matthias. *Gemeinschaftsmahl und Mahlgemeinschaft: Soziologie und Liturgie frühchristlicher Mahlfeiern*. Tübingen: Francke Verlag, 1996.

Koch, Ernst. "Paulusexegese und Bundestheologie: Bullingers Auslegung von Gal 3:17–26." In *Histoire de l'exégèse au XVIe siècle*, edited by Olivier Fatio and Pierre Fraenkel, 342–50. Geneva: Droz, 1979.

———. *Die Theologie der Confessio Helvetica Posterior*. Beiträge zur Geschichte und Lehre der Reformierten Kirche 27. Neukirchen: Neukirchener Verlag des Erziehungsvereins, 1968.

Koch, Reinhold. *Erbe und Auftrag: Das Abendmahlsgespräch in der Theologie des 20. Jahrhunderts*. Munich: Chr. Kaiser, 1957.

Köhler, Walther. *Dogmengeschichte als Geschichte des christlichen Selbstbewusstseins: Das Zeitalter der Reformation*. Zurich: Max Neihans, 1951.

———. *Das Marburger Religionsgespräch 1529*. Leipzig: M. Heinsius Nachfolger Eger & Sievers, 1929.

———. "Zu Zwinglis ältester Abendmahlsauffassung." *Zeitschrift für Kirchengeschichte* 45 (1926–1927): 399–408.

———. "Zum Abendmahlsstreite zwischen Luther und Zwingli." In *Lutherstudien. Zur 4 Jahrhundertfeier der Reformation*, Veröffentlicht von den Mitarbeitern der Weimarer Lutherausgabe, 114–39. Weimar: Böhlau, 1917.

———. "Zum Gedächtnis der ersten evangelischen Abendmahlsfeier in Zürich." *Neue Züricher Zeitung*, no. 531 (1925).

———. "Zur Abendmahls Kontroverse in der Reformationszeit insbesondere zur Entwicklung der Abendmahlslehre Zwinglis." *Zeitschrift für Kirchengeschichte* 47 (1928): 47–56.

———. "Zur Geschichte der privaten Abendmahlsfeier." *Zwingliana* 3, no. 2 (1913): 58–64.

———. *Zwingli und Luther. Ihr Streit über das Abendmahl nach seinen politischen und religiösen Beziehungen.* Quellen und Forschungen zur Reformations Geschichte 6–7. Vol. 1: Leipzig, 1924. Vol. 2: Gütersloh, 1953.

Krauth, Charles P. "Calvin on the Lord's Supper." In *The Conservative Reformation and Its Theology*, 493–502. Philadelphia: Lippincott, 1871.

Kretchmar, Georg. "Abendmahl: III/1. Altekirche." In *Theologisches Realenzyklopädie*, 1:59–89. Berlin: Walter de Gruyter, 1977.

Krodel, Gottfried. "The Lord's Supper in the Theology of the Young Luther." *Lutheran Quarterly* 13 (1961): 19–33.

Krönler, Hans. "Der Kult der Eucharistie in Sprache und Volkstum der deutschen Schweiz, Schriften der Schweizer, Gesellschaft für Volkskunde XXXIII." Diss., Frieburg Basel, 1949.

Krüger, Friedhelm. *Bucer und Erasmus.* Wiesbaden: F. Steiner Verlag, 1970.

Krusche, Werner. *Das Wirken des Heiligen Geistes nach Calvin.* Göttingen: Vandenhoeck & Ruprecht, 1957.

Kühn, Ulrich. "Abendmahl und Opfer." In *Eucharistie. Beiträge zur Theologie der "Erneuerten Agende,"* edited by Alexander Völker, 61–75. Berlin: Evangelische Haupt-Bibelgesellschaft, 1993.

Landgraf, Artur Michael. "Die in der Frühscholastik klassische Frage Quid sumit mus." In *Dogmensgeschichte der Frühscholastik* III/2, 207–22. Regensburg: Putset, 1955.

———. *Einführung in die Geschichte der Theologischen Literatur der Frühscholastik.* Regensburg: Gregorius-Verlag, 1948.

Lang, August. *Der Evangelienkommentar Martin Butzers und die Grundzüge seiner Theologie.* Studien zur Geschichte der Theologie und der Kirche, Bd II., edited by N. Bonwetsch and R. Seeberg. Leipzig: Dieterich'sche Verlags-Buchhandlung Theodore Weicher, 1900.

Lang, Bernhard. "The West-Side Story (2) Calvin's Theory of Christ's Spiritual Presence." In *Sacred Games: A History of Christian Worship*, 322–27. New Haven, CT: Yale University Press, 1997.

Larson, Mark J. "Moving beyond Zwingli: The Calvinist Doctrine of the Lord's Supper." *Outlook* 54, no. 4 (2004): 11–13.

Laskey, Dennis Alan. "In Faith and Fervent Love: The Concept of Communio in Luther's Understanding of the Lord's Supper." ThD diss., Lutheran School of Theology at Chicago, 1983.

Lecerf, Auguste. "The Liturgy of the Holy Supper at Geneva in 1542." *Reformed Liturgy* 3, no. 2 (1966–67): 17–24.

Lecordier, Gaston. *La Doctrine de l'Eucharistie chez saint Augustin.* Paris: Lecoffre, 1930.

Lécuyer, Joseph. "La sacrifice selon saint Augustin." In *Augustinus Magister*, Congrès international augustinien 1954, 905–14. Paris: Études augustiniennes, 1954–55.

Leijenhorst, Cees. "Place, Space and Matter in Calvinist Physics." *Monist* 84, no. 4 (2001): 520–41.

Leith, John H. *Assembly at Westminster: Reformed Theology in the Making*. Richmond, VA: John Knox Press, 1973.

Leo the Great. "Sermon 74:2." In *St Leo the Great: Sermons*. Translated by Jane Patricia Freeland and Agnes Josephine Conway. Vol. 93, The Fathers of the Church: A New Translation, 326 Washington DC: The Catholic University Press, 1996.

Leuschner, Immanuel. "Bullinger und Calvin einigen sich in der Abendmahlsfrage." In *Heinrich Bullinger, Vater der reformierten Kirche*, edited by Fritz Blanke and Immanuel Leuschner, 216–24. Zurich: Theologischer Verlag, 1990.

Lies, Lothar. "Realpräsenz bei Luther und den Lutheranern Heute." *Zeitschrift für Katholische Theologie* 119 (1997): 181–219.

Lietzmann, Hans. *Mass and Lord's Supper*. Translated by Dorothea H. G. Reeve. Leiden: E. J. Brill, 1953–55.

Lindberg, Carter. *The European Reformations*. Oxford: Blackwell, 1996.

Locher, Gottfried W. *Im Geist und in der Wahrheit: Die reformatorische Wendung im Gottesdienst zu Zürich*. Neukirchen: K. Moers, 1957.

———. *Streit unter Gästen*. Zurich: Theologischer Verlag, 1972.

———. *Die Theologie Huldrych Zwinglis im Lichte seiner Christologie*. Zurich: Zwingli-Verlag, 1952.

———. "Die theologische und politische Bedeutung des Abendmahlsstreites im Licht von Zwinglis Briefen." *Zwingliana* 13, no. 5 (1971): 281–304.

———. *Zwingli's Thought: New Perspectives*. Leiden: E. J. Brill, 1981.

———. *Die Zwinglische Reformation im Rahmen der europäischen Kirchengeschichte*. Göttingen: Vandenhoeck & Ruprecht, 1979.

Lohse, Bernard, ed. *Der Durchbruch der reformatorischen Erkenntnis bei Luther*. Darmstadt: Wissenschaftliche Buchgesellschaft, 1968.

———, ed. *Der Durchbruch der reformatorischen Erkenntnis bei Luther: Neuere Untersuchungen*. Stuttgart: F. Steiner Verlag Wiesbaden, 1988.

———. *Martin Luther: An Introduction to His Life and Work*. Translated by Robert C. Schultz. Philadelphia: Fortress Press, 1986.

Loofs, Friedrich. "Abendmahl II." In *Realencyklopädie für protestantische Theologie und Kirche*, 3rd ed. Leipzig: J. C. Hinrich, 1896.

Lord, Albert Bates. *The Singer of Tales*. Edited by Stephen Mitchell and Gregory Nagy. Cambridge, MA: Harvard University Press, 2000.

Lortz, Joseph. *Die Reformation in Deutschland*. Vols. 1–2. Freiburg, 1939–1940. Translated as *The Reformation in Germany* (New York: Herder & Herder, 1968).

———. "Sakramentales Denken beim jungen Luther." In *Lutherjahrbuch 1969*, 9–40. Göttingen: Vandenhoeck & Ruprecht, 1969.

———. *Wie kam es zur Reformation?* Einsiedeln: Johannes Verlag, 1955. Translated by Otto M. Knab as *How the Reformation Came* (New York: Herder & Herder, 1964).

Lubac, Henri de. *Corpus Mysticum: l'eucharistie et l'Église au Moyen âge*. 2nd ed. Paris: Aubier, 1949.

Luther, Martin. *D. Martin Luthers Werke: Kritische Gesamtausgabe*. Weimar: Hermann Böhlaus, 1888.

———. *Luther's Works*. Edited by Jaroslav Pelikan and Helmut T. Lehmann. 55 vols. St. Louis: Concordia Publishing House; Philadelphia: Fortress Press, 1955–.

MacCulloch, Diarmaid. *Thomas Cranmer*. New Haven, CT: Yale University Press, 1996.

Macdonald, Allan J. *Berengar and the Reform of Sacramental Doctrine*. London: Longmans, Green, 1930. Reprint, Merrick, NY: Richwood Publishing Co., 1977.

———, ed. *The Evangelical Doctrine of Holy Communion*. London: SPCK, 1936.

Mack, Burton. *A Myth of Innocence*. Philadelphia: Fortress Press, 1988.

MacLeod, Donald. "Calvin into Hyppolytus?" In *To Glorify God: Essays on Modern Reformed Liturgy*, edited by Bryan Spinks and Iain Torrance, 255–67. Grand Rapids: Eerdmans, 1999.

MacMullen, Ramsay. *Christianizing the Roman Empire (A.D. 100–400)*. New Haven, CT: Yale University Press, 1984.

Macy, Gary. *The Banquet's Wisdom*. New York: Paulist Press, 1992.

———. "The Doctrine of Transubstantiation in the Middle Ages." *Journal of Ecclesiastical History* 45 (1994): 11–41. Reprinted in *Treasures from the Store-room*. Collegeville, MN: Liturgical Press, 1999.

———. "Quid Mus Sumit as a Pastoral Question." *Researches de Théologie anci-enne et médiévale* 58 (1991): 157–66.

———. *The Theologies of the Eucharist in the Early Scholastic Period*. Oxford: Clar-endon Press; New York: Oxford University Press, 1984.

———. *Treasures from the Storeroom*. Collegeville, MN: Liturgical Press, 1999.

Magenot, E. "Eucharistie du XIIe a la fin du XVe siécle." In *Dictionnaire de théologie catholique*, 5:1304–20. Paris, 1913.

Mann, Frido. *Das Abendmahl beim jungen Luther*. Munich: M. Hueber, 1971.

Mannermaa, Tuomo. *Christ Present in Faith: Luther's View of Justification*. Edited by Kirsi Stjerna. Minneapolis: Fortress Press, 2005.

———. "Justification and Theosis in Lutheran-Orthodox Perspective." In *Union with Christ: The New Finnish Interpretation of Luther*, edited by Carl E. Braaten and Robert W. Jenson, 25–41. Grand Rapids: Eerdmans, 1998.

———. "Theosis als Thema der finnischen Lutherforschung." In *Luther und Theosis*, 11–26. Helsinki: Luther-Agricola-Gesellschaft; Erlangen: Luther-Akademie Ratzeburg, 1990.

———. "Why Is Luther So Fascinating?" In *Union with Christ: The New Finnish Interpretation of Luther*, edited by Carl E. Braaten and Robert W. Jenson, 1–20. Grand Rapids: Eerdmans, 1998.

Marcel, Pierre. "La communication du Christ avec les siens: A parole et la cène." *La Revue Réformée* 37 (1986): 1–64.

Martelet, Gustave. *Résurrection, eucharistie, et genèse de l'homme; chemins théologiques d'un renouveau chrétien*. Paris: Desclée, 1972. Translated by René Hague as *The Risen Christ and the Eucharistic World* (New York: Sea-bury Press, 1976).

Martyn, J. Louis. *History and Theology in the Fourth Gospel.* Nashville: Abingdon Press, 1979.

Marxsen, Willi. *Das Abendmahl als christologisches Problem.* Gütersloh: Gütersloher Verlagshaus Gerd Mohn, 1960. Translated by Lorenz Neiting as *The Lord's Supper as a Christological Problem* (Philadelphia: Fortress Press, 1970).

———. *The Beginnings of Christology; together with The Lord's Supper as a Christological Problem.* Translated by Paul J. Achtemeier and Lorenz Nieting. Introduction by John Reumann. Philadelphia: Fortress Press, 1979.

———. "Christology in the NT." In *The Interpreter's Dictionary of the Bible: Supplementary Volume.* Nashville: Abingdon Press, 1976.

———. "Jesus of Nazareth: An Event." In *Jesus and the Church: The Beginnings of Christianity,* selected, translated, and introduced by Philip E. Devenish, 55–75. Philadelphia: Trinity Press International, 1992.

———. "The Limits to the Possibility of Christological Assertions." In *Witness and Existence: Essays in Honor of Schubert M. Ogden,* edited by Philip E. Devenish and George L. Goodwin, translated by Philip E. Devenish, 43–54. Chicago: University of Chicago Press, 1989.

———. "The Meals of Jesus and the Lord's Supper of the Church." In *Jesus and the Church: The Beginnings of Christianity,* selected, translated, and introduced by Philip E. Devenish, 137–46. Philadelphia: Trinity Press International, 1992.

———. *Das Neue Testament als Buch der Kirche.* Gütersloh: Gütersloher Verlagshaus Gerd Mohn, 1966. Translated by James E. Mignard as *The New Testament as the Church's Book* (Philadelphia: Fortress Press, 1966).

———. *New Testament Foundations for Christian Ethics.* Translated by O. C. Dean Jr. Edinburgh: T. & T. Clark, 1993.

———. *Die Sache Jesu geht weiter.* Gütersloh: Gütersloher Verlagshaus Gerd Mohn, 1976.

———. "Toward the New Testament Grounding of Baptism." In *Jesus and the Church: The Beginnings of Christianity,* selected, translated, and introduced by Philip E. Devenish, 147–71. Philadelphia: Trinity Press International, 1992.

Mason, Matthew W. "A Spiritual Banquet: John Calvin on the Lord's Supper." *Churchman* 117, no. 4 (2003): 329–46.

Mathison, Keith A. *Given for You: Reclaiming Calvin's Doctrine of the Lord's Supper.* Phillipsburg: Presbyterian & Reformed, 2002.

Maxwell, William D. *An Outline of Christian Worship: Its Developments and Forms.* London: Oxford University Press, 1949.

Mayer, Cornelius. "Die Feier der Eucharistice als Selbstdarstellung der Kirche nach der Lehre des hl. Augustinus." In *Der hl. Augustinus als Seersorger, Augustinus-Colloquium 20–24 Mai, 1991,* 94–102. St. Ottilien: EOS-Verlag, 1992.

McArthur, A. Allan. *The Evolution of the Christian Year.* London: SCM Press, 1953.

McCabe, Herbert. "Eucharistic Change." *Priests and People* 8, no. 6 (1994): 217–21.

McCoy, Charles S., and J. Wayne Baker. *Fountainhead of Federalism: Heinrich Bullinger and the Covenant Tradition.* Louisville, KY: Westminster/John Knox Press, 1991.

McCracken, George E., trans. and ed. *Early Medieval Theology.* Library of Christian Classics 9. Philadelphia: Westminster Press, 1955.

McCue, James F. "The Doctrine of Transubstantiation from Berengar through Trent: The Point at Issue." *Harvard Theological Review* 61 (1968): 385–430.

———. "Luther and the Change in the Understanding of Sacrament." In *Lutherjahrbuch 1985,* 282–83. Göttingen: Vandenhoeck & Ruprecht, 1985.

McDonnell, Kilian. "Calvin's Eucharistic Doctrine." *Reformed Liturgics* 5, no. 2 (Fall 1968): 13–21.

———. *John Calvin, the Church and the Eucharist.* Princeton, NJ: Princeton University Press, 1967.

McGiffert, Arthur Cushman. *Christianity as History and Faith.* New York: Charles Scribner's Sons, 1934.

McGinn, Bernard. *The Presence of God: A History of Western Christian Mysticism.* New York: Crossroad, 1991–.

McGowan, Andrew Brian. "'Is There a Liturgical Text in the Gospel?' The Institution Narratives and Their Early Interpretive Communities." *Journal of Biblical Literature* 118, no. 1 (1999): 73–87.

———. "The Meals of Jesus and the Meals of the Church: Eucharistic Origins and Admission to Communion." In *Studia Patristica Diversa: Essays in Honor of Paul E. Bradshaw,* edited by Maxwell E. Johnson and L. Edward Phillips, 101–15. Portland, OR: Pastoral Press, 2004.

McGrath, Alistair E. "John Calvin and Late Medieval Thought." *Archiv für Reformationsgeschichte* 77 (1986): 58–78.

McKim, Donald K. *Theological Turning Points.* Atlanta: John Knox Press, 1988.

McLelland, Joseph C. "Lutheran-Reformed Debate on the Eucharist and Christology." In *Marburg Revisited,* edited by Paul C. Empie and James I. McCord, 39–54. Minneapolis: Augsburg, 1966.

McLelland, Joseph C. "Meta-Zwingli or Anti-Zwingli? Bullinger and Calvin in Eucharistic Concord." In *Huldrych Zwingli, 1484–1531: A Legacy of Radical Reform. Papers from the 1984 International Zwingli Symposium,* edited by E. J. Furcha, 179–95. Montreal: McGill University Faculty of Religious Studies, 1985.

Meinhold, Peter. "Abendmahl und Opfer nach Luther." In *Abendmahl und Opfer,* edited by Peter Meinhold and Erwin Iserloh, 35–73. Stuttgart: Schwabenverlag, 1960.

Meyer, Boniface. "Calvin's Eucharistic Doctrine: 1536–39." *Journal of Ecumenical Studies* 4, no. 1 (1967): 47–65.

———. "Sacramental Theology in the Institutes of John Calvin." *American Benedictine Review* 15 (1964): 360–80.

Miéville, H. *La sainte cène d'après Ulrich Zwingli.* Lausanne: Georges Bridel, 1871.

Milavec, Aaron. "The Pastoral Genius of the Didache: An Analytical Translation and Commentary." In *Christianity,* edited by Jacob Neusner, Ernest S. Frerichs, and Amy-Jill Levine, 89–125 Atlanta: Scholars Press, 1989.

Miller, Allen O., and M. Eugene Osterhaven, trans. *The Heidelberg Catechism: 400th Anniversary Edition*. New York: United Church Press, 1962.

Mitchell, Nathan. *Cult and Controversy: The Worship of the Eucharist outside Mass*. New York: Pueblo Publishing, 1982.

Mohlberg, L. C., ed. *Liber Sacramentorum Romanae Aeclesiae Ordinis Anni Circuli*. Rerum Ecclesiasticarum Documenta, Series Major, 4. Rome: Herder, 1960.

Moloney, Raymond. *The Eucharist*. London: Geoffrey Chapman, 1995.

Moore-Keish, Martha L. "Calvin, Sacraments, and Ecclesiology." In *Call to Worship: Liturgy, Music, Preaching and the Arts*, edited by Theodore A. Gill Jr., 25–41. Louisville, KY: Geneva Press, 2002.

Mottu, Henry. "Nos convictions réformées au sujet de la saints cène." *Les Cahiers Protestants* (October 1987): 5–11.

Müller, E. F. Karl, ed. *Die Bekenntnisschriften der reformierten Kirche*. Leipzig: A. Deichert (Georg Böhme), 1903. Reprint, Waltrop: Spenner, 1999.

Naegle, August. *Die Eucharistie Lehre des heiligen Johannes Chrysostomus, des Doctor Eucharistiae*. Strassburg: Herder, 1900.

Nagel, Norman. "The Presence of Christ's Body and Blood in the Sacrament of the Altar according to Luther." *Concordia Theological Monthly* 39 (1968): 227–38.

Naphy, William G. *Calvin and the Consolidation of the Genevan Reformation*. Louisville, KY: Westminster John Knox Press, 2003.

Neuser, Wilhelm. "Martin Bucer als Mittler im Abendmahlsstreit (1530/31)." In *Kaum zur glauben. Von der Häresie und dem Umgang mit ihr*, edited by Athina Lexutt and Vicco von Bülow, 140–61. Rheinbach-Merzbach: CMZ-Verlag, 1998.

———. *Reformierte Bekenntnisschriften 1/1*. Edited by Heiner Faulenbach and Eberhard Busch, in conjunction with Emidio Campi et al. Neukirchen-Vluyn: Neukirchener, 2002.

———. *Die Tauflehre des Heidelberger Katechismus: Eine aktuelle Lösung des Problems der Kindertaufe*. Munich: Chr. Kaiser Verlag, 1967.

———. "Zwinglis Abendmahlsbrief an Thomas Wyttenbach (1523)." In *Wegen en gestalten in het gereformeerd protestantisme*, 35–46. Amsterdam: Ton Bolland, 1976.

Neusner, Jacob. "The Pharisees: Jesus' Competition." In *Judaism in the Beginning of Christianity*, 45–61. Philadelphia: Fortress Press, 1984.

Nevin, John Williamson. *My Own Life: The Early Years*. Papers of the Eastern Chapter, Historical Society of the Evangelical and Reformed Church, no. 1. Lancaster, PA, 1964.

———. *The Mystical Presence: A Vindication of the Reformed or Calvinistic Doctrine of the Holy Eucharist*. Philadelphia: J. B. Lippincott, 1846.

———. *The Mystical Presence and Other Writings on the Eucharist*. Edited by Bard Thompson and George H. Bricker. Lancaster Series on the Mercersburg Theology. Boston and Philadelphia: United Church Press, 1966.

———. *The Mystical Presence and the Doctrine of the Reformed Church on the Lord's Supper*. Edited by Linden J. DeBie. Mercersburg Theology Study Series 1. Eugene, OR: Wipf & Stock, 2012.

Nichols, James Hastings, ed. *The Mercersburg Theology*. New York: Oxford University Press, 1966.

Nicholson, Brian. "Calvin's Doctrine of the Spiritual Presence of Christ in the Lord's Supper." *Antithesis* 2, no. 2 (1991): 35–38.

Niebuhr, Richard R. *Schleiermacher on Christ and Religion.* New York: Charles Scribner's Sons, 1964.

Niemeyer, H. A., ed. *Collectio confessionum in ecclesiis reformatis publicatarum.* Leipzig: Klinkhardt, 1840.

Niesel, Wilhelm, ed. *Bekenntnisschriften und Kirchenordnungen der nach Gottes Wort reformierten Kirchen.* 3rd ed. Zollikon-Zurich: Evangelischer Verlag, 1940.

———. *Calvin-Bibliographie, 1901–1959.* Munich: C. Kaiser, 1961.

———. *Calvins Lehre vom Abendmahl im Lichte seiner letzen Aniwort an Westphal.* 2nd ed. Munich: Chr. Kaiser Verlag, 1935.

———. *The Theology of Calvin.* Translated by Harold Knight. Philadelphia: Westminster Press, 1956.

———. "Zwinglis 'spätere' Sakramentsanschauung." *Theologische Blätter* 11 (1932): 12–17.

Oberman, Heiko. *Forerunners of the Reformation: The Shape of Late Medieval Thought.* New York: Holt, Rinehart & Winston, 1966.

———. *The Harvest of Medieval Theology.* Cambridge, MA: Harvard University Press, 1963.

———. *The Impact of the Reformation.* Grand Rapids: Eerdmans, 1994.

———. *Luther: Man between God and the Devil.* New Haven, CT: Yale University Press, 1989.

———. *Masters of the Reformation.* Cambridge: Cambridge University Press, 1981.

Ogden, Schubert M. *Doing Theology Today.* Valley Forge, PA: Trinity Press, 1996.

———. *Faith and Freedom: Toward a Theology of Liberation.* Rev. and enl. ed. Nashville: Abingdon Press, 1989.

———. *Is There Only One True Religion or Are There Many?* Dallas: Southern Methodist Press, 1992.

———. *On Theology.* San Francisco: Harper & Row, 1986.

———. *The Point of Christology.* San Francisco: Harper & Row, 1982.

———. *The Reality of God and Other Essays.* New York: Harper & Row, 1966.

———. "Sources of Religious Authority in Liberal Protestantism." *Journal of the American Academy of Religion* 44 (1976): 403–16.

———. *The Understanding of Christian Faith.* Eugene, OR: Cascade Books, 2010.

———. "What Is Theology?" In *On Theology,* 1–21. San Francisco: Harper & Row, 1986.

———, and Van A. Harvey. "How New Is the 'New Quest of the Historical Jesus'?" In *The Historical Jesus and the Kerygmatic Christ,* edited by Carl E. Braaten and Roy A. Harrisville. New York: Abingdon Press, 1964.

Old, Hughes Oliphant. "Biblical Wisdom Theology and Calvin's Understanding of the Lord's Supper." In *Calvin Studies VI,* edited by John H. Leith, 77–86. Davidson, NC, 1992.

Ong, Walter. *Interfaces of the Word: Studies in the Evolution of Consciousness and Culture.* Ithaca, NY: Cornell University Press, 1971.

———. *Orality and Literacy: The Technologizing of the Word.* London and New York: Routledge, 2002.

———. *The Presence of the Word: Some Prolegomena for Cultural and Religious History.* New Haven, CT: Yale University Press, 1967.

Opitz, Peter. "Bullinger's Decades: Instructions in Faith and Conduct." In *Architect of Reformation: An Introduction to Heinrich Bullinger, 1504–1575,* edited by Bruce Gordon and Emidio Campi, 102–3. Grand Rapids: Baker Academic, 2004.

———. "Eine Theologie der Gemeinschaft im Zeitalter der Glaubensspaltung." *Zwingliana* 31 (2004): 199–214.

———. *Heinrich Bullinger als Theologe. Eine Studie zu seinen "Decades."* Zurich: Theologischer Verlag, 2004.

Osborne, Thomas. "Faith, Philosophy, and the Nominalist Background to Luther's Defense of the Real Presence." *Journal of the History of Ideas* 63 (2002): 63–82.

Osterhaven, Maurice Eugene. "Eating and Drinking Christ: The Lord's Supper as an Act of Worship in the Theology and Practice of John Calvin." *Reformed Review* 37 (1983–84): 83–93.

———. "The Sacraments." In *The Faith of the Church: A Reformed Perspective on Its Historical Development,* 125–54. Grand Rapids: Eerdmans, 1982.

Ozment, Steven E. *The Age of Reform.* New Haven, CT: Yale University Press, 1980.

———. *Homo Spiritualis.* Leiden: E. J. Brill, 1969.

———. *Protestants: The Birth of a Revolution.* New York: Doubleday, 1993.

———. *The Reformation in the Cities.* New Haven, CT: Yale University Press, 1975.

Pannier, Jacques. *Les origines de la confession de foi et de la discipline des église réformées de France.* Paris: F. Alcan, 1936.

Parker, T. H. L. *John Calvin: A Biography.* Philadelphia: Westminster Press, 1975.

Partee, Charles. "Calvin's Central Dogma Again." *Sixteenth Century Journal* 18, no. 2 (1987): 191–99.

Patrologiae Cursus Completus. Series Graeca. Edited by J.-P. Migne. Paris, 1857–91.

Patrologiae Cursus Completus. Series Latina. Edited by J.-P. Migne. Paris, 1844–91.

Patterson, Steven J. *Beyond the Passion: Rethinking the Death and Life of Jesus.* Minneapolis: Fortress Press, 2004.

Payne, John B. *Erasmus: His Theology of the Sacraments.* N.p.: M. E. Bracheter, 1970.

Pelikan, Jaroslav. *The Growth of Medieval Theology (600–1300).* Vol. 3 of *The Christian Tradition: A History of the Development of Doctrine.* Chicago: University of Chicago Press, 1978.

———. *Luther the Expositor.* St. Louis: Concordia Publishing House, 1959.

Perrin, Norman. *Rediscovering the Teaching of Jesus.* New York: Harper & Row, 1967.

Pesch, Otto. "Thomas von Aquino/Thomismus/Neuthomismus." In *Theologische Realenzyklopädie*, 33:433–74. New York and Berlin: Walter de Gruyter, 2002.

Pestalozzi, Carl. *Heinrich Bullinger: Leben und ausgewählte Schriften*. Elberfeld: R. L. Fridrechs, 1858.

Peters, Albrecht. *Realpräsenz, Luthers Zeugnis von Christ Gegenwart im Abendmahl*. Berlin: Luther Verlagshaus, 1960.

Peura, Simo. "Christ as Favor and Gift: The Challenge of Luther's Understanding of Justification." In *Union with Christ: The New Finnish Interpretation of Luther*, edited by Carl E. Braaten and Robert W. Jenson, 42–69. Grand Rapids: Eerdmans, 1998.

———. "What God Gives Man Receives: Luther on Salvation." In *Union with Christ: The New Finnish Interpretation of Luther*, edited by Carl E. Braaten and Robert W. Jenson, 76–95. Grand Rapids: Eerdmans, 1998.

Portalié, Eugène. *A Guide to the Thought of Saint Augustine*. Translated by Ralph J. Bastian. Chicago: H. Regnery Co., 1960.

Potter, G. R. *Zwingli*. Cambridge: Cambridge University Press, 1976.

Pound, Ezra. "A Pact." In *Ezra Pound: New Selected Poems and Translations*, edited by Richard Sieburth, 39. New York: New Directions Books, 2010.

Power, David N. "Eucharist." In *Systematic Theology II: Roman Catholic Perspectives*, edited by Francis Schüssler Fiorenza and John P. Galvin, 261–88. Minneapolis: Fortress Press, 1991.

———. *The Eucharistic Mystery*. New York: Crossroad, 1994.

Pratzner, Ferdinand. *Messe und Kreuzesopfer, Die Krise der sakramentalen Idee bei Luther und in der mittelalterlichen Scholastik*. Vienna: Herder, 1970.

Prenter, Regin. "A Lutheran Doctrine of Eucharistic Sacrifice?" *Studia Theologica* 19 (1965): 189–99.

Procter, Francis. *A New History of the Book of Common Prayer*. Revised by Walter Howard Frere. London: Macmillan & Co., 1955.

Pruett, Gordon E. "A Protestant Doctrine of the Eucharistic Presence." *Calvin Theological Journal* 10, no. 2 (November 1975): 142–74.

Quere, Ralph W. "Changes and Constants: Structure in Luther's Understanding of the Real Presence in the 1520s." *Sixteenth Century Journal* 16, no. 1 (1985): 48–53.

———. *Melanchthon's Christum Cognoscere: Christ's Efficacious Presence in the Eucharistic Theology of Melanchthon*. Nieuwkoop: B. De Graaf, 1977.

Radbertus, Pascasius. *De corpore et sanguine domini. Epistola ad Fredugardum*. Corpus Christianorum Continuatio Mediaevalis 16. Turnholti: Typographi Brepols, 1969.

Rahner, Karl. "The Theology of Symbol." In *Theological Investigations*, 4:221–52. Baltimore: Helicon, 1966.

Raitt, Jill. *The Eucharistic Theology of Theodore Beza. Development of the Reformed Doctrine*. Chambersburg, PA: American Academy of Religion, 1972.

———. "Roman Catholic New Wine in Reformed Old Bottles? The Conversion of the Elements in the Eucharistic Doctrines of Theodore Beza and Edward Schillebeeckx." *Journal of Ecumenical Studies* 8 (1971): 581–604.

Redeker, Martin. *Schleiermacher: Life and Thought.* Translated by John Wallhauser. Philadelphia: Fortress Press, 1973.

Reformierte Bekenntnisschriften. Vols. 1/1, 1/2, 1/3. Edited by Heiner Faulenbach and Eberhard Busch, in conjunction with Emidio Campi et al. Neukirchen-Vluyn: Neukirchener, 2002, 2006, 2007.

Reformierte Bekenntnisschriften. Vols. 2/1, 2/2. Edited by Andreas Mühling and Peter Opitz, in conjunction with Emidio Campi et al. Neukirchen-Vluyn: Neukirchener, 2009.

Reid, W. Stanford. "The Lord's Supper and Church Unity in the Thought of John Calvin." *Theological Forum* 12 (July 1985): 2–6.

Remy, Jochen. "Die 'Kölner Reformation' und ihre Bedeutung für die englische Kirchengeschichte. Anmerkung zu einer Verhältnisbestimmung zwischen dem 'Einfältigen Bedenken' und dem 'Book of Common Prayer.'" *Veröffentlichungen des Kölnischen Geschichtsvereins* 67 (1993): 119–40.

Rhols, Jan. *Reformed Confessions: Theology from Zurich to Barmen.* Translated by John Hoffmeyer. Introduction by Jack L. Stotts. Louisville, KY: Westminster John Knox Press, 1998.

Richardson, Cyril. *Zwingli and Cranmer on the Eucharist.* Evanston, IL: Seabury Western Theological Seminary, 1949.

Riggs, John W. *Baptism in the Reformed Tradition: An Historical and Practical Theology.* Columbia Series in Reformed Theology. Louisville, KY: Westminster John Knox Press, 2002.

———. "Emerging Ecclesiology in Calvin's Baptismal Thought." *Church History* 64, no. 1 (1995): 29–43.

———. "Eschatology of Table Sharing: On the Origins of Christian Worship." *Eden Journal* 1, no. 2 (May 1992): 45–60.

———. "From Gracious Table to Sacramental Elements: The Tradition-History of Didache 9 and 10." *Second Century* 4 (1984): 83–102.

———. *Postmodern Christianity.* Harrisburg, PA: Trinity Press International, 2003.

———. "The Sacred Food of Didache 9–10 and Second-Century Ecclesiologies." In *The Didache in Context,* edited by Clayton N. Jefford, 256–62. Leiden: E. J. Brill, 1995.

———. Theological commentary for Ninth Sunday after the Ephiphany. In *Feasting on the Word: Year B, Vol. 1* edited by David L. Bartlett and Barbara Brown Taylor, 422-27. Louisville, KY: Westminster John Knox Press, 2008.

Rodolphe, Peter. "Calvin et le liturgie d'après l'Institution." *Ètudes théologiques et religieuses* 60, no. 3 (1985): 385– 401.

Rogers, Jack. *Presbyterian Creeds: A Guide to the Book of Confessions.* Philadelphia: Westminster Press, 1985.

Rogge, Joachim. *Virtus und Res: Um die Abendmahlswirklichkeit bei Calvin.* Stuttgart: Calwer Verlag, 1965.

Rordorf, Willy. *Sunday.* Translated by A. A. K. Graham. Philadelphia: Westminster Press, 1968.

Rorem, Paul. *Calvin and Bullinger on the Lord's Supper.* Nottingham: Grove Books, 1989.

————. "Calvin and Bullinger on the Lord's Supper, part 1, The Impasse." *Lutheran Quarterly* 2, no. 2 (1988): 155–84.

————. "Calvin and Bullinger on the Lord's Supper, part 2, The Agreement." *Lutheran Quarterly* 2, no. 3 (1988): 357–89.

————. "The Consensus Tigurinus (1549): Did Calvin Compromise?" In *Calvinus sacrae scripturae professor: Calvin as Confessor of Holy Scripture*, edited by Wilhelm H. Neuser, 72–90. Grand Rapids: Eerdmans. 1994.

Rubin, Miri. *Corpus Christi: The Eucharist in Late Medieval Culture.* Cambridge and New York: Cambridge University Press, 1991.

Rückert, H. "Das Eindringen der Tropuslehre in die schweizerische Auffassung vom Abendmahl." *Archiv für Reformationsgeschichte* 37 (1940): 199–221.

Rüetschi, Kurt J. "Bucer und Bullinger in ihren Persönlichen Beziehungen." In *Martin Bucer and Sixteenth-Century Europe: Actes du Colloque de Strasbourg, 28–31 Août 1991*, vol. 1, edited by Christian Krieger and Marc Lienhard, 429–39. Leiden: E. J. Brill, 1993.

Rupprecht, Johannes. *Hermann Bezzel als Theologe.* Munich: C. Kaiser, 1925.

Salu, M. B., trans. *The Ancrene Riwle.* Notre Dame, IN: Notre Dame University Press, 1956.

Sanders, E. P. *Jesus and Judaism.* Philadelphia: Fortress Press, 1985.

Sanders, Paul. "Heinrich Bullinger et le 'Zwinglianisme Tardif' aux Lendemains du 'Consensus Tigurinus.'" *Zwingliana* 19 (1992): 307–23.

Sasse, Herman. "The Bedeutung der Realpräsenz." *Lutherischer Rundblick* 9 (1961): 70–87.

————. *This Is My Body: Luther's Contention for the Real Presence in the Sacrament of the Altar.* Minneapolis: Augsburg Publishing House, 1959.

Scaer, David. "In Response to Bengt Hägglund: Did Luther and Melanchthon Agree on the Real Presence?" *Concordia Theological Quarterly* 44 (1980): 141–47.

Schäfer, Rolf. "Zum Problem der Gegenwart Christi im Abendmahl." *Zeitschrift für Theologie und Kirche* 84 (1987): 195–214.

Schaff, Philip. *Bibliotheca Symbolica Ecclesiae Universalis: The Creeds of Christendom.* 3 vols. 4th ed. New York: Harper & Bros., 1887-1919.

————. "The Second Helvetic Confession. A.D. 1566." Vol. 3, *Bibliotheca Symbolica Ecclesiae Universalis: The Creeds of Christendom*, 4th ed., 1:390–95. New York: Harper & Bros., 1919.

Schempp, Paul. "Das Abendmahl bei Luther." In *Paul Schempp: Gesammelte Aufsätze*, 88–106. Munich: Chr. Kaiser, 1960.

Schillebeeckx, Eduard. *Christ the Sacrament of Encounter with God.* New York: Sheed & Ward, 1963.

Schleiermacher, Friedrich. *The Christian Faith.* Philadelphia: Fortress Press, 1976.

————. *Der christliche Glaube nach den Grundsätzen der evangelischen Kirche im Zusammenhange dargestellt.* 7th ed. Edited by Martin Redeker. Berlin: Walter de Gruyter, 1960.

Schmidt, Karl Ludwig. "Abendmahl: I. im Neuen Testament." In *Die Religion in Geschichte und Gegenwart*, 1:6–16. Tübingen: J. C. B. Mohr, 1927.

Schmidt-Clausing, Fritz. *Zwingli*. Berlin: Walter de Gruyter, 1965.

———. *Zwingli als Liturgiker. Eine liturgiegeschichtliche Untersuchung*. Göttingen: Vandenhoeck & Ruprecht, 1952.

Schmitz, Josef. *Gottesdienst im altchristlichen Mailand: Eine liturgiewissenschaftliche Untersuchung über Initiation and Messfeier während des Jahres der Zeit des Bischofs Ambrosius*. Cologne: Peter Hanstein, 1975.

Schoedel, William R. *Ignatius of Antioch*. Philadelphia: Fortress Press, 1985.

Schrenk, D. G. "Zwinglis Hauptmotiv in der Abendmahlslehre und das Neue Testament." *Zwingliana* 5, no. 4 (1930): 176–85.

Schrenk, Gottlob. *Gottesreich und Bund im älteren Protestantismus*. Darmstadt: Wissenschaftliche Buchgesellschaft, 1967.

Schubert, H. von. "Das Marburger Gespräche als Anfang der Abendmahlskonkordie." *Zeitschrift für Kirchengeschichte* 30 (1909): 60–78.

Schultheß-Rechberg, Gustav von. *Heinrich Bullinger: Der Nachfolger Zwinglis*. Schriften des Vereins für Reformationsgeschichte 82. Halle: Verein für Reformationsgeschichte, 1904.

Schüssler Fiorenza, Elisabeth. *In Memory of Her*. New York: Crossroad, 1983.

Schwab, Wolfgang. *Entwicklung und Gestalt der Sakramententheologie bei Martin Luther*. Frankfurt: P. Lang, 1977.

Schweizer, Eduard. "Abendmahl: I. in NT." In *Die Religion in Geschichte und Gegenwart*, 1:10–21. Tübingen: J. C. B. Mohr, 1957.

———. *The Lord's Supper according to the New Testament*. Philadelphia: Fortress Press, 1967.

Schweizer, Julius. *Reformierte Abendmahlsgestaltung in der Schau Zwinglis*. Basel: F. Reinhardt, 1954.

Scott, C. A. "Zwingli's Doctrine of the Lord's Supper." *Expositor* 3 (1901): 161–71.

Seebass, Gottfried. "Bucer—Forschung seit dem Jubiläumsjahr 1991." *Theologische Rundschau* 62 (1997): 271–300.

Seeberg, Reinhold. *Text-Book of the History of Doctrines*. Translated by Charles E. Hay. Grand Rapids: Baker Book House, 1983.

Seeley, David. *The Noble Death*. Sheffield: Sheffield Academic Press, 1990.

Semmelroth, Otto. *The Preaching Word: On Theology of Proclamation*. Translated by John Jay Hughes. New York: Herder & Herder, 1965.

Sibley, Laurence C., Jr. "The Church as Eucharistic Community: Observations on John Calvin's Early Eucharistic Theology (1536–1545)." *Worship* 81, no. 3 (2007): 249–67.

Smith, Dennis E. *From Symposium to Eucharist*. Minneapolis: Fortress Press, 2003.

———. *From Symposium to Eucharist*. Minneapolis: Augsburg Fortress, 2003.

———. "The Last Supper." In *The New Interpreter's Dictionary of the Bible*, 3:582–85. Nashville: Abingdon Press, 2008.

———. "Table Fellowship and the Historical Jesus." In *Religious Propaganda and Missionary Competition in the New Testament World: Essays Honoring Dieter Georgi*, edited by Lukas Bormann, Kelly del Tredici, and Angela Standhartinger, 135–62. Leiden: E. J. Brill, 1994.

Smith, Morton. *Jesus the Magician*. San Francisco: Harper & Row, 1978.

————. "Pauline Worship as Seen by Pagans." *Harvard Theological Review* 73 (1980): 241–49.

Smits, Luchesius. *Saint Augustin dans l'oeuvre de Jean Calvin.* Vol. 1, *Etude de Critique Litteraire.* Assen: Van Gorcum, 1956.

Sommerlath, Ernst. "Das Abendmahl bei Luther." In *Vom Sakrament des Altars,* edited by Herman Sasse, 95–132. Leipzig: Dörffling & Francke, 1941.

————. "Luthers Lehre von der Realpräsenz in Abendmahl im Zusammenhang mit seiner Gottesanschauung nach den Abendmahlsschriften von 1527–1528." In *Das Erbe Martin Luthers, Festschrift für Ludwig Ihmels,* edited by R. Jelke, 320–28. Leipzig: Dörffling & Francke, 1928.

————. *Der Sinn des Abendmahls nach Luthers Gedanken über des Abendmahl, 1527/29.* Leipzig: Dörffling & Francke, 1930.

Sources chrétiennes, edited by H. de Lubac and Jean Daniélou. Paris: Éditions du Cerf, 1946–.

Spijker, Willem van't. "Bucer's Influence on Calvin: Church and Community." In *Martin Bucer: Reforming Church and Community,* edited by David Frederick Wright, 32–44. New York: Cambridge University Press, 1994.

————. *Calvin: A Brief Guide to His Life and Thought.* Translated by Lyle D. Bierma. Louisville, KY: Westminster John Knox Press, 2009.

————. "De Leer van de Doop bij Zwingli, Bullinger en Bucer." In *Rondom de Doopvont,* edited by Willem van't Spijker, 221–62. Kampen, Netherlands: De Groot Goudriaan, 1983.

Spruyt, Bart Jan. *Cornelius Henrici Hoen (Hoenius) and His Epistle on the Eucharist (1525).* Leiden: Brill, 2006.

Staedtke, Joachim. "Bullingers Theologie—eine Fortsetzung der Zwinglischen?" In *Bullinger-Tagung 1975,* edited by Ulrich Gäbler and Endre Zsindely, 87–98. Zurich: Instituts für Schweizerische Reformationsgeschichte, 1977.

————. *Die Theologie des Jungen Bullinger.* Studien zur Dogmengeschichte und Systematische Theologie 16. Zurich: Zwingli-Verlag, 1962.

————. "Voraussetzungen der Schweizer Abendmahlslehre." *Theologische Zeitschrift* 16 (January/February 1960): 19–32.

Staehelin, Rudolf. *Huldreich Zwingli, sein Leben und Wirken.* 2 vols. Basel: B. Schwabe, 1895–97.

Steinmetz, David C. "The Theology of Calvin and Calvinism." In *Reformation Europe: A Guide to Research,* edited by Steven Ozment, 211–32. St. Louis: Center for Reformation Research, 1982.

Steinmetz, David. "Scripture and the Lord's Supper in Luther's Theology." *Interpretation* 37 (1983): 253–65.

Stephens, Peter. "The Sacraments in the Confessions of 1536, 1549, and 1566: Bullinger's Understanding in the Light of Zwingli's." *Zwingliana* 33 (2006): 51–76.

Stephens, W. P. *The Holy Spirit in the Theology of Martin Bucer.* Cambridge: Cambridge University Press, 1970.

————. *The Theology of Huldrych Zwingli.* Oxford: Clarendon Press, 1986.

Stephenson, John R. "The Holy Eucharist: At the Center or Periphery of the Church's Life in Luther's Thinking?" In *A Lively Legacy: Essays in Honor of Robert Preuss*, edited by Kurt E. Marquat, John R. Stephenson, and Bjarne W. Teigen, 154–63. Fort Wayne, IN: Concordia Theological Seminary, 1985.

———. *The Lord's Supper*. St. Louis: Luther Academy, 2003.

———. "Martin Luther and the Eucharist." *Scottish Journal of Theology* 36 (1983): 447–61.

———. "Sanctification and the Lord's Supper." In *The Pieper Lectures: Sanctification, New Life in Christ*, edited by John A. Maxfield, 44–54. St. Louis: Concordia Historical Institute and the Luther Academy, 2003.

Stock, Ursula. *Die Bedeutung der Sakramente in Luthers Sermons von 1519*. Leiden: E. J. Brill, 1982.

Stone, Darwell. *A History of the Doctrine of the Eucharist*. London: Longmans, Green, 1909.

Stookey, Laurence Hull. "Calvin: Virtualism." In *Eucharist: Christ's Feast with the Church*, 55–62. Nashville: Abingdon Press, 1993.

Strasser, Otto. "Der Consensus Tigurinus." *Zwingliana* 9 (1949): 1–16.

Strobel, August. *Ursprung und Geschichte des frühchristlichen Osterkalenders*. Berlin: Akademie-Verlag, 1977.

Strohl, Henri. "Bucer et Calvin." *Bulletin de Histoire du Protestantisme francaise* 87 (1938): 354–56.

Strohl, Jane E. "God's Self-Revelation in the Sacrament of the Altar." In *By Faith Alone*, edited by Joseph A. Burgess and Marc Kolden, 97–109. Grand Rapids: Eerdmans, 2004.

Stumpf, Johann. *Beschreibung des Abendmahlsstreites*. Edited by Fritz Büsser. Zurich: Verlag Berichthaus, 1960.

Stupperich, Robert. "Strassburgs Stellung im Beginn des Sakramentsstreits." *Archiv für Reformationsgeschichte* 38 (1941): 249–72.

Süss, Theobald. "La présence réelle du Christ dans l'eucharist d'après les recherches protestantes actuelles." *Revue des sciences philosophiques et théologiques* 53 (1969): 433–57.

Sykes, Stephen, and John Booty. *The Study of Anglicanism*. London: SPCK, 1988.

Talley, Thomas. *The Origins of the Liturgical Year*. Collegeville, MN: Liturgical Press, 1991.

Tamburello, Dennis. *Union with Christ: John Calvin and the Mysticism of St. Bernard*. Louisville, KY: Westminster John Knox Press, 1994.

Tappert, Theodore G. *The Book of Concord: The Confessions of the Evangelical Lutheran Church*. Philadelphia: Fortress Press, 2000.

———. "Meaning and Practice in the Reformation." In *Meaning and Practice of the Lord's Supper*, edited by Helmut Lehmann, 85–109. Philadelphia: Muhlenberg, 1961.

Taussig, Hal. *In the Beginning Was the Meal: Social Experimentation and Early Christian Identity*. Minneapolis: Augsburg Fortress Press, 2009.

Taylor, Michael J. "Calvin." In *The Protestant Liturgical Renewal: A Catholic Viewpoint*, 82–92. Westminster, MD: Newman Press, 1963.

Theissen, Gerd. *The Social Setting of Pauline Christianity: Essays on Corinth.* Edited and translated by John H. Schütz. Philadelphia: Fortress Press, 1982.

Thomas, J. Heywood. "Logic and Metaphysics in Luther's Eucharistic Theology." *Renaissance and Modern Studies* 23 (1979): 147–59.

Thompson, Bard, ed. *Liturgies of the Western Church.* New York: World Publishing Co., 1961.

Thompson, Nicholas. *Eucharistic Sacrifice and Patristic Tradition in the Theology of Martin Bucer, 1534–1546.* Leiden and Boston: Brill, 2005.

Thurian, Max. "The Real Presence." In *The Eucharistic Memorial,* translated by J. G. Davies, 108–24. Richmond: John Knox Press, 1961.

Tice, Terrence N. *Schleiermacher.* Nashville: Abingdon Press, 2006.

———. *Schleiermacher Bibliography (1784–1984): Updating and Commentary.* Princeton, NJ: Princeton Theological Seminary, 1985.

———. "Schleiermacher Bibliography: Update 1987." *New Athenaeum/Neues Athenaeum* 1 (1989): 280–350.

———. "Schleiermacher Bibliography: Update 1990." *New Athenaeum/ Neues Athenaeum* 2 (1991): 131–65.

———. "Schleiermacher Bibliography: Update 1994." *New Athenaeum/Neues Athenaeum* 4 (1995): 139–94.

———. *Schleiermacher Bibliography: With Brief Introductions, Annotations, and Index.* Princeton, NJ: Princeton Theological Seminary, 1966.

———. *Schleiermacher's Sermons: A Chronological Listing and Account.* Lewiston, NY: E. Mellen Press, 1997

Tinker, Melvin. "Language, Symbols, and Sacraments: Was Calvin's View of the Lord's Supper Right?" *Churchman* 112, no. 2 (1998): 131–49.

Tori, Mitchell. "Luther and Cajetan on the Sacrifice of the Mass." *Logia 9,* no. 4 (2000): 29–36.

Torrance, Thomas F. *The Hermeneutics of John Calvin.* Edinburgh: Scottish Academic Press, 1988.

Tracy, James D. "Humanism and the Reformation." In *Reformation Europe: A Guide to Research,* edited by Steven Ozment, 33–57. St. Louis: Center for Reformation Research, 1982.

Troeltch, Ernst. *The Social Teaching of the Christian Churches.* Translated by Olive Wyon. New York: Macmillan, 1931.

Tylenda, Joseph N. "Calvin and Christ's Presence in the Supper—True or Real." *Scottish Journal of Theology* 27 (1974): 65–75.

———. "Calvin and Westphal: Two Eucharistic Theologies in Conflict." In *Calvin's Books: Festschrift Dedicated to Peter De Klerk on the Occasion of His Seventieth Birthday,* edited by Wilhelm H. Neuser, Herman J. Selderhuis, and Wilhem van't Spijker, 99–122. Heerenveen: J. J. Groen, 1997.

———. "Calvin on Christ's True Presence in the Lord's Supper." *American Ecclesiastical Review* 155 (November 1966): 321–33.

———. "The Calvin-Westphal Exchange: The Genesis of Calvin's Treatises against Westphal." *Calvin Theological Journal* 9, no. 2 (November 1974): 182–209.

————. "The Ecumenical Intentions of Calvin's Early Eucharistic Teaching." In *Reformatio Perennis*, edited by Brian A. Gerrish, 27–47. Pittsburgh: Pickwick Press, 1981.

————. "A Eucharistic Sacrifice in Calvin's Theology?" *Theological Studies* 37 (1976): 456–66.

Van der Lof, L. J. "Eucharistie et présence réelle selon saint Augustin." *Revue des Études Augustiniennes* 10, no. 4 (1964): 295–304.

Vatja, Vilmos. "Das Abendmahl. Gegenwart Christi—Feier der Gemeinschaft-Eucharistiches Opfer." In *Confessio Augustana und Confutatio: der Augsburger Reichstag 1530 und die Einheit der Kirche: internationales Symposion der Gesellschaft zur Herausgabe des Corpus Catholicorum in Augsburg vom 3.–7. September 1979*, edited by Erwin Iserloh, 545–77. Münster, 1980.

Venema, Cornelis P. *Heinrich Bullinger and the Doctrine of Predestination: Author of "the Other Reformed Tradition"?* Grand Rapids: Baker Academic, 2002.

————. "Heinrich Bullinger's Correspondence on Calvin's Doctrine of Predestination, 1551–1553." *Sixteenth Century Journal* 17 (1986): 449.

Vermes, Geza. *Jesus the Jew*. London: Collins, 1973.

Vernet, F. "Eucharistie du IXe a la fin du XIe siécle." In *Dictionnaire de théologie catholique* 5:1222. Paris, 1913.

Wainwright, Geoffrey. "Berengar of Tours," In *Encyclopedia of Religion*, 2:112-13. New York: Macmillan, 1987.

Walker, G. S. M. "The Lord's Supper in the Theology and Practice of Calvin." In *Calvin: A Collection of Essays*, edited by G. E. Duffield, 131–48. Grand Rapids: Eerdmans, 1966.

Walker, Williston. *John Calvin: The Organizer of Reformed Protestantism, 1509–1564*. New York: G. P. Putnam's Sons, 1906.

Wallace, Ronald S. *Calvin's Doctrine of the Word and Sacrament*. Edinburgh: Oliver & Boyd, 1953.

————. *Geneva and the Reformation: A Study of Calvin as Social Reformer, Churchman, Pastor, and Theologian*. Grand Rapids: Baker Book House, 1988.

Walser, Peter. *Die Prädestination bei Heinrich Bullinger im Zusammenhang mit seiner Gotteslehre*. Studien zur Dogmengeschichte und Systematischen Theologie 11. Zurich: Zwingli-Verlag, 1957.

Walton, Robert C. "Heinrich Bullinger 1504–1575." in *Shapers of Religious Traditions in Germany, Switzerland, and Poland 1560–1600*, edited by Jill Raitt, 69–87. New Haven, CT: Yale University Press, 1981.

————. "Let Zwingli Be Zwingli." In *Prophet, Pastor, Protestant: The Work of Huldrych Zwingli after Five Hundred Years*, edited by E. J. Furcha and H. Wayne Pipkin, 171–90. Allison Park, PA: Pickwick Publications, 1984.

Weinstein, Donald. "In Whose Image and Likeness? Interpretations of Renaissance Humanism." *Journal of the History of Ideas* 33 (1972): 165–76.

Weisz, Leo. "Johannes Stumpfs Geschichte des Abendmahlsstreites." *Zwingliana* 5, no. 4 (1930): 193–221.

Wendel, François. *Calvin: The Origins and Development of His Religious Thought*. Translated by Philip Mairet. London: William Collins & Sons, 1963.

Wengert, Timothy. "'We Will Feast Together in Heaven Forever': The Epistolary Friendship of John Calvin and Philip Melanchthon." In *Melanchthon in Europe: His Work and Influence beyond Wittenberg*, edited by Karin Maag, 19–44. Grand Rapids: Baker, 1999.

White, James F. *Introduction to Christian Worship*. 3rd ed. Nashville: Abingdon Press, 2000.

Wicks, Jared. "'Fides Sacramenti–Fides Specialis': Luther's Development in 1518." In *Luther's Reform: Studies on Conversion and the Church*, 117–47. Mainz: Verlag P. von Zabern, 1992.

Wilhelmi, Thomas, Bernd Paul, Michael Mermann, and Danièle Fischer, eds. *Bucer-Bibliographie/Bibliographie Bucer 1975–1998*. Strasbourg: Association des Publications de la Faculté de Théologie Protestante, 1999.

Williams, Sam. *Jesus' Death as a Saving Death*. Missoula, MT: Scholars Press, 1975.

Willis, E. David. "Calvin's Use of Substantia." In *Calvinus Ecclesiae Genevensis Custos*, edited by Wilhelm H. Neuser, 289–301. Frankfurt: Peter Lang, 1984.

———. "A Reformed Doctrine of the Eucharist and Ministry and Its Implications for Roman Catholic Dialogues." *Journal of Ecumenical Studies* 21, no. 2 (Spring 1984): 295–309.

Wilsøff, Carl. *The Gift of Communion: Luther's Controversy with Rome on Eucharistic Sacrifice*. Translated by Joseph M. Shaw. Minneapolis: Augsburg, 1964.

Woodruff, Jennifer Lynn. "John Calvin, the Wesleys, and John Williamson Nevin on the Lord's Supper." *Methodist History* 41, no. 4 (2003): 159–78.

Zachman, Randall C. *The Assurance of Faith: Conscience in the Theology of Martin Luther and John Calvin*. Minneapolis: Fortress Press, 1993.

———. *Image and Word in the Theology of John Calvin*. Notre Dame, IN: University of Notre Dame Press, 2007.

———. *John Calvin as Teacher, Pastor, and Theologian*. Grand Rapids: Baker Academic, 2006.

Zwingli, Huldrych. *An Account of the Faith*. In *The Latin Works and the Correspondence of Huldreich Zwingli*, vol. 2, edited by Samuel Macauley Jackson and William John Hinke. Philadelphia: Heidelberg Press, 1922.

———. *Confessionum in ecclesiis reformatis publicatarum*. Leipzig: Klinkhardt, 1840. English translation in *Reformed Confessions of the Sixteenth Century*, edited by Arthur C. Cochrane (Philadelphia: Westminster Press, 1966).

———. *Huldreich Zwinglis sämtliche Werke*. Vol. 1. Edited by Emil Egli, Georg Finsler, et al. Corpus Reformatorum. Berlin: C. A. Schwetschke und Sohn, 1905.

———. *Huldreich Zwinglis sämtliche Werke*. Vols. 2–5, 7–12. Edited by Emil Egli, Georg Finsler, et al. Corpus Reformatorum. Leipzig: M. Heinsius Nachfolger, 1908–28.

———. *Huldreich Zwinglis sämtliche Werke*. Vols. 6/1, 6/2, 13–14. Edited by Emil Egli, Georg Finsler, et al. Corpus Reformatorum. Zurich: Verlag Berichthaus, 1944–82.

———. *On True and False Religion*. In *The Latin Works of Huldreich Zwingli*, edited by Samuel Macauley Jackson. Philadelphia: Heidelberg Press, 1929.

AUTHOR INDEX

Alber, Matthew, 56–57, 58, 62–63, 76, 186n7, 188n10, 191nn 52–58, 192n60
Albert the Great, 24–25, 169n165
Alcuin, 11
Alexander of Hales, 38, 169n166
Althaus, Paul, 38, 41, 175n24, 178nn27, 44, 47; 179n50, 180nn59, 64
Ambrose of Milan, 11, 13–14, 16, 20, 25, 27, 34–35, 54, 100, 141, 161n72, 162n76, 163nn96, 97; 164n104, 170n180
Aquinas, Thomas. *See* Thomas Aquinas
Aristotle, 24, 25, 49, 179n56, 183n123, 185n3
Augustine of Hippo, ix, x, 11, 13–17, 19, 20, 25, 27, 33–36, 39–40, 50, 54, 59, 61–63, 65, 67, 72–74, 80–82, 85–86, 89–103, 104–7, 109–10, 112–17, 119, 122, 130, 141–42, 152, 161n72, 162n76, 163–64nn101–6, 165nn111–12, 118–19; 170n181, 172n1, 184n152, 185n4, 190–91n50,196n111, 210nn19–20; 213nn73–74; 218n154, 221n164, 225n19

Baillie, Donald M., 134, 137–39
Barclay, Alexander, 57–58, 85–86, 186n7, 188nn17, 20; 211nn24–26, 218n156
Barth, Karl, xi, 112, 134–39, 142, 151–52, 227n43, 232n98, 233n142, 234nn143– 53, 237n34
Batiffol, Pierre, 14, 35, 85, 161n72, 164n102
Baur, August, 56, 58, 186n7, 187n8

Beckmann, Joachim, 85, 205n8, 210nn18, 20
Berengar of Tours, 19–20, 24, 64, 162n76, 166n141, 167n142, 169n165, 170n176
Betz, Johannes, ix, 14, 161nn65, 70; 162n82, 163nn88, 90–93, 95; 163nn99, 101; 165n121
Beza, Theodore, 204n1, 207–8n8, 216n127, 239n57
Biel, Gabriel, 24, 114
Blanke, Fritz, 57–58, 186n7, 188n17, 194n91, 207n8, 218n155, 219n156
Bodenstein, Andreas. *See* Karlstadt
Bonaventure, 24, 169n166
Brenz, Johannes, 78, 196n109, 202n174
Bucer, Martin, x, xii, 45, 48, 55, 57, 72, 74–80, 82–83, 91–92, 95, 99–101, 107, 109, 114–15, 130, 142, 181n76, 182n109, 188n15, 199nn149–51, 200nn152–55, 201nn156–59, 161–65; 202nn167, 174; 203nn178, 180–86; 204nn187–89, 209n8, 220n156
Budé, Guillaume, 83
Bugenhagen, John, 46, 48, 50, 199–200n151
Bullinger, Heinrich, x, 67, 74, 103–11, 112–15, 117–18, 121–22, 124–25, 130, 142, 195n99, 207–8n8, 218nn155, 218–20n156, 220–21n157, 221nn158–60, 162–65; 222nn166–79; 223nn180–91, 195; 224n7, 226n36, 227n37, 229n66
Bultmann, Rudolf, 2–3, 152, 153n1, 154n12, 159n50, 216n125, 237nn34, 36; 237–38n45

SUBJECT INDEX

Ambrosian, 11, 35, 161n72, 162n76
Anabaptists, viii, 50
Anglican. *See* Church of England
Anglican Catechism, 123–24
annihilation, 21, 25, 34, 55
Articles of Religion, 114, 230n78
Augsburg Confession, 72, 101
   Variata, ix, 97, 101
Augustinian, ix, 15, 18–20, 35–37, 39,
   54, 59, 61, 66, 73, 89–95, 97–98,
   102–3, 105, 107, 112–17, 119,
   122, 142, 152, 161n72, 162n76,
   165n112, 165n127, 172n1,
   178n48, 184n152, 193n79,
   221n161, 226n33

banquet, 1–2, 4, 6, 9, 23, 56, 106,
   156n22, 158n34
baptism, vii–xii, 16, 26–28, 30–31, 39,
   43–45, 50, 67, 87–90, 93, 105, 108,
   119, 122–27, 135–36, 138, 141,
   170n177, 183n132, 212nn49, 52;
   234n152, 236n20
Baptist, vii, 136
Belgic Confession, 114, 120, 170n185,
   171nn196, 201, 202; 226n35,
   228n59, 229n62
Bible
   Mark, x, 3, 5, 141, 146, 154–55n16,
     180n66
   Synoptic Gospels, 8, 41, 159n45
   John, 8–9, 26, 48–50, 53, 61–65,
     69–70, 75–78, 80, 81–82, 86, 91,
     93–96, 100–102, 104, 106, 109,
     112, 117, 119–20, 126, 128, 130,
     141, 191n50, 196n111, 201n165,
     202n167, 204n189, 221nn159,
     161; 228n50

1 Corinthians, x, 6–7, 36, 43, 53, 80,
   98, 117, 122, 149, 157n26
Ephesians, 94, 117
Bullinger-like, 113, 119, 124, 142, 224n7

Calvin-like, 137, 139, 142
Canons of Dort, 29, 171n196
Catholicism, vii–xiii, 9–33, 34–36, 40,
   42, 71, 81–82, 85–86, 92, 95, 102–
   3, 109, 128, 135, 138, 142, 144–45,
   156n20, 168n158, 172n220,
   174n23, 178–79n50, 189n28,
   203n182, 230n71, 232n109,
   238n49, 239n51, 239n57
   Roman Catholic Mass, xii, 22, 37,
     41–42, 45, 56, 58–60, 66, 67, 76,
     83, 104, 116, 122, 138, 180nn66,
     69; 189n28, 230n71
chaburah, 3
Christ
   presence in Supper
     body and blood, ix, 9–13, 16–25,
       34, 41, 44, 46–48, 52–54, 55,
       59–61, 63, 65, 79, 85–87, 90,
       92–94, 96–99, 102, 105–7, 110,
       113–17, 120–25, 128–29, 133,
       141–42, 149, 151, 163n89,
       164n104, 167n150, 169n166,
       184n1, 186n6, 189n24, 190n47,
       210n22, 215n106, 216n126,
       234n170
     metabolic, x, 11, 14–17, 19–21,
       25, 34–36, 44, 50, 53–54, 59–61,
       63, 81, 107, 141–42, 162n76,
       164n104
     metabolic real presence, 35, 36,
       38, 40, 43, 44, 46, 52–55, 60, 63,
       74–76, 78, 81, 100, 103